KINANTHROPOMETRY AND EXERCISE PHYSIOLOGY LABORATORY MANUAL

SECOND EDITION

Volume 1: Anthropometry
Tests, procedures and data

Edited by Roger Eston and Thomas Reilly

London and New York

First edition published 1996 by E & FN Spon,
an imprint of the Taylor & Francis Group

Second edition published 2001 by Routledge
2 Park Square, Milton Park, Abingdon, Oxon, OX14 4RN

Simultaneously published in the USA and Canada by Routledge
270 Madison Ave, New York NY 10016

Routledge is an imprint of the Taylor & Francis Group

Transferred to Digital Printing 2005

© 1996 E & F N Spon; 2001 Roger Eston and Thomas Reilly for selection and
editorial matter; individual contributors their contribution

Typeset in Palatino by Bookcraft Ltd, Stroud, Gloucestershire

British Library Cataloguing in Publication Data
A catalogue record for this book is available from the British Library

Library of Congress Cataloging in Publication Data
A catalog record for this book has been requested

ISBN 0–415–23613–4 (pbk)
ISBN 0–415–23612–6 (hbk)

Printed and bound by Antony Rowe Ltd, Eastbourne

KINANTHROPOMETRY AND EXERCISE PHYSIOLOGY LABORATORY MANUAL

SECOND EDITION

VOLUME 1: ANTHROPOMETRY

This is the second edition of the highly successful *Kinanthropometry and Exercise Physiology Laboratory Manual*. Developed as a key resource for lecturers and students of kinanthropometry, sports science, human movement and exercise physiology, this edition is thoroughly revised and completely up-to-date. Now divided into two volumes – *Anthropometry* and *Exercise Physiology* – this manual provides:

- help in the planning and conduct of practical sessions
- comprehensive theoretical background on each topic, and up-to-date information so that there is no need for additional reading
- seven entirely new chapters providing a balance between kinanthropometry and physiology
- eleven self-standing chapters in each volume which are independent of each other, enabling the reader to pick out topics of interest in any order
- a wide range of supporting diagrams, photographs and tables

Volume 1: Anthropometry covers body composition, proportion, size, growth and somatotype and their relationship with health and performance; methods for evaluating posture and range of motion; assessment of physical activity and energy balance with particular reference to the assessment of performance in children; the relationship between anthropometry and body image; statistics and scaling methods in kinanthropometry and exercise physiology.

Volume 2: Exercise Physiology covers the assessment of muscle function including aspects of neuromuscular control and electromyography, the oxygen transport system and exercise including haematology, lung and cardiovascular function; assessment of metabolic rate, energy and efficiency including thermoregulation; and assessment of maximal and submaximal energy expenditure and control, including the use of heart rate, blood lactate and perceived exertion.

An entire one-stop resource, these volumes present laboratory procedures next to real-life practical examples with appropriate data. In addition, each chapter is conveniently supplemented by a complete review of contemporary literature, as well as theoretical overviews, offering an excellent basic introduction to each topic.

Dr Roger Eston is Reader and Head of the School of Sport, Health and Exercise Sciences, University of Wales, Bangor, and **Professor Thomas Reilly** is Director of the Research Institute for Sport and Exercise Sciences, Liverpool John Moores University. Both editors are practising kinanthropometrists and collaborate in conducting workshops for the British Association for Sport and Exercise Sciences.

CONTENTS

CONTRIBUTORS

G. ATKINSON
Research Institute for Sport and Exercise
    Sciences,
Liverpool John Moores University, Henry
    Cotton Building,
Webster Street, Liverpool L3 2ET, UK

G. BEUNEN
Center for Physical Development Research,
Faculty of Physical Education and
    Physiotherapy,
K.U. Leuven, Tervuursevest 101,
B–3001 Leuven (Heverlee), Belgium

C. BOREHAM
Department of Sport and Exercise Sciences,
University of Ulster,
Shore Road, Newtownabbey,
Co Antrim BT37 0XY, UK

J. BORMS
Human Biometry and Health Promotion,
Vrije Universiteit Brussel,
Brussels, Belgium

J.E.L. CARTER
Department of Exercise and Nutritional
    Sciences,
San Diego State University,
San Diego, California, USA

P.H. DANGERFIELD
Department of Human Anatomy,
The University of Liverpool,
Liverpool, UK

W. DUQUET
Department of Human Biometry,
Vrije Universiteit Brussel,
Brussels, Belgium

M.R. HAWES
Faculty of Kinesiology,
University of Calgary,
Calgary, Alberta
Canada

A.D. MARTIN
School of Human Kinetics,
University of British Colombia,
Vancouver, Canada

A. NEVILL
School of Sport, Performing Arts and Leisure,
University of Wolverhampton,
Walsall, UK

T. OLDS
School of Physical Education, Exercise and
    Sport Studies,
University of South Australia,
Underdale, Australia

T. REILLY
Research Institute for Sport and Exercise
    Science,
Liverpool John Moores University,
Liverpool, UK

A.V. ROWLANDS
School of Sport, Health and Exercise Sciences,
University of Wales, Bangor, UK

E. VAN PRAAGH
Exercise Physiology,
Université Blaise Pascal,
Clermont-Ferrand, France

P. VAN ROY
Department of Experimental Anatomy,
Vrije Universiteit Brussel,
Brussels, Belgium

E. M. WINTER
Sport Science Research Institute,
Sheffield Hallam University,
Sheffield, UK

PREFACE

The subject area referred to as kinanthropometry has a rich history although the subject area itself was not formalized until the International Society for Advancement of Kinanthropometry was established in Glasgow in 1986. The Society supports its own international conferences and publication of Proceedings linked with these events. It also facilitates the conduct of collaborative research projects on an international basis. Until the publication of the first edition of *Kinanthropometry and Exercise Physiology Laboratory Manual; Tests, Procedures and Data* by the present editors in 1996, there was no laboratory manual which would serve as a compendium of practical activities for students in this field. The text was published under the aegis of the International Society for Advancement of Kinanthropometry in an attempt to make good the deficit.

Kinanthropometrists are concerned about the relation between structure and function of the human body, particularly within the context of movement. Kinanthropometry has applications in a wide range of areas including, for example, biomechanics, ergonomics, growth and development, human sciences, medicine, nutrition, physical education and sports science. Initially, the book was motivated by the need for a suitable laboratory resource which academic staff could use in the planning and conduct of class practicals in these areas. The content of the first edition was designed to cover specific teaching modules in kinanthropometry and other academic programmes, mainly physiology, within which kinanthropometry is sometimes subsumed. It was intended also to include practical activities of relevance to clinicians, for example in measuring metabolic functions, muscle performance,

physiological responses to exercise, posture and so on. In all cases the emphasis is placed on the anthropometric aspects of the topic. In the second edition all the original chapters have been updated and an additional seven chapters have been added, mainly concerned with physiological topics. Consequently, it was decided to separate the overall contents of the second edition into two volumes, one focusing on anthropometry practicals whilst the other contained physiological topics.

The content of both volumes is oriented towards laboratory practicals but offers much more than a series of laboratory exercises. A comprehensive theoretical background is provided for each topic so that users of the text are not obliged to conduct extensive literature searches in order to place the subject in context. Each chapter contains an explanation of the appropriate methodology and, where possible, an outline of specific laboratory-based practicals. This is not always feasible, for example in studying growth processes in child athletes. Virtually all aspects of performance testing in children are reviewed and special considerations with regard to data acquisition on children are outlined in Volume 1. Methodologies for researchers in growth and development are also described in this volume and there are new chapters devoted to performance assessment for field games, assessment of physical activity and energy balance, and anthropometry and body image.

The last two chapters in Volume 1 are concerned with basic statistical analyses and scaling procedures which are designed to inform researchers and students about data handling. The information should promote proper use of common statistical techniques for analysing data obtained on human subjects as well as help to avoid common abuses of basic statistical tools.

The content of Volume 2 emphasizes physiology but includes considerations of kinanthropometric aspects of the topics where appropriate. Practical activities of relevance to clinicians are covered, for example in measuring metabolic and cardiovascular functions, assessing muscle performance, physiological and haematological responses to exercise, and so on. The chapters concerned with electromyography, haematology, cardiovascular function, and limitations to submaximal exercise performance are new whilst material in the other chapters in this volume has been brought up to date in this second edition.

Many of the topics included within the two volumes called for unique individual approaches and so a rigid structure was not imposed on contributors. Nevertheless, in each chapter there is a clear set of aims for the practicals outlined and a comprehensive coverage of the theoretical framework. As each chapter is independent of the others, there is an inevitable re-appearance of concepts across chapters, including those of efficiency, metabolism, maximal performance and issues of scaling. Nevertheless, the two volumes represent a collective set of experimental exercises for academic programmes in kinanthropometry and exercise physiology.

It is hoped that the revised edition in two volumes will stimulate improvements in teaching and instruction strategies in kinanthropometry and physiology. In this way we will have made a contribution towards furthering the education of the next generation of specialists concerned with the relationship between human structure and function.

Roger Eston
Thomas Reilly

INTRODUCTION

The first edition of this text was published in 1996. Until its appearance, there was no laboratory manual serving as a compendium of practical activities for students in the field of kinanthropometry. The text was published under the aegis of the International Society for Advancement of Kinanthropometry, in particular its working group on 'Publications and Information Exchange' in an attempt to make good the deficit. The book has been used widely as the subject area became firmly established on undergraduate and postgraduate programmes. The necessity to update the content after a four-year period is a reflection of the field's expansion.

Kinanthropometry is a relatively new term although the subject area to which it refers has a rich history. It describes the relationship between structure and function of the human body, particularly within the context of movement. The subject area itself was formalized with the establishment of the International Society for Advancement of Kinanthropometry at Glasgow in 1986. The Society supports its own international conferences and publication of Proceedings linked with these events.

Kinanthropometry has applications in a wide range of areas including, for example, biomechanics, ergonomics, growth and development, human sciences, medicine, nutrition, physical education and sports science. The book was motivated by the need for a suitable laboratory resource which academic staff could use in the planning and conduct of class practicals in these areas. The content was designed to cover specific teaching modules in kinanthropometry and other academic programmes, such as physiology, within which

kinanthropometry is sometimes incorporated. It was intended also to include practical activities of relevance to clinicians, for example in measuring metabolic functions, muscle performance, physiological responses to exercise, posture and so on. In all cases the emphasis is placed on the anthropometric aspects of the topic.

In the current revised edition the proportion of physiology practicals has been increased, largely reflecting the ways in which physiology and anthropometry complement each other on academic programmes in the sport and exercise sciences.

The six new chapters have a physiological emphasis (focusing on electromyography, haematology, cardiovascular function, submaximal limitations to exercise, assessment of physical activity and energy balance), except for the final chapter on the links between anthropometry and body image. Of the fifteen chapters retained from the first edition, four have incorporated new co-authors with a view to providing the most authoritative contributions available.

As with the first edition, the content is oriented towards laboratory practicals but offers much more than prescription of a series of laboratory exercises. A comprehensive theoretical background is provided for each topic so that users of the text are not obliged to conduct extensive literature reviews in order to place the subject in context. Each chapter contains an explanation of the appropriate methodology and where possible an outline of specific laboratory-based practicals. This is not always feasible, for example in studying growth processes in child athletes. In such cases, virtually all aspects of performance testing in children are covered and special considerations with regard to data acquisition on children are outlined. Methodologies for researchers in growth and development are also described.

Many of the topics included in this text called for unique individual approaches and so it was not always possible to have a common structure for each chapter. In the majority of cases the laboratory practicals are retained until the end of that chapter, as the earlier text provides the theoretical framework for their conduct. Despite any individual variation from the standard structure, together the contributions represent a collective set of exercises for an academic programme in kinanthropometry. The relative self-sufficiency of each contribution also explains why relevant concepts crop up in more than one chapter, for example, concepts of efficiency, metabolism, maximal oxygen uptake, scaling and so on.

The last section contains two chapters which are concerned with basic statistical analysis and are designed to inform researchers and students about data handling. This advice should help promote proper use of common statistical techniques for analysing data obtained on human subjects as well as help to avoid common abuses of basic statistical tools.

It is hoped that this text will stimulate improvement in teaching and instruction strategies in the application of laboratory techniques in kinanthropometry and physiology. In this way we will have continued to make our contribution towards the education of the next generation of specialists concerned with relating human structure to its function.

Roger Eston
Thomas Reilly

PART ONE

BODY COMPOSITION, PROPORTION AND GROWTH

IMPLICATIONS FOR HEALTH AND PERFORMANCE

Michael R. Hawes and Alan D. Martin

1.1 AIMS

The aims of this chapter are to develop understanding in:
- body composition models,
- chemical versus anatomical partitioning,
- levels of validity and the underlying assumptions of a variety of methods,
- the theory and practice of the best-known techniques: underwater weighing, plethysmography, dual-energy X-ray absorptiometry, skinfolds and bioelectric impedance,
- the importance of body fat distribution and how it is measured, and
- sample specificity and the need for caution in applying body composition equations.

1.2 INTRODUCTION

The assessment of body composition is common in fields as diverse as medicine, anthropology, ergonomics, sport performance and child growth. Much interest still centres on quantifying body fatness in relation to health status and sport performance, but there are good reasons to measure the amounts of other constituents of the body. As a result, interest in techniques for assessing body composition has grown significantly in recent years as new technologies have been applied to compositional problems. The traditional method of densitometry is no longer regarded as the criterial standard for determining percent body fat because of better appreciation of the frequent violation of one of its basic assumptions. Despite the increasing number of methods for assessing body composition, validation is still the most serious issue, and because of this there is confusion over whether one method is more accurate than another. In this chapter we will examine the important methods, investigate their validation hierarchy, provide practical details for assessing many body constituents, and suggest directions for future research.

It is common to explain human structure in terms of increasing organizational complexity ranging from atoms and molecules to the anatomical, described as a hierarchy of cell, tissue, organ, system and organism. Body composition can be viewed as a fundamental problem of quantitative anatomy which may be approached at any organizational level, depending on the nature of the constituents of interest (Figure 1.1). Knowledge of the interrelationship of constituents within a given level or between levels is also important, and may be useful for indirectly estimating the size of a particular compartment (Wang *et al.*, 1992).

1.3 LEVELS OF APPROACH

At the first level of composition are the masses of approximately 50 elements which comprise the **atomic level**. Total body mass is 98% determined by the combination of oxygen, carbon, hydrogen, nitrogen, calcium and phosphorus, with the remaining 44 elements comprising less than 2% of total body mass (Keys and Brozek, 1953). Technology is available for

Kinanthropometry and Exercise Physiology Laboratory Manual: Tests, Procedures and Data. 2nd Edition, Volume 1: Anthropometry
Edited by RG Eston and T Reilly. Published by Routledge, London, June 2001

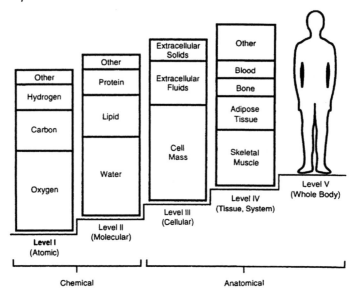

Figure 1.1 The five levels of human body composition (adapted from Wang *et al.*, 1992).

measurement *in vivo* of all of the major elements found in humans. Current methods usually involve exposure of the subject to ionizing radiation which places severe restrictions upon the utility of this approach. Examples of body composition analysis at this level are the use of whole-body potassium-40 (^{40}K) counting to determine total body potassium, or the use of neutron activation to estimate the body's nitrogen or calcium. The primary importance of the atomic level is the relationship of specific elements to other levels of organization, as, for example, in estimating total body protein stores from its nitrogen content. The great scarcity of the required instrumentation makes this level inaccessible to all but a few researchers.

The **molecular level** of organization is made up of more than 100,000 chemical compounds, which may be reduced to five main chemical groupings – lipid, water, protein, carbohydrate (mainly glycogen) and mineral. Some confusion arises with the term lipid, which may be defined as those molecules that are insoluble in water but soluble in organic solvents such as ether. Though there are many forms of lipid found in the human body, by far the most common is triglyceride, the body's

main caloric reservoir, with a relatively constant density of 0.900 g ml^{-1}. Other forms of lipid typically comprise less than 10% of total body lipid and have varying densities, for example phospholipids (1.035 g ml^{-1}) and cholesterol (1.067 g ml^{-1}) (Keys and Brozek, 1953). Lipid is often categorized as 'essential' or 'nonessential' on the basis of function. Essential (or non-adipose) lipids are those without which other structures could not function, for example lipid found in cell membranes and nervous tissue. Though commonly taken to be about 3–5% of body mass, data from the only 5 cadavers in which non-adipose lipid has been measured suggest much greater variability (Martin and Drinkwater, 1991). The term fat is sometimes used to refer to adipose tissue. To avoid confusion, the term fat will be used interchangeably with the term lipid and will not refer to adipose tissue.

Any measure of total body fat (such as percent fat by underwater weighing or skinfold calliper) gives a single value that amalgamates all body fat regardless of function or location. The remainder, after removal of all fat, is the fat-free mass (FFM), composed of fat-free muscle, fat-free bone, fat-free adipose tissue and so on. The lean body mass (LBM) is the FFM with the inclusion of the essential (non-adipose) lipids; however, LBM is sometimes erroneously used as a synonym for FFM. It should be clear that there is no means of direct *in vivo* measurement of the fat compartment, so fat must always be estimated indirectly, as, for example, by measuring body density. Other molecular compartments may be estimated by isotope dilution (total body water), dual-energy X-ray absorptiometry (bone mineral content) or neutron activation analysis of nitrogen (total body protein).

At the **cellular** level the body is divided into total cell mass, extracellular fluid (ECF) and extracellular solids (ECS). The total cell mass is comprised of all the different types of cells including adipocytes, myocytes and osteocytes. There is no direct method of measuring discrete cell masses or total cell mass.

The ECF includes intravascular plasma and extravascular plasma (interstitial fluid). This fluid compartment is predominantly water and acts as a medium for the exchange of gases, nutrients and waste products, and may be estimated by isotope dilution methods. The ECS includes organic substances such as collagen and elastin fibres in connective tissue and inorganic elements such as calcium and phosphorus which are found predominantly in bone. The ECS compartment cannot be directly measured although several of its components may be estimated by neutron activation analysis.

The fourth level of organization includes **tissues**, **organs** and **systems** which, although of differing levels of complexity, are functional arrangements of tissues. The four categories of tissue are connective, epithelial, muscular and nervous. Adipose and bone are forms of connective tissue which, together with muscle tissue, account for about 75% of total body mass. Adipose tissue consists of adipocytes together with collagen and elastin fibres which support the tissue. It is found predominantly in the subcutaneous region of the body but is also found in smaller quantities surrounding

organs, within tissue such as muscle (interstitial) and in the bone marrow (yellow marrow). The density of adipose tissue ranges from about 0.92 g ml^{-1} to 0.96 g ml^{-1} according to the proportions of its major constituents, lipid and water, and declines with increasing body fatness.

There is no direct method for the *in vivo* measurement of adipose tissue mass but advances in medical imaging technology (ultrasound, magnetic resonance imaging, computed tomography) allow accurate estimation of the areas of adipose and other tissues from cross-sectional images of the body. Tissue areas from adjacent scans may be combined by geometric modelling to predict regional and even total volumes accurately, if the whole body is scanned. Although there is limited access and high cost associated with these techniques, they have the potential to serve as alternative criterion methods for the validation of more accessible and less costly methods for the assessment of body composition.

Bone is a specialized connective tissue with an elastic protein matrix, secreted by osteocytes, onto which is deposited a calcium phosphate based mineral, hydroxyapatite, which provides strength and rigidity. The density of bone varies considerably according to such factors as age, sex and activity level. The range of fresh bone density in cadaveric subjects has been reported as 1.18–1.33 g ml^{-1} (Martin *et al.*, 1986). The mass of bone mineral may be accurately estimated by dual energy X-ray absorptiometry (DEXA), but DEXA bone densities are areal densities, i.e. g cm^{-2}, and are therefore subject to bone size artefacts.

Muscle tissue is found in three forms, skeletal, visceral and cardiac. Its density is relatively constant at about 1.065 g ml^{-1} (Forbes *et al.*, 1953; Mendez and Keys, 1960), although the quantity of interstitial adipose tissue within the tissue will introduce some variability. Surprisingly, there are few methods for quantifying the body's muscle mass; of these, the medical imaging techniques appear to be the most accurate, while anthropometry and urinary creatinine excretion have both been used.

The other tissues, nervous and epithelial, have been regarded as less significant tissues in body composition analysis. As a result, attempts have not been made to quantify these tissues; they are usually regarded as residual tissues.

The **whole-body** or organismic level of organization considers the body as a single unit dealing with overall size, shape, surface area, density and external characteristics. Clearly these characteristics are the most readily measured and include stature, body mass and volume.

The five levels of organization of the body provide a useful framework within which the different approaches to body composition may be situated. It is evident that there must be interrelationships between levels which may provide quantitative associations facilitating estimates of previously unknown compartments. The understanding of interrelationships between levels of complexity also helps guard against erroneous interpretation of data determined at different levels. As an example, body lipid is typically assessed at the molecular level while the quantity of muscle tissue, in a health and fitness setting, is addressed at the tissue or system level by circumference measurements and correction for skinfold thicknesses. The two methods are incompatible in the sense that they overlap by both including the interstitial lipid compartment.

Since the whole-body level is not strictly a compositional level and the atomic and cellular levels are of very limited interest to most people, the organizational system reduces to two levels, the molecular and tissue levels. This is then identical to the two-level system proposed by Martin and Drinkwater (1991), the **chemical** and **anatomical** levels, a system which will be used here.

1.4 VALIDITY

The validity of a method is the extent to which it accurately measures a quantity whose true value is known. Body composition analysis is unusual in that only cadaver dissection can give truly valid measures, but almost no validation has been carried out this way. In fact, there is not a single subject for whom body density and body fat (by dissection and ether extraction) have been measured. This has resulted in the acceptance of an indirect method, densitometry, as the criterion for fat estimation.

In addition to the five levels of organization, there are three levels of validation in body composition, as, for example, in the assessment of body fat. At level I, total fat mass is measured directly by cadaver dissection, i.e. ether extraction of lipid is carried out for all tissues of the body. At level II, some quantity other than fat is measured (e.g. body density or the attenuation of an X-ray beam in DEXA), and a quantitative relationship is established to enable estimation of fat mass from the measured quantity. At level III, an indirect measure is again taken (e.g. skinfold thickness or bioelectrical impedance) and a regression equation against a level II method, typically densitometry, is derived. Thus level III methods are *doubly* indirect in that they incorporate all the assumptions of the level II method they are calibrated against, as well as having their own inherent limitations. The regression approach also means that methods such as skinfold thickness measurement are highly sample-specific, since the quantitative relationship between skinfold thickness and body density depends on many variables including body hydration, bone density, relative muscularity, skinfold compressibility and thickness, body fat patterning and the relative amount of intra-abdominal fat. This, along with the use of different subsets of skinfold sites, is why there are several hundred equations in the literature for estimating fat from skinfolds.

Calibration of level III methods against densitometry also precludes the possibility of *validating* any level III method against densitometry, as this is merely a circular argument. For example, the computed percent body fat by bioelectric impedance analysis

(BIA) cannot be validated by underwater weighing, on the basis that both methods give similar values, because the BIA equations are based on regression against percent fat by underwater weighing. To validate BIA against densitometric values, the actual impedance values derived from the BIA machine should be used. It should be clear that assessment of body composition is far from an exact science and all methods should be scrutinized for the validity of their underlying assumptions. For the purposes of this chapter, it is convenient to separate assessment methods by the type of constituent they measure: chemical or anatomical.

1.5 THE CHEMICAL MODEL

A model may consist of any number of components, with the simple requirement that when added together they give total body mass. At the chemical level, the body is broken down into various molecular entities. An example of a four-component chemical model might be fat, water, bone mineral and a residual component (i.e. all the fat-free, bone mineral-free, dry constituents). Ryde *et al.* (1998) used a five compartment model of body composition comprising fat and fat-free mass (FFM), where FFM = water + protein + minerals + glycogen, to calculate body fat changes in ten overweight women on a 10 week very low calorie diet. The simplest chemical model is the well-known two-component model consisting of the fat mass and the fat-free mass (FFM). Since the great majority of body composition techniques have this partition as their aim, this will be covered in some detail here.

1.5.1 DENSITOMETRY: UNDERWATER WEIGHING AND PLETHYSMOGRAPHY

The two-component chemical densitometric model: Densitometry is an approach to estimating body fatness based on the theory that the proportions of fat mass and fat-free mass can be calculated from the known densities of the two

compartments and the measured whole-body density (D_b) (Keys and Brozek, 1953). In essence, the theory is based on the following assumptions and procedures. (For the complete derivation see Martin and Drinkwater, 1991.)

The body, of mass M, is divided into a fat component of mass FM and density d_f, and a fat-free component of mass FFM and density d_{ffm}. The masses of the two components must add up to the body's mass (M), and the volumes (mass/density) of the two components must add up to the body's volume. The basic equation for predicting percent body fat ($BF\%$) from body density is derived from the above principles, and is:

$$BF\% = \frac{1}{D_b} \cdot \frac{(d_f \cdot d_{ffm})}{(d_{ffm} - d_f)} - \frac{d_f}{(d_{ffm} - d_{fm})} \times 100 \quad (1.1)$$

This equation contains three unknowns; it is solved by assuming values for d_f and d_{ffm} and measuring D. The standard assumptions are $d_f = 0.900$ g ml^{-1} and $d_{ffm} = 1.100$ g ml^{-1}; although, as explained in more detail later, the numeric value of d_{ffm} has been questioned recently as more accurate estimates have become available. Siri's equation for percent body fat is derived when the respective values of 0.9 and 1.1 are used in equation 1.1.

$$BF\% = \frac{495}{D_b} - 450$$

When d_{ffm} is given a value of 1.113 g ml^{-1} (Schutte *et al.*, 1984), the following equation is derived:

$$BF\% = \frac{437}{D_b} - 393$$

Underwater weighing: Whole-body density, D, is then determined, usually by measuring body volume by underwater weighing or similar technique (Figure 1.2). Underwater, or hydrostatic, weighing is based on Archimedes' principle which states that the upthrust on a body fully submerged in a fluid is equal to the weight of fluid that it displaces. Therefore the weight of water displaced by a submerged body is its weight in air minus its weight in water. Dividing this by the density of water gives the body's gross volume. This must be corrected for lung volume and gastrointestinal gas. If the underwater weight is obtained when the subject has completely exhaled (residual volume), then this value must be subtracted from the body's gross volume, along with a correction for gastrointestinal gas, usually taken to be 100 ml. Though some systems measure residual volume at the same time as the underwater weight, it is typically determined outside the underwater weighing tank, by the subject exhaling maximally and then breathing within a closed system that contains a known quantity of pure oxygen (Wilmore *et al.*, 1980). Nitrogen is an inert gas, hence the quantity of N_2 inhaled and exhaled as part of air does not change in response to metabolic processes. Therefore the quantity of N_2 in the lungs after maximum exhalation is representative of the residual volume. This remaining N_2 is diluted by a known quantity of pure oxygen during several breaths of the closed circuit gas. Analysis of the resulting gas mixture from the closed circuit system yields the dilution factor of N_2, and since N_2 is present in a fixed proportion in air, the residual volume can be calculated. This procedure and the necessary calculations are described in section 1.9.3.

If these procedures are carried out by an experienced technician, the determination of corrected body density is both accurate and precise. Assumptions about the component densities must be scrutinized. The fat compartment of the body consists primarily of triglyceride which has a constant density of very close to 0.900 g ml⁻¹. There are small quantities of other forms of lipid in the body located in the nervous system and within the membrane of all cells. Though the density of these lipids is greater than that of triglyceride, the relatively small quantity of each has little effect upon overall density of body lipid. Thus the density of body fat may be accepted as relatively constant at 0.900 g ml⁻¹. However the

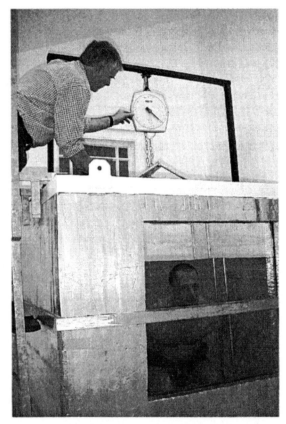

Figure 1.2 Underwater weighing procedure for calculating body density.

second assumption is much less tenable, since the density of the FFM has never been measured, and the value of 1.100 g ml⁻¹ assigned by Behnke *et al.* (1942) more than 50 years ago was acknowledged to be only an estimate (Keys and Brozek, 1953). In the absence of a direct measurement this value has remained in use, and it is only with the recent ability to measure bone mineral density (BMD), along with data from the Brussels Cadaver Study and elsewhere, that the extent of the variability of the fat-free density has been appreciated. On the basis of available evidence, the standard deviation of the fat-free density has been estimated at 0.02 g ml⁻¹ (Martin and Drinkwater, 1991). This may not appear to be problematic, since it corresponds to a coefficient of variation of less than 2%. However, equation (1.1) is particularly sensitive to changes in fat-free density. An example will demonstrate this. If a lean male has a whole-body density, $D = 1.070$ g ml^{-1}, then estimated body fat by Siri's equation is 12.6%. If his fat-free density is actually 1.12 g ml^{-1} rather than the assumed value of 1.100 g ml^{-1}, then from equation (1.1) his true fat is 19.1%. Conversely, if his fat-free density is 1.080 g ml^{-1}, his true fat is 4.7% (Figure 1.3). In the former situation Siri's equation gives a 43% underestimate, in the latter a 168% overestimate. Subjects with fat-free densities greater than 1.100 g ml^{-1} will have their percent fat underestimated by Siri's equation. This can lead to anomalous values that are lower than the generally accepted lower limit for essential fat of about 3–4%. Some athletes who combine leanness with a high fat-free density may even yield a negative percent fat, which occurs when the measured whole-body density is greater than 1.100 g ml^{-1}. Ethnic factors also contribute to error. Schutte *et al.* (1984) have estimated that fat-free density in Black Americans is 1.113 g ml^{-1}. If this is true, then there is an underestimate of about 5% fat in assuming a fat-free density of 1.100 g ml^{-1} in a non-athletic Black population whose whole-body densities are in the range 1.06–1.10 g ml^{-1}. The error will be greater in an athletic population, particularly in 'power athletes', whose bone density is high. Conversely, those with low fat-free densities, such as older subjects, especially women, will have their percent fat overestimated. This is also true for lean female athletes with chronic amenorrhoea, and its resultant bone loss. Densitometric evaluation of percent fat in children requires a sliding value for fat-free density from the 1.063 g ml^{-1} for newborns suggested by Lohman *et al.* (1984), to the adult value of 1.100 g ml^{-1} at physical maturity, but it is difficult to attribute a particular value to a given child, without information on sexual maturation. On the basis of varying estimates of d_{ffm}, formulae for converting whole body density to percent body fat have been derived for different populations. These have been summarized by Heyward and Stolarczyk (1996) and Going (1996).

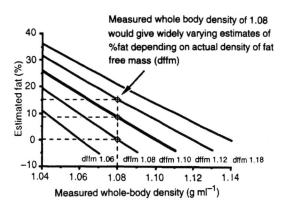

Figure 1.3 Siri's equation for estimation of percent fat plotted for different values of assumed density of fat free mass (dffm) (adapted from Martin and Drinkwater, 1991).

Plethysmography: Though body volume for the determination of body density has primarily been assessed by underwater weighing and Archimedes' principle, a more direct approach is to measure the volume of a fluid that the body displaces. Simple water displacement, while in principle an excellent approach, is limited in practice by the difficulty of measuring accurately the change in water level before and after submersion of the body. Gas displacement was described in 1963 with a focus on infants, but technical difficulties prevented wider use. There is a resurgence of interest however, and currently one commercial system is available, the BOD POD (Life Measurement Instruments Inc., Concord, California). This equipment consists of a test chamber large enough to hold an adult, separated by a diaphragm from a reference chamber. Vibration of the diaphragm induces pressure changes which allow determination of the test chamber volume, first with, then without, the subject, permitting the measurement of the subject's volume (Dempster and Aitkins, 1995). A number of corrections are required for surface area, clothing and lung volume. Reliability appears to be good, but the method underestimated percent fat in athletes compared to underwater weighing and DEXA (Collins *et al.*, 1999).

Currently, plethysmography appears to be less accurate than underwater weighing in determining body density, and is also subject to the same error as underwater weighing when using Siri's, or similar, equation to convert density into percent fat. At this time it appears that accuracy must be improved for this method to gain wider acceptance.

Because of the uncertainty regarding the assumption of constancy of the FFM and the potentially large errors that result, it is not reasonable to rely on densitometry alone as a criterion method for percent fat any more. This is of particular importance since, as will be detailed shortly, most indirect methods are, in effect, calibrated against densitometry. While there is no current replacement, many researchers agree that DEXA, with some improvements, will fulfil that role in the future (Kohrt, 1998).

1.5.2 DUAL-ENERGY X-RAY ABSORPTIOMETRY

Bone densitometry instruments have evolved from single- to dual-photon to dual-energy X-ray absorptiometry (DEXA) over the last three decades and widespread availability of whole-body scanners has made their use for determining body composition far more feasible (Lohman, 1996). The DEXA unit consists of a bed on which the subject lies supine, while a collimated dual-energy X-ray beam from a source under the bed passes through the subject. The beam's attenuation is measured by detectors above the subject, and both source and detector move so that either the whole body or selected regions of the subject are scanned in a rectilinear fashion (Figure 1.4). Some systems use a pencil beam, others use an array of beams and detectors for faster scanning. The dual energy of the beam allows quantification of two components in each pixel. In boneless regions these are fat and a lean component. It should be noted that the lean component is actually all the fat-free, bone mineral-free constituents – this is not muscle, as some mistakenly believe. In bone mineral-containing pixels, the three-component system must be reduced to two components, bone mineral and a soft tissue component which contains an assumed fat-to-lean ratio. Strategies for estimating this ratio vary by manufacturer but consist in part of extrapolation of the measured fat-to-lean ratios of soft tissue pixels adjacent to bone. In this way, the fat, bone mineral and lean content of each pixel is determined (Kohrt, 1995). Summing these for all

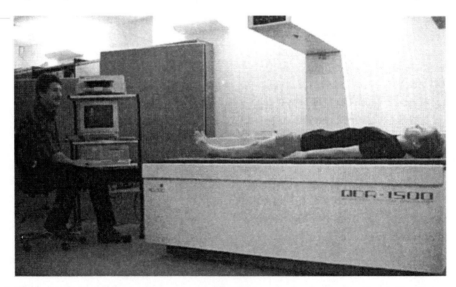

Figure 1.4 Dual energy X-ray absorptiometer procedure for assessing body density and body composition.

University of Wales, Bangor

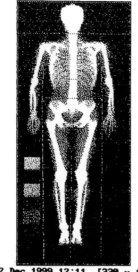

·02.Dec.1999 12:11 [330 x 150]
Hologic QDR-1500 (S/N 1522)
Enhanced Whole Body V5.72

A12029902   Thu 02.Dec.1999 11:43
Name: A R
Comment:
I.D.: 22   Sex: F
S.S.#:   - -   Ethnic: W
ZIPCode: Height: 173.00 cm
Scan Code: SP Weight: 59.2 kg
BirthDate: 02.Feb.74   Age: 25
Physician:
Image not for diagnostic use

TOTAL BMC and BMD CV is < 1.0%
C.F.   1.011   1.093   1.000

Region	Area (cm2)	BMC (grams)	BMD (gms/cm2)
L Arm	100.47	155.77	0.827
R Arm	186.45	154.98	0.831
L Ribs	156.12	123.41	0.790
R Ribs	140.75	112.04	0.796
T Spine	165.42	100.12	1.089
L Spine	68.35	89.93	1.316
Pelvis	290.48	418.71	1.403
L Leg	368.85	517.87	1.404
R Leg	361.57	515.29	1.425
SubTot	1934.46	2268.12	1.172
Head	228.92	512.44	2.239
TOTAL	2163.38	2700.56	1.285

HOLOGIC

Region	BMC (grams)	Fat (grams)	Lean (grams)	Lean+BMC (grams)	Total (grams)	% Fat (%)
L Arm	155.8	694.1	1942.2	2097.9	2792.0	24.9
R Arm	155.8	679.7	2090.1	2245.1	2924.7	23.2
Trunk	924.2	4274.9	24083.9	25008.1	29283.0	14.6
L Leg	517.9	2596.8	6630.1	7148.0	9744.8	26.6
R Leg	515.3	2650.9	6766.1	7281.4	9932.3	26.7
SubTot	2268.1	10896.3	41512.4	43780.6	54676.9	19.9
~Head	512.4	654.8	3090.0	3610.4	4265.2	15.4
TOTAL	2700.6	11551.1	44610.4	47391.0	58942.1	19.6

~assumes 17.0% brain fat
LBM 73.2% water

HOLOGIC

Figure 1.5 Analysis of body composition of the female in Figure 1.4 using a Hologic QDR–1500 pencil beam DEXA technique. Note that the sum of the individual predicted masses equates very closely to the actual whole body mass of the subject, a factor which is essential for the validity of the technique.

pixels gives the composition of the whole body (Figure 1.5). Thus DEXA uses a three-component chemical model of the body, and can therefore be compared with underwater weighing. Comparison of percent fat by underwater weighing and DEXA show differences that are correlated with BMD, probably reflecting the effect of BMD on the fat-free density.

Dual-energy X-ray absorptiometry is a level II method in that the component values are calibrated against standards. The quality of the body composition assessment is therefore dependent only on the theoretical and practical aspects of the DEXA technology. It does not rely on calibration against underwater weighing, unlike skinfold assessment.

A whole-body DEXA scan can give regional composition as well as whole-body values, but precision values are considerably poorer than for the whole body. The default breakdown consists of six to seven regions: head, torso, pelvis and four limbs, but other segments can be defined by the operator. Since DEXA does not suffer the basic weakness of densitometry, in that there is no requirement for constant density of the FFM, it has the potential to become the new criterial standard for fat estimation. It is also relatively independent of fluctuations in hydration, as water excess or deficit has been shown to affect only the lean component – as it should. Nevertheless, attempts at validation by carcass analysis have been equivocal. Although recent evidence is promising, more work is needed in this area to establish validity (Prior *et al.*, 1997; Kohrt, 1998). Comparison with underwater weighing is confounded by the different manufacturers' detection, calibration and analysis techniques, as well as by differing types of beam and specifics of the analysis software. Despite these difficulties, there is optimism among researchers that with continued improvement, DEXA will at some point become the criterial standard for body fat assessment. It appears that that time is still some years away.

1.5.3 LEVEL III METHODS

The defining characteristic of a level III method is that it uses an equation that represents an empirically-derived mathematical relationship between its measured parameter and percent fat by the level II method – almost always underwater weighing (though with the rise in acceptance of DEXA, more DEXA-based equations are likely to be published, e.g. Stewart *et al.*, 2000; Eston *et al.*, 2001). This relationship is derived by regression analysis, and typically is a simple linear regression, linear regression of a logarithmic variable, or a quadratic curve fit. Thus all level II methods are *doubly indirect*, and as such, they are vulnerable to the errors and assumptions associated with

underwater weighing, as well as those deriving from their own technique, whether this be skinfold callipers, bioelectrical impedance, infrared interactance or some other approach.

Skinfold thickness: There is good face validity to the idea that a representative measure of the greatest depot of body fat (i.e. subcutaneous) might provide a reasonable estimate of total body fat. This notion becomes less tenable as a greater understanding emerges with respect to various patterns of subcutaneous fat depots and different proportions of fat in the four main storage areas. However, the fact that so many equations have been derived for estimating percent body fat from skinfold thicknesses suggests the need for caution, and an examination of the assumptions underlying the use of skinfold callipers reinforces this.

The skinfold method measures a double fold of skin and subcutaneous adipose by means of callipers which apply a constant pressure over a range of thicknesses (Figure 1.6). In converting this linear distance into a percent fat value, various assumptions are required (Martin *et al.*, 1985). Initially, one must accept that a compressed double layer of skin and subcutaneous adipose is representative of an uncompressed single layer of adipose tissue. This implies that the skin thickness is either negligible or constant and that adipose tissue compresses in a predictable manner. Clearly skin thickness will comprise a greater proportion of a thin skinfold compared to a thicker skinfold and its relationship cannot be regarded as constant. In addition it has been shown that skin thickness varies from individual to individual as well as from site to site, which suggests that it cannot be regarded as negligible (Martin *et al.*, 1992). With respect to compressibility, the evidence suggests that adipose tissue compressibility varies with such factors as age, gender, site, tissue hydration and cell size. The dynamic nature of compressibility is readily observed when callipers are applied to a skinfold and a rapid decline in the needle gauge occurs. The lipid fraction of adipose tissue must also be constant if skinfold thickness is to be indicative of total body lipid. Adipose tissue includes structures other than fat molecules; these include cell membranes, nuclei and organelles. In a relatively empty adipocyte the proportion of fat to other structures may be quite low while a relatively full adipocyte will occupy a proportionately greater volume. Orpin and Scott (1964) suggested that fat content of adipose tissue may range between 5.2% and 94.1% although Martin *et al.* (1994) suggested a general range of 60–85%.

The previous three assumptions relate to the measurement of a single skinfold. There remain two assumptions that must be considered with respect to the validity of skinfold

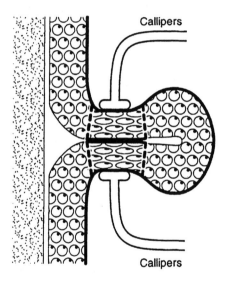

Skin

◐ Subcutaneous adipose tissue

◯ Deformed adipose tissue

▦ Underlying muscle

Figure 1.6 Schematic section through a skinfold at measurement site (adapted from Martin *et al.*, 1985). The calliper jaws exert a constant pressure over a wide range of openings. The skinfold includes skin which varies in thickness from site to site and individual to individual; adipose tissue of variable compressibility and varying proportionate volume occupied by cell membranes, nuclei, organelles and lipid globules.

thickness as a predictor of total body fat. The first deals with the assumption that a limited number of skinfold sites in some way represents the remaining subcutaneous adipose tissue, i.e. the distribution of fat shows some regularity from one person to another. Despite the two general patterns of fat distribution, android – central predominance, and gynoid – gluteofemoral predominance, fat patterns are quite individual. The final assumption is that a limited number of subcutaneous sites are representative of fat deposited non-subcutaneously (omentum, viscera, bone marrow and interstices). While there is some evidence that internal fat increases with subcutaneous fat, this relationship is affected by many variables, particularly age.

The procedure for generating percent fat equations for level III methods can be illustrated by examining the classic approach of Durnin and Womersley (1974). They measured body density (*D*) by underwater weighing, as well as the sum of four skinfolds on 481 men and women, categorized by age and sex. The resulting plots showed a curvilinear shape, so they used the $\log_{10}$ of the sum of the four skinfolds to linearize the relationship and then carried out a linear regression to establish the constants of the equation. As an example, their equation for 20–29-year-old men is:

$$D = 1.1631 - 0.0632 \times \log_{10}(\Sigma 4 \; SF)$$

Siri's equation can then be used to calculate percent fat.

It is important to note that the slopes and intercepts were different for all their sex and age groups, demonstrating that the relationship between body density and the sum of skinfolds differed. Put another way, people from different age and sex groups who have the same sum of skinfolds have different body densities. For a given sum of skinfolds, men have higher body density than women mainly because of higher bone density, greater muscularity and the women's tendency to have more subcutaneous fat in the gluteofemoral region which is not assessed by the four skinfolds that they chose. Similarly, for a given sum of skinfolds, older men have lower body density than young men because of increasing internalization of fat, as well as a decline in muscle mass and bone density. There are other factors such as skin thickness and skinfold compressibility whose variability potentially affects the relationship between skinfolds and body density.

In view of the complexity of percent fat prediction from skinfold thicknesses, some guidelines are helpful when choosing an equation to estimate percent fat in a particular subject. It is important to select an equation that has been derived from a sample whose characteristics (ethnicity, age, sex, athletic status, health status, and so on) are similar to those of the subject to be measured. Equations with few skinfolds cannot detect deviations in fat patterning, so it is better to use equations with skinfold sites that include arm, leg and trunk. Not all equations are based on the same type of skinfold calliper, and since these give different readings for a given skinfold, choice of calliper becomes important. Proper site location and correct technique will help minimize error.

An alternative approach to the use of skinfold measurement is to sum the skinfold thicknesses to form a simple indicator of fatness. Use of this measure avoids many of the untenable assumptions that are inherent in the calculation of percent fat from skinfold thicknesses. This approach can be useful when normative values for the sum of skinfolds are available, as the sum can then be converted into a percentile, showing an individual's relative standing within a population.

Bioelectrical Impedance: Bioelectrical impedance analysis (BIA) is a method of body composition analysis that has become increasingly popular for its ease, portability and moderate cost. The electrical properties, particularly impedance, of living tissue, have been used for more than 50 years to describe and measure certain tissue or organ functions. In recent years bioelectrical impedance has been used to quantify the fat-free mass (FFM) allowing the proportion of body fat to be calculated. The method is based on the electrical properties of hydrous and anhydrous tissues and their electrolyte content. Many reviews of the subject have been published (e.g. Lukaski, 1987; Van Loan, 1990; Oldham, 1996).

Nyboer *et al.* (1943) demonstrated that electrical impedance could be used to determine biological volume. On application of a low voltage to a biological structure, a small alternating current flows through it, using the intra- and extracellular fluids as a conductor and cell membranes as capacitors. The FFM, including the non-lipid components of adipose tissue, contain virtually all of the water and electrolytes of the body and thus the FFM is almost totally responsible for conductance of an electrical current. Impedance to the flow of an electrical current is a function of the resistance and reactance of the conductor. The complex geometry and bioelectrical properties of the human body are confounding factors, but in principle, impedance may be used to estimate the bioelectrical volume of the FFM since it is related to the length and cross-sectional area of the conductor. Equations to estimate either total body water (TBW) or FFM have been developed by regression against criterion methods such as tritium dilution for TBW and densitometry for FFM.

The impedance of biological structures can be measured with electrodes applied to the hands and feet, an excitation current of 800 μA at 50 kHz and a bioelectrical impedance analyser that measures resistance and reactance. Recommended electrode placement varies however, and it now appears that proximal placement may reduce error (Lukaski, 1996). The resulting impedance value (though many systems use only the resistive component) is then entered into an appropriate equation. Many equations have been published to predict the FFM from BIA for various population subsets by age and sex (e.g. Van Loan, 1990). The most frequently occurring component in these equations is the resistive index, which is the square of stature, divided by resistance. Other variables that have been included in prediction equations include height, weight, sex, age, various limb circumferences, reactance, impedance, standing height, arm length and bone breadths. The reported r^2 or R^2 values range between 0.800 and 0.988 with standard error of the estimate (SEE) ranging from 1.90 to 4.02 kg (approximately 2–3%). Slightly lower correlations ($R^2 = 0.76 - 0.92$) have been reported for the prediction of percent fat with an SEE of 3–4%.

Bioelectrical impedance analysis appears to be a safe, simple method of estimating the fat and fat-free masses, but some cautions are needed. As has been discussed previously, the 'criterion' methods are prone to considerable error, which will be propagated into the BIA measurement. As with all level II methods, BIA equations tend to be population specific with generally poor characteristics of fit for a large heterogeneous population. For example, Hodgdon and Fitzgerald (1987) found that a single manufacturer's equation generally overestimated individuals with low percent fat and underestimated individuals with high percent fat. In order to improve the heterogeneity of BIA prediction equations, various anthropometric variables have been introduced (e.g. Segal *et al.*, 1988). By using a large, heterogeneous population, they found that prediction of percent fat improved when gender and fatness specific equations were developed. The fatness specific equations require a priori determination of degree of fatness (< or > 20% and 30% for males and females respectively) by means of anthropometric techniques. In addition the prediction equations included height², mass and age as independent variables. The measurement is influenced by electrode placement, dehydration, exercise, heat and cold exposure, and a conductive surface (Lukaski, 1996), leading to the following recommendations for testing procedures (Heyward, 1991):

- No eating or drinking for 4 hours before the test
- No exercise for 12 hours before the test
- Urinate within 30 minutes before the test

- No alcohol consumption within 48 hours before the test
- No diuretics within 7 days before the test

additionally

- Inaccuracies may be introduced during the pre-menstrual period for women (Gleichauf and Roe, 1989)
- The changing pattern of water and mineral content of growing children suggests that a child-specific prediction equation should be used (Houtkooper *et al.*, 1989; Eston *et al.*, 1990; 1993)

Near infrared interactance (NIR): This technique uses a spectrophotometer and a fibre-optic probe which emits a beam of electromagnetic radiation in the near infrared region. The beam is directed into the body at a specified location, such as the biceps skinfold site, and the return of the scattered and reflected energy is measured to give an optical density. It is unclear why this gives a measure of body fat, but, with the addition of other designated variables (typically some combination of height, weight, age, frame size, and an exercise factor), regression against body density by underwater weighing leads to a prediction equation for percent fat. Comparison studies with other techniques have not demonstrated any advantage of NIR over other techniques. Some found that the method increasingly under-predicted densitometrically determined percent fat as subject fatness increased (Elia *et al.*, 1990), or that the sum of three or seven skinfolds was a better predictor of percent fat determined by underwater weighing than either NIR or BIA (Stout *et al.*, 1996). Correlation coefficients with percent fat determined by underwater weighing fat were moderate and standard errors were too high for accurate prediction (Cassady *et al.*, 1993), despite the large proportion of the variation in percent fat that was explained by the non-NIR variables. Overall, this method does not appear to offer any improvement over existing level III methods.

1.5.4 BODY MASS INDEX AS A MEASURE OF FATNESS

Body weight is often thought of as a measure of fatness, and this perception is reinforced by the use of height–weight tables as an indicator of health risk and life expectancy by the life insurance industry. Superficially it would appear that weight per unit of height is a convenient expression that reflects body build and body composition, and variations of this index have been a recurring theme in anthropometry for over 150 years following the pioneer work of Adolphe Quetelet (1796–1874). The simple ratio of weight to height may appear to be the most informative expression but it expresses a three-dimensional measure (weight) in relation to a one-dimensional measure. Since three-dimensional measures vary as the cube of a linear measure, dimensional consistency would be better served by the expression of mass to the cube of height, a ratio known as the *Ponderal Index*. This is not the end of the discussion however, because a further complicating factor arises since body shape changes as height increases (Ross *et al.*, 1987). Since the objective of the ratio is to examine weight in relative independence of height, several authors have concluded that w/ht^2 – with weight in kg and height in m – is the most appropriate index, and this has been termed the *Body Mass Index* (BMI), the inverse of which was previously known as the *Quetelet Index*.

The BMI has gained acceptance because in many epidemiological studies it shows a moderate correlation with estimates of body fat. However, some of these studies also show very similar correlation values between BMI and estimates of lean body mass. In some populations the BMI is influenced to almost the same degree by the lean and fat compartments of the body, suggesting that it may be as much a measure of lean tissue as it is of fat. Unfortunately, only the correlation values between estimates of body fat and BMI have been used to promote the use of this ratio for individual counselling with respect to health status, diet, weight loss and other fitness factors. On an individual basis, people of the same height will vary with respect to frame size, tissue densities and proportion of various tissues. People may be heavy for their height because of a large, dense skeleton and large muscle mass while others may be as heavy for their height because they carry excess adipose tissue. On an individual basis it would be erroneous to consider relative weight as a measure of obesity or fatness – the scientific evidence is not nearly strong enough to suggest a basis for individual health decisions (Keys *et al.*, 1972; Garn *et al.*, 1986). In summary, BMI is a good indicator of fatness in populations whose overweight individuals are overweight because of fatness, a condition which may hold for certain populations such as all American adults, but not for others such as athletes, for whom it is completely inappropriate.

1.6 THE ANATOMICAL MODEL

The anatomical model has been largely neglected since the rise of densitometry as the criterion method gave dominance to the chemical model. This is unfortunate since, for many applications, anatomical components are of more interest. Elite male athletes will show fat values that are typically in the range 6–12%, regardless of sport. However, measures of total and regional muscularity are considerably better at discriminating between athletes in different sports. Similarly, skeletal mass has been neglected and the chemical component, bone mineral content, has been the common measure of bone status. A strong argument can be made for the use of adipose tissue as a fatness measure since in lean people the amount of total body *fat* has almost no anatomical or physiological meaning. Despite the fact that, by their very nature, anatomical components have both anatomical and physiological significance, there are few proven techniques for estimating them.

1.6.1 ADIPOSE TISSUE

Surprisingly, there are no equations to estimate adipose tissue mass from skinfolds, BIA or any other level III method. The only current approach is the use of the medical imaging techniques such as computerized tomography (CT), magnetic resonance imaging (MRI) or ultrasound. Though these methods depend on very different physical principles, from the viewpoint of body composition analysis they are very similar. Each gives a cross-sectional view at a selected level of the body, from which areas of different tissues can be quantified. This quantification can be done with scan analysis software, or by scanning the resulting radiograph into a microcomputer for subsequent image analysis. A single scan is unable to yield adipose or any other tissue mass, however. It is at best, an indicator of fatness in that region of the body. Adipose tissue volumes of a selected region, or of the whole body, can be calculated by geometric modelling of areas from a series of contiguous scans. A plot of adipose tissue area from each scan against the distance of the scan from one extremity of the body (foot) shows the distribution of adipose tissue along the body, and the area under this curve gives total adipose tissue volume. Multiplying this by adipose tissue density gives adipose tissue mass. This approach has also used ultrasound imaging at measured points on the arm and thigh to estimate segmental fat and lean mass volumes (Eston *et al.*, 1994). While medical imaging techniques could be used as a criterion measure against which level III methods, particularly skinfolds, could be calibrated, this has not yet been done, and only a small number of subjects have been investigated in this manner. However, CT and MRI have proved very useful in the study of intra-abdominal adiposity, which is discussed in a later section.

1.6.2 MUSCLE

The quantity and proportion of body fat have remained a focal point in body composition analysis because of the perceived negative relationship of fatness to health, fitness and sport performance. It is evident to many working with high-performance athletes that knowledge of the changing total and regional masses of muscle in an athlete is an equal or perhaps more significant factor in sport performance. Estimation of total and regional muscle mass has not received the same attention as estimation of fat mass although it could be argued that there is more variability, and therefore a greater need to know, amongst athletes in muscle mass than in body fat. Anatomical (tissue-based) models for estimating total muscle mass have been proposed by Matiegka (1921), Heymsfield *et al.* (1982), Drinkwater *et al.* (1986), and Martin *et al.* (1990). The early approach of Matiegka (1921) was based on the recognition that total muscle mass was in large part reflected by the size of muscles on the extremities. Thus, he proposed that muscle mass could be predicted by using skinfold-corrected diameters of muscle from the upper arm, the forearm, the thigh and calf multiplied by stature, and an empirically derived constant. Drinkwater *et al.* (1986) attempted to validate Matiegka's formula using the evidence of the Brussels Cadaver Study and proposed modifications to the original mathematical constant. Martin *et al.* (1990) published equations for the estimation of muscle mass in men, based on cadaver evidence. Data from six unembalmed cadavers were used to derive a regression equation to predict total muscle mass. The proposed equation was subsequently validated by predicting the known muscle masses from a separate cohort of five embalmed cadavers ($r^2 = 0.93$, SEE 1.58 kg, approximately 0.5%) and comparing the results to estimates derived from the equations of Matiegka (1921) and Heymsfield *et al.* (1982). The equation recommended by Martin *et al.* (1990) predicted muscle mass more accurately than the other two equations, which substantially underestimated the muscle mass of what must be regarded as a limited sample. Martin *et al.* (1990) attempted to minimize the specificity of their equation by ensuring that

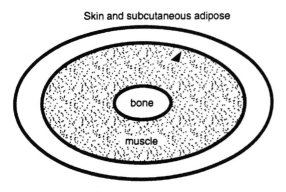

Skin and subcutaneous adipose

Figure 1.7 Schematic view of the derivation of estimated muscle and bone area from a measurement of external girth. There are inherent assumptions that the perimeters are circular and that a single skinfold measure is representative of the entire subcutaneous layer of the section. Muscle and bone area = $\pi ((c/2\pi) - (SF/2))^2$, where c = girth measure (cm), SF = skinfold (cm).

the upper and lower body were both represented in the three circumference terms.

Several of the above methods are based on the geometric model of extremity girths describing a circle and a single skinfold as representative of a constant subcutaneous layer overlying a circular muscle mass. A simple formula predicts the skinfold corrected geometric properties of the combined muscle and bone tissue (Figure 1.7).

$$\text{muscle and bone} = \pi \left(\frac{c}{2\pi} - \frac{SF}{2} \right)^2$$

where c is girth measure (cm) and SF is skinfold (cm).

Further, the volume of the segments of the limb have been predicted by use of the formula for a truncated cone. The anthropometric/geometric model has been found consistently to overestimate muscle area when compared to areas measured from computed tomography and magnetic resonance images (de Koning *et al.*, 1986; Baumgartner *et al.*, 1992). Nevertheless, the correlation between anthropo-

metrically derived areas and imaged areas has been shown to be very high, $r > 0.9$.

The relationship of cross-sectional area of muscle to force output is well established (Ikai and Fukunaga, 1968). Knowledge of the changing size of muscle resulting from particular training regimens is therefore important information for a coach evaluating the effect of the programme and for the motivation of the athlete (Hawes and Sovak, 1994). Size of muscle relative to body mass may provide information on a young athlete's stage of development and readiness for certain categories of skill development; changing size of muscle may reflect the effectiveness of a particular exercise or activity; diminished size may reflect a lack of recovery time (over-training) or in-season response to changing patterns of training. In all instances regular feedback of results to the coach may provide early information for adjustment or enhancement of the training regimens.

1.6.3 BONE

The skeleton is a dynamic tissue responding to environmental and endocrine changes by altering its shape and its density. Nevertheless it is less volatile than either muscle or adipose tissue and its influence upon human performance has been largely neglected. Matiegka (1921) proposed that skeletal mass could be estimated from an equation that included stature, the maximum diameter of the humerus, wrist, femur and ankle and a mathematical constant. Drinkwater *et al.* (1986) attempted to validate the proposed equation against recent cadaver data and found that an adjustment to Matiegka's constant produced a more accurate estimate in their sample of older, cadaveric persons. Drinkwater *et al.* (1986) commented that the true value of the coefficient probably lies between the original and their calculated value. An estimation of bone mass within a prototypical model may provide insight into structural factors that contribute to athletic success. In a longitudinal study of high performance synchronized swimmers, Hawes and Sovak (1993) found that the world and Olympic champion had disproportionally narrow bone diameters compared to other synchronized swimmers competing at the international level. Since positive buoyancy contributes to the ease of performing exercises above water, a relatively small mass of the most dense body tissue might be construed as a morphological advantage in athletes of otherwise equal abilities.

1.7 BODY FAT DISTRIBUTION

The relationship between increasing body fat and health risk is generally accepted, even though two people with the same percent fat may have very different risks of cardiovascular-related diseases. This anomaly was addressed over 50 years ago by Vague (1947), who noted two general patterns of fat distribution on the body, which he designated as android and gynoid because of their predominance in males and females respectively. Greater health risk is associated with the android pattern of trunk deposition than the gynoid pattern of gluteofemoral deposition. The use of medical imaging techniques to quantify abdominal adiposity has demonstrated that it is the intra-abdominal adipose tissue that is associated with the highest health risk. Both MRI and CT have been used successfully to measure adipose compartments of the abdomen. The full procedure is to take a series of consecutive scans that cover the whole abdominal region. Areas of subcutaneous and internal adipose tissue are determined from each scan and the corresponding volumes are generated since the distance between scans is known. However, a single scan at the level of the umbilicus shows a very high correlation ($r > 0.9$) with intra-abdominal adipose tissue volume (Abate *et al.*, 1997). These methods are very expensive, and are more use in research than in screening or individual evaluation.

The simplest approach to quantifying fat distribution is the use of the ratio of waist circumference to hip circumference (WHR). Waist circumference is variously taken at the waist narrowing, the umbilicus, or other skeletally-determined locations, while hip circumference is taken at the maximum gluteal girth. Bjorntorp (1984) suggested that a ratio of 1:1 in men is indicative of a significant elevation in the risk of ischaemic heart and cerebrovascular disease. The corresponding ratio representing increased risk for women is 0.8:1. The robustness of the association of WHR with health risk factors in large-scale epidemiological studies has been underscored by a substantial body of research that demonstrates important metabolic differences between abdominal and gluteofemoral adipose tissue. A tentative explanation for why women of reproductive age have great difficulty in reducing gynoid fat deposits is that gluteofemoral adiposity is an evolutionary adaptation to store fat for the energy-demanding lactational phase of childbearing; studies show that lipolysis in this region is facilitated by the endocrine environment of lactation. Thus, though some women may want to reduce excess gluteofemoral fat, its presence is often more of an aesthetic issue than a health issue. As a general summary, this ratio appears to have some utility in the assessment of health risk although it should be used with caution.

1.8 OTHER CONSIDERATIONS

This chapter has presented an overview of the issues surrounding the quantification of body composition *in vivo*. There are several issues in body composition that must be resolved before the field can advance to maturity. The most important is the absence of validation and the consequent lack of a true criterion method. While DEXA is well placed to assume this role for percent fat, some methodological improvements are needed before then. Considerable work has been done in recent years on multicomponent models which estimate body fat by equations incorporating a number of measured variables, such as body density, total body water, and bone mineral content. In this way it is hoped that the improvement in prediction is not offset by the increased error inherent in the measurement of many variables. A detailed description of this approach is given elsewhere (Heymsfield *et al.*, 1996). The second problem is the traditional focus on the chemical model, specifically fat. This has meant that sport scientists and others have few proven tools for quantifying body constituents that have physiological and anatomical meaning, particularly muscle. The advances in medical imaging discussed here may help to address this issue, but these methods are expensive and difficult for many to access.

Other methods of assessing body composition have been developed and successfully used in the field. The use of percentile rankings against a normative database gives much useful information. One such approach is the 'O' Scale system (Ross *et al.*, 1986), which therefore avoids the use of biological constants whose limitations have been discussed at length. An individual is plotted on two parallel nine point scales for adiposity, measured by sum of skinfolds and body weight relative to normative data (>22,000 Canadian subjects) for age and sex. The resulting graph provides separately, the individual status of body weight and adiposity relative to a normal population. Thus an individual who appears to be heavy for a given height may be shown as heavy for the reason of a high adiposity value or may be heavy despite a low adiposity value implying a relative high value for adipose free tissues, particularly muscle and bone. The scales are sensitive to change over relatively short time periods and are well suited for monitoring progress within a training or fitness regimen. A norm-based approach has also been advocated for children (Martin and Ward, 1996).

In summary, care must be taken in applying body composition methods because of their sample specificity and poor validation. Because of this the best use of body composition techniques is probably for repeated measures in the same individuals over a period of time to investigate change due to growth, ageing or some intervention. The following laboratory exercises are designed to provide an introduction to a variety of body composition assessment procedures.

1.9 PRACTICAL 1: DENSITOMETRY

1.9.1 PURPOSE

- To determine body composition by densitometry

1.9.2 METHODS

1. The subject should report to the laboratory several hours postprandial. A form-fitting swimsuit is the most appropriate attire.
2. Height, body mass and age should be recorded using the methods specified in Practical 3.
3. Determination of total body density.

Facilities will vary from custom-built tanks to swimming pools. The following is an outline of the major procedures:

- Determine the tare weight of the suspended seat or platform together with weight belt.
- Record the water temperature and barometric pressure.
- The subject should enter the tank and ensure that all air bubbles (clinging to hair or trapped in swimsuit) are removed.

- Subjects who may have difficulty in maintaining full submersion should attach a weight belt of approximately 3 kg.
- The subject quietly submerses while sitting or squatting on the freely suspended platform and exhales to a maximum. Drawing the knees up to the chest will facilitate complete evacuation of the lungs. The subject remains as still as possible and the scale reading is recorded.
- This procedure is repeated 4 – 5 times with the most consistent highest value accepted as the underwater weight.
4. Determination of residual volume (*RV*).

- *RV* is the volume of air remaining in the lungs following a maximal exhalation.
- *RV* may be measured by the N_2 dilution method or estimated from age and height.
- If the *RV* is to be measured, there is evidence to suggest that the procedure should be completed with the subject submersed to the neck in order to approximate the pressure acting on the lungs in a fully submersed position.
- The equipment used to determine *RV* will vary from laboratory to laboratory. The fundamental procedure is as follows:
  - The gas analyser should be calibrated according to manufacturer's specifications.
  - A three-way T-valve is connected to a 5 litre anaesthetic bag, a pure oxygen tank and a spirometer. The system (spirometer, bag, valve and tubing) should be flushed with oxygen three times. On the fourth occasion a measured quantity (approximately 5 litres) of oxygen is introduced into the spirometer bell, the O_2 valve is closed and the T-valve opened to permit the O_2 to pass into the anaesthetic bag. The bag is closed off with a spring clip and is removed from the system together with the T-valve. A mouthpiece hose is attached to the T-valve.
  - The subject prepares by attaching a nose clip and immersing to the neck in the tank. The mouthpiece is inserted and the valve opened so that the subject is breathing room air. When comfortable the subject exhales maximally drawing the knees to the chest in a similar posture to that adopted during underwater weighing since *RV* is affected by posture (see Chapter 3 Volume 2, by Eston). At maximum exhalation the T-valve is opened to the pure O_2 anaesthetic bag and the subject takes 5–6 regular inhalation–exhalation cycles. On a signal the subject again exhales maximally and the T-valve to the anaesthetic bag is closed. The subject removes the mouthpiece and breathes normally. The anaesthetic bag is attached to the gas analysers and values for the CO_2 and O_2 are recorded.
  - Measurement of *RV* should be repeated several times to ensure consistent results.

1.9.3 CALCULATION OF RESIDUAL VOLUME AND DENSITY

(a) Measured residual volume (Wilmore *et al.*, 1980)

$$RV = \frac{VO_2 \text{(ml)} \times FEN_2}{0.798 - FEN_2} - DS\text{(ml)} \times BTPS$$

where:
$\dot{V}O_2$ is the volume of O_2 measured into the anaesthetic bag (~5 litres)

FEN$_2$ is the fraction of N$_2$ at the point where equilibrium of the gas analyser occurred calculated as:

$$[100\% - (\%O_2 + \%CO_2)] / 100$$

DS is the dead space of mouthpiece and breathing valve (calculated from the specific situation)

BTPS is the body temperature pressure saturated correction factor which corrects the volume of measured gas to ambient conditions of the lung according to Table 1.1.

Table 1.1 BTPS Correction Factors

Gas temp. (°C)	Correction factor	Gas temp. (°C)	Correction factor
20.0	1.102	24.0	1.079
20.5	1.099	24.5	1.077
21.0	1.096	25.0	1.074
21.5	1.093	25.5	1.071
22.0	1.091	26.0	1.069
22.5	1.089	26.5	1.065
23.0	1.085	27.0	1.062
23.5	1.082	27.5	1.060

(b) Predicted residual volume

Men: $RV = 0.0115$ (age) $+ 0.019$ (*ht* in cm) $- 2.240$ (Boren *et al.*, 1966)

Women: $RV = 0.0210$ (age) $+ 0.023$ (*ht* in cm) $- 2.978$ (Boren *et al.*, 1966)

Estimated *RV* (Boren *et al.*, 1966) has been shown to have a standard error of measurement (SEM) of 0.29 litres when compared to an actual *RV* of 0.13 litres in athletes (Morrow *et al.*, 1985). Transformed to percent fat units this represents a SEM of 2.0% fat. The SEM of measured *RV* was 0.2% fat. Alternative equations for the prediction of *RV* in adults and children are available (see Eston, Chapter 3, Volume 2).

1.9.4 BODY DENSITY CALCULATIONS

$$Body\,Volume\,(V_b) = \frac{(mass\,in\,air\ -\ mass\,in\,water)}{density\,of\,water\,corrected\,for\ water\,temperature} \qquad Body\,Density\,(D_b) = \frac{mass\,in\,air}{(V_b - trapped\,air)}$$

where:
   trapped air = residual lung volume + tubing dead space + 100 ml (100 ml is the conventional allowance for gastrointestinal gases) and the correction for water temperature is according to Table 1.2.

Table 1.2   Water Temperature Correction

H_2O temp.	Density of H_2O
25.0	0.997
28.0	0.996
31.0	0.995
35.0	0.994
38.0	0.993

%Fat according to Siri (1956) = [(4.95 / body density) − 4.50] × 100
%Fat according to Brozek *et al.* (1963) = [(4.57 / body density) − 4.142] × 100

Interpretation

Table 1.3 is based on the normative data from Katch and McKardle (1983) and Durnin and Womersley (1974). It should be noted that 'obesity' is often defined as >25% fat for men and >30% fat for women, although this should be interpreted with caution.

Table 1.3

Age (years)	%Fat (mean±SD)	
	Men	Women
17–30	15±5	25±5
30–50	23±7	30±6
50–70	28±8	35±6

1.10 PRACTICAL 2: MEASUREMENT OF SKINFOLDS

1.10.1 PURPOSE

- To develop the technique of measuring skinfolds
- To compare various methods of computing estimates of proportionate fatness

1.10.2 METHODS

A well-organized and established set of procedures will ensure that test sessions go smoothly and that there can be no implication of impropriety when measuring subjects. The procedures should include:

- Prior preparation of equipment and recording forms
- Arrangements for a suitable space which is clean, warm and quiet
- Securing the assistance of an individual who will record values
- Forewarning the subjects that testing will occur at a given time and place
- Ensuring that females bring a bikini style swimsuit to facilitate measurement in the abdominal region and that males wear loose fitting shorts or speed swimsuit
- The measurer's technique must include recognition and respect for the notion of personal space and sensitive areas
- Great care must be taken in the consistent location of measurement sites as defined in Figures 1.8 to 1.15 and section 1.10.3
- Recognition that the data are very powerful in both a positive and *negative* sense. Young adolescents in particular are very sensitive about their body image and making public specific or implied information on body composition values may have a negative effect on an individual

(a) Skinfold measurements – general technique

- A warm room and easy atmosphere will help the subject to relax which will help you to manipulate the skinfold
- During measurement the subject should stand erect but relaxed through the shoulders and arms
- The site should be marked with a washable felt pen
- The objective is to raise a double fold of skin and subcutaneous adipose leaving the underlying muscle undisturbed
- All skinfolds are measured on the right side of the body
- The measurer takes the fold between thumb and forefinger of the left hand – this procedure is facilitated by a slight rolling and pulling action
- The calliper is held in the right hand and the pressure plates of the calliper are applied perpendicularly to the fold and 1 cm below or to the right of the fingers depending on the direction of the raised skinfold (e.g., see Figure 8.4)
- The calliper is held in position for 2 s prior to recording the measurement to the nearest 0.2 mm (the grasp is maintained throughout the measurement)
- All skinfolds should be measured three times with at least a 2 minute interval to allow the tissue to restore to its uncompressed form; the median value is the accepted value

(b) Secondary computation of fatness

There are over 100 equations for predicting fatness from skinfold measurements. The fact that these equations sometimes predict quite different values for the same individual leads to the conclusion that the equations are population-specific, i.e. the equation only accurately predicts the criterion value (usually densitometrically determined) for the specific population in the validation study, and when applied to other populations the equation loses its validity. This diversity will be illustrated if you compute estimates of percent fat from the following frequently used equations. It should be observed that while inter-individual comparisons of percent fat may not be valid for many of the reasons previously discussed, intra-individual comparisons of repeated measurements may provide useful information. The summation of skinfold values will also provide comparative values avoiding some of the assumptions associated with estimates of proportionate fatness.

(c) Percent fat equations (skinfold sites shown in Table 1.4)

Parizkova (1978) – ten sites

$$\%\text{Fat} = 39.572 \log X - 61.25 \text{ (females } 17 - 45 \text{ years)}$$
$$\%\text{Fat} = 22.32 \log X - 29.00 \text{ (males } 17 - 45 \text{ years)}$$

where:

$$X = \Sigma10 \text{ skinfolds as specified (mm)}$$

Durnin and Womersley (1974) – four sites

$$\text{body density} = 1.1610 - 0.0632 \log\Sigma4 \text{ (men)}$$
$$\text{body density} = 1.1581 - 0.0720 \log\Sigma4 \text{ (women)}$$
$$\text{body density} = 1.1533 - 0.0643 \log\Sigma4 \text{ (boys)}$$
$$\text{body density} = 1.1369 - 0.0598 \log\Sigma4 \text{ (girls)}$$
$$\%\text{Fat (Siri, 1956)} = [(4.95 / \text{body density}) - 4.5] \times 100$$

where:

$$\Sigma4 = \Sigma4 \text{ skinfolds as specified (mm)}$$

Jackson and Pollock (1978) – three sites

$$\text{body density of males} = 1.1093800 - 0.0008267 (\Sigma3_M) + 0.0000016 (\Sigma3_M)^2 - 0.0002574 (X2)$$

Jackson et al. (1980) – three sites (females)

$$\text{body density of females} = 1.099421 - 0.0009929 (\Sigma3_F) + 0.0000023 (\Sigma3_F)^2 - 0.0001392 (X2)$$
$$\%\text{Fat (Siri, 1956)} = [(4.95 / \text{body density}) - 4.5] \times 100$$

where:

$$\Sigma3_M = \Sigma3 \text{ skinfolds (mm) as specified for males}$$
$$\Sigma3_F = \Sigma3 \text{ skinfolds (mm) as specified for females}$$
$$X2 = \text{age (years)}$$

Jackson and Pollock (1978) – seven sites

body density of males = $1.112 - 0.00043499\ (\Sigma 7) + 0.00000055\ (\Sigma 7)^2 - 0.00028826\ (X2)$

Jackson et al. (1980) – seven sites

body density of females = $1.097 - 0.00046971\ (\Sigma 7) + 0.00000056\ (\Sigma 7)^2 - 0.00012828\ (X2)$

%Fat (Siri, 1956) = $[(4.95\ /\ \text{body density}) - 4.5] \times 100$

where:

$\Sigma 7 = \Sigma 7$ skinfolds as specified (mm)

$X2$ = age (years)

Table 1.4 Summary of skinfold sites used in selected equations for prediction of percent fat

Reference	*Parizkova (1978)*	*Jackson et al. (1980)*	*Jackson and Pollock, (1978)*	*Jackson et al. (1980)*	*Jackson and Pollock (1978)*	*Durnin and Womersley (1974)*
Sum of skinfolds	$\Sigma 10$	$\Sigma 3$	$\Sigma 3$	$\Sigma 7$	$\Sigma 7$	$\Sigma 4$
Population	*M & F*	*Female*	*Male*	*Female*	*Male*	*M & F*
Skinfold site						
Cheek	*					
Chin	*					
Pectoral (chest 1)	*		*	*	*	
Axilla (midaxillary)				*	*	
Chest 2	*					
Abdomen	*					
Abdominal			*	*	*	
Iliac crest*	*					*
Suprailium		*		*	*	
Subscapular	*			*	*	*
Triceps	*	*		*	*	*
Biceps						*
Patella	*					
Midthigh		*	*	*	*	
Proximal calf	*					

*Termed 'suprailiac' by Durnin and Womersley (1974) and 'iliocristale' by Parizkova (1978).

1.10.3 LOCATIONS OF SKINFOLD SITES

All measurements are taken on the right side of the body

Cheek *horizontal* skinfold raised at the midpoint of the line connecting the tragus (cartilaginous projection anterior to the external opening of the ear) and the nostrils (Figure 1.8).

Chin *vertical* skinfold raised above the hyoid bone: the head is slightly lifted but the skin of the neck must stay loose (Figure 1.8).

Pectoral (Chest 1) *oblique* skinfold raised along the borderline of the pectoralis major between the anterior axillary fold and the nipple.
Females measurement is taken at ⅓ of the distance between anterior axillary fold and nipple.
Males measurement is taken at ½ of the distance between anterior axillary fold and nipple (Figure 1.9).

Axilla *vertical* skinfold raised at the level of the xiphosternal junction (midaxillary) on the midaxillary line (Figure 1.10).

Chest 2 *horizontal* skinfold raised on the chest above the 10th rib at the point of intersection with the anterior axillary line – slight angle along the ribs (Figure 1.10).

Abdomen *horizontal* fold raised 3 cm lateral and 1 cm inferior to the umbilicus (Figure 1.11).

Abdominal *vertical* fold raised at a lateral distance of approximately 2 cm from the umbilicus (Figure 1.11).

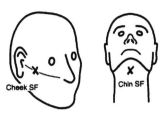

Figure 1.8 Location of the cheek and chin skinfold sites.

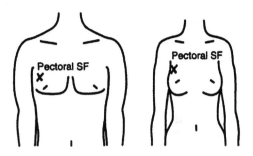

Figure 1.9 Location of the pectoral skinfold sites.

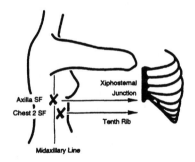

Figure 1.10 Location of the axilla and chest 2 skinfold sites.

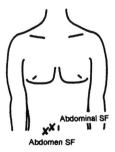

Figure 1.11 Location of the abdominal skinfold sites.

Iliac crest *diagonal* fold raised immediately above the crest of the ilium on a vertical line from the mid-axilla (Figure 1.12). This skinfold was referred to as the Suprailiac by Durnin and Womersley (1974) and Iliocristale by Parizkova (1978).

Suprailium *diagonal* fold above the crest of the ilium at the point where an imaginary line would come down from the anterior axillary border (Figure 1.12). It is slightly anterior to the iliac crest.

Supraspinale *diagonal* skinfold following the natural cleavage lines of the skin. It is raised 5–7 cm above the anterior superior iliac spine on a line from the anterior axillary border to the spinale (Figure 1.12). This skinfold is used for somatotyping (Chapter 2) and is more anterior than the suprailium (Figure 1.12).

Subscapular *oblique* skinfold raised 1 cm below the inferior angle of the scapula at approximately 45° to the horizontal plane following the natural cleavage lines of the skin (Figure 1.13).

Triceps *vertical* skinfold raised on the posterior aspect of the m. triceps, exactly halfway between the olecranon process and the acromion process when the hand is supinated (Figure 1.13).

Biceps *vertical* skinfold raised on the anterior aspect of the biceps, at the same horizontal level as the triceps skinfold skin (Figure 1.13).

Patella *vertical* skinfold in the mid-sagittal plane raised 2 cm above the proximal edge of the patella. The subject should bend the knee slightly (Figure 1.14).

Midthigh *vertical* skinfold raised on the anterior aspect of the thigh midway between the inguinal crease and the

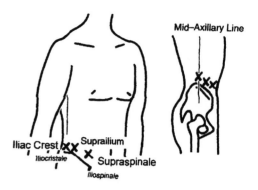

Figure 1.12 Location of the skinfold sites in the iliac crest region.

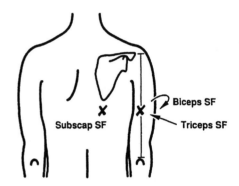

Figure 1.13 Location of the biceps, triceps and subscapular skinfold sites.

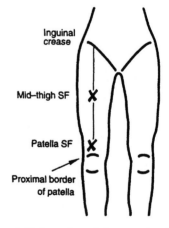

Figure 1.14 Location of the anterior thigh skinfold sites.

proximal border of the patella (Figure 1.14). The knee should be flexed at an angle of 90° with the subject in a seated position or the subject could stand with the foot placed on a box.

Proximal calf *vertical* skinfold raised on the posterior aspect of the calf in the mid-sagittal plane 5 cm inferior to the fossa poplitea (Figure 1.15).

Medial calf *vertical* skinfold raised on the medial aspect of the calf at the level of the maximum circumference (Figure 1.15). The subject may be sitting or have the foot placed on a box.

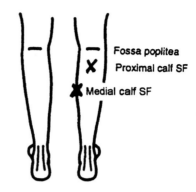

Figure 1.15 Location of the proximal and medial calf skinfold site.

1.11 PRACTICAL 3: PROPORTIONATE WEIGHT, DISTRIBUTION OF ADIPOSE TISSUE AND FAT-FREE MASS

1.11.1 PURPOSE

- To evaluate body mass index
- To evaluate waist to hip ratio as a measure of fat patterning
- To determine fat-free mass by bioelectrical impedance

1.11.2 METHOD: BODY MASS INDEX (BMI)

- BMI = body mass (kg) / stature^2 (m)
- Describes weight for height
- Often used in epidemiological studies as a measure of obesity
- A high BMI means proportionately high weight for height

(a) Stature

- As height is variable throughout the day (see Chapter 4, section 4.8, Dangerfield), the measurement should be performed at the same time for each test session (height may still vary due to activities causing compression of the intervertebral discs, i.e. running)
- All stature measurements should be taken with the subject barefoot
- The **Frankfurt Plane** refers to the position of the head when the line joining the orbitale (lower margin of eye socket) to the tragion (notch above tragus of the ear) is horizontal
- There are several techniques for measuring height which yield slightly different values. The following technique is recommended:

(b) Stature against a wall

- Subject stands erect, feet together against a wall on a flat surface at a right angle to the wall mounted stadiometer
- A stadiometer consists of a vertical board with an attached metric rule and a horizontal headboard that slides to contact the vertex
- The heels, buttocks, upper back and (if possible) cranium should touch the wall
- The subject's head should be in the Frankfurt Plane, arms relaxed at sides
- The subject is instructed to inhale and stretch up
- The measurer slides the headboard of the stadiometer down to the vertex and records the measurement to the nearest 0.1 cm

(c) Body mass

- Use a calibrated beam-type balance
- The subject should be weighed without shoes and in minimal clothing
- For best results, repeated measurements should be taken at the same time of day, in the same state of hydration and nourishment after voiding (preferably first thing in the morning – 12 hours after ingesting food)
- Measurement is recorded to the nearest 0.1 kg

(d) Interpretation

- Values ≤ 19 or ≥ 26 are considered to place an individual in health risk zones according to morbidity and mortality data for males and females 2–60 years. These values should be considered within the context of the discussion presented previously.

1.11.3 METHOD: WAIST-TO-HIP RATIO (WHR)

- WHR = waist girth / hip girth
- May be used in conjunction with trunk skinfolds to determine whether excess fat is being carried in the trunk region
- A high WHR combined with high trunk skinfolds has been shown to be associated with increased morbidity, glucose intolerance, hyperinsulinaemia, blood lipid disorders and mortality
- A high WHR with low skinfolds may be associated with high trunk muscle development

(a) Tape technique (cross-handed technique)

- The metal case of the measure is held in the right hand and the stub end is controlled by the left hand
- Girths are measured with the tape at right angles to the long axis of the bone
- The tape is pulled out of its case and around the body segment by the left hand, the two hands are crossed intersecting the tape at the zero mark
- The aim is to obtain the circumference of the part with the tape in contact with, but not depressing, the fleshy contour

(b) Waist girth

- The subject stands erect, abdomen relaxed, arms at sides, feet together
- The measurer stands facing subject and places a steel tape measure around the subject's natural waist (the obvious narrowing between the rib and the iliac crest)
- If there is no obvious waist, find the smallest horizontal circumference in this region
- Measurement is taken at the end of a normal expiration to the nearest 0.1 cm

(c) Hip girth

- The subject stands erect, buttocks relaxed, feet together, preferably wearing underwear or swimsuit
- The measurer stands to one side of the subject and places the steel tape measure around the hips at the horizontal level of greatest gluteal protuberance (usually at the level of the symphysis pubis)
- Check that the tape is not compressing the skin and record to the nearest 0.1 cm

(d) Interpretation

- Values of ≥ 0.90 (males) and ≥ 0.80 (females) are considered to place an individual in health risk zones according to morbidity and mortality data for males and females 20–70 years. These values should be considered within the context of the discussion presented previously.

1.11.4 METHOD: BIOELECTRICAL IMPEDANCE ANALYSIS (BIA)

- Based on the electrical conductance characteristics of hydrous (fat-free) and anhydrous (fat component) tissues
- The impedance to the flow of an electrical current is a function of resistance and reactance and is related to length and cross-sectional area of the conductor (the hydrous or fat-free tissue)
- The unit of electrical resistance (Ω) is most commonly used to represent impedance

(a) Test conditions

Prior to testing the subject should:

- Not have had anything to eat or drink in the previous 4 hours
- Not have exercised within the previous 12 hours
- Not have consumed alcohol within the previous 48 hours
- Not have used diuretics within the previous 7 days
- Have urinated within the previous 30 minutes

(b) Anthropometric procedures (tetrapolar method)

- As defined by the manufacturer (if using the pre-programmed function of the unit) or according to the equation of choice
- The subject should lie supine on a table with the legs slightly apart and the right hand and foot bare

- Four electrodes are prepared with electro-conducting gel and attached at the following sites (or as per manufacturer's instructions)
- Just proximal to the dorsal surface of the third metacarpal-phalangeal joint on the right hand
- On the dorsal surface of the right wrist adjacent to the head of the ulna
- On the dorsal surface of the right foot just proximal to the second metatarsal-phalangeal joint
- On the anterior surface of the right ankle between the medial and lateral malleoli
- The subject should lie quietly while the analyser is turned on and off
- The subject should lie quietly for 5 minutes before repeating the procedure.

(c) Calculations

- As per manufacturer's instructions

  or

- Females: FFM (kg) = 4.917 + 0.821 (ht^2/R) (Lukaski *et al.*, 1986)
- Males: FFM (kg) = 5.214 + 0.827 (ht^2/R) (Lukaski *et al.*, 1986)
- FFM (kg) = 17.7868 + 0.00098(ht^2) + 0.3736M − 0.0238R − 4.2921(sex) − 0.1531(age)

                                  (Van Loan and Mayclin, 1987)

where:
  ht = height (cm)
  R = resistance (Ω)
  M = mass (kg)
  sex for males = 0, females = 1
  age in years.

1.12 PRACTICAL 4: ESTIMATION OF MUSCLE MASS AND REGIONAL MUSCULARITY

1.12.1 PURPOSE

- To develop the technique required to estimate total and regional muscularity

1.12.2 METHODS

Matiegka (1921) – males and females

$$M \text{ (kg)} = [(CDU + CDF + CDT + CDC)/8]^2 \times ht \text{ (cm)} \times 6.5 \times 0.001$$

$$M \% = (M \text{ (kg)} / \text{body mass}) \times 100$$

where:

$$CDU = \frac{(\text{max upper arm girth})}{\pi} - \text{triceps } SF \text{ (cm)}$$

$$CDF = \frac{(\text{max forearm girth})}{\pi} - \frac{(\text{forearm } SF1 \text{ (cm)} + \text{forearm } SF2 \text{ (cm)})}{2}$$

$$CDT = \frac{(\text{midthigh girth})}{\pi} - \text{thigh } SF \text{ (cm)}$$

$$CDC = \frac{(\text{max calf girth})}{\pi} - \text{proximal calf } SF \text{ (cm)}$$

- *ht* is stature in cm
- Variables for computing corrected diameters are defined on the following pages
- *CD* is the corrected diameter of *U* = upper arm, *F* = forearm, *T* = thigh, *C* = calf
- Note that skinfolds should be expressed in cm, i.e. scale reading on the skinfold calliper/ 10

Martin et al. (1990) – males only

$$M \text{ (kg)} = [ht \times (0.0553CTG^2 + 0.0987FG^2 + 0.0331CCG^2) - 2445] \times 0.001$$

$$M \% = (M \text{ (kg)} / \text{body mass}) \times 100$$

where:
ht is stature in cm
CTG is the corrected thigh girth = thigh girth – π (front thigh *SF*/10)
FG is the maximum forearm girth
CCG is the corrected calf girth = calf girth – π (medial calf *SF*/10)

1.12.3 DETERMINATION OF VARIABLES RELATED TO ESTIMATION OF MUSCLE MASS

Stature (*ht*) as before (Practical 3)

Maximum upper arm girth (cm)

- The girth measurement of the upper arm at the insertion of the deltoid muscle
- The subject stands erect with the arm abducted to the horizontal, the measurer stands behind the arm of the subject, marks the insertion of the deltoid muscle and measures the girth perpendicular to the long axis of the arm

Maximum forearm girth (cm)

- The maximum circumference at the proximal part of the forearm (usually within 5 cm of the elbow)
- The subject stands erect with the arm extended in the horizontal plane with the hand supinated, the measurer stands behind the subject's arm and moves the tape up and down the forearm (perpendicular to the long axis) until the maximum circumference of the forearm is located

Mid thigh girth (cm)

- The girth taken at the midpoint between the trochanterion and the tibiale laterale
- The subject stands erect, feet 10 cm apart and weight evenly distributed, the measurer crouches to the right side, palpates and marks the trochanterion and the tibiale laterale. The midpoint is found using a tape or anthropometer
- The girth is taken at this level, perpendicular to the long axis of the thigh

Maximum calf girth (cm)

- The subject stands erect, feet 10 cm apart and weight evenly distributed, the measurer crouches to the right side, and moves the tape up and down the calf, perpendicular to the long axis until the greatest circumference is located

Triceps skinfold (cm)

- As before (Practical 2)

Thigh skinfold (cm)

- As before (Practical 2)

Proximal calf skinfold (cm)

- As before (Practical 2)

Medial calf skinfold (cm)

- A vertical skinfold taken on the medial aspect of the calf at the level of maximum calf girth, the subject stands with the right foot on a platform, flexing the knee and hip to 90°

Forearm 1 (lateralis) (cm)

- A vertical skinfold taken at the level of maximum forearm girth on the lateral aspect of the forearm with the hand supinated

Forearm 2 (volaris) (cm)

- A vertical skinfold taken at the level of maximum forearm girth taken on the anterior aspect of the forearm with the hand supinated

1.13 PRACTICAL 5: ESTIMATION OF SKELETAL MASS

- An indication of skeletal robustness that correlates highly with bone breadths at the elbow, wrist, knee and ankle

1.13.1 PURPOSE

- To develop the technique required to estimate skeletal mass by anthropometry

1.13.2 METHODS

Matiegka (1921) – males and females.

$$S \text{ (kg)} = [(HB + WB + FB + AB)/4]^2 \times ht \times 1.2 \text{ kg} \times 0.001$$

$$S \% = (S \text{ (kg)} / \text{body mass}) \times 100$$

where:
HB is biepicondylar humerus
WB is bistyloideus
FB is biepicondylar femur
AB is bimalleolar; *ht* is height in cm

Drinkwater et al. (1986) – males and females

$$S \text{ (kg)} = [(HB + WB + FB + AB)/4]^2 \times ht \times 0.92 \text{ kg} \times 0.001$$

$$S \% = (S \text{ (kg)} / \text{body mass}) \times 100$$

where variables are as defined previously.

1.13.3 DETERMINATION OF VARIABLES RELATED TO ESTIMATION OF SKELETAL MASS

- Landmarks for bone breadth measurements should be palpated with the fingers, then the anthropometer is applied firmly to the bone, compressing soft tissue when necessary

Stature (*ht*) as before (Practical 3)

Biepicondylar humerus breadth

- The distance between medial and lateral epicondyles of the humerus when the shoulder and elbow are flexed
- The measurer palpates the epicondyles and applies the blades of an anthropometer or small spreading calliper at a slight upward angle while firmly pressing the blades to the bone

Bistyloideus breadth

- The distance between the most prominent aspects of the styloid processes of the ulna and radius
- The subject flexes the elbow and the hand is pronated so that the wrist is horizontal
- The styloid processes are palpated and the anthropometer is applied firmly to the bone

Biepicondylar femur breadth

- The distance between the most medial and lateral aspects of the femoral condyles (epicondyles)
- The subject stands with the weight on the left leg and the right knee flexed (the foot may rest on a raised surface or the subject may sit with the leg hanging)
- The measurer crouches in front of the subject, palpates the femoral condyles and applies the anthropometer at a slight downward angle while firmly pressing to the bone

Bimalleolar breadth

- The maximum distance between the most medial and lateral extensions of the malleoli
- The subject stands erect with the weight evenly distributed over both feet
- The measurer palpates the malleoli and applies the anthropometer firmly to the bone
- A horizontal distance is measured, but the plane between the malleoli is oblique

1.14 ANTHROPOMETRIC LANDMARKS AND MEASUREMENT DEFINITIONS

These definitions are aligned with those of the International Society for the Advancement of Kinanthropometry, and are used here with permission of Turnpike Electronic Publications (www.tep2000.com) from whose CD-ROM, Anthropometry Illustrated, they are abridged.

1.14.1 LANDMARK DEFINITIONS

Vertex (V) The vertex is the most superior point in the mid-sagittal plane on the skull when the head is held in the Frankfurt Plane.

Gnathion (GN) The gnathion is the most inferior border of the mandible in the mid-sagittal plane.

Suprasternale (SST) The suprasternal notch is located at the superior border of the sternal notch (or incisura jugularis) in the mid-sagittal plane.

Mesosternale (MST) The mesosternale is the point located on the corpus sterni at the intersection of the mid-sagittal plane and the transverse plane at the mid-level of the fourth chondrosternal articulation.

Epigastrale (EG) The epigastrale is the point on the anterior surface of the trunk at the intersection of the mid-sagittal plane and the transverse plane through the most inferior point of the tenth rib.

Thelion (TH) The thelion is the breast nipple.

Omphalion (OM) The omphalion is the mid-point of the navel or umbilicus.

Symphysion (SY): The symphysion forms the superior border of the symphysis pubis at the mid-sagittal plane.

Acromiale (A) The acromiale is the point located at the superior and external border of the acromion process when the subject is standing erect with relaxed arms.

Radiale (R) The radiale is the point at the proximal and lateral border of the head of the radius.

Stylion (STY) The stylion is the most distal point on the styloid process of the radius. The stylion radiale is located in the so-called anatomical snuffbox (the triangular area formed when the thumb is extended at the first carpal-metacarpal joint, the area being defined by the raised tendons of the abductor pollicus longus, the external pollicus brevis and the extensor pollicus longus). It is the most distal point of the styloid process of the radius.

Dactylion (DA) The dactylion is the tip of the middle finger (third digit). It is the most distal point on the hand. The tips of the other digits are designated as the first, second, fourth, and fifth dactylions (the thumb being the first digit).

Metacarpale Radiale (MR) The metacarpale radiale is the most lateral point on the distal head of the second metacarpal of the hand (located either on the outstretched hand or when gripping a dowel or pencil).

Metacarpale Ulnare (MU) The metacarpale ulnare is the most medial point on the distal head of the fifth metacarpal of the hand (located either on the outstretched hand or when gripping a dowel or pencil).

Iliocristale (IC) The iliocristale is the most lateral point on the iliac crest. This is the site for locating the iliac crest skinfold that is immediately superior.

Iliospinale (IS) The iliospinale is the inferior aspect of the anterior superior iliac spine. The iliospinale is the undermost tip of the anterior superior iliac spine, *not* the most anterior curved aspect.

Spinale (SPI) The spinale is a less exact term for the iliospinale.

Trochanterion (TRO) The trochanterion is the most superior point on the greater trochanter of the femur, *not* the most lateral point.

Tibiale Mediale (TM) The tibiale mediale (or tibiale internum) is the most superior point on the margo glenoidalis of the medial border of the head of the tibia.

Tibiale Laterale (TL) The tibiale laterale (or tibiale externum) corresponds to the previously defined tibiale mediale but is located on the lateral border of the head of the tibia (*not* to be confused with the more inferior capitum fibulare).

Sphyrion Laterale (SPH) The sphyrion laterale is on the malleolare mediale (or internum). It is the most distal tip of the malleolare mediale (or tibiale). It can be palpated most easily from beneath and dorsally (it is the distal tip, *not* the outermost point of the malleolare).

Sphyrion Fibulare (SPH F) The sphyrion fibulare is the most distal tip of the malleolare laterale (or externum) of the fibula. It is more distal than the sphyrion tibiale.

Pternion (PTE) The pternion is the most posterior point on the heel of the foot when the subject is standing.

Acropodion (AP) The acropodion is the most anterior, distal point on the longest phalange of the foot when the subject is standing. The subject's toenail may be clipped to locate this landmark when measuring.

Metatarsale Tibiale (MT T) The metatarsale tibiale is the most medial point on the head of the first metatarsal of the foot when the subject is standing.

Metatarsale Fibulare (MT F) The metatarsale fibulare is the most lateral point on the head of the fifth metatarsal of the foot when the subject is standing.

Cervicale (C) The cervicale is the most posterior point on the spinous process of the seventh cervical vertebra.

Gluteale (GA) The gluteale is the distal point in the mid-sagittal plane at the arch of the sacrococcygeal fusion.

1.14.2 MEASUREMENT DEFINITIONS

Stretch Stature The maximum distance from the floor to the vertex of the head, when the head is held in the Frankfurt Plane and a gentle traction force is applied.

Stretch Sitting Height The distance from the vertex of the head to the base of the sitting surface when the seated subject is instructed to sit tall and when gentle traction is applied to the mandible.

Body Weight The force of gravity acting on the mass of the body.

Armspan The distance from the left to the right dactylion of the hands when the palms are facing forward on the wall and the outstretched arms are abducted to the horizontal with the shoulders.

Lengths

Acromial–Radiale Length (Arm) The distance from the acromiale to the radiale.

Radiale–Stylion Length (Forearm) The distance from the radiale to the stylion.

Mid-stylion–Dactylion Length (Hand) The shortest distance from the mid-stylion line to the dactylion III.

Iliospinale Height (Obtained height plus box height) Projected height from the box or tabletop to the iliospinale landmark.

Trochanterion Height (Obtained height plus box height) Projected height from the box or tabletop to the trochanterion landmark.

Trochanterion–Tibiale Laterale Length (Thigh) The distance from the trochanterion to the tibiale laterale.

Tibiale Laterale Height (Leg) Distance from the box to the tibiale laterale landmark.

Tibiale Mediale–Sphyrion Tibiale (Tibia Length) Direct length from tibiale mediale to sphyrion tibiale.

Foot Length The distance between the acropodion and pternion (i.e. the most distal toe and posterior surface of the heel).

Breadths

Biacromial Breadth The distance between the most lateral points on the acromion processes when the subject stands erect with the arms hanging loosely at the sides.

Biiliocristal Breadth The distance between the most lateral points on the superior border of the iliac crest.

Transverse Chest Breadth The distance between the most lateral aspects of the thorax at the mesosternale level.

Anterior–Posterior Chest Depth The depth of the chest at the mesosternale level obtained with spreading calliper or anthropometer with recurved branches used as a sliding calliper.

Biepicondylar Humerus Breadth Distance between medial and lateral epicondyles of the humerus when the arm is raised forward to the horizontal and the forearm is flexed to a right angle at the elbow.

Wrist Breadth The bistyloid breadth when the right forearm is resting on a table or the subject's thigh and the hand flexed at the wrist to an angle of about $90°$.

Hand Breadth The distance between the metacarpale laterale and metacarpale mediale when the subject firmly grasps a pencil.

Biepicondylar Femur Breadth The distance between medial and lateral epicondyles of the femur when the subject is seated and the leg is flexed at the knee to form a right angle with the thigh.

Ankle Breadth The distance between the maximum protrusions of the medial tibial malleolus and the lateral fibular malleolus.

Foot Breadth The distance between the metatarsale fibulare and the metatarsale tibiale.

Girths

Head Girth The maximum perimeter of the head when the tape is located immediately superior to the glabellar point (mid-point between brow ridges).

Neck Girth The perimeter of the neck taken immediately superior to the larynx (Adam's apple).

Arm Girth (Relaxed) The perimeter distance of the right arm parallel to the long axis of the humerus when the subject is standing erect and the relaxed arm is hanging by the sides.

Arm Girth (Flexed and Tensed) The maximum circumference of the flexed and tensed right arm raised to the horizontal position.

Forearm Girth The maximal girth of the right forearm when the hand is held palm up and relaxed.

Wrist Girth The perimeter of the right wrist taken distal to the styloid processes.

Chest Girth The end-tidal perimeter of the chest at mesosternale level.

Waist Girth The perimeter at the level of the noticeable waist narrowing located approximately half way between the costal border and iliac crest.

Omphalion Girth (Abdominal) The perimeter distance at the level of the omphalion or mid-point of the umbilicus or navel.

Gluteal Girth (Hip) The perimeter at the level of the greatest posterior protuberance and at approximately the symphysion pubis level anteriorly.

Thigh Girth (Upper) The perimeter of the right thigh which is measured when the subject stands erect, weight equally distributed on both feet, and assists by holding clothing out of the way.

Mid-Thigh Girth The perimeter distance of the right thigh perpendicular to the long axis of the femur at the marked mid-trochanterion-tibiale level.

Calf Girth The maximum perimeter of the calf when the subject stands with weight equally distributed on both feet.

Ankle Girth The perimeter of the narrowest part of the lower leg superior to the sphyrion tibiale.

Skinfold Thicknesses

See descriptions in Practical 2.

ACKNOWLEDGEMENT

The authors acknowledge with thanks the contribution of Kate Plant and Daniela Sovak in the preparation of the laboratory activities; Steve Hudson in providing a graduate student perspective in the preparation of the text; and Dale Oldham for the preparation of computer generated illustrations. We are also very grateful to Turnpike Electronic Publications Inc. for permission to use excerpts from its CD-ROM.

REFERENCES

Abate, N.A., Garg, A., Coleman, R.D., *et al.* (1997). Prediction of total subcutaneous abdominal, intraperitoneal and retroperitoneal adipose tissue masses in men by a single axial MRI scan. *American Journal of Clinical Nutrition*, **65**, 403–8.

Baumgartner, R.N., Rhyne, R.L., Troup, C., *et al.* (1992). Appendicular skeletal muscle areas assessed by magnetic resonance imaging in older persons. *Journal of Gerontology*, **47**, M67–72.

Behnke, A.R., Feen, B.G. and Welham, W.C. (1942). Specific gravity of healthy men. *Journal of the American Medical Association*, **118**, 495–8.

Bjorntorp, P. (1984). Hazards in subgroups of human obesity. *European Journal of Clinical Investigations*, **14**, 239–41.

Boren, H.G., Kory, R.C. and Syner, J.C. (1966). The Veterans Administration – Army Cooperative Study on Lung Function II: The lung volume and its subdivisions in normal man. *American Journal of Medicine*, **41**, 96–114.

Brozek, J., Grande, F., Anderson, J.T. and Keys, A. (1963). Densitometric analysis of body composition: revision of some quantitative assumptions. *Annals of the New York Academy of Sciences*, **110**, 113–40.

Cassady, S.L., Nielsen, D.H., Janz, K.F., *et al.* (1993). Validity of near infra-red body composition analysis in children and adolescents. *Medicine and Science in Sports and Exercise*, **25**, 1185–91.

Collins, M.A., Millard-Stafford, M.L., Sparling, P.B., *et al.* (1999). Evaluation of the BOD POD for assessing body fat in collegiate football players.

Medicine and Science in Sports and Exercise, **31**, 1350–6.

De Koning, F.L., Binkhorst, R.A., Kauer, J.M.G. and Thijssen, H.O.M. (1986). Accuracy of an anthropometric estimate of the muscle and bone area in a transversal cross-section of the arm. *International Journal of Sports Medicine*, **7**, 246–9.

Dempster, P. and Aitkins, S. (1995). A new air displacement method for the determination of human body composition. *Medicine and Science in Sports and Exercise*, **27**, 1692–7.

Drinkwater, D.T., Martin, A.D., Ross, W.D. and Clarys, J.P. (1986). Validation by cadaver dissection of Matiegka's equations for the anthropometric estimation of anatomical body composition in adult humans. In *The 1984 Olympic Scientific Congress Proceedings–Perspectives in Kinanthropometry*. ed. J.A.P. Day (Human Kinetics, Champaign, IL), pp. 221–7.

Durnin, J.V.G.A. and Womersley, J. (1974). Body fat assessed from total body density and its estimation from skinfold thickness: measurements on 481 men and women aged from 16 to 72 years. *British Journal of Sports Medicine*, **32**, 77.

Elia, M., Parkinson, S.A. and Diaz, E. (1990). Evaluation of near infra-red interactance as a method for predicting body composition. *European Journal of Clinical Nutrition*, **44**, 113–21.

Eston, R.G., Rowlands, A.V. and Rosalia, S. (2001). Prediction of DXA – determined whole body density from skinfolds: empirical evidence for including the thigh skinfold. *Journal of Sports Sciences*, in press.

Eston, R.G., Evans, R. and Fu, F. (1994). Estimation of body composition in Chinese and British males by ultrasonic assessment of segmental adipose tissue volume. *British Journal of Sports Medicine*, **28**, 9–13.

Eston, R.G., Cruz, A., Fu, F. and Fung, L. (1993). Fat-free mass estimation by bioelectrical impedance and anthropometric techniques in Chinese children. *Journal of Sports Sciences*, **11**, 241–7.

Eston, R.G., Kreitzman, S., Lamb, K.L., *et al.* (1990). Assessment of fat-free mass by hydrodensitometry, skinfolds, infra-red interactance and electrical impedance in boys and girls aged 11–12 years. *Journal of Sports Sciences*, **8**, 174–5.

Forbes, R.M., Cooper, A.R. and Mitchell, H.H. (1953). The composition of the adult human body as determined by chemical analysis. *Journal of Biological Chemistry*, **203**, 359–66.

Garn, S.M., Leonard, W.R. and Hawthorne, V.M. (1986). Three limitations of the body mass index. *American Journal of Clinical Nutrition*, **44**, 996–7.

Gleichauf, C.N. and Roe, D.A. (1989). The menstrual cycle's effect on the reliability of bioimpedance measurements for assessing body composition. *American Journal of Clinical Nutrition*, **50**, 903–7.

Going, S.B. (1996). Densitometry. In *Human Body Composition*. eds. A.F.Roche, S.B Heymsfield and T.G. Lohman (Human Kinetics, Champaign, IL), pp. 3–23.

Hawes, M.R. and Sovak, D. (1993). Skeletal ruggedness as a factor in performance of Olympic and national calibre synchronized swimmers. In *Kinanthropometry IV*. eds. W. Duquet and J.A.P. Day (E. & F.N. Spon, London), pp. 107–13.

Hawes, M.R. and Sovak, D. (1994). Morphological prototypes, assessment and change in young athletes. *Journal of Sport Sciences*, **12**, 235–42.

Heymsfield, S.B., Wang, Z.M. and Withers, R.T. (1996). Multicomponent molecular level models of body composition. In *Human Body Composition*. eds. A.F. Roche, S.B. Heymsfield and T.G. Lohman (Human Kinetics, Champaign, IL), pp. 129–48.

Heymsfield, S.B., McManus, C., Smith, J., *et al.* (1982). Anthropometric measurement of muscle mass: revised equations for calculating bone-free arm muscle area. *American Journal of Clinical Nutrition*, **36**, 680–90.

Heyward, V.H. (1991). *Advanced Fitness Assessment and Exercise Prescription*. (Human Kinetics, Champaign, IL).

Heyward, V.H. and Stolarczyk, L.M. (1996). *Applied Body Composition Assessment*. (Human Kinetics, Champaign, IL), pp. 7–15.

Hodgdon, J.A. and Fitzgerald, P.I. (1987). Validity of impedance predictions at various levels of fatness. *Human Biology*, **59**, 281–98.

Houtkooper, L.B., Lohman, T.G., Going, S.B. and Hall, M.C. (1989). Validity of bioelectrical impedance for body composition assessment in children. *Journal of Applied Physiology*, **66**, 814–21.

Ikai, M. and Fukunaga, T. (1968). Calculation of muscle strength per unit cross-sectional area of human muscle by means of ultrasonic measurement. *Internationale Zeitschrift für Angewandte Physiologie*, **26**, 26–32.

Jackson, A.S. and Pollock, M.L. (1978). Generalized equations for predicting body density of men. *British Journal of Nutrition*, **40**, 497–504.

Jackson, A.S., Pollock, M.L. and Ward A. (1980).

Generalized equations for predicting body density of women. *Medicine and Science in Sports and Exercise*, **12**, 175–82.

Katch, F. and McArdle, W. (1983). *Nutrition, Weight Control and Exercise*, 2nd edn. (Lea and Febiger, Philadelphia).

Keys, A. and Brozek, J. (1953). Body fat in adult man. *Physiological Reviews*, **33**, 245–345.

Keys, A., Fidanza, F., Karvonen, M.J., *et al.* (1972). Indices of relative weight and obesity, *Journal of Chronic Diseases*, **25**, 329–43.

Kohrt, W.M. (1995). Body composition by DXA: tried and true? *Medicine and Science in Sports and Exercise*, **27**, 1349–53.

Kohrt, W.M. (1998). Preliminary evidence that DXA provides an accurate assessment of body composition. *Journal of Applied Physiology*, **84**, 372–7.

Lohman, T.G. (1996). Dual-energy X-ray absorptiometry. In *Human Body Composition*. eds. A.F. Roche, S.B. Heymsfield and T.G. Lohman (Human Kinetics, Champaign, IL), pp. 63–78.

Lohman, T.G., Slaughter, M.H., Boileau, R.A., *et al.* (1984). Bone mineral measurements and their relation to body density in children, youth and adults. *Human Biology*, **56**, 667–79.

Lukaski, H.C. (1987). Methods for the assessment of human body composition: traditional and new. *American Journal of Clinical Nutrition*, **46**, 537–56.

Lukaski, H.C. (1996). Biological indexes considered in the derivation of the bioelectrical impedance analysis. *American Journal of Clinical Nutrition*, **64 (Suppl)**, 397S–404S.

Lukaski, H.C., Bolonchuk, W.W., Hall, C.B. and Siders, W.A. (1986). Validation of tetrapolar bioelectric impedance method to assess human body composition. *Journal of Applied Physiology*, **60**, 1327–32.

Martin, A.D. and Drinkwater, D.T. (1991). Variability in the measures of body fat. *Sports Medicine*, **11**, 277–88.

Martin A.D. and Ward, R. (1996). Body composition of children. In *Measurement in Pediatric Exercise Science*. ed. D. Docherty (Human Kinetics, Champaign, IL), pp. 87–126.

Martin, A.D., Daniel, M., Drinkwater, D.T. and Clarys, J.P. (1994). Adipose tissue density, estimated adipose lipid fraction and whole-body adiposity in male cadavers. *International Journal of Obesity*, **18**, 79–93.

Martin, A.D., Drinkwater, D.T., Clarys, J.P. and Ross, W.D. (1986). The inconstancy of the fat-free mass: a reappraisal with applications for densitometry. In *Kinanthropometry III. Proceedings of the VII Commonwealth and International Conference on Sport, Physical Education, Dance, Recreation and Health*. eds. T.J. Reilly, J. Watkins and J. Borms (E. & F.N. Spon, London), pp. 92–7.

Martin, A.D., Ross, W.D., Drinkwater, D.T. and Clarys, J.P. (1985). Prediction of body fat by skinfold calliper: assumptions and cadaver evidence. *International Journal of Obesity*, **9**, 31–9.

Martin, A.D., Spenst, L.F., Drinkwater, D.T. and Clarys, J.P. (1990). Anthropometric estimation of muscle mass in men. *Medicine and Science in Sports and Exercise*, **22**, 729–33.

Martin, A.D., Drinkwater, D.T., Clarys, J.P., *et al.* (1992). Effects of skin thickness and skinfold compressibility on skinfold thickness measurement. *American Journal of Human Biology*, **6**, 1–8.

Matiegka, J. (1921). The testing of physical efficiency. *American Journal of Physical Anthropology*, **4**, 223–30.

Mendez, J. and Keys, A. (1960). Density and composition of mammalian muscle. *Metabolism*, **9**, 184–7.

Morrow, J.R., Bradley, P.W. and Jackson, A.S. (1985). Residual volume prediction errors with trained athletes. *Medicine and Science in Sports and Exercise*, **17**, 204.

Nyboer, J., Bagno, S. and Nims, L.F. (1943). The electrical impedance plethysmograph and electrical volume recorder. Washington: National Research Council, Committee on Aviation.

Oldham, N.M. (1996). Overview of bioelectric impedance analysers. *American Journal of Clinical Nutrition*, **64 (Suppl)**, 405S–412S.

Orpin, M.J. and Scott, P.J. (1964). Estimation of total body fat using skin fold caliper measurements. *New Zealand Medical Journal*, **63**, 501–7.

Parizkova, J. (1978). Lean body mass and depot fat during ontogenesis in humans. In *Nutrition, Physical Fitness and Health: International Series on Sport Sciences*, **7**. eds. J. Parizkova and V.A. Rogozkin (University Park Press, Baltimore), pp. 24–51.

Prior, B.M., Cureton, K.J., Modlesky, C.M., *et al.* (1997). In vivo validation of whole body composition estimates from dual-energy X-ray absorptiometry. *Journal of Applied Physiology*, **83**, 623–30.

Ross, W.D., Martin, A.D. and Ward R. (1987). Body composition and aging: theoretical and methodological implications. *Collegium Anthropologicum*, **11**, 15–44.

Ross, W.D., Eiben, O.G., Ward, R., *et al.* (1986). Alternatives for conventional methods of human body composition and physique assessment. In *The 1984 Olympic Scientific Congress Proceedings: Perspectives in Kinanthropometry.* ed. J.A.P. Day (Human Kinetics, Champaign, IL), pp. 203–20.

Ryde, S.J.S., Eston, R.G., Laskey, M.A., *et al.* (1998). Changes in body fat: measurements by neutron activation, densitometry and dual energy X-ray absorptiometry. *Applied Radiation and Isotopes,* **49**, 507–9.

Schutte, J.E., Townsend, E.J., Huff, J., *et al.* (1984). Density of lean body mass is greater in Blacks than in Whites. *Journal of Applied Physiology,* **456**, 1647–9.

Segal, K.R., Van Loan, M., Fitzgerald, P.I., *et al.* (1988). Lean body mass estimation by bioelectrical impedance analysis: a four-site cross-validation study. *American Journal of Clinical Nutrition,* **47**, 7–14.

Siri, W.E. (1956). Body composition from fluid spaces and density: analysis of methods. *University of California Radiation Laboratory Report* **UCRL no. 3349**.

Stewart, A.D. and Hannan, W.J. (2000). Prediction of fat and fat-free mass in male athletes using dual energy X-ray absorptiometry as the reference method. *Journal of Sports Sciences,* **18(4)**, 263-74.

Stout, J.R., Housh, T.J., Eckerson, J.M., *et al.* (1996). Validity of methods for estimating percent body fat in young women. *Strength and Conditioning Journal,* **10**, 25–9.

Vague, J. (1947). La differenciation sexuelle, facteur déterminant des formes de l'obèsité. *Presse Med.,* **30**, 339–40.

Van Loan, M.D. (1990). Bioelectrical impedance analysis to determine fat-free mass, total body water and body fat. *Sports Medicine,* **10**, 205–17.

Van Loan, M.D. and Mayclin, P. (1987). Bioelectrical impedance analysis: is it a reliable estimator of lean body mass and total body water? *Human Biology,* **59**, 299–309.

Wang, Z.M., Pierson Jr., R.N. and Heymsfield, S.B. (1992). The five-level model: a new approach to organizing body-composition research. *American Journal of Clinical Nutrition,* **56**, 19–28.

Wilmore, J.H., Vodak, P.A., Parr, R.B., *et al.* (1980). Further simplification of a method for determination of residual lung volume. *Medicine and Science in Sports and Exercise,* **12**, 216–18.

SOMATOTYPING

William Duquet and J. E. Lindsay Carter

2.1 AIMS

The aims in this chapter are to:
- define the meaning of the terms 'endomorphy', 'mesomorphy' and 'ectomorphy',
- provide an understanding of the somatotype rating so that the student can visualize the body type of a subject with a given somatotype,
- explain how to calculate an anthropometric somatotype,
- distinguish the dominance of a certain component within a person, and to relate this to a certain somatotype category,
- describe how to plot and interpret somatotypes on a somatochart,
- highlight possible stabilities or instabilities of the individual phenotypical appearance,
- compare global somatotypes between subjects and between samples,
- understand the specific advantages of using a somatotype method over single trait or index methods.

2.2 HISTORY

Somatotyping is a method for describing the human physique in terms of a number of traits that relate to body shape and composition. The definition of the traits, and the form of the scales that are used to describe the relative importance of the traits, vary from one body type method to the other. Attempts to establish such methods date from Hippocrates, and continue to the present time. Excellent reviews of

these early methods were published by Tucker and Lessa (1940a, 1940b) and by Albonico (1970).

A classic approach, that led to the presently most used method, was introduced by Sheldon *et al.* (1940). Their most important contribution to the field lies in the combination of the basic ideas of two other methods. The first was Kretschmer's (1921) classification, with three empirically determined and visually rated body build extremes, with each subject being an amalgam of the three 'poles'. The second was the analytical, anthropometrically determined body build assessment of Viola (1933), in which the ratio of trunk and limb measures and thoracic and abdominal trunk values are expressed proportionate to a 'normotype'. In Sheldon's method an attempt is made to describe the genotypical morphological traits of a person in terms of three components, each on a 7-point scale. This genotypic approach, the rigidity of the closed 7-point ratings, and also a lack of objectivity of the ratings, made the method unattractive to most researchers, especially in the field of kinanthropometry.

From these three principal criticisms, and in addition those of Heath (1963), emerged a new method, created by Heath and Carter (1967). It was partly influenced by ideas from Parnell (1954, 1958). They proposed a phenotypic approach, with open rating scales for three components, and ratings that can be estimated from objective anthropometric measurements. The Heath–Carter somatotype method is the

Kinanthropometry and Exercise Physiology Laboratory Manual: Tests, Procedures and Data. 2nd Edition, Volume 1: Anthropometry
Edited by RG Eston and T Reilly. Published by Routledge, London, June 2001

most universally applied, and will be used in this laboratory manual. The most extensive description of the method, its development and applications can be found in Carter and Heath (1990). Two other original methods were introduced by Lindegård (1953) and by Conrad (1963). They are less used than the Heath–Carter method.

2.3 THE HEATH–CARTER SOMATOTYPE METHOD

2.3.1 DEFINITIONS

(a) Somatotype

A somatotype is a quantified expression or description of the present morphological conformation of a person. It consists of a three-numeral rating, for example, 3.5–5–1. The three numerals are always recorded in the same order, each describing the value of a particular component of physique.

(b) Anthropometric and photoscopic somatotypes

The principal rating of the component values is based on a visual inspection of the subject, or his or her photograph, preferably a front, a side and a back view, taken in minimal clothing. This rating is called the photoscopic (or anthroposcopic) somatotype rating. If the investigator cannot perform a photoscopic rating, the component values can be estimated from a combination of anthropometric measurements. The calculated three-numeral rating is then called the anthropometric somatotype. The recommended somatotyping procedure is a combination of an anthropometric followed by a photoscopic evaluation.

(c) Components

A component is an empirically defined descriptor of a particular aspect or trait of the human body build. It is expressed as a numeral on a continuous scale that theoretically starts at zero and has no upper limit. The ratings are

rounded to the half-unit. In practice, no ratings lower than one-half are given (as a particular body build trait can never be absolutely absent), and a rating of more than seven is extremely high.

(d) Endomorphy

The first component, called endomorphy, describes the relative degree of fatness of the body, regardless of where or how it is distributed. It also describes corresponding physical aspects such as roundness of the body, softness of the contours, relative volume of the abdominal trunk, and distally tapering of the limbs.

(e) Mesomorphy

The second component, called mesomorphy, describes the relative musculoskeletal development of the body. It also describes corresponding physical aspects such as the apparent robustness of the body in terms of muscle or bone, the relative volume of the thoracic trunk, and the possibly hidden muscle bulk.

(f) Ectomorphy

The third component, called ectomorphy, describes the relative slenderness of the body. It also describes corresponding physical aspects such as the relative 'stretched-out-ness', the apparent linearity of the body or fragility of the limbs, in absence of any bulk, be it muscle, fat or other tissues.

(g) Somatotype category

Category is the more qualitative description of the individual somatotype, in terms of the dominant component or components. For example, a subject with a high rating on mesomorphy and an equally low rating on endomorphy and on ectomorphy, will be called a mesomorph or a balanced mesomorph. The complete list with possible categories and corresponding dominance variations is given in Practical 2 of this chapter.

2.3.2 ASSESSMENT

(a) Anthropometric somatotype

The anthropometric somatotype can be calculated from a set of 10 measurements: height, weight, four skinfolds (triceps, subscapular, supraspinale, and medial calf), two biepicondylar breadths (humerus and femur), and two girths (upper arm flexed and tensed, and calf). Descriptions of measurement techniques are given later.

(b) Photoscopic somatotype

The photoscopic somatotype can only be rated objectively by persons who have trained to attain the necessary skill, and whose rating validity and reliability is established against the evaluations of an experienced rater. This part of the procedure is therefore not included in the present text. It is, however, generally accepted that the anthropometric evaluation gives a fair estimate of the photoscopic procedure. Important deviations are only found in subjects with a high degree of dysplasia in fat or muscle tissue.

Many researchers, who do not use photographs or visual inspection, or who lack experience in rating photoscopically, report the anthropometric somatotype only. In reporting a somatotype, researchers should therefore always mention the method used.

2.3.3 FURTHER ELABORATION

The differences or similarities in somatotypes of subjects or groups of subjects can be visualized by plotting them on a somatochart (see Practical 1). A somatotype rating can be thought of as being a vector, or a point in a three-coordinate system, in which each axis carries a somatotype component scale. The somatochart is the orthogonal projection of this three-coordinate system, parallel to the bisector of the three axes, on a two-dimensional plane.

The somatotype is an entity and should be treated as such. One possible qualitative technique is the use of somatotype categories. A quantitative technique is the use of the SAD or Somatotype Attitudinal Distance, which is the difference in component units between two somatotypes, or in terms of the somatochart, the three-dimensional distance between two points.

In time series of somatotypes of the same subject, the ongoing changes in somatotype can be expressed by adding the consecutive SADs. This sum is called the Migratory Distance (*MD*).

These further elaborations will be covered in the Practicals.

2.3.4 MEASUREMENT TECHNIQUES

The descriptions are essentially the same as in Carter and Heath (1990). The following techniques should ideally be used for subsequent calculation of the Heath–Carter anthropometric somatotype. Where the choice is possible, measures should be taken both on left and right sides, and the largest measure should be reported. In large-scale surveys, measuring on the right side is preferable.

The anthropometric equipment needed includes a weighing scale, a stadiometer (a height scale attached on a wall and a Broca plane) or an anthropometer for measuring the height, a skinfold calliper, a small sliding or spreading calliper for the breadths, and a flexible steel or fibreglass tape for the girths.

(a) Weight

The subject, in minimal clothing, stands in the centre of the scale platform. Record body mass to the nearest tenth of a kilogram if possible. A correction is made for clothing so that nude weight is used in subsequent calculations. Avoid measuring body mass shortly after a meal.

(b) Height

The subject stands straight, against an upright wall with a stadiometer or against an anthropometer, touching the wall or the anthropometer with back, buttocks and both heels. The head is oriented in the Frankfurt Plane (i.e. the lower border of the eye socket and the upper border of the ear opening should be on a horizontal line). The subject is instructed to stretch upward and take and hold a full breath. Lower the Broca plane or the ruler until it touches the vertex firmly, but without exerting extreme pressure.

(c) Skinfolds

Raise a fold of skin and subcutaneous tissue at the desired site firmly between thumb and forefinger of the left hand, and pull the fold gently away from the underlying muscle. Hold the calliper in the right hand and apply the edge of the plates on the calliper branches 1 cm below the fingers, and allow them to exert their full pressure before reading the thickness of the fold after about two seconds. Harpenden or Holtain callipers are recommended.

Triceps skinfold

The subject stands relaxed, with the arm hanging loosely. Raise the triceps skinfold at the midline on the back of the arm at a level halfway between the acromion and the olecranon processes. (See Figure 1.13.)

Subscapular skinfold

The subject stands relaxed. Raise the subscapular skinfold adjacent to the inferior angle of the scapula in a direction which is obliquely downwards and outwards at 45°. (See Figure 1.13.)

Supraspinale skinfold

The subject stands relaxed. Raise the fold 5 to 7 cm above the anterior superior iliac spine on a line to the anterior axillary border and in a direction downwards and inwards at 45°. (See Figure 1.12.)

Medial calf skinfold

The subject sits with the legs slightly spread. The leg that is not being measured can be bent backwards to facilitate the measurement. Raise a vertical skinfold on the medial side (aspect) of the leg, at the level of the maximum girth of the calf. (See Figure 1.15.)

(d) Breadths

Biepicondylar humerus breadth

The subject holds the shoulder and elbow flexed to 90°. Measure the width between the medial and lateral epicondyles of the humerus. In this position, the medial epicondyle is always somewhat lower than the lateral. Apply the calliper at an angle approximately bisecting the angle of the elbow. Place firm pressure on the cross-branches of the calliper in order to compress the subcutaneous tissue.

Biepicondylar femur breadth

The subject sits, or stands upright with one foot on a pedestal, with the knee bent at a right angle. Measure the greatest distance between the lateral and medial epicondyles of the femur. Place firm pressure on the cross-branches in order to compress the subcutaneous tissue.

(e) Girths

Upper arm girth, flexed and tensed

The subject holds the upper arm horizontally and flexes the elbow 45°, clenches the hand and maximally contracts the elbow flexors and extensors. Take the measurement at the greatest girth of the arm. The tape should not be too loose, but should not indent the soft tissue either.

Standing calf girth

The subject stands with the feet slightly apart. Place the tape horizontally around the calf and measure the maximum circumference. The tape should not be too loose, but should not indent the soft tissue either.

2.4 RELEVANCE OF SOMATOTYPING

Why should you use somatotyping? Of what value is it in exercise and sports science? These are important questions that are often asked.

The somatotype gives an overall summary of the physique as a unified whole. Its utility is in the combination of three aspects of physique into a somatotype rating. It combines the appraisal of adiposity, musculoskeletal robustness and linearity into the three-numbered rating and conjures up in your mind a visual image of the three aspects of the physique. The adiposity is related to the relative fatness or endomorphy, the relative muscle and bony robustness is related to the fat-free body or mesomorphy, and the linearity or ectomorphy gives an indication of the bulkiness or mass relative to stature in the physique. From a few simple measurements, the somatotype gives a useful summary of a variety of possible measures or observations that can be made on the body.

The somatotype tells you what kind of physique you have, and how it looks. It has been used to describe and compare the physiques of athletes at all levels of competition and in a variety of sports. Somatotypes of athletes in selected sports are quite different from each other, whereas somatotypes are similar in other sports. Somatotyping has also been used to describe changes in physique during growth, ageing, and training, as well as in relation to physical performance. The somatotype is a general descriptor of physique. If more precise questions are asked, such as 'What is the growth rate in upper extremity bone segments?', then different and specific measures need to be taken.

Two examples illustrate how the somatotype gives more information than some typical measures of body composition. First, the somatotype indicates the difference between individuals with the same level of fatness. An elite male bodybuilder, gymnast and long distance runner may each have the same estimate of percent body fat at 5%. All three are low in percentage body fat, but this fact alone does not tell you the important differences between the physiques of these athletes. They differ considerably in their muscle, bone and linearity. The bodybuilder may be a 1–9–1, the gymnast a 1–6–2, and the runner a 1–3–5 somatotype. They are all rated '1' in endomorphy, but they have completely different ratings on mesomorphy and ectomorphy. The somatotype describes these differences.

As a second example, two males with the same height and body mass, and therefore the same body mass index (BMI), can have physiques that look completely different. If they are both 175 cm tall and weigh 78 kg, they will have a BMI value of 25.5, and a somatotype height-weight ratio of 41.0. Their somatotypes are 6–3–1 and 3–6–1. They are completely different looking physiques. Both have low linearity (1 in ectomorphy), but the BMI does not tell you anything about their specific differences in body composition as inferred from their opposite ratings of 6 (high) and 3 (low) in endomorphy or in mesomorphy.

In both the examples above, the potential performance characteristics for the subjects would be quite different because of the differences in mesomorphy and ectomorphy in the first example, and in endomorphy and mesomorphy in the second example.

2.5 PRACTICAL 1: CALCULATION OF ANTHROPOMETRIC SOMATOTYPES

2.5.1 INTRODUCTION

The aim of this practical is to learn how to calculate anthropometric somatotypes, using the classical approach and using some fast calculation formulae, and to learn how to plot the results on a somatochart.

2.5.2 METHODS

Endomorphy is estimated from the relation between the component value and the sum of three skinfold measures, relative to the subject's height.

Mesomorphy is estimated from the deviation of two girths and two breadths from their expected values, relative to the subject's height.

Ectomorphy is estimated from the relation between the component value and the reciprocal of the Ponderal Index, or height over cube root of weight ratio.

(a) Steps for the manual calculation of the anthropometric somatotype

The following is a guide in 16 steps for calculating the anthropometric somatotype by means of the Heath–Carter somatotype rating form (Figures 2.1 and 2.2). Endomorphy is calculated in steps 2 to 5, mesomorphy in steps 6 to 10, and ectomorphy in steps 11 to 14. A worked example, in which these steps were followed, is given in Figure 2.1.

The measurements for subject B171 were: body mass: 59.5 kg; height: 165.6 cm; triceps skinfold: 11.3 mm; subscapular skinfold: 10.0 mm; supraspinale skinfold: 6.5 mm; calf skinfold: 12.0 mm; humerus breadth: 6.4 cm; femur breadth: 8.8 cm; biceps girth: 27.2 cm; calf girth: 37.1 cm.

Step 1 Record the identification data in the top section of the rating form.

Step 2 Record the values obtained from each of the four skinfold measurements.

Step 3 Sum the values of the triceps, subscapular and supraspinale skinfolds; record this sum in the box opposite 'Sum 3 skinfolds'. Correct for height by multiplying this sum by 170.18 / height (cm).

Step 4 Circle the closest value in the 'Sum 3 skinfolds' scale to the right. The scale reads vertically from high to low in columns and horizontally from left to right in rows. 'Lower limit' and 'upper limit' on the rows provide exact boundaries for each column. These values are circled if the 'Sum 3 skinfolds' figure is closer to the limit than to the midpoint.

Step 5 In the row 'Endomorphy' circle the value directly under the column circled in Step 4.

Step 6 Record the subject's height and the diameters of the humerus and the femur in the appropriate boxes. Make the corrections for skinfolds for the girths of biceps and calf as follows: convert triceps and calf skinfold to cm by dividing them by 10; subtract converted triceps skinfold from the biceps girth; subtract converted calf skinfold from calf girth.

Step 7 On the height scale directly to the right of the recorded height box, circle the value nearest to the measured height of the subject.

Step 8 For each bone diameter and girth, circle the figure nearest the measured value in the adjacent row. (If the measurement falls midway between the two values, circle the lower value. This conservative procedure is used because the largest girths and diameters are recorded.)

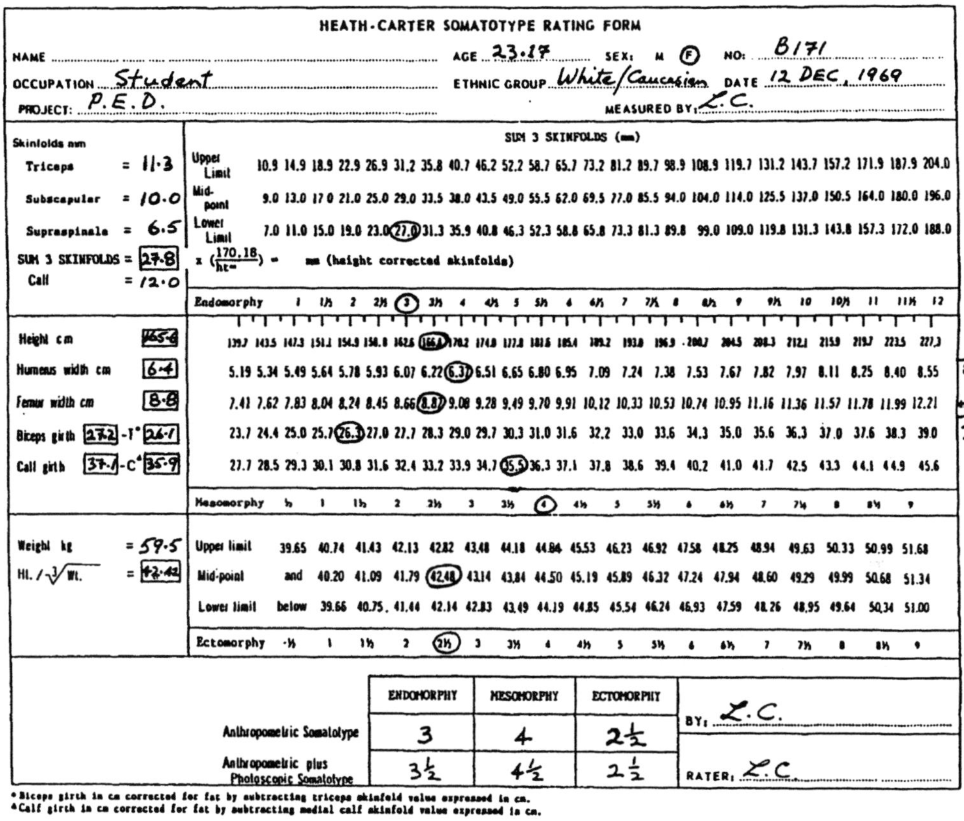

HEATH-CARTER SOMATOTYPE RATING FORM

NAME .... AGE *23.17* SEX: M Ⓕ NO: *B171*

OCCUPATION *Student* ETHNIC GROUP *White/Caucasian* DATE *12 DEC, 1969*

PROJECT: *P.E.D.* MEASURED BY: *L.C.*

Skinfolds mm

SUM 3 SKINFOLDS (mm)

Triceps = 11·3   Upper Limit   10.9 14.9 18.9 22.9 26.9 31.2 35.8 40.7 46.2 52.2 58.7 65.7 73.2 81.2 89.7 98.9 108.9 119.7 131.2 143.7 157.2 171.9 187.9 204.0

Subscapular = 10.0   Mid-point   9.0 13.0 17.0 21.0 25.0 29.0 33.5 38.0 43.5 49.0 55.5 62.0 69.5 77.0 85.5 94.0 104.0 114.0 125.5 137.0 150.5 164.0 180.0 196.0

Supraspinale = 6·5   Lower Limit   7.0 11.0 15.0 19.0 23.0 (27.0) 31.3 35.9 40.8 46.3 52.3 58.8 65.8 73.3 81.3 89.8 99.0 109.0 119.8 131.3 143.8 157.3 172.0 188.0

SUM 3 SKINFOLDS = 27.8   x ($\frac{170.18}{ht=}$) = mm (height corrected skinfolds)

Call = 12.0

Endomorphy   1   1½   2   2½   ③   3½   4   4½   5   5½   6   6½   7   7½   8   8½   9   9½   10   10½   11   11½   12

Height cm   165·4   139.3 143.5 147.3 151.1 154.9 158.8 162.6 (166.4) 170.2 174.0 177.8 181.6 185.4 189.2 193.0 196.9 200.7 204.5 208.3 212.1 215.9 219.7 223.5 227.3

Humerus width cm   6·4   5.19 5.34 5.49 5.64 5.78 5.93 6.07 6.22 (6.37) 6.51 6.65 6.80 6.95 7.09 7.24 7.38 7.53 7.67 7.82 7.97 8.11 8.25 8.40 8.55

Femur width cm   8·8   7.41 7.62 7.83 8.04 8.24 8.45 8.66 (8.87) 9.08 9.28 9.49 9.70 9.91 10.12 10.33 10.53 10.74 10.95 11.16 11.36 11.57 11.78 11.99 12.21

Biceps girth   27.2 -1° 26·1   23.7 24.4 25.0 25.7 (26.3) 27.0 27.7 28.3 29.0 29.7 30.3 31.0 31.6 32.2 33.0 33.6 34.3 35.0 35.6 36.3 37.0 37.6 38.3 39.0

Calf girth   37·4 -C° 35·9   27.7 28.5 29.3 30.1 30.8 31.6 32.4 33.2 33.9 34.7 (35.5) 36.3 37.1 37.8 38.6 39.4 40.2 41.0 41.7 42.5 43.3 44.1 44.9 45.6

Mesomorphy   ½   1   1½   2   2½   3   3½   ④   4½   5   5½   6   6½   7   7½   8   8½   9

Weight kg = 59·5   Upper limit   39.65 40.74 41.43 42.13 42.82 43.48 44.18 44.86 45.53 46.23 46.92 47.58 48.25 48.94 49.63 50.33 50.99 51.68

Ht. /³√ Wt. = 42.42   Mid-point   and   40.20 41.09 41.79 (42.48) 43.14 43.84 44.50 45.19 45.89 46.32 47.24 47.94 48.60 49.29 49.99 50.68 51.34

Lower limit   below   39.66 40.75 41.44 42.14 42.83 43.49 44.19 44.85 45.54 46.24 46.93 47.59 48.26 48.95 49.64 50.34 51.00

Ectomorphy   -½   1   1½   2   (2½)   3   3½   4   4½   5   5½   6   6½   7   7½   8   8½   9

	ENDOMORPHY	MESOMORPHY	ECTOMORPHY	
Anthropometric Somatotype	3	4	2½	BY: *L.C.*
Anthropometric plus Photoscopic Somatotype	3½	4½	2½	RATER: *L.C.*

° Biceps girth in cm corrected for fat by subtracting triceps skinfold value expressed in cm.
ᶜ Calf girth in cm corrected for fat by subtracting medial calf skinfold value expressed in cm.

1/8 = ·125
+4·0
4·13

Figure 2.1 Example of a completed anthropometric somatotype rating.

Step 9 Deal in this step only with columns as units, not with numerical values.
Check the circled deviations of the values for widths and girths from the circled value in the height column. Count the column deviations to the right of the height column as positive deviations, with columns as units. Deviations to the left are negative deviations. Calculate the algebraic sum of the deviations (D). Use this formula: Mesomorphy = $(D/8) + 4$.

Step 10 In the row 'Mesomorphy' circle the closest value for the mesomorphy calculated in Step 9. (If the point is midway between two values, circle the value closest to 4 on the scale. This conservative regression toward 4 guards against spuriously extreme ratings.)

Step 11 Record body mass (kg).

Step 12 Obtain the value for height divided by cube root of weight (HWR) from a nomograph or by calculation. Record HWR in the appropriate box. Note: the HWR can be calculated easily using a hand calculator. A nomogram can be found in Carter and Heath (1990), p. 273.

Step 13 Circle the closest value in the HWR scale. Circle the upper or lower limit if the HWR is closer to this limit than to the midpoint of the column.

HEATH-CARTER SOMATOTYPE RATING FORM

NAME .... AGE .... SEX: M F NO: ....

OCCUPATION .... ETHNIC GROUP.................................... DATE ....

PROJECT: .... MEASURED BY:..

SUM 3 SKINFOLDS (mm)

Skinfolds mm

Triceps = | Upper Limit | 10.9 14.9 18.9 22.9 26.9 31.2 35.8 40.7 46.2 52.2 58.7 65.7 73.2 81.2 89.7 98.9 108.9 119.7 131.2 143.7 157.2 171.9 187.9 204.0

Subscapular = | Mid-point | 9.0 13.0 17.0 21.0 25.0 29.0 33.5 38.0 43.5 49.0 55.5 62.0 69.5 77.0 85.5 94.0 104.0 114.0 125.5 137.0 150.5 164.0 180.0 196.0

Supraspinale = | Lower Limit | 7.0 11.0 15.0 19.0 23.0 27.0 31.3 35.9 40.8 46.3 52.3 58.8 65.8 73.3 81.3 89.8 99.0 109.0 119.8 131.3 143.8 157.3 172.0 188.0

SUM 3 SKINFOLDS = ☐ x $(\frac{170.18}{ht=})$ = mm (height corrected skinfolds)
Call =

Endomorphy   1   1½   2   2½   3   3½   4   4½   5   5½   6   6½   7   7½   8   8½   9   9½   10   10½   11   11½   12

Height cm = ☐   139.7 143.5 147.3 151.1 154.9 158.8 162.6 166.4 170.2 174.0 177.8 181.6 185.4 189.2 193.0 196.9 .200.7 204.5 208.3 212.1 215.9 219.7 223.5 227.3

Humerus width cm = ☐   5.19 5.34 5.49 5.64 5.78 5.93 6.07 6.22 6.37 6.51 6.65 6.80 6.95 7.09 7.24 7.38 7.53 7.67 7.82 7.97 8.11 8.25 8.40 8.55

Femur width cm = ☐   7.41 7.62 7.83 8.04 8.24 8.45 8.66 8.87 9.08 9.28 9.49 9.70 9.91 10.12 10.33 10.53 10.74 10.95 11.16 11.36 11.57 11.78 11.99 12.21

Biceps girth ☐ -T° ☐   23.7 24.4 25.0 25.7 26.3 27.0 27.7 28.3 29.0 29.7 30.3 31.0 31.6 32.2 33.0 33.6 34.3 35.0 35.6 36.3 37.0 37.6 38.3 39.0

Calf girth ☐ -C° ☐   27.7 28.5 29.3 30.1 30.8 31.6 32.4 33.2 33.9 34.7 35.5 36.3 37.1 37.8 38.6 39.4 40.2 41.0 41.7 42.5 43.3 44.1 44.9 45.6

Mesomorphy   ½   1   1½   2   2½   3   3½   4   4½   5   5½   6   6½   7   7½   8   8½   9

Weight kg = | Upper limit | 39.65 40.74 41.43 42.13 42.82 43.48 44.18 44.84 45.53 46.23 46.92 47.58 48.25 48.94 49.63 50.33 50.99 51.68

HL. / ∛ Wt. = ☐ | Mid-point | and | 40.20 41.09 41.79 42.48 43.14 43.84 44.50 45.19 45.89 46.32 47.24 47.94 48.60 49.29 49.99 50.68 51.34

| Lower limit | below | 39.66 40.75 41.44 42.14 42.83 43.49 44.19 44.85 45.54 46.24 46.93 47.59 48.26 48.95 49.64 50.34 51.00

Ectomorphy   ½   1   1½   2   2½   3   3½   4   4½   5   5½   6   6½   7   7½   8   8½   9

	ENDOMORPHY	MESOMORPHY	ECTOMORPHY	
Anthropometric Somatotype				BY: ....
Anthropometric plus Photoscopic Somatotype				RATER: ....

* Biceps girth in cm corrected for fat by subtracting triceps skinfold value expressed in cm.
* Calf girth in cm corrected for fat by subtracting medial calf skinfold value expressed in cm.

Figure 2.2 The Heath-Carter somatotype rating form.

Step 14 In the row 'Ectomorphy' circle the ectomorphy value directly under the circled HWR.

Step 15 Record the circled values for each component in the row 'Anthropometric Somatotype'. (If a photoscopic rating is available, the rater should record the final decision in the row 'Anthropometric and Photoscopic Somatotype'.)

Step 16 The investigator signs the box to the right of the recorded rating.

Note: If in Step 7 the recorded height is closer to the midpoint than to the two adjacent column values, place a vertical arrow between the two values. Continue to work treating this as a half column, calculating half units for the deviations in Step 9.

(b) Formulae for the calculation of the anthropometric somatotype by computer

The formulae in Table 2.1 were derived from the scales of the somatochart.

Table 2.1 Formulae for the calculation of the anthropometric Heath-Carter somatotype by calculator or computer

Endomorphy	$= -0.7182 + 0.1451X - 0.00068X^2 + 0.0000014X^3$
Endomorphy	$= 0.858HB + 0.601FB + 0.188AG + 0.161CG - 0.131SH + 4.5$
Ectomorphy	$= 0.732HWR - 28.58$

$$\text{(if } HWR > 40.74)$$

$$= 0.463HWR - 17.615$$

$$\text{(if } 39.65 < HWR \leq 40.74)$$

$$= 0.5$$

$$\text{(if } HWR \leq 39.65)$$

Where: $X = \Sigma 3$ skinfolds, corrected for height; HB = humerus breadth; FB = femur breadth; AG = corrected arm girth; CG = corrected calf girth; SH = standing height; HWR = height over cube root of mass.

(c) Formulae for plotting somatotypes on the somatochart

The exact location of a somatotype on the somatochart (Figure 2.3) can be calculated using the formulae:

$$X = \text{ectomorphy} - \text{endomorphy}$$

$$Y = 2 \times \text{mesomorphy} - (\text{endomorphy} + \text{ectomorphy})$$

In our example, a subject with somatotype 3.0–4.0–2.5 is plotted with the following coordinates:

$$X = 2.5 - 3.0 = -0.5$$

$$Y = 2 \times 4.0 - (3.0 + 2.5) = 2.5$$

2.5.3 TASKS

A group of 6 adult subjects was measured. The results are shown in Table 2.2.

1. Calculate the anthropometric somatotype for each subject. Use copies of the somatotype rating form (Figure 2.2), and follow the example of Figure 2.1.
2. Calculate the anthropometric somatotype for each subject, using the formulae given in Table 2.1.
3. Check all calculations by rounding the second series of results to the half-unit, and comparing the results with the first calculations.

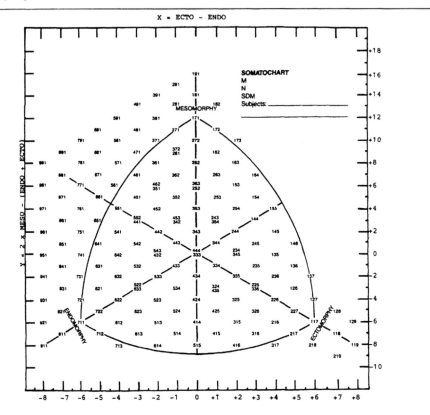

Figure 2.3 Somatotype for plotting somatotypes. (From Carter, 1980.)

Table 2.2   Anthropometric measurements of 6 adult male subjects

Subject:	1	2	3	4	5	6
Mass (kg)	82.0	67.7	60.5	64.4	82.4	80.8
Height (cm)	191.7	175.3	160.0	171.5	180.6	188.3
Triceps skinfold (mm)	7.0	5.0	3.0	4.2	11.2	17.1
Subscapular skinfold (mm)	6.0	7.0	5.0	5.7	8.8	12.1
Supraspinale skinfold (mm)	4.0	3.0	3.0	3.6	7.1	11.5
Medial calf skinfold (mm)	9.0	4.0	3.0	3.0	9.9	12.0
Humerus breadth (cm)	7.3	7.0	6.5	6.6	7.4	6.5
Femur breadth (cm)	10.1	9.4	8.9	9.7	9.2	9.1
Upper arm girth (cm) (flexed and tensed)	33.2	35.7	34.4	29.5	36.1	36.5
Standing calf girth (cm)	36.0	34.4	36.4	34.5	40.6	38.6

2.6 PRACTICAL 2: COMPARISON OF SOMATOTYPES OF DIFFERENT GROUPS

2.6.1 INTRODUCTION

The aim in this practical is to learn how to compare anthropometric somatotypes, using the somatotype category approach and using SAD techniques.

2.6.2 METHODS

There are many ways to analyse somatotype data. The easiest way is to consider each component separately, and to treat it like any other biological variable, using descriptive and inferential statistics.

However, the somatotype is more than three separate component values. Two subjects with an identical value for one of the components can nevertheless have completely different physiques, depending on the values of the two other components. For example, a somatotype 2–6–2 is completely different from a somatotype 2–2–6, but they both have the same endomorphy value. It is precisely the combination of the three component values into one expression that is the strength of the somatotype concept. Hence, techniques were developed to analyse the somatotype as a whole: among them, somatotype categories and SAD techniques (see Duquet and Hebbelink, 1977; Duquet, 1980; Carter *et al.*, 1983).

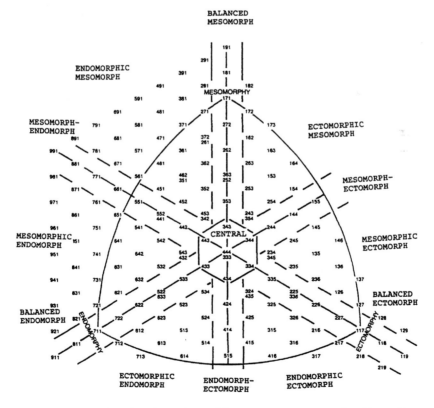

Figure 2.4 A somatochart showing the regions of the somatotype categories. (From Carter, 1980.)

(a) Somatotype categories

Carter and Heath (1990) defined 13 somatotype categories, shown as areas in Figure 2.4. The exact definitions are as follows:

Central type No component differs by more than one unit from the other two.

Balanced endomorph Endomorphy is dominant and mesomorphy and ectomorphy are equal (or do not differ by more than one-half unit).

Mesomorphic endomorph Endomorphy is dominant and mesomorphy is greater than ectomorphy.

Mesomorph–endomorph Endomorphy and mesomorphy are equal (or do not differ by more than one-half unit), and ectomorphy is smaller.

Endomorphic mesomorph Mesomorphy is dominant and endomorphy is greater than ectomorphy.

Balanced mesomorph Mesomorphy is dominant and endomorphy and ectomorphy are equal (or do not differ by more than one-half unit).

Ectomorphic mesomorph Mesomorphy is dominant and ectomorphy is greater than endomorphy.

Mesomorph–ectomorph Mesomorphy and ectomorphy are equal (or do not differ by more than one-half unit), and endomorphy is smaller.

Mesomorphic ectomorph Ectomorphy is dominant and mesomorphy is greater than endomorphy.

Balanced ectomorph Ectomorphy is dominant and endomorphy and mesomorphy are equal (or do not differ by more than one-half unit).

Endomorphic ectomorph Ectomorphy is dominant and endomorphy is greater than mesomorphy.

Endomorph–ectomorph Endomorphy and ectomorphy are equal (or do not differ by more than one-half unit), and mesomorphy is lower.

Ectomorphic endomorph Endomorphy is dominant and ectomorphy is greater than mesomorphy.

This classification can be simplified into seven larger groupings:

Central type No component differs by more than one unit from the other two.

Endomorph Endomorphy is dominant, mesomorphy and ectomorphy are more than one-half unit lower.

Endomorph–mesomorph Endomorphy and mesomorphy are equal (or do not differ by more than one-half unit), and ectomorphy is smaller.

Mesomorph Mesomorphy is dominant, endomorphy and ectomorphy are more than one-half unit lower.

Mesomorph–ectomorph Mesomorphy and ectomorphy are equal (or do not differ by more than one-half unit), and endomorphy is smaller.

Ectomorph Ectomorphy is dominant, endomorphy and mesomorphy are more than one-half unit lower.

Ectomorph–endomorph Endomorphy and ectomorphy are equal (or do not differ by more than one-half unit), and mesomorphy is lower.

(b) Somatotype Attitudinal Distance

Table 2.3 Formulae for calculation of SAD parameters

$$SAD(A;B) = \sqrt{(end(A) - end(B))^2 + (mes(A) - mes(B))^2 + (ect(A) - (ect(B))^2}$$

$$SAM(X) = \sum_i \frac{SAD(\overline{X} - X_i)}{N_x}$$

$$SAV(X) = \sum_i \frac{SAD(\overline{X} - X_i)^2}{N_x}$$

Where: SAD = Somatotype Attitudinal Distance; SAM = Somatotype Attitudinal Mean; SAV = Somatotype Attitudinal Variance; *end* = endomorphy rating; *mes* = mesomorphy rating; *ect* = ectomorphy rating; A = an individual or a group; B = an individual or a group; X = a group; X_i = an individual member of group X; $\overline{X}$ = somatotype mean of group X; N_x = number of subjects in group X.

The SAD is the exact difference, in component units, between two somatotypes (if A and B are subjects), or between two somatotype group means (if A and B are group means), or between the group mean and an individual somatotype (if A and B are a group mean and a subject, respectively).

Like other parametric statistics, the SAD can be used to calculate differences, hence mean deviations and variances. Table 2.3 also gives formulae for calculating the Somatotype Attitudinal Mean and the Somatotype Attitudinal Variance (SAV). The SAM and the SAV describe the magnitude of the absolute scatter of a group of somatotypes around the group mean. The SAD can lead to relatively simple parametric statistical treatment for calculating differences and correlations of whole somatotypes. Multivariate techniques may be more appropriate, but are also more complicated (Cressie *et al.*, 1986).

2.6.3 TASKS

Two groups of female middle distance runners, one at international level and the other at national level, were measured. The calculated somatotypes are shown in Table 2.4.

Table 2.4 Somatotypes of 6 national-level and 10 international-level female middle distance runners (data from Day *et al.*, 1977)

International	*National*
1.5–3.0–3.5	2.0–3.5–4.0
1.0–3.0–5.0	2.0–4.0–4.0
1.5–3.0–4.5	3.5–4.5–2.0
1.0–2.0–6.0	2.5–3.5–3.0
2.0–3.0–4.0	1.5–3.5–4.5
1.5–3.0–4.0	2.5–4.0–3.0
2.5–2.0–4.0	
1.0–4.0–3.0	
2.0–3.0–4.0	

1. Separate component analysis.

- Calculate the means and standard deviations of each separate component for each group
- Calculate the significance of the differences between the two groups for each component separately – use 3 *t*-tests for independent means
- Discuss the difference between the two groups in terms of their component differences

2. Global somatotype analysis: location on the somatochart.

- Locate and plot each somatotype on a copy of Figure 2.3 by means of the *X*–*Y* coordinates
- Do the same for the two somatotype means
- Discuss this visual impression of the difference between the two samples: is there a difference in location of the means? Is there a difference in dispersion of the individual somatotypes between the two groups?

3. Global somatotype analysis: somatotype categories.

- Determine the somatotype category for each subject of the two groups
- Construct a cross-tabulation with the two groups as rows, and the different somatotype categories as columns
- Discuss the difference in somatotype category frequencies between the two groups
- Use chi-square to calculate the significance of the difference between the two groups with regard to the somatotype categories. (Note that larger cell frequencies are necessary for a meaningful interpretation of chi-square.)

4. Global somatotype analysis: *SAD* techniques.

- Calculate the *SAV* for each group, using the formulae in Table 2.3
- Check the difference in scatter between the two groups by describing the *SAM* of each group, and by means of an *F*-test on their *SAV*s
- Calculate the difference in location between the two groups, by means of the *SAD* between the mean somatotypes (use the formula in Table 2.3)

2.7 PRACTICAL 3: ANALYSIS OF LONGITUDINAL SOMATOTYPE SERIES

2.7.1 INTRODUCTION

The aim in this practical is to learn how to perform an analysis of a longitudinal series of somatotypes, using the somatochart approach and using *SAD* techniques.

2.7.2 METHODS

Analysis of time series in biological sciences must take into account the specific fact that the measurement series are within-subject factors. This can be achieved for illustrative purposes by connecting the consecutive plots of a particular measurement with time for the same subject. The classic way would be the evolution with time of the separate component values. The somatotype entity can be preserved by connecting the consecutive plots on the somatochart. Quantitative analysis of the changes is possible with MANOVA techniques with a within-subject design.

A simple quantitative way to describe the total change in somatotype with time is the Migratory Distance or MD. The MD is the sum of the *SAD* values, calculated from each consecutive pair of somatotypes of the subject:

$$MD(a; z) = SAD(a; b) + SAD(b; c) + \ldots\ldots + SAD(y; z)$$

where: a = first observation; b = second observation; $\ldots\ldots$; z = last observation; $SAD(p; q)$ = change from somatotype p to somatotype q.

2.7.3 TASKS

A group of children was measured annually from aged six until their seventeenth birthdays. The anthropometric somatotypes were calculated using the formulae in Table 2.1. The results are given in Table 2.5.

Table 2.5 Consecutive somatotypes of 6 children from their sixth to their seventeenth birthday (data from Duquet *et al.*, 1993)

Subjects	1	2	3	4	5	6
Age						
6	2.7–5.3–2.5	2.0–5.7–1.6	3.2–3.9–3.5	2.7–4.8–2.2	1.7–3.6–3.3	2.9–4.7–2.1
7	3.4–5.2–2.0	2.4–4.7–2.1	2.6–3.4–4.3	1.6–4.4–3.1	1.7–3.2–4.4	3.6–4.5–2.3
8	4.2–5.2–1.6	2.3–4.5–2.3	2.3–2.3–5.3	1.6–4.1–3.5	1.6–3.2–4.2	4.6–4.7–1.8
9	4.8–5.6–1.3	2.3–4.6–2.4	2.1–2.0–5.3	1.8–3.8–4.3	1.3–2.9–4.2	6.2–5.1–1.0
10	5.3–5.8–1.2	2.2–4.7–2.6	2.1–2.1–5.5	1.5–3.4–4.3	1.6–2.8–4.4	6.9–5.1–0.7
11	6.0–6.0–1.3	2.0–4.7–2.4	1.8–1.8–5.6	1.6–3.3–4.5	1.8–2.5–4.8	7.7–5.4–0.7
12	7.2–5.7–1.3	1.9–5.0–2.4	1.5–1.1–6.1	1.3–3.0–4.8	2.2–2.7–4.1	8.3–5.6–0.5
13	7.5–5.9–0.5	1.5–5.2–2.8	2.4–1.2–5.5	1.1–2.8–5.0	2.9–2.8–3.4	8.4–5.8–0.5
14	6.3–5.9–0.8	1.1–5.2–3.1	2.2–1.1–6.0	1.2–2.5–5.1	3.5–2.9–3.5	8.6–5.9–0.5
15	3.8–5.3–1.7	1.3–5.3–2.8	2.0–1.2–5.5	1.6–2.5–4.9	3.7–3.0–2.9	8.0–5.9–0.5
16	3.0–5.4–1.6	1.8–5.5–2.6	2.4–1.0–5.4	1.7–2.3–4.6	3.8–3.2–2.7	7.9–6.2–0.5
17	2.9–5.5–1.6	1.5–5.4–2.7	1.8–0.8–6.0	1.9–2.6–4.5	2.8–2.9–3.5	8.3–6.4–0.5

1. Plot the changes of each component with time. Construct diagrams with age on the horizontal axis, and the component value on the vertical axis. Prepare one complete line diagram per child, on which the evolution of each component is shown. Discuss the change in individual component values for each child with age, and also the dominance situations from age to age.

2. Calculate the *X–Y* coordinates of each somatotype. Locate the consecutive somatotypes of each child on a copy of Figure 2.3, using the formulae given in Practical 1. Use one somatochart per child. Discuss the change in global somatotype and the change in component dominances with age for each child.
3. Calculate the Migratory Distance for each child. Use the formulae given above. Calculate also the mean *MD* per child. Discuss the differences in *MD* between the children, and compare with the somatochart profiles.

2.8 PRACTICAL 4: VISUAL INSPECTION OF SOMATOTYPE PHOTOGRAPHS: AN INTRODUCTION TO PHOTOSCOPIC SOMATOTYPING

2.8.1 INTRODUCTION

The aim of this practical is to demonstrate how to perform a visual evaluation of the degree of presence or absence of each component in an individual by means of a somatotype photograph, and to learn to evaluate the somatotype dominance situation within this individual.

2.8.2 METHODS

A visual evaluation of the somatotype should be based on careful reading of the descriptions of the components in definitions 2.3.1 (c), (d), (e) and (f) or on the more detailed descriptions in Carter and Heath (1990). This practical should be seen as an introduction, to obtain a first impression of the technique. Expertise should be gained by comparing your own ratings with those of an experienced rater. The steps to follow in this first approach are given in the following tasks.

2.8.3 TASKS

Figure 2.5 shows somatotype photographs of the same child taken at ages 7.4, 10.0, 12.5, 14.5 and 17.0.

1. Read the definition of endomorphy, and try to decide through visual inspection at which age the child has the lowest level of endomorphy, at which age the second lowest level, and so on.
2. Next, draw an *X–Y* coordinate graph, in which the horizontal axis represents the age points, and the vertical axis represents the level of endomorphy. Do not try yet to attach a scale to the vertical axis. Try to draw a broken line that indicates, to your best impression, the way endomorphy eventually changes with age in the child.
3. Proceed in the same way with the component mesomorphy, and construct the polygon for mesomorphy on a separate page.
4. Proceed in the same way with the component ectomorphy, and construct the polygon for ectomorphy on a third page.

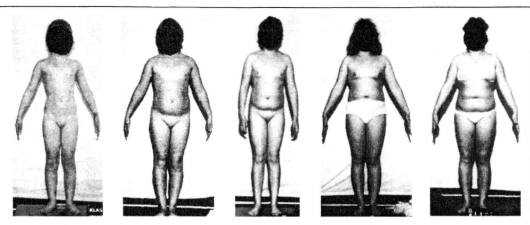

Figure 2.5 Somatotype photographs of the same child taken at ages 7.4, 10.0, 12.5, 14.5 and 17.0.

5. Compare visually on the first photograph the level of each component at the lowest age, and try to decide if one or two components are less or more dominant than the other, or if they are of equal importance. Give your visual impression of the somatotype category at this age, using the definitions given in Practical 2.
6. Now superimpose the three polygons. Shift one or more lines up or downwards if necessary, according to your photoscopic impression of the relative dominance of the components at this age.
7. Continue in the same way for each age.
8. Compare the diagram obtained with the ones that resulted from Task 1 of Practical 3. Try to find out which of the six subjects in Table 2.5 corresponds to the child in Figure 2.5.
9. Check if your visual impressions correspond to the anthropometric somatotype assessment at each age. Make the necessary corrections, and try to fit the scale of the vertical axis.

REFERENCES

Albonico, R. (1970). *Mensch-Menschen-Typen. Entwicklung und Stand der Typenforschung.* (Birkhauser Verlag, Basel).

Carter, J.E.L. (1980). *The Heath-Carter Somatotype Method.* (San Diego State University Syllabus Service, San Diego, CA).

Carter, J.E.L. and Heath, B.H. (1990). *Somatotyping – Development and Applications.* (Cambridge University Press, Cambridge).

Carter, J.E.L., Ross, W.D., Duquet, W. and Aubry, S.P. (1983). Advances in somatotype methodology and analysis. *Yearbook of Physical Anthropology,* **26**, 193–213.

Conrad, K. (1963). *Der Konstitutionstypus. Theoretische Grundlegung und praktischer Bestimmung.* (Springer, Berlin).

Cressie, N.A.C., Withers, A.T. and Craig, N.P. (1986). The statistical analysis of somatotype data. *Yearbook of Physical Anthropology,* **29**, 197–208.

Day, J.A.P., Duquet, W. and Meersseman, G. (1977). Anthropometry and physique type of female middle and long distance runners, in relation to speciality and level of performance. In *Growth and Development; Physique.* ed. O. Eiben (Akademiai Kiado, Budapest), pp. 385–97.

Duquet, W. (1980). Studie van de toepasbaarheid van de Heath & Carter-somatotypemethode op kinderen van 6 tot 13 jaar. (Applicability of the Heath-Carter somatotype method to 6 to 13 year old children.) Ph.D Dissertation, Vrije Universiteit Brussel, Belgium.

Duquet, W. and Hebbelinck, M. (1977). Application of the somatotype attitudinal distance to the study of group and individual somatotype status and relations. In *Growth and Development; Physique.* ed. O. Eiben (Akademiai Kiado, Budapest), pp. 377–84.

Duquet, W., Borms, J., Hebbelinck, M., *et al.* (1993). Longitudinal study of the stability of the somatotype in boys and girls. In *Kinanthropometry IV*. eds. W. Duquet and J.A.P. Day (E. & F.N. Spon, London) pp. 54–67.

Heath, B.H. (1963). Need for modification of somatotype methodology. *American Journal of Physical Anthropology*, **21**, 227–33.

Heath, B.H. and Carter, J.E.L. (1967). A modified somatotype method. *American Journal of Physical Anthropology*, **27**, 57–74.

Kretschmer, E. (1921). *Körperbau und Charakter*. (Springer Verlag, Berlin).

Lindegård, B. (1953). Variations in human body build. *Acta Psychiatrica et Neurologica*, **Suppl 86**, (Munksgård, Copenhagen).

Parnell, R.W. (1954). Somatotyping by physical anthropometry. *American Journal of Physical Anthropology*, **12**, 209–40.

Parnell, R.W. (1958). *Behaviour and Physique*. (E. Arnold, London).

Sheldon, W.H., Stevens, S.S. and Tucker, W.B. (1940). *The Varieties of Human Physique*. (Harper and Brothers, New York).

Tucker, W.B. and Lessa, W.A. (1940a). Man: a constitutional investigation. *The Quarterly Review of Biology*, **15**, 265–89.

Tucker, W.B. and Lessa, W.A. (1940b). Man: a constitutional investigation (continued). *The Quarterly Review of Biology*, **15**, 411–55.

Viola, G. (1933). *La costituzione individuale*. (Cappelli, Bologna).

PHYSICAL GROWTH, MATURATION AND PERFORMANCE

Gaston Beunen

3.1 AIMS

This chapter aims to familiarize students with growth evaluation, the assessment of sexual and skeletal maturation and the evaluation of physical performance as assessed with the Eurofit test battery.

3.2 INTRODUCTION

Growth, maturation and development are three concepts that are often used together and sometimes considered as synonymous. Growth is a dominant biological activity during the first two decades of life. It starts at conception and continues until the late teens or even the early twenties for a number of individuals. Growth refers to the increase in size of the body as a whole or the size attained by the specific parts of the body. The changes in size are outcomes of: (a) an increase in cell number or hyperplasia, (b) an increase in cell size or cell hypertrophy, and (c) an increase in intercellular material, or accretion. These processes occur during growth but the predominance of one or another process varies with age. For example, the number of muscle cells (fibres), is already established shortly after birth. The growth of the whole body is traditionally assessed by the changes in stature measured in a standing position, or for infants, in supine position (recumbent length). To assess the growth of specific parts of the body, appropriate anthropometric techniques have been described (Weiner and Lourie, 1969; Carter,

1982; Cameron, 1984; Lohman *et al.*, 1988; Simons *et al.*, 1990).

3.2.1 DEFINITION OF CONCEPTS

Maturation refers to the process of becoming fully mature. It gives an indication of the distance that is travelled along the road to adulthood. In other words, it refers to the tempo and timing in the progress towards the mature biological state. Biological maturation varies with the biological system that is considered. Most often the following biological systems are examined: sexual maturation, morphological maturation, dental maturation and skeletal maturation. Sexual maturation refers to the process of becoming fully sexually mature, i.e. reaching functional reproductive capability. Morphological maturation can be estimated through the percentage of adult stature that is already attained at a given age. Skeletal and dental maturation refers respectively to a fully ossified adult skeleton or dentition (Tanner, 1962, 1989; Malina and Bouchard, 1991).

Development is a broader concept, encompassing growth, maturation, learning, and experience (training). It relates to becoming competent in a variety of tasks. Thus one can speak of cognitive development, motor development and emotional development as the child's personality emerges within the context of the particular culture in which the child was born and reared. Motor development is the

Kinanthropometry and Exercise Physiology Laboratory Manual: Tests, Procedures and Data. 2nd Edition, Volume 1: Anthropometry
Edited by RG Eston and T Reilly. Published by Routledge, London, June 2001

process by which the child acquires movement patterns and skills. It is characterized by continuous modification based upon neuromuscular maturation, growth and maturation of the body, residual effects of prior experience and new motor experiences per se (Malina and Bouchard, 1991). Postnatal motor development is characterized by a shift from primitive reflex mechanisms towards postural reflexes and definite motor actions. It further refers to the acquisition of independent walking and competence in a variety of manipulative tasks and fundamental motor skills, such as running, skipping, throwing, catching, jumping, climbing, and hopping (Keogh and Sugden, 1985). From school age onwards, the focus shifts towards the development of physical performance capacities traditionally studied in the context of physical fitness or motor fitness projects. Motor fitness includes cardiorespiratory endurance, anaerobic power, muscular strength and power, local muscular endurance (sometimes called functional strength), speed, flexibility and balance (Pate and Shephard, 1989; Simons *et al.*, 1969, 1990).

3.2.2 HISTORICAL PERSPECTIVE

According to Tanner (1981) the earliest surviving statement about human growth appears in a Greek elegy of the sixth century BC. Solon the Athenian divided the growth period into hebdomads, that is, successive periods of seven years each. The infant (literally, while unable to speak) acquires deciduous teeth and sheds them before the age of seven. At the end of the next hebdomad the boy shows the signs of puberty (beginning of pubic hair), and in the last period the body enlarges and the skin becomes bearded (Tanner, 1981, p.1).

Anthropometry was not born of medicine or science but of the arts. Painters and sculptors needed instructions about the relative proportions of legs and trunks, shoulders and hips, eyes and forehead and other parts of the body. The inventor of the term anthropometry was a German physician, Johan Sigismund Elsholtz (1623–88). It is interesting to note that at this time there was not very much attention given to absolute size but much more to proportions. Note also that the introduction of the 'mètre' occurred only in 1795 and even then other scales continued to be used.

The first published longitudinal growth study of which we have record was made by Count Philibert Guéneau de Montbeillard (1720–85) on request of his close friend Buffon (Tanner, 1981). The growth and the growth velocity curves of Montbeillard's son are probably the best known curves in auxology (study of human growth). They describe growth and its velocity from birth to adulthood, which have been widely studied since then in various populations (see, for example, Eveleth and Tanner, 1990). Growth velocity refers to the growth over a period of time. Very often velocity is used to indicate changes in stature over a period of one year.

Another significant impetus in the study of growth was given by the Belgian mathematician Adolphe Quetelet (1796–1874). He was in many ways the founder of modern statistics and was instrumental in the foundation of the Statistical Society of London. Quetelet collected data on height and weight and fitted a curve to the succession of means. According to his mathematical function the growth velocity declines from birth to maturity and shows no adolescent growth spurt. This confused a number of investigators until the 1940s (Tanner, 1981, p.134). At the beginning of the nineteenth century there was an increased interest in the growing child due to the appalling conditions of the poor and their children. A new direction was given by the anthropologist Franz Boas (1858–1942). He was the first to realize the individual variation in tempo of growth and was responsible for the introduction of the concept of physiological age or biological maturation. A number of longitudinal studies were then initiated in the 1920s in the USA and later in Europe. These studies served largely as the basis of our present knowledge on physical growth and maturation (Tanner, 1981; Malina and Bouchard, 1991).

3.2.3 FITNESS AND PERFORMANCE

In several nations there is great interest in developing and maintaining the physical fitness levels of the citizens of all age levels, but special concern goes to the fitness of youth. Physical fitness has been defined in many ways. According to the American Academy of Physical Education 'physical fitness is the ability to carry out daily tasks with vigor and alertness, without undue fatigue and with ample energy to engage in leisure time pursuits and to meet the above average physical stresses encountered in emergency situations' (Clarke, 1979).

Often the distinction is made between an organic component and a motor component. The organic component is defined as the capacity to adapt to and recover from strenuous exercise, and relates to energy production and work output. The motor component relates to the development and performance of gross motor abilities. Since the beginning of the 1980s the distinction between health-related and performance-related physical fitness has come into common use (Pate and Shephard, 1989). Health-related fitness is then viewed as a state characterized by an ability to perform daily activities with vigour, and traits and capacities that are associated with low risk of premature development of the hypokinetic diseases (i.e. those associated with physical inactivity) (Pate and Shephard, 1989, p.4). Health-related physical fitness includes cardiorespiratory endurance, body composition, muscular strength and flexibility. Performance-related fitness refers to the abilities associated with adequate athletic performance, and encompasses components such as isometric strength, power, speed-agility, balance and hand–eye coordination.

Since Sargent (1921) proposed the vertical jump as a physical performance test for men, considerable change has taken place both in the conceptualization of physical performance and physical fitness and also about measurement. In the early days the expression 'general motor ability' was used to indicate one's 'general' skill. The term was similar to the general intelligence factor used at that time. Primarily under the influence of Brace (1927) and McCloy (1934) a fairly large number of studies were undertaken and a multiple motor ability concept replaced the general ability concept. There is now considerable agreement among authors and experts that the fitness concept is multi-dimensional and several abilities can be identified. An ability refers to a more general trait of the individual which can be inferred from response consistencies on a number of related tasks, whereas skill refers to the level of proficiency on a specific task or limited group of tasks. A child possesses isometric strength since he or she performs well on a variety of isometric strength tests.

Considerable attention has been devoted to fitness testing and research in the USA and Canada. The President's Council on Youth Fitness, the American Alliance for Health, Physical Education, Recreation and Dance (AAHPER, 1958, 1965; AAHPERD, 1988) and the Canadian sister organization (CAHPER, 1965) have done an outstanding job in constructing and promoting fitness testing in schools. Internationally the fundamental works of Fleishman (1964) and the International Committee for the Standardization of Physical Fitness Tests (now the International Council for Physical Activity and Fitness Research) (Larson, 1974) have received considerable attention and served, for example, as the basis for nationwide studies in Belgium (Hebbelinck and Borms, 1975; Ostyn et al., 1980; Simons et al., 1990). Furthermore, the fitness test battery constructed by Simons et al. (1969) served as the basis for studies in The Netherlands (Bovend'eerdt et al., 1980) and for the construction of the Eurofit test battery (Adam et al., 1988).

In the following section three laboratory practicals will be outlined focusing on standards of normal growth, biological maturity status and evaluation of physical fitness.

3.3 STANDARDS OF NORMAL GROWTH

3.3.1 METHODOLOGICAL CONSIDERATIONS

Growth data may be used in three distinct ways: (1) to serve as a screening device in order to identify individuals who might benefit from special medical or educational care; (2) to serve as control in the treatment of ill children (the paediatric use); and (3) as an index of the general health and nutritional status of the population or sub-population (Tanner, 1989). Standards of normal growth usually include reference data for attained stature or any other anthropometric dimension and, where available, also reference values for growth velocity. Reference values for attained stature are useful for assessing the present status to answer the question: 'Is the child's growth normal for his/her age and sex?' Growth velocity reference values are constructed to verify the growth process.

Reference charts of attained height, usually referred to as growth standards or curves, are constructed on the basis of cross-sectional studies. In such studies representative samples of girls and boys stemming from different birth cohorts and consequently of different age groups are measured once.

It has to be remembered that the outer percentiles such as the 3rd and 97th are subject to considerably greater sample error than the mean or the 50th percentile (Goldstein, 1986; Healy, 1986). The precision of estimates of population parameters, such as the mean, depends on the sample size and the variability in the population. If $\overline{X}$ is the sample mean, then the 95% confidence values, a and b, are two values such that the probability that the true population mean lies between them is 0.95. If the distribution of the measurement is Gaussian, then for a simple random sample a and b are given by:

$$a = \overline{X} + 1.96SE_{mean}$$

$$b = \overline{X} - 1.965SE_{mean}$$

where SE_{mean} is the standard error of the mean = $\dfrac{SD}{\sqrt{n-1}}$ and SD is the standard deviation.

From these formulae it can be easily seen that for a given population variance the confidence intervals decrease when the sample size increases. Major standardizing studies use samples of about 1000 subjects in each sex and age group but 500 subjects normally produce useful percentiles (Eveleth and Tanner, 1990). Representative samples can be obtained in several ways, the most commonly used being simple random samples and stratified samples. In a simple random sample each subject has an equal chance of being selected in the sample and each subject in the population must be identifiable. In a stratified sample, significant strata are identified and in each stratum a sample is selected. A stratification factor is one that serves for dividing the population into strata or subdivisions of the population, such as ethnic groups or degree of urbanization. The stratification factor is selected because there is evidence that this factor affects, or is related to, the growth process.

Growth velocity standards or reference values can be obtained only from longitudinal studies. In a longitudinal study a representative sample of boys and/or girls from one birth cohort is measured repeatedly at regular intervals. The frequency of the measurements depends on the growth velocity and also on the measurement error. During periods of rapid growth it is necessary to increase the frequency of the measurements. For stature, for example, it is recommended to carry out monthly measurements during the first year of life and to measure every three months during the adolescent growth spurt. Although some recent evidence (Lampl *et al.*, 1992) suggests that there is much more variation in growth velocity, with periods of rapid change (stepwise or saltatory increase) followed by periods of no change (stasis), when growth is monitored over very short periods of time (days or weeks).

Cross-sectional standards for growth are most often presented as growth charts. Such charts are constructed from the means and standard deviations or from the percentiles of the different sex and age groups. Conventionally, the 3rd, 10th, 25th, 50th, 75th, 90th, and 97th percentiles are displayed. The 3rd and 97th percentile delineate the outer borders of what is considered as 'normal' growth. This does not imply that on a single measurement one can decide about the 'abnormality' of the growth process. Children with statures outside the 3rd and 97th percentile need to be examined further.

Since growth is considered as a regular process over large (years) time intervals, a smooth continuous curve is fitted to the sample statistics (means, means ± 1(2) × SD, different percentiles P3, P10, P25, P50, P75, P90, P97). The series of sample statistics can be graphically smoothed, by eye, or a mathematical function can be fitted to the data. This mathematical function is selected so that it is simple and corresponds closely to the observations. In a common procedure a smooth curve is drawn through the medians (means). This can be done by fitting non-linear regressions to narrow age groups and estimating the centre of the group. The age groups are then shifted to the next age interval, resulting in a number of overlapping intervals in which corrected (estimated) medians are identified. The next step is to estimate the other percentiles, taking into account the corrections that have been made to the medians in the first step. This can be done by using the residuals from the fitted 50th percentile curve within each age group to estimate the other percentiles. This procedure can be improved by setting up a general relationship between the percentiles we want to estimate and the 50th percentile (Goldstein, 1984).

3.3.2 MATHEMATICAL BASIS OF VELOCITY CURVES

Longitudinal growth velocity reference values are obtained from the analysis of individual growth data. Individual growth curves are fitted to the serial measurements of each child. For many purposes graphical fits (Tanner *et al.*,

1966) are sufficient, but mathematical curves may also be employed (Goldstein, 1979; Marubini and Milani, 1986; Jolicoeur *et al.*, 1992). Most mathematical curves or models presently in use are developed for growth in stature. Some models have also been applied for a few body dimensions, such as body mass and diameters. The mathematical functions can be divided into two classes: structural models and non-structural.

3.3.3 STRUCTURAL MODELS

In the structural models the mathematical function, usually a family of functions or mathematical model, imposes a well-defined preselected shape to the growth curves that are fitted to the data. If the function reflects underlying processes, then the parameters of the function may have biological meaning (Bock and Thissen, 1980). Jenss and Bayley (1937) proposed a model to describe the growth process from birth to eight years. This model includes a linear and an exponential term in which the linear part describes the growth velocity and the exponential part describes growth deceleration. Several other functions have been used to describe the growth during the adolescent period (Deming, 1957; Marubini *et al.*, 1972; Hauspie *et al.*, 1980). More recently, various models have also been proposed to describe the whole growth period from birth to adulthood (Preece and Baines, 1978; Bock and Thissen, 1980; Jolicoeur *et al.*, 1992). Preece and Baines (1978) have derived a family of mathematical models to describe the human growth curve from the differential equation:

$$\frac{dh}{dt} = s(t)(h_1 - h) \tag{1}$$

Where: h = height; h_1 = adult height; and $s(t)$ is a function of time.

Model 1, in which $s(t)$ was defined by

$$\frac{ds}{dt} = (s_1 - s)(s - s_0) \tag{2}$$

was especially accurate and robust, containing only five parameters. The function is

Table 3.1 Mean values for parameters in model 1 (after Preece and Baines, 1978)

| | Boys (n = 35) | | Girls (n = 23) | |
	Mean	SD	Mean	SD
h_1	174.6	6.0	163.4	5.1
h_θ	162.9	5.6	152.7	5.2
S_0	0.1124	0.0126	0.1320	0.0181
S_1	1.2397	0.1683	1.1785	0.1553
θ	14.60	0.93	12.49	0.74

Key:
h_1 adult height
S_0 rate constant related to prepubertal velocity
S_1 rate constant related to peak height velocity
θ time parameter, near to age at peak height velocity
Exact values of the growth characteristics (take-off, peak velocity) can be mathematically derived.

$$h = h_1 - \frac{2(h_1 - h_\theta)}{\exp[S_0(t-\theta)] + \exp[S_1(t-\theta)]} \quad (3)$$

where: h_θ and h_1 (adult height) are two height parameters; θ is a time parameter; and s_0 and s_1 are rate constants having dimensions inverse of time.

From Equation 3 the velocity and acceleration function can be calculated. The position of the maximum and minimum growth velocity can be calculated from the acceleration curve and subsequently age at 'take-off', age at 'peak height velocity' height and velocity at these points can be obtained. Table 3.1 gives the mean values for British adolescents.

growth parameters obtained from the graphical or mathematical curve fitting are then combined to form the so-called mean constant growth curve and by differentiation the mean constant growth velocity curve.

For most growth studies cross-sectional standards have been published. Tanner (1989) has argued that 'tempo-conditional' standards, meaning standards that allow for differences in the tempo of growth between children, are much finer instruments to evaluate normality of growth. Such conditional standards combine information from longitudinal and cross-sectional studies. Other conditional standards can be used such as standards for height that allow for height of parents (Tanner, 1989).

3.3.4 NON-STRUCTURAL MODELS

For the non-structural approach, polynomials using various fitting techniques have been applied (Van't Hof *et al.*, 1976; Largo *et al.*, 1978; Gasser *et al.*, 1984). The use of increments or difference scores between observations of adjacent intervals is often not indicated. The regularity of the growth process is overlooked, two measurement errors are involved in each increment, and successive increments are negatively related (Van't Hof *et al.*, 1976). The individual

3.3.5 GROWTH EVALUATION

Depending on the number of students in the class, 30–50 secondary school girls and/or boys from the local school can be measured. Exact identification, including birth date and date of measurement, name and address and parents' heights should be asked in a small enquiry addressed to the parents. At the same time informed consent to conduct the study can be obtained. Furthermore, consent has to

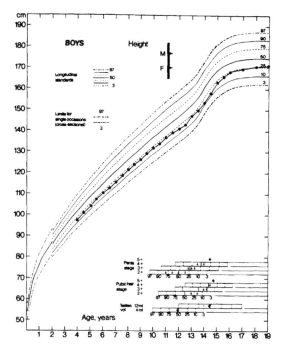

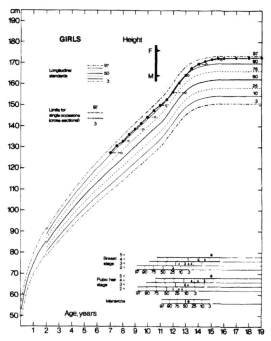

Figure 3.1 Standards of height for British boys, with normal boy plotted. (Reprinted by permission of the publishers from *Fetus into Man: Physical Growth from Conception to Maturity* by J. M. Tanner, Harvard University Press, Cambridge, MA, Copyright, 1978, 1989 by J. M. Tanner.)

Figure 3.2 Standards of height for British girls, with normal girl plotted. (Reprinted by permission of the publishers from *Fetus into Man: Physical Growth from Conception to Maturity* by J. M. Tanner, Harvard University Press, Cambridge, MA, Copyright, 1978, 1989 by J. M. Tanner.)

be obtained from the school administration. It is also advisable to obtain approval for the project by the local medical ethics committee.

Included here are standards for British children (Figures 3.1 and 3.2) (Tanner, 1989). If these standards are used for the evaluation of the school children, then height should be measured according to the procedures described by Tanner (Tanner, 1989, pp.182–6). If local standards are available these should be used and the measuring techniques that were used in constructing these standards should be adopted. The measuring technique is all important and each student needs to get experienced with the measuring techniques, preferably by conducting a preliminary intra- and inter-observer study with an experienced anthropometrist.

Once the data are collected each individual measurement is plotted against the reference standards. Chronological age should be converted to decimal age expressed in years and tenths of a year, (i.e. to calculate the decimal age the year is divided by 10 not 12). Using Table 3.2 the child's birth date is recorded, e.g. a child born on 26 June 1985 has the birthday 85.482. The date of the observation is, for example, 15 October 1999 recorded as 99.786. Age at examination is obtained by simple subtraction, e.g. 99.786 – 85.482 = 14.304 rounded to 14.30 years.

Table 3.3 presents data from two boys followed at annual intervals (data from the Leuven Longitudinal Study of Belgian Boys, Ostyn *et al.*, 1980). To assess the growth process of these boys their data can be plotted against the British reference data (ignoring small differences between Belgian and British populations) (Figure 3.1).

Table 3.2 Decimals of year

	1	2	3	4	5	6	7	8	9	10	11	12
	Jan	Feb	Mar	Apr	May	Jun	Jul	Aug	Sep	Oct	Nov	Dec
1	000	085	162	247	329	414	496	581	666	748	833	915
2	003	088	164	249	332	416	499	584	668	751	836	918
3	005	090	167	252	334	419	501	586	671	753	838	921
4	008	093	170	255	337	422	504	589	674	756	841	923
5	011	096	173	258	340	425	507	592	677	759	844	926
6	014	099	175	260	342	427	510	595	679	762	847	929
7	016	101	178	263	345	430	512	597	682	764	849	932
8	019	104	181	266	348	433	515	600	685	767	852	934
9	022	107	184	268	351	436	518	603	688	770	855	937
10	025	110	186	271	353	438	521	605	690	773	858	940
11	027	112	189	274	356	441	523	608	693	775	860	942
12	030	115	192	277	359	444	526	611	696	778	863	945
13	033	118	195	279	362	447	529	614	699	781	866	948
14	036	121	197	282	364	449	532	616	701	784	868	951
15	038	123	200	285	367	452	534	619	704	786	871	953
16	041	126	203	288	370	455	537	622	707	789	874	956
17	044	129	205	290	373	458	540	625	710	792	877	959
18	047	132	208	293	375	460	542	627	712	795	879	962
19	049	134	211	296	378	463	545	630	715	797	882	964
20	052	137	214	299	381	466	548	633	718	800	885	967
21	055	140	216	301	384	468	551	636	721	·803	888	970
22	058	142	219	304	386	471	553	638	723	805	890	973
23	060	145	222	307	389	474	556	641	726	808	893	975
24	063	148	225	310	392	477	559	644	729	811	896	978
25	066	151	227	312	395	479	562	647	731	814	899	981
26	068	153	230	315	397	482	564	649	734	816	901	984
27	071	156	233	318	400	485	567	652	737	819	904	986
28	074	159	236	321	403	488	570	655	740	822	907	989
29	077		238	323	405	490	573	658	742	825	910	992
30	079		241	326	408	493	575	660	745	827	912	995
31	082		244		411		578	663		830		997

After Tanner and Whitehouse (1984). With permission of Castlemead Publications.

Table 3.3   Growth characteristics of two 'normal boys'

	Age (years)	Height (cm)	Body mass (kg)	Subscapular skinfolds (mm)	Triceps (mm)
Case 1	13	149.6	40.0	4.1	10.2
	14	154.2	43.0	5.1	9.6
	15	162.9	50.0	7.1	9.0
	16	169.8	55.0	5.6	8.4
	17	173.4	63.0	7.9	6.2
	18	175.3	65.0	7.3	7.2
Case 2	13	158.5	48.5	7.6	10.8
	14	166.2	53.0	7.0	10.9
	15	172.3	57.5	6.2	8.6
	16	176.6	64.0	11.6	8.4
	17	177.8	67.0	10.2	8.0
	18	178.1	68.5	8.8	7.5

3.3.6 INTERPRETATION OF THE RESULTS

As expected the heights of the children are scattered over the growth chart. In order to evaluate the growth status, it is advisable to calculate the mid-parent percentile. This is the average of the percentile that corresponds to the height of the father and of the mother. (The sex-specific growth charts are of course used to define these percentiles.) If one takes the mid-parent height percentile as the 'target', a band of ±10 cm for boys and ±9 cm for girls can be plotted (use copies of the reference chart) for each child and the observed height should fall within this band. It is unlikely that a child with two small parents, at 25th percentile, will have a stature above the 75th percentile, the upper limit of the previously mentioned growth band. On the other hand it is to be expected that a child from two tall parents, at 75th percentile, will have a stature at or even somewhat above the 75th percentile.

For the interpretation of the individual data it is important to know that the mean age at peak height velocity is about 14 years with a standard deviation of 1 year for boys in both the British and Belgian populations.

The following questions can be considered: (1) are these two boys small, average, tall for their age?; (2) are they early, average or late maturers?; (3) do they have adequate body mass for their size? To answer these questions reference data are needed for body mass, body mass index and/or skinfolds (for boys 14 years of age see Table 3.5).

3.3.7 FURTHER RECOMMENDATIONS

It should be remembered that the reported parents' heights are much more subject to error than when measured. In a growth clinic it is common practice that the parents' heights are measured.

If the height of only one parent is available, the height of the other parent can be estimated by adding, for father's height, or subtracting, for mother's height, 13 cm from the height reported by the mother or father, respectively.

If the British reference curves are used it should be kept in mind that there are large interpopulation differences and that, even within a population, differences may occur due to ethnicity, social status or degree of urbanization, to name a few reasons, (see, for example, Eveleth and Tanner, 1990).

3.4 BIOLOGICAL MATURATION: SKELETAL AGE

3.4.1 METHODOLOGICAL CONSIDERATIONS

It is well documented that somatic characteristics, biological maturation and physical performance are interrelated, and that young elite athletes exhibit specific maturity characteristics (Beunen, 1989; Malina and Bouchard, 1991). Young elite male athletes are generally advanced in their maturity status whereas young female athletes show late maturity status, especially in skating, gymnastics and ballet dancing. The assessment of biological maturity is thus a very important indicator of the growing child. It is therefore a valuable tool in the hands of experienced kinanthropometrists and all other professionals involved in the evaluation of the growth and development of children.

3.4.2 ASSESSMENT OF SEXUAL MATURATION

As mentioned already, several biological systems can be used to assess biological maturity status. In assessing sexual maturation the criteria described by Reynolds and Wines (1948, 1951) synthesized and popularized by Tanner (1962) are most often used. They should not be referred to as Tanner's stages since they were in use long before Tanner described them in *Growth at Adolescence*. Furthermore, there is considerable difference in the stages for pubic hair, breast or genital development. For breast, pubic hair, and genital development, five discrete stages are described (Tanner, 1962).

The breast development stages, which

follow Reynolds and Wines (1948) are illustrated in Figure 3.3.

Stage 1 Pre-adolescent: elevation of papilla only.

Stage 2 Breast bud stage: elevation of breast and papilla as small mound. Enlargement of areolar diameter.

Stage 3 Further enlargement and elevation of breast and areola, with no separation of their contours.

Stage 4 Projection of areola and papilla to form a secondary mound above the level of the breast.

Stage 5 Mature stage: projection of papilla only due to recession of the areola to the general contour of the breast.

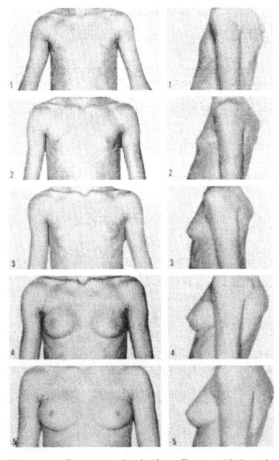

Figure 3.3 Breast standards (from Tanner, 1962, with permission).

The genital development stages are illustrated in Figure 3.4.

Stage 1 Pre-adolescent: Testes, scrotum and penis are of about the same size and proportion as in early childhood.

Stage 2 Enlargement of scrotum and of testes. The skin of the scrotum reddens and changes in texture. Little or no enlargement of penis at this stage.

Stage 3 Enlargement of penis, which occurs at first mainly in length. Further growth of testes and scrotum.

Stage 4 Increased size of penis with growth in breadth and development of glands. Further enlargement of testes and scrotum; increased darkening of scrotal skin.

Stage 5 Genitalia adult in size and shape. No further enlargement takes place after stage 5 is reached; it seems, on the contrary, that the penis size decreases slightly from the immediately post-adolescent peak (Reynolds and Wines, 1951).

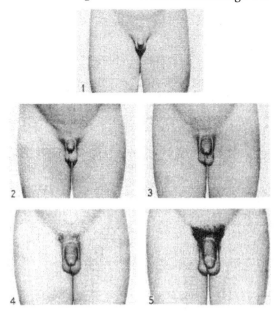

Figure 3.4 Genital standards. (from Tanner, 1962, with permission).

The pubic hair stages are illustrated in Figure 3.5, for boys and girls.

Stage 1 Pre-adolescent: The vellus over the pubes is not further developed than that over the abdominal wall, i.e. no pubic hair.

Stage 2 Sparse growth of long, slightly pigmented downy hair, straight or only slightly curled, appearing chiefly at the base of the penis or along the labia.

Stage 3 Considerably darker, coarser and more curled. The hair spreads sparsely over the junction of the pubes. It is at this stage that pubic hair is first seen in the usual type of black and white photograph of the entire body; special arrangements are necessary to photograph stage 2 hair.

Stage 4 Hair now resembles adult in

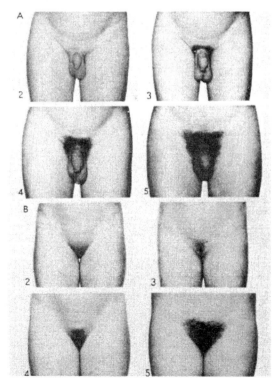

Figure 3.5 Pubic hair standards: (a) boys; (b) girls. (from Tanner, 1962, with permission).

type, but the area covered by it is still considerably smaller than in the adult. No spread to the medial surface of the thighs.

Stage 5 Adult in quantity and type with distribution of the horizontal (or classically 'feminine') pattern. Spread to medial surface of thighs but not up linea alba or elsewhere above the base of the inverse triangle.

These stages must be assigned by visual inspection of the nude subject or from somatotype photographs from which the specific areas are enlarged. Given the invasiveness of the technique, self-inspection has been proposed as an alternative but more information is needed on its reliability and validity before it can be used in epidemiological research.

Age at menarche, defined as the first menstrual flow, can be obtained retrospectively by interrogating a representative sample of sexually mature women. Note, however, the influence of error of recall. The recall data are reasonably accurate for group comparisons. The information obtained in longitudinal or prospective studies is of course much more accurate, but here other problems inherent to longitudinal studies interfere. In the status quo technique, representative samples of girls expected to experience menarche are interrogated. The investigator records whether or not menstrual periods have started at the time of investigation. Reference standards can be constructed using probits or logits for which the percentage of menstruating girls at each age level is plotted against chronological age, whereafter a probit or logit is fitted through the observed data. Morphological age can be assessed by means of the age at peak height velocity, i.e. the age at which the maximum growth velocity in height occurs. This requires a longitudinal study. An alternative method of defining morphological age is to use percentage of predicted height.

3.4.3 PREDICTION OF ADULT HEIGHT

The actual height is then expressed as a percentage of adult height. The problem here is to define adult height. Several techniques have been developed for the prediction of adult height. The techniques developed by Bayley (1946), Roche *et al.* (1975a) and Tanner *et al.* (1983) seem to be the most accurate and most commonly used. The predictors in these techniques are actual height, chronological age, skeletal age, and, in some techniques, parental height and/or age at menarche for girls. Based on data of the Fels Longitudinal Study, Wainer *et al.* (1978) demonstrated that in American white children reasonable accuracy can be obtained in predicting adult stature when skeletal age is replaced by chronological age. Khamis and Roche (1994) also showed that when current stature, current weight, and mid-parent stature are used as predictors, the errors of prediction are only slightly larger then those for the Roche–Wainer–Thissen method (1975a) which requires skeletal age. More recently, based on data of the Leuven Longitudinal Study on Belgian Boys, Beunen *et al.* (1997) proposed the Beunen–Malina method for predicting adult stature. In this method adult stature is predicted from four somatic dimensions: current stature, sitting height, subscapular skinfold, triceps skinfold, and chronological age. In the age range 13–16 years, the accuracy of the Beunen–Malina method compares favourably with the original Tanner–Whitehouse method (Tanner *et al.,* 1983). For boys aged 12.5–13.5 years, for example, adult stature can be predicted using the following regression equation (Beunen *et al.,* 1997):

adult stature = 147.99 cm + 0.87 stature (cm)
     − 0.77 sitting height (cm)
     + 0.54 triceps skinfold (mm)
     − 0.64 subscapular skinfold (mm)
     − 3.39 chronological age (years)

The main advantage of the Beunen-Malina method is that it is non-invasive and does not require the assessment of skeletal age based on radiographs. It is however clear that the original Tanner–Whitehouse method (Tanner *et al.*, 1983) is to be preferred when radiographs of the hand and wrist are available. It should also be noted that the Beunen–Malina method is only for boys.

In this respect it is of interest to note that at 2 years of age, boys attain nearly 50% of their adult stature, whereas girls reach this landmark at 1.5 years. Boys reach 75% of adult stature at about 9 years and girls at 7.5 years. Finally 90% is reached at about 13.5 years in boys and at 11.5 years in girls (Tanner, 1989). This clearly demonstrates that already at two years of age girls are biologically more mature than boys and that this advancement increases with age to reach a difference of about 2 years at adolescence. Until now, no practical useful technique has been developed to assess 'shape age' as another indicator of morphological maturity.

3.4.4 DENTAL AND SKELETAL TECHNIQUES

Dental maturity can be estimated from the age of eruption of deciduous or permanent teeth or from the number of teeth present at a certain age (Demirjian, 1978). Eruption is, however, only one event in the calcification process and has no real biological meaning. For this reason, Demirjian *et al.* (1973) constructed scales for the assessment of dental maturity, based on the principles that Tanner *et al.* (1983) developed for the estimation of skeletal age.

Skeletal maturity is the most commonly used indicator of biological maturation. It is widely recognized as the best single biological maturity indicator (Tanner, 1962). Three main techniques are presently in use: the atlas technique, first introduced by Todd (1937) and later revised by Greulich and Pyle (1950, 1959), the bone-specific approach developed by Tanner *et al.* (1983), the bone-specific approach developed by Roche *et al.* for the knee (1975b) and for the hand (1988).

3.4.5 SKELETAL AGE ASSESSMENT: TWII SYSTEM

In this section the assessment of skeletal age according to the Tanner–Whitehouse method (TWII) (Tanner *et al.*, 1983) will be introduced.

The TWII is a bone-specific approach which means that all the bones of a region of the body are graded on a scale and then combined to give an estimate of the skeletal maturation status of that area. The TWII system is developed for the hand and wrist. In this area 28 ossification centres of long, short and round bones are found, including primary ossification centres (round bones) and secondary ossification centres (epiphyses of the short and long bones). The primary ossification centres of the short and long bones develop before birth and form the diaphyses. The secondary centres of the short and long bones generally develop after birth and form the epiphyses. For each centre a sequence of developmental milestones is defined. Such a milestone indicates the distance that has been travelled along the road to full maturity, meaning the adult shape and fusion between epiphysis and diaphysis for short and long bones. Such a sequence of milestones is invariant, meaning that the second milestone occurs after the first but before the third. Based on careful examination of longitudinal series of normal boys and girls, stages of skeletal maturity were defined for all the bones in the hand and wrist. The stages are described in a handbook for the assessment of skeletal age (Tanner *et al.*, 1983). Each stage is indicated by a letter. Stages are converted to weighted maturity scores. These scores are defined in such a way as to minimize the overall disagreement between the scores assigned to the different bones over the total standardizing sample. Furthermore, a biological weight is assigned to the scores so that, for example, the distal epiphysis of the radius and ulna are given four times more weight than the metacarpals or phalanges of the third and fifth finger. Three scales are available: one for 20 bones of the hand and wrist (TWII scale), one for the 13 short and long bones (RUS scale; radius, ulna and short bones), and one for the carpal bones (CARP scale). Although 28 bone centres develop post-natally in the hand and wrist, only 20 bones are assessed in the total TWII system. Since the metacarpals and phalanges, considered row-wise, show considerable agreement in their maturity status, only the first, third, and fifth fingers are estimated. Once the maturity stages are assigned to the bones, the stages are converted to maturity scores using one of the three scales. The scores are then simply added to form the overall maturity score for the hand and wrist (TWII scale), the long and short bones (RUS scale) or the carpals (CARP scale). For these overall maturity scores reference data are then constructed for a population, (e.g. Tanner *et al.*, 1983; Beunen *et al.*, 1990). Very often the maturity score is converted into skeletal age, which is the corresponding chronological age when, on the average, an overall maturity score is reached. In the Belgian population a TWII score of 848 corresponds to a skeletal age of 13.5 years, and this is exactly the same in the British population. At other age levels, however, there are considerable differences between Belgian and British children.

3.4.6 PRACTICAL EXERCISE

In assessing skeletal age, radiographs have to be taken in a standard position and with standard equipment (for instructions see Tanner *et al.*, 1983). The descriptions and directions of the authors should also be carefully followed. This implies that the written criteria for the stages should be carefully studied and followed. The illustrations are only a guide for the identification of the stages. They represent the upper and lower limit of a given stage. For the assignment of stages the first criterion of the previous stage must be clearly visible and, in the case of only one criterion, this must be present. If there are two criteria, one of the two must be present. When three criteria are described, two of the three must be visible. Depending on the scale (TWII, RUS, CARP) the corresponding scores for each sex must be given, then summed and compared to reference standards for the population.

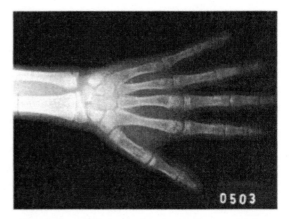

Figure 3.6 Radiograph of the hand and wrist of a Belgian boy (I).

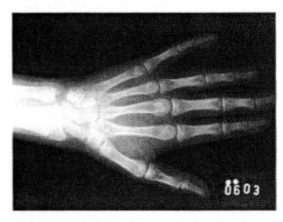

Figure 3.7 Radiograph of the hand and wrist of a Belgian boy (II).

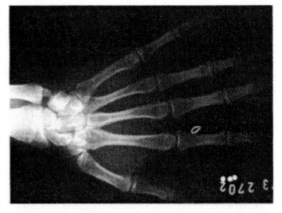

Figure 3.8 Radiograph of the hand and wrist of a Belgian boy (III).

Name : ....   Name of assessor : ....

Sex : ....   Christian name : ....

Date of birth (day / month / year)

Date of x-ray

bone	stage	score	RUS	bone	stage	score	CARP
Radius				Capitate			
Ulna				Hamate			
Metacarpal I				Triquetral			
Metacarpal II							
Metacarpal V				Lunate			
Prox. Phal. I				Scaphoid			
Prox. Phal. III							
Prox. Phal. V				Trapezium			
Mid. Phal. I				Trapezoid			
Mid. Phal. V				Tot. Carp–score			
				CARP–skel. age			
Dist. Phal. II							
Dist. Phal. III				Total TW2–score			
Dist. Phal. V				TW2–skel. age			
Total RUS–score				Chronological age			
RUS–skel. age							

In each ☐ one digit is filled in ; do not note 9 for 9 years but note 09

Figure 3.9 Scoring sheet for skeletal age assessment.

In order to familiarize students with the system, three radiographs (Figures 3.6–3.8) are included for which the three maturity scores can be obtained. A scoring sheet is shown in Figure 3.9. As described above, the instructions in the handbook (Tanner *et al.*, 1983) should be carefully followed and the bones are rated in the same order as indicated on the scoring sheet.

The scores obtained should then be compared with those of an experienced observer. In this case the ratings can be compared with those of the author (see the Appendix at the end of this chapter). His ratings show considerable agreement with those of the originators of the method (Beunen and Cameron, 1980). The differences between the students' ratings and those of the expert need to be discussed, and if time permits, a second rating can be done with at least a one-week interval.

In most cases the student will experience that he/she is able to obtain fairly close agreement between his/her ratings and those of the expert. This does not at all imply that the student is now experienced. From intra- and inter-observer studies conducted in our laboratory, it appears that before one becomes experienced about 500 radiographs have to be assessed. The assessor also needs to verify his/her own intra-observer reliability and has to compare his/her ratings with those of an expert.

As previously mentioned skeletal age is an important variable in the regression equations for predicting adult height. Given the characteristic physical structure of athletes, and the role of stature in this respect, it can be easily understood that the estimation of adult stature can be a useful factor in an efficient guidance of young athletes.

Finally, it should be mentioned that skeletal age correlates moderately to highly with other indicators of biological maturity such as sexual maturity and morphological maturity. The association with dental maturity is considerably lower. The associations are, however, never strong enough to allow individual prediction but they are strong enough to indicate the maturation status of a group of children or populations. This means that when a group of female gymnasts is markedly delayed in sexual maturity, the group is also likely to be delayed in skeletal maturity (Beunen, 1989; Malina and Bouchard, 1991).

3.5 PHYSICAL FITNESS

3.5.1 METHODOLOGICAL CONSIDERATIONS

As mentioned earlier the physical fitness concept and its measurement have evolved over time and recently the distinction between health- and performance-related fitness has been introduced. Table 3.4 gives an overview of test batteries that have been used and, more importantly, for which reference values have been constructed. For the test batteries included in Table 3.4 attempts were made to obtain tests that are objective, standardized, reliable, and valid (for more information about test construction see Safrit (1973) and Anastasi (1988)). For most of the batteries, nationwide reference values were constructed. Attempts have also been made to construct criterion-referenced norms (Blair *et al.*, 1989). Within the context of the health-related fitness concept, standards of required fitness levels were created by expert panels, e.g. 42 ml kg^{-1} min^{-1} for $\dot{V}O_2$ max in young men and 35 ml kg^{-1} min^{-1} for young women. Very little empirical evidence is available to create such criterion-related standards for the other health-related fitness items.

From Table 3.4 it is clear that in most batteries the same components are included and that quite often the same tests are proposed. Note of course that test batteries that are intended to evaluate health-related fitness do not incorporate performance-related items. With increasing awareness about safety and risks involved in testing, some testing procedures have been adapted, e.g. sit-ups were originally tested with straight legs and hands crossed behind the neck whereas in more recent procedures the arms are crossed over the chest, the knees are bent and the subject curls to a position in which the elbows touch the knees or thighs. In the latter procedure there is less risk of causing low-back pain.

In order to construct reference values for a population, large representative samples of boys and girls from different age levels must be examined. The same principles apply as for the construction of growth standards discussed previously. The data obtained must be transferred into reference scales so that the individual scores can be evaluated and test results can be compared. Most often reference values are reported in percentile scales but raw scores can

Table 3.4 Fitness components and test items in selected physical fitness test batteries

Fitness Component	Test Batteries									
	AAHPER youth fitness test (1958)	Fleishman (1964)	AAHPER youth fitness test (1965)	CAHPER (1965)	Simons et al. (1969)	ICPFT Larson (1974)	Fitnessgram (1987)	NCYFS II Ross & Pate (1987)	AAHPERD Physical Best (1988)	EUROFIT Adam et al. (1988)
Health-related components										
Cardio-respiratory endurance	660 yard run–walk	660 yard run–walk	660 yard run–walk	300 yard	step test	600–800–1000–1500–2000 m run	1 min walk–run for time	0.5 min run–walk 1 min run–walk	1 min run	endurance shuttle run (Léger & Lambert, 1982) bicycle ergometer test
Body composition	—	—	—	—	triceps–subscapular–suprailiac–calf skinfolds	—	triceps–calf skinfolds	triceps–subscapular–calf skinfold	triceps–calf skinfolds	triceps–biceps–subscap.–suprailiac–calf skinfold
Flexibility	—	turn and twist bend, twist and touch	—	—	sit and reach	forward trunk flexion or sit and reach	sit and reach	sit and reach	sit and reach	sit and reach
Upper body muscular endurance and strength	pull-ups	pull-ups	pull-ups (boys) flexed arm hang (girls)	flexed arm hang	flexed arm hang	flexed arm hang (girls and children)	pull-ups	pull-ups modified	pull-ups	flexed arm hang
Abdominal muscular endurance and strength	sit-ups	leg lifts	sit-ups	sit-ups	leg lifts	sit-ups (bent knees)	sit-ups (bent knees)	sit-ups (bent knees)	sit-ups (curl to sitting position)	sit-ups (bent knees)

continued on next page

Table 3.4 Fitness components and test items in selected physical fitness test batteries (cont.)

Fitness Component	Test Batteries									
	AAHPER youth fitness test (1958)	Fleishman (1964)	AAHPER youth fitness test (1965)	CAHPER (1965)	Simons et al. (1969)	ICPFT Larson (1974)	Fitnessgram (1987)	NCYFS II Ross & Pate (1987)	AAHPERD Physical Best (1988)	EUROFIT Adam et al. (1988)
Performance-related components										
Static (isometric) strength	—	handgrip	—	—	arm pull	handgrip	—	—	—	—
Explosive strength	standing long jump	softball throw	standing long jump	standing long jump	vertical jump	standing long jump	—	—	—	—
Anaerobic power	softball throw	—	softball throw	—	—	—	—	—	—	—
Running speed	50 yard dash shuttle run	100 yard shuttle run	50 yard dash shuttle run	50 yard dash 40 yard shuttle run	50 m shuttle run	50 m dash 40 m shuttle run	shuttle run (optional)	—	—	50 m shuttle run
Speed of limb movement	—	—	—	—	plate tapping	—	—	—	—	plate tapping
Balance	—	one foot balance	—	—	need established	—	—	—	—	flamingo balance
Coordination	—	—	—	—	stick balance	—	—	—	—	—

also be transformed into standard scales (z-scores), normalized standard scales (transformed into a normalized distribution) or age norms (motor age and motor coefficient as in the original Osereztky motor development scale). Probably none of these scales can be considered as the best and much depends on the needs of the test constructor and the needs of those who intend to use the test.

3.5.2 PHYSICAL FITNESS TESTING

Similarly to what has been explained in the growth evaluation section (section 3.2.5), a number of secondary school children can be examined on a physical fitness test battery. In selecting a test battery, it should be kept in mind that appropriate and recent reference values need to be available, and that the battery selected has been constructed according to well-established scientific procedures (see above). Furthermore, all the equipment necessary for adequate testing needs to be available.

The Eurofit test battery (Adam *et al.*, 1988) was selected for this purpose. Selected Normative values from the Eurofit test battery items for British and Dutch children are shown in Tables 8.6 and 8.7. Reference values of the Belgian population are also available (Lefevre *et al.*, 1993). Table 3.4 shows that this battery includes health- and performance-related fitness items. If the Eurofit tests are examined and the reference values of 14-year-old Belgian children (Tables 3.5 and 3.6) are used, then only 14-year-old children should

Table 3.5 Profile chart of the Eurofit test for 14-year-old boys

	P3	P10	P25	P50	P75	P90	P97
Anthropometry							
Height (cm)	153.2	157.7	162.3	167.4	172.5	176.9	181.0
Weight (kg)	38.6	42.5	47.0	52.9	60.1	68.0	77.5
Triceps skinfold (mm)		5.9	6.9	8.4	11.4	16.0	
Biceps skinfold (mm)		3.2	3.6	4.3	5.1	9.5	
Subscapular skinfold (mm)		5.1	5.7	6.3	7.9	10.9	
Suprailiac skinfold (mm)		3.8	4.2	4.8	6.9	11.2	
Calf skinfold (mm)		5.9	7.2	8.9	12.1	17.2	
Sum skinfolds (mm)		25.5	28.7	32.7	43.6	65.9	
Physical performance							
Flamingo balance (n)		24.9	19.5	14.8	11.0	7.8	
Plate tapping (s)		14.2	13.0	11.8	10.8	10.1	
Sit and reach (cm)		11.2	16.0	21.0	25.7	29.5	
Standing long jump (cm)		164.5	179.6	194.2	208.0	221.0	
Handgrip (N)		25.3	29.0	33.4	38.0	42.6	
Sit-ups (n)		20.0	22.8	25.4	27.8	29.9	
Flexed arm hang (cm)		5.1	13.6	23.2	34.0	45.8	
Shuttle run (s)		23.3	22.2	21.2	20.4	19.7	
Endurance shuttle run (n)		4.9	6.3	7.8	9.3	10.6	

be tested. In the reference tables, 14 years includes 14.00 to 14.99-year-old children.

Before the test session in the secondary school all pupils should be familiarized with the test procedure. It is advisable first to study the test instructions and descriptions (Adam *et al.*, 1988), then to organize a demonstration session during which the tests are correctly demonstrated and then to practise the test with peers of the same class as subjects. Once the training period has finished, the session of testing in the school can be planned. As for the evaluation of growth, informed consent is needed from the parents and school, and for older children from the

adolescents themselves. Care should be taken that children at risk are identified. The recommendations of the American College of Sports Medicine should be followed to identify individuals at risk (American College of Sports Medicine, 1991). Generally children who are allowed to participate in physical education classes can be tested, taking into account that some are only allowed to participate in some exercise sessions.

Obviously the general recommendations for administering the Eurofit tests should be carefully followed. The individual scores are recorded on a special sheet (Figure 3.10). Once

Table 3.6 Profile chart of the Eurofit test for 14-year-old girls

	P3	P10	P25	P50	P75	P90	P97
Anthropometry							
Height (cm)	149.2	153.5	157.6	162.2	166.6	170.6	174.4
Weight (kg)	39.7	43.5	47.6	52.9	59.4	66.7	75.4
Triceps skinfold (mm)		9.0	11.0	14.2	18.7	24.4	
Biceps skinfold (mm)		4.6	5.9	8.1	11.7	16.9	
Subscapular skinfold (mm)		7.0	8.2	10.0	13.7	19.7	
Suprailiac skinfold (mm		5.5	7.1	9.4	13.6	19.7	
Calf skinfold (mm)		9.7	12.4	16.4	22.0	29.0	
Sum skinfolds (mm)		38.3	46.4	59.1	79.4	107.2	
Physical performance							
Flamingo balance (n)		27.6	20.7	15.4	11.3	7.5	
Plate tapping (s)		14.2	13.1	12.1	11.2	10.6	
Sit and reach (cm)		16.9	21.9	26.9	31.4	34.8	
Standing long jump (cm)		140.0	152.5	166.0	179.4	191.6	
Handgrip (N)		20.2	22.9	25.8	28.9	31.7	
Sit-ups (n)		15.9	18.6	21.0	23.4	25.8	
Flexed arm hang (cm)		0.0	2.8	7.5	14.4	23.1	
Shuttle run (s)		24.2	23.3	22.3	21.4	20.7	
Endurance shuttle run (n)		2.9	3.7	4.8	6.1	7.2	

the tests are administered the individual scores are converted to reference scales. For this purpose reference scales of the Eurofit test battery for 14-year-old boys and girls are provided (Table 3.5 and 3.6 after Lefevre *et al.*, 1993).

Name : ....   Christian name : ....

School : ....   Class : ....

Date of birth   :

day   month   year

Test date   :

Test	Procedure	Score	Result
Triceps skinfold*	–	mm	
Biceps skinfold*	–	mm	
Subscapular skinfold*	–	mm	
Suprailiac skinfold*	–	mm	
Calf skinfold*	–	mm	
Flamingo balance	1 trial	number min^{-1}	
Plate tapping	1 trial	time s 25 $cycle^{-1}$	
Sit and reach	2 trials	cm	
Standing long jump	2 trials	cm	
Handgrip	2 trials	kg	
Bent arm hang	1 trial	s	
Shuttle run	1 trial	s	
Endurance shuttle run	1 trial	number	

For measuring procedures follow the directions of the Eurofit manual. It is good practice to measure all the skinfolds once, repeat the measurements and verify if the difference is not larger than 10%. If so take another measurement and average the results. The test order as given on this sheet should be respected

Figure 3.10 Pro-forma for recording the Eurofit test results.

3.5.3 INTERPRETATION AND DISCUSSION

Each individual test score is plotted against the profiles given in Table 3.5 for boys and Table 3.6 for girls. From this profile the fitness level can be evaluated. As a guideline the test results of a Belgian 14-year-old boy (Jan) will be discussed (Table 3.7).

Jan seems to perform above average in two of the five health-related fitness items (endurance and flexibility). His skinfolds are quite high, and he performs below the median for muscular endurance and strength of the upper body and abdomen (bent arm hang and sit-ups). For his health-related condition it can be concluded that his cardiorespiratory endurance is above average for his sex and age but that given the rather high skinfolds his performance can probably be improved. To do this, Jan needs to be sufficiently active (endurance-type activities) and control his energy intake (most probably excessive amounts of fat, or carbohydrates from soft drinks, sweets, snacks and so on). Furthermore, his muscular endurance and strength are weak and need to be improved. Note the negative influence of fatness (adiposity) on these items. For the performance-related items quite large variability among tests is observed. Balance is excellent, and static strength is average. Note the positive influence of fatness on static

Table 3.7 Individual profile of a 14-year-old Belgian boy (Jan)

	P3	P10	P25	P50	P75	P90	P97
Anthropometry							
Height (cm)	153.2	157.7	162.3	167.4	172.5	176.9	181.0
Weight (kg)	38.6	42.5	47.0	52.9	60.1	68.0	77.5
Triceps skinfold (mm)		5.9	6.9	8.4	11.4	16.0	
Biceps skinfold (mm)		3.2	3.6	4.3	5.1	9.5	
Subscapular skinfold (mm)		5.1	5.7	6.3	7.9	10.9	
Suprailiac skinfold (mm		3.8	4.2	4.8	6.9	11.2	
Calf skinfold (mm)		5.9	7.2	8.9	12.1	17.2	
Sum skinfolds (mm)		25.5	28.7	32.7	43.6	65.9	
Physical performance							
Flamingo balance (n)		24.9	19.5	14.8	11.0	7.8	
Plate tapping (s)		14.2	13.0	11.8	10.8	10.1	
Sit and reach (cm)		11.2	16.0	21.0	25.7	29.5	
Standing long jump (cm)		164.5	179.6	194.2	208.0	221.0	
Handgrip (N)		25.3	29.0	33.4	38.0	42.6	
Sit-ups (n)		20.0	22.8	25.4	27.8	29.9	
Flexed arm hang (cm)		5.1	13.6	23.2	34.0	45.8	
Shuttle run (s)		23.3	22.2	21.2	20.4	19.7	
Endurance shuttle run (n)		4.9	6.3	7.8	9.3	10.6	

strength. Jan scores poorly on tests that require explosive actions and speed (standing long jump, shuttle run and plate tapping). Undoubtedly, these poor performance levels will have an effect on Jan's sport-specific skills. He will thus profit largely from an improvement in these capacities. In conclusion, Jan needs a general conditioning programme in which the weak performance capacities are trained.

In interpreting the results, one should bear in mind that all tests and measurements are affected by measurement error. Therefore small differences in test results should be ignored. Furthermore, the selection of the Eurofit tests was based on the factor-analytic studies of Simons *et al.* (1969, 1990). In these studies it was shown that, when fitness factors are rotated to an oblique configuration, the factors showed only small intercorrelations; consequently the interrelationship between fitness items is low. This implies that it is very unlikely that a boy or girl would perform well on all items; generally there is some variation between tests. Note, however, that outstanding athletes perform above the median for most or all items. Note also that the tests correlate with somatic dimensions and biological maturity status. Static strength (handgrip) is positively correlated with height and body mass. Tests in which the subject performs against his own weight or part of it, for example, tests of muscular endurance and power are negatively correlated with height and weight. From the above it is also clear that in assessing the performance capacities and especially in guiding and prescribing exercise programmes, the assessment of habitual physical activity and of nutritional status add significantly to the advice and guidance.

SUMMARY

After a few historical notes this chapter considers growth evaluation, assessment of biological maturation and physical fitness evaluation. For each of the three sections the concept, assessment and evaluation techniques are explained and a detailed description is given of a practical. For the growth and physical fitness evaluation, a small project is described in which data are collected and afterwards evaluated. For skeletal age assessment, X-rays are assessed according to the Tanner–Whitehouse technique. Each section ends with a number of recommendations and a short discussion of the evaluation and techniques that have been used. Additional details concerning the assessment of growth, maturation and performance are given by Boreham and Van Praagh in Chapter 8.

APPENDIX

Estimation according to the author of this chapter. (For his intra- and inter-observer reliability see Beunen and Cameron, 1980.)

Estimations radiograph Figure 3.6: Boy
Radius: G, Ulna: E, MCI: F, MCIII: F, MCV: E, PPI: F, PPIII: F, PPV: F, MPIII: F, MPV: F, DPI: E, DPIII: F; DPV: F

Capitate: G, Hamate: G, Triquetral: G, Lunate: G, Schaphoid: G, Trapezium: G, Trapezoid: H

Estimations radiograph Figure 3.7: Boy
Radius: H, Ulna: G, MCI: G, MCIII: G, MCV: G, PPI: G, PPIII: G, PPV: G, MPIII: G, MPV: F, DPI: G, DPIII: G; DPV: F

Capitate: H, Hamate: H, Triquetral: H, Lunate: H, Schaphoid: H, Trapezium: H, Trapezoid: H

Estimations radiograph Figure 3.8: Boy
All bones have reached the adult stage
RUS age: adult, CARP age: adult, TWII 20-bone age: adult

REFERENCES

AAHPER (1958). *Youth Fitness Test Manual*, AAHPER, Washington, DC.

AAHPER (1965). *Youth Fitness Test Manual*, revised edn. AAHPER, Washington, DC.

AAHPERD (1988). *The AAHPERD Physical Best Program*, AAHPERD, Reston, VA.

Adam, C., Klissouras, V., Ravassolo, M., *et al.* (1988). *Eurofit. Handbook for the Eurofit Test of Physical*

Fitness. Council of Europe, Committee for the Development of Sport, Rome.

American College of Sports Medicine (1991). *Guidelines for Exercise Testing and Prescription*. (Lea and Febiger, Philadelphia).

Anastasi, A. (1988). *Psychological Testing*. (Macmillan, New York).

Bayley, N. (1946). Tables for predicting adult height from skeletal age and present height. *Journal of Pediatrics*, **28**, 49–64.

Beunen, G. (1989). Biological age in pediatric exercise research. In *Advances in Pediatric Sport Sciences*, vol. 3, *Biological Issues*. ed. O. Bar-Or (Human Kinetics, Champaign, IL), pp. 1–39.

Beunen, G. and Cameron, N. (1980). The reproducibility of TW2 skeletal age assessment by a self-taught assessor. *Annals of Human Biology*, **7**, 155–62.

Beunen, G., Lefevre, J., Ostyn, M., *et al.* (1990). Skeletal maturity in Belgian youths assessed by the Tanner-Whitehouse method (TW2). *Annals of Human Biology*, **17**, 355–76.

Beunen, G., Malina, R.M., Lefevre, J., *et al.* (1997). Prediction of adult stature and non-invasive assessment of biological maturation. *Medicine and Science in Sports and Exercise*, **29**, 225–30.

Blair, N., Clarke, D.G., Cureton, K.J. and Powell, K.E. (1989). Exercise and fitness in childhood: implications for a lifetime of health. In *Perspectives in Exercise and Sports Medicine. Youth and Exercise and Sports*, vol. 2. eds. C.V. Gisolfi and D.R. Lamb (Benchmark Press, Indianapolis), pp. 401–30.

Bock, R.D. and Thissen, D. (1980). Statistical problems of fitting individual growth curves. In *Human Physical Growth and Maturation. Methodologies and Factors*. eds. F.E. Johnston, A.F. Roche and C. Susanne (Plenum Press, New York), pp. 265–90.

Bovend'eerdt, J.H.F., Bernink, M.J.E., van Hijfte, T. (1980). *De MOPER Fitness Test. Onderzoeksverslag*. (De Vrieseborch, Haarlem).

Brace, D.K. (1927). *Measuring Motor Ability*. (Barnes, New York).

CAHPER (1965). *Fitness Performance Test Manual for Boys*. CAHPER, Toronto.

Cameron, N. (1984). *The Measurement of Human Growth*. (Croom Helm, London).

Carter, J.E.L. ed. (1982). *Physical Structure of Olympic Athletes. Part I. The Montreal Olympic Games Anthropological Project. Medicine and Sport 16*. (Karger, Basel).

Clarke, H.H. (1979). Academy approves physical fitness definition. *Physical Fitness News Letter*, **25**, 1.

Deming, J. (1957). Application of the Gompertz curve to the observed pattern of growth in length of 48 individual boys and girls during the adolescent cyclus of growth. *Human Biology*, **29**, 83–122.

Demirjian, A. (1978). Dentition. In *Human Growth: Postnatal Growth*, vol. 2. eds. F. Falkner and J.M. Tanner (Plenum Press, New York), pp. 413–44.

Demirjian, A., Goldstein, H. and Tanner, J.M. (1973). A new system for dental age assessment. *Human Biology*, **45**, 211–27.

Eveleth, P.B. and Tanner, J.M. (1990). *Worldwide Variation in Human Growth*. (Cambridge University Press, Cambridge).

Fitnessgram Users Manual (1987). Institute for Aerobics Research, Dallas, TX.

Fleishman, E.A. (1964). *The Structure and Measurement of Physical Fitness*. (Prentice Hall, Englewood Cliffs, NJ).

Gasser, T., Köhler, W., Müller, H-G., Kneip, A., *et al.* (1984). Velocity in physical changes associated with adolescence in girls. *Annals of Human Biology*, **11**, 397–411.

Goldstein, H. (1979). *The Design and Analysis of Longitudinal Studies. Their Role in the Measurement of Change*. (Academic Press, London).

Goldstein, H. (1984). Current developments in the design and analysis of growth studies. In *Human Growth and Development*. eds. J. Borms, R. Hauspie, A. Sand, *et al.* (Plenum Press, New York), pp. 733–52.

Goldstein, H. (1986). Sampling for growth studies. In *Human Growth: a Comprehensive Treatise*, 2nd edn, vol. 3. eds. F. Falkner and J.M. Tanner (Plenum Press, New York), pp. 59–78.

Greulich, W.W. and Pyle, I. (1950, 1959). *Radiographic Atlas of Skeletal Development of the Hand and Wrist*. (Stanford University Press, Stanford, CA).

Hauspie, R.C., Wachholder, A., Baron, G., *et al.* (1980). A comparative study of the fit of four different functions to longitudinal data for growth in height of Belgian Boys. *Annals of Human Biology*, **7**, 347–58.

Healy, M.J.R. (1986). Statistics of growth standards. In *Human Growth: a Comprehensive Treatise*, 2nd edn, vol. 3. eds. F. Falkner and J.M. Tanner (Plenum Press, New York), pp. 47–58.

Hebbelinck, M. and Borms, J. (1975). *Biometrische Studie van een Reeks Lichaamskenmerken en Lichamelijke Prestatietests van Belgische Kinderen uit het Lager Onderwijs*. Centrum voor Bevolkings - en Gezinsstudiën (C.B.G.S.), Brussels.

Jenss, R.M. and Bayley, M. (1937). A mathematical method for studying the growth of a child. *Human Biology*, **9**, 556–63.

Jolicoeur, P., Pontier, J. and Abidi, H. (1992). Asymptotic models for the longitudinal growth of human stature. *American Journal of Human Biology*, **4**, 461–8.

Keogh, J. and Sugden, D. (1985). *Movement Skill Development*. (MacMillan, New York).

Khamis, H.J. and Roche, A.F. (1994). Predicting adult stature without using skeletal age: the Khamis-Roche method. *Pediatrics*, **94**, 504–7.

Lampl, M., Veldhuis, J.D. and Johnson, M.L. (1992). Saltation and stasis: a model of human growth. *Science*, **258**, 801–3.

Largo, R.H., Gasser, Th., Prader, A., et al. (1978). Analysis of the adolescent growth spurt using smoothing spline functions. *Annals of Human Biology*, **5**, 421–34.

Larson, L.A. ed. (1974). *Fitness, Health, and Work Capacity: International Standards for Assessment*. (Macmillan, New York).

Lefevre, J., Beunen, G., Borms, J., et al. (1993). *Eurofit Testbatterij. Leiddraad bij Testafneming en Referentie-research*. BLOSO-Jeugdsportcampagne, Brussels.

Lohman, T.G., Roche, A.F. and Martorell, R. eds. (1988). *Anthropometric Standardization Reference Manual*. (Human Kinetics, Champaign, IL).

McCloy, C.H. (1934). The measurement of general motor capacity and general motor ability. *Research Quarterly*, **Suppl 5**, 46–61.

Malina, R.M. and Bouchard, C. (1991). *Growth, Maturation, and Physical Activity*. (Human Kinetics, Champaign, IL).

Marubini, E. and Milani, S. (1986). Approaches to the analysis of longitudinal data. In *Human Growth: a Comprehensive Treatise*, 2nd edn, vol. 3. eds. F. Falkner and J.M. Tanner (Plenum Press, New York), pp. 33–79.

Marubini, E., Resele, L.F., Tanner, J.M. and Whitehouse, R.H. (1972). The fit of the Gompertz and logistic curves to longitudinal data during adolescence on height, sitting height, and biacromial diameter in boys and girls of the Harpenden Growth Study. *Human Biology*, **44**, 511–24.

Ostyn, M., Simons, J., Beunen, G., et al. (1980). *Somatic and Motor Development of Belgian Secondary School Boys. Norms and Standards*. (Leuven University Press, Leuven).

Pate, R. and Shephard, R. (1989). Characteristics of physical fitness in youth. In *Perspectives in Exercise Science and Sports Medicine. Youth, Exercise and Sport*, vol. 2. eds. C.V. Gisolfi and D.R. Lamb (Benchmark Press, Indianapolis), pp. 1–45.

Preece, M.A. and Baines, M.J. (1978). A new family of mathematical models describing the human growth curve. *Annals of Human Biology*, **5**, 1–24.

Reynolds, E.L. and Wines, J.V. (1948). Individual differences in physical changes associated with adolescence in girls. *American Journal of Diseases of Children*, **75**, 329–50.

Reynolds, E.L. and Wines, J.V. (1951). Physical changes associated with adolescence in boys. *American Journal of Diseases of Children*, **82**, 529–47.

Roche, A.F., Wainer, H. and Thissen, D. (1975a). Predicting adult stature for individuals. *Monographs in Pediatrics*, **3**, 1–114.

Roche, A.F., Wainer, H. and Thissen, D. (1975b). *Skeletal Maturity: Knee Joint as a Biological Indicator*. (Plenum Press, New York).

Roche, A.F., Chumlea, W.C. and Thissen, D. (1988). *Assessing the Skeletal Maturity of the Hand-Wrist: Fels Method*. (Thomas, Springfield).

Ross, J.G. and Pate, R.R. (1987). The national children and youth fitness study II: A summary of findings. *Journal of Physical Education, Recreation and Dance*, **56**, 45–50.

Safrit, M.J. (1973). *Evaluation in Physical Education. Assessing Motor Behavior*. (Prentice Hall, Englewood Cliffs, NJ).

Sargent, D.A. (1921). The physical test of a man. *American Physical Education Review*, **26**, 188–94.

Simons, J., Beunen, G., Ostyn, M., *et al.* (1969). Construction d'une batterie de tests d'aptitude motrice pour garçons de 12 à 19 ans par le méthode de l'analyse factorielle. *Kinanthropologie*, **1**, 323–62.

Simons, J., Beunen G.P., Renson, R., *et al.* eds. (1990). *Growth and Fitness of Flemish Girls. The Leuven Growth Study*. HKP Sport Science Monograph Series 3. (Human Kinetics, Champaign, IL)

Tanner, J.M. (1962). *Growth at Adolescence*. (Blackwell Scientific Publications, Oxford).

Tanner, J.M. (1981). *A History of the Study of Human Growth*. (Cambridge University Press, Cambridge).

Tanner, J.M. (1989). *Fetus into Man. Physical Growth from Conception to Maturity*. (Harvard University Press, Cambridge, MA).

Tanner, J.M., Whitehouse, R.H. and Takaiski, M. (1966). Standards from birth to maturity for height, weight, height velocity and weight velocity. *Archives of Diseases of Childhood*, **41**, 454–71, 613–35.

Tanner, J.M., Whitehouse, R.H., Cameron, N., *et al.* (1983). *Assessment of Skeletal Maturity and Prediction of Adult Height (TW2 method)*. (Academic Press, London).

Todd, J.W. (1937). *Atlas of Skeletal Maturation: Part 1. Hand*. (Mosby, London).

Van't Hof, M.A., Roede, M.J. and Kowalski, C.J. (1976). Estimation of growth velocities from individual longitudinal data. *Growth*, **40**, 217–40.

Wainer, H., Roche, A.F. and Bell, S. (1978). Predicting adult stature without skeletal age and without parental data. *Pediatrics*, **61**, 569–72.

Weiner, J.S. and Lourie, J.A. (1969). *Human Biology*. (F.A. Davis, Philadelphia).

PART TWO

GONIOMETRIC ASPECTS OF MOVEMENT

Peter H. Dangerfield

4.1 AIMS

The aims of this chapter are to:
- review the nature and definition of posture,
- examine various techniques of assessing the upright position and normal status,
- consider abnormalities in posture and their effects on performance with particular reference to the consequences for sporting activities.

4.2 INTRODUCTION

Maintenance of the upright posture by humans is unique among mammals and primates. During human evolution, as the hindlimbs progressively assumed the role of locomotion, the vertebral column adapted from a horizontal compressed structure to a vertical weight-bearing rod. Its relationship with the pelvic girdle distally and the skull proximally also changed. The centre of gravity of primates has also evolved, being shifted backwards towards the hindlimbs as the length and musculature of the hindlimbs increased. At the same time, to reduce energy expenditure in countering needless body rotation about the centre of gravity, forces for forward propulsion passed through the centre of gravity. Early changes in body form also allowed primates to adopt sitting positions with the forelimb being freed for manipulative functions. The flexibility of the vertebral column has also increased along with the size of the vertebrae which, in the lumbar region, has developed to cope with increased compression forces resulting from an upright posture. Additionally, changes in the role of the sternum and abdominal muscles in maintaining less truncal stiffness has resulted in the wide shallow chest of humans with a reduced angulation of the ribs.

Adopting an upright posture and acquiring freedom to use the upper limb, independently of the legs, has increased the dynamic demands on the vertebral column. It developed the capability to produce and accumulate moments of force while transmitting and concentrating forces from other parts of the body. These forces include dynamic compressive forces, in which the intervertebral disc acts as a flexible link, lowering the resonant frequency of the spine. This then allows the spinal musculature and ligaments to dissipate energy. As a consequence, changing to an upright posture has resulted not only in specific human functional abilities, but also unique functional disabilities which can have implications in sporting and physical activities. Such conditions might include spinal curvatures of an acquired type, or the problems sometimes developed by sports participants and professional musicians due to degenerative disease of the lumbar spine and other joints or as a consequence of repetitive injury or sprains. These may be accompanied by body asymmetry, which itself might adversely affect the normal posture and inertial properties of the body. This subject has recently been reviewed in detail elsewhere (Dangerfield, 1994).

Posture can be studied from a number of different aspects. These include evolution of bipedalism and the upright position, changes

Kinanthropometry and Exercise Physiology Laboratory Manual: Tests, Procedures and Data. 2nd Edition, Volume 1: Anthropometry
Edited by RG Eston and T Reilly. Published by Routledge, London, June 2001

during development in infancy and childhood, mechanisms of physiological control and its role in health and its importance in sport, exercise and ergonomics. It is therefore important to understand the concept of posture and to examine some of the methods that have been developed to assess it, allowing investigation of the factors that influence it in different states, such as rest and movement.

While a clear definition of posture in the context of the upright stance of the human is difficult, it is generally accepted that it is possible to define both static and dynamic posture. Static posture is a consequence of a state of muscular and skeletal balance within the body and this creates stability by an orientation of the constituent parts of the body in space at any moment in time. The least energy will be used by the body to achieve this stable state and any departure from it will lead to imbalance and the development of bad posture, a situation encountered in a range of medical circumstances. Bad posture may also be a problem for sports coaches and their trainees.

It is very rare for a normal individual to remain in a static position since the daily routines of life are essentially dynamic and involve movement. Dynamic posture is the state the segments of the body adopt when undertaking movement. Posture is always the relative orientation of the constituent parts of the body in space at any moment in time. Thus, maintaining an upright position requires constant dynamic adjustment by muscles in the trunk and limbs, under the automatic and conscious control of the central nervous system to counter the effects of gravity. Posture should therefore be regarded as a position assumed by the body before it makes its next move (Roaf, 1977).

Assessment of posture requires consideration of the human body in an upright stance, in readiness for the next movement. This is ideally measured using standard anthropometric equipment and methodologies. For example, if the working day includes sitting, sitting height should be measured. Good posture has been developed in cultures where sitting cross-legged leads to strong back muscles (Roaf, 1977).

4.3 CURVATURES AND MOVEMENT OF THE VERTEBRAL COLUMN

The normal vertebral column possesses well-marked curvatures in the sagittal plane in the cervical, thoracic, lumbar and pelvic regions. Three million years of evolution have caused rounding of the thorax and pelvis as an adaptation to bipedal gait. In infancy, functional muscle development and growth exert a major influence on the way the curvatures in the column take shape and also on changes in the proportional size of individual vertebrae, in particular in the lumbar region. The lumbar curvature becomes important for maintaining the centre of gravity of the trunk over the legs when walking commences. In addition, changes in body proportions exert a major influence on the subsequent shape of the curvatures in the column.

The cervical curvature is lordotic (Greek: I bend); that is, the curvature is convex in the anterior direction. It is the least marked vertebral curvature and extends from the atlas to the second thoracic vertebra. The thoracic curve is kyphotic (Greek: bent forwards); in other words the curvature is concave in the anterior direction (Figure 4.1). It extends from the second to the twelfth thoracic vertebrae. This curvature is caused by the increased posterior depth of the thoracic vertebral bodies. It appears to be at its minimum during the pubertal growth spurt (Willner and Johnson, 1983). The lumbar curve is naturally lordotic and has a greater magnitude in the female. It extends from the twelfth thoracic vertebra to the lumbosacral angle, with an increased convexity of the last three segments due to greater anterior depth of intervertebral discs and some anterior wedging of the vertebral bodies. The curvature develops in response to gravitational forces, which arise as the child assumes the upright position during sitting and standing, and to the forces exerted between the psoas major and

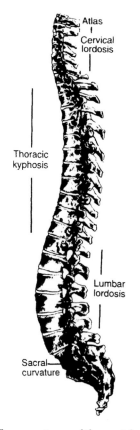

Figure 4.1 The curvatures of the vertebral column.

thoracic region, as elsewhere any lateral flexion is always accompanied by some rotation (Davis, 1959).

When physical tasks are undertaken, the body should normally be in a relaxed position which evokes the least postural stress. If forces are imposed on the body that create stress, the risk of damage to biological structures increases. This is referred to as postural strain (Weiner, 1982). Postural strain causes prolonged static loading in affected muscles.

The loading of the spine is localized in the erector spinae muscles and prolonged loading eventually leads to pain; for example, pain is a common result of sitting uncomfortably in a badly designed chair. The eventual result of excessive strain will be an injury. In the context of the spine, the more inappropriate the strain on the vertebral column, the greater is the likelihood of back injury. The lumbar region of the spine is the most susceptible to athletic and other injuries and can affect up to 80% of the population (Alexander, 1985). The reasons for the high risk of injury are due to the fundamental weakness of the structure itself, loading forces encountered in everyday living such as body weight, muscle contractions and external loading, and recreational and sporting activities. These all contribute to the development of postural strain and injury.

Injury itself is caused by activities that increase weight loading, rotational stresses or back arching. The result is damage to the intervertebral disc, ligaments or muscles, and secondary consequences which affect the sciatic and other nerves. Severe trauma might result in a fracture to the vertebral column. Symptoms of damage will include pain, stiffness and numbness or paraesthesia. It is also important to identify whether the pain was sudden in onset, such as after lifting an object or more gradual without any obvious antecedent. Such back pain is often difficult to quantify or even prove to be a physical problem and not psychosomatic. Objective quantification is difficult (D'Orazio, 1993). Therefore, as the medical problems of diagnosis, treatment and

abdominal muscles and the erector spinae muscle. The lordosis increases steadily during growth (Willner and Johnson, 1983). Within the pelvis, the curve is concave anteroinferior and involves the sacrum and coccygeal vertebrae, extending from the lumbosacral joint to the apex of the coccyx.

The cervical and lumbar regions of the vertebral column are the most mobile regions, although, with the exception of the atlantooccipital and atlantoaxial joints, little movement is possible between each adjacent vertebra. It is a summation of movement throughout the vertebral column which permits the human to enjoy a wide range of mobility. Anatomically, the movements are flexion and extension, lateral flexion to the left or right and rotation. Anatomical circumduction occurs only in the mid-

rehabilitation, as well as the extensive range of biomechanical and other investigations possible in this field, are beyond the scope of this chapter, the reader should consult the appropriate orthopaedic and other literature.

4.4 DEFINING AND QUANTIFICATION OF POSTURE

4.4.1 INERTIAL CHARACTERISTICS

When maintaining an erect and well-balanced position, with little muscle activity, the line of gravity of the body extends in a line from the level of the external auditory meatus, anterior

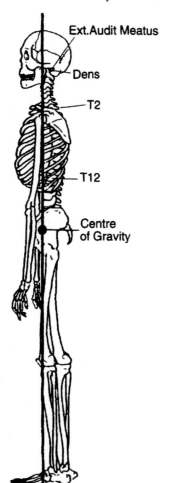

Figure 4.2 The line of centre of gravity of the body.

to the dens of the axis, anterior to the body of the second thoracic vertebra and the body of the twelfth thoracic vertebra and the fifth lumbar vertebra to lie anterior to the sacrum (Klausen, 1965) (Figure 4.2). As a result, the vertebral bodies and intervertebral discs act as a weight-bearing pillar from the base of the skull to the sacrum. Furthermore, there is a cephalocaudal increase in the cross-sectional surface area of the discs and vertebral bodies (Pal and Routal, 1986). There is also a sexual dimorphism, with females having a lower width to depth ratio than males, due to the heavier body build of the male (Taylor and Twomey, 1984).

4.4.2 ANTHROPOMETRY AND POSTURE

Extensive literature is available which details anthropometric techniques, applied to the field of biology, medicine and ergonomics (Weiner and Lourie, 1969; Hrdlicka, 1972; Cameron, 1986; Pheasant, 1986; Lohman *et al.*, 1988; Burwell and Dangerfield, 1992). All anthropometric techniques are similar, although the definition of the measured dimensions may vary. Direct surface measurements employ devices for measuring length, height and mass such as the stadiometer for height and sitting height and the anthropometer for limb segment and pelvic or shoulder width. In the context of posture, anthropometry has been extensively employed in medicine in the study of scoliosis (spinal curvature) (see Burwell and Dangerfield, 1992; Cole *et al.*, 2000). Indirect methods include ultrasound, X-rays (conventional radiographs and computerized tomography (CT)) and magnetic resonance imaging (MRI) (Figure 4.3). By taking several readings at different places in different planes, three-dimensional descriptions of body shape may be obtained.

Biostereometrics refers to the spatial and spatio-temporal analysis of form and function based on analytical geometry. It deals with three-dimensional measurements of biological subjects that vary with time, due to factors

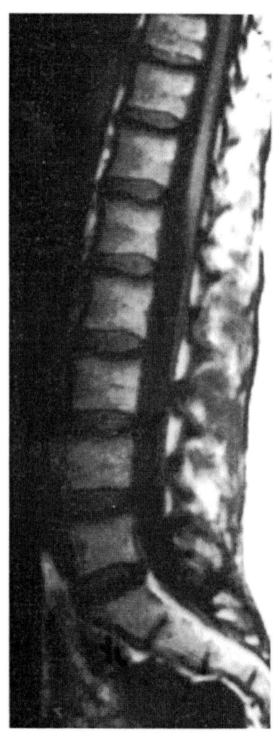

Figure 4.3 MRI image of the lumbar spine.

such as growth and movement. Adapted to sport and movement science, biostereometrics enables dynamic movement and technical performance in any particular sport to be studied. Only recently have researchers come to accept this concept of dynamic movement. This is due in part to the complexity of movement and the additional difficulty in analysing data from such studies as this analysis requires expensive and powerful computers. In consequence, assessment of body shape, particularly in biomechanics and medicine, has been governed by the illusion that the body should be examined in the anatomical position, standing still and maintaining this position like a shop dummy. This is clearly unrealistic.

It is difficult, without a clear definition of the term *Posture*, to offer precise and clear methods for measuring and thus quantifying it. As a result, methods used to quantify body shape can by inference be applied to the understanding of posture.

4.5 ASSESSMENT OF POSTURE AND BODY SHAPE

Methods employed in assessment of body shape can be considered in two groups:

1. Measurements in a static phase of posture.
2. Measurements in dynamic and changing posture.

4.5.1 MEASUREMENTS IN A STATIC PHASE OF POSTURE

These measurements involve quantification of the normal physiological curves of the vertebral column, usually in the erect position. By the adoption of a standardized position (usually an erect position), the measurement can then tested for reproducibility (Ulijaszek and Lourie, 1994).

4.5.2 SUBJECTIVE MEASUREMENT OF STATIC POSTURE

Static posture is usually assessed subjectively using a rating chart (Bloomfield *et al.*, 1994).

The subject stands in the upright position and is observed against the chart.

4.5.3 OBJECTIVE MEASUREMENT OF SPINAL LENGTH, CURVATURE AND SPINAL SHRINKAGE

Clinical and biological measurement of spinal length, curvature and shrinkage is needed to understand fully the effect of posture on the human body. This applies in both sport and medical contexts.

Various techniques are available to assess posture. These range from invasive criterion techniques such as conventional radiography and computerized tomography, which involve potential exposure to ionizing radiation, and magnetic resonance imaging. Other techniques involve light-based systems which negate the risks of ionizing radiation exposure. Simpler and less expensive manual techniques of assessing posture are also widely used. These techniques are summarized below.

4.5.4 NON-INVASIVE MANUAL TECHNIQUES OF ASSESSING POSTURE

Accurate measurement of height and length can be achieved using anthropometric equipment such as the Harpenden Stadiometer and Anthropometer (Holtain Ltd., Crymych, Dyfed, Wales). Such equipment is portable and may be carried to field conditions allowing lengths such as biacromial diameter, tibial length, or other parameters to be measured (Figure 4.4). These instruments incorporate a counter recorder for ease of reading, which reduces the likelihood of recording error.

Profile measurements which can be used to assess body angles, such as that between the spine and the vertical, may be recorded photographically. Such records are permanent and offer the opportunity to record changes in posture and position over time, such as before and after athletic events. While traditional drawbacks were related to the expense of film and time, this is no longer the case if digital cameras are employed. High-quality digital

Figure 4.4 Holtain anthropometer used to measure tibial length. A counter recorder is employed which gives an instant and accurate read-out of length.

images can be downloaded to a computer and examined and analysed as required.

The most commonly assessed passive movement is spinal flexion. This is frequently done by visual inspection in the medical clinical situation, and thus is often undertaken inaccurately. Alternatively, it is feasible to measure spinal flexion using a simple tape to measure the increase in spinal length, in different positions of flexion or extension, between skin markings made over the spinous processes.

In order to achieve accuracy in measurements in spinal flexion, goniometers and inclinometers are used. These simple instruments can measure a wide range of other spinal and pelvic angles and positions to a high degree of accuracy and reproducibility.

(a) The Debrunner Kyphometer

The kyphometer is a device that was developed to measure the angles of kyphosis and lordosis within the vertebral column (Figures 4.5 and 4.6) (Straumann Ltd., Welwyn Garden City, England). A dial indicates the angle between the instrument's feet when placed on the spine. The angle of thoracic kyphosis is estimated by placing the feet over the T1 vertebra and T12. This measurement is both

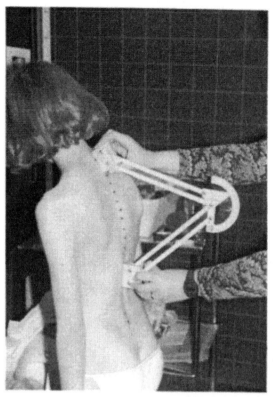

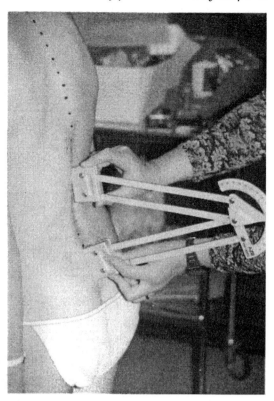

Figure 4.5 Using the kyphometer to measure thoracic kyphosis on a subject. The angle is read off the dial on the instrument.

Figure 4.6 Measuring lumbar lordosis using the kyphometer.

accurate and reproducible. The angle decreases with inspiration and increases again with expiration and so care should be taken to standardize the measurement technique with the appropriate stage of the respiratory cycle (Salisbury and Porter, 1987). Lumbar lordosis is measured between T12 and L1 vertebrae and is also affected by the respiration cycle. It is likewise affected by sexual dimorphism between the male and female subject, being larger in post-pubertal females. However, experience has found that lumbar kyphosis is less easy to measure accurately than thoracic kyphosis. (Dangerfield *et al.*, 1987). Both these measurements have been experimentally correlated with the same measurements undertaken on erect spinal radiographs (Dangerfield *et al.*, 1987; Hellsing *et al.*, 1987; Ohlen *et al.*, 1989).

(b) Goniometers

The goniometer is widely used both in clinical situations, for example by orthopaedic surgeons and physiotherapists, and in research programmes. The instrument is a simple tool that can measure limb and trunk joint angles and also flexions within the spine. It offers a rapid and low-cost method of quantifying posture and spinal mobility by the measurement of angles in the spine, such as the proclive and declive angles (Figures 4.7, 4.8 and 4.9). These angles can be expanded to measurements at each level of the vertebral column and can thus give accurate indications of the shape of the entire vertebral column. Ranges of spinal mobility may be useful in studying athletic performance but again due allowance should be made for age and sex (Tsai and Wredmark, 1993).

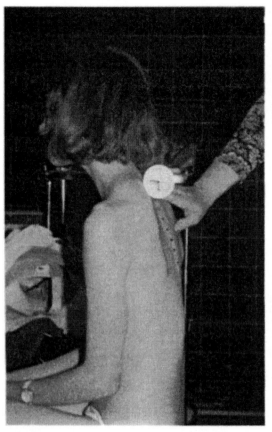
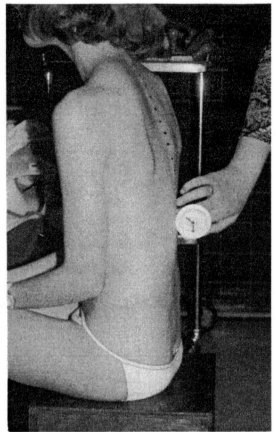

Figure 4.7 A goniometer used to measure the proclive angle, the angle between the spine and vertical at the level of the 7th cervical vertebra.

Figure 4.8 Measuring the angle at the thoracolumbar junction.

The same instrument may be used to assess the lateral flexibility of the spine by placing the dial over T1 vertebra and then asking the subject to flex to the right and to the left. This measurement is useful in assessing spinal movement in patients with deformity or arthritic diseases. Techniques for skin marking may also facilitate simple but accurate measurement of spinal flexion, and offer a useful measure of physical movement (MacRae and Wright, 1969; Rae *et al.*, 1984).

(c) The scoliometer

Other goniometers have been specially devised for studying the spine in scoliosis clinics. The OSI Scoliometer is used, for example, to quantify the hump deformity of scoliosis in the coronal plane (Orthopedic Systems Inc., Union City, CA, USA). A ball bearing in a glass tube aligns itself to the lowest point of the tube when placed across the hump-deformity, permitting a reading of the angle of trunk inclination (ATI) from a scale on the instrument (Figure 4.10). This angle is a measure of the magnitude of the ribcage or lumbar deformity, associated with the lateral curvature of the spine.

(d) Other methods

Another method for quantifying body shape is to reproduce the outline of the structure under consideration using a rod-matrix device or a flexicurve. Contour outlines of the trunk, in

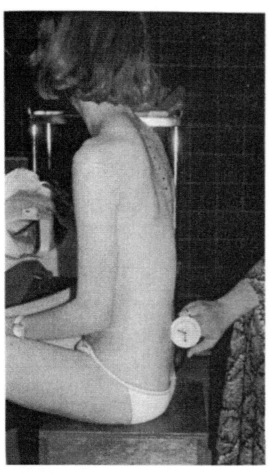

Figure 4.9 Measuring the declive angle at the lumbar-sacral junction.

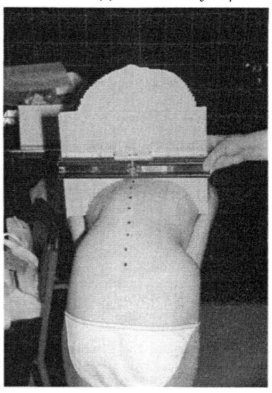

Figure 4.11 Formulator Body Contour Tracer used to record cross-sectional shape of the thorax in a patient with scoliosis (a lateral curvature of the spine causing a rib-hump deformity and asymmetry of the thorax).

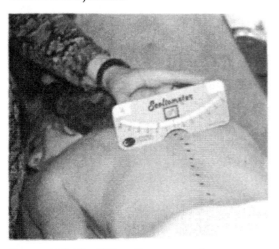

Figure 4.10 The OSI scoliometer used to measure the Angle of Trunk Inclination (ATI) in the spine of a scoliosis subject lying prone.

both the horizontal and vertical planes, can be measured using a rod-matrix device such as the Formulator Body Contour Tracer (Danger-field and Denton, 1986) (Figure 4.11) or a flexicurve (Tillotson and Burton, 1991). Both these methods give a permanent record of shape by tracing the outline obtained onto paper but suffer from the tedium of use if more than one tracing is required. They are used in recording ribcage shape and thoracic and lumbar lordosis, and in athletes may be applied to assessment of lumbar movements following exercise.

These techniques are simple to employ but can be time-consuming and laborious in practical use. Accuracy depends on experience of the observer and careful use of the instrument. Furthermore, reproducibility of data collection is essential. Unfortunately, in assessing movement and posture related to the spine, the technique used is often flawed, due to practical difficulties in separating one particular movement from another within a complex anatomical structure.

4.6 OTHER CLINICAL METHODS OF POSTURE ASSESSMENT

4.6.1 PHOTOGRAPHIC METHODS

Moiré photography employs optical interference patterns to record the three-dimensional shape of a surface. It has been used to evaluate pelvic and trunk rotation and also trunk deformity (Willner, 1979; Suzuki *et al.*, 1981; Asazuma *et al.*, 1986).

Stereophotogrammetry, originally developed for cartography, has been adopted in the evaluation of structural deformity of the trunk and for posture measurement. Two cameras are used to take overlapping pairs of photographs. These can be analysed to produce a three-dimensional contour map of the subject and can be described as points in terms of x, y and z coordinates (Sarasate and Ostman, 1986). This technique has found limited application in the study of scoliosis, a condition in which the vertebral column develops a lateral curvature and vertebral rotation, frequently leading to severe physical deformity (Figure 4.12). Scoliotic curvatures may be due to primary pathological conditions but can also result from leg length inequality or muscle imbalance encountered in sports such as tennis, or discus and javelin throwing (Burwell and Dangerfield, 1992).

An extension of this technique is stereoradiography where two X-ray images are used instead of photographs. This technique is invasive and potentially hazardous due to the use

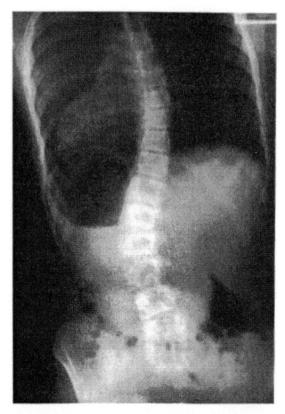

Figure 4.12 A patient with scoliosis: a condition in which the vertebral column develops a lateral curvature and vertebral rotation, frequently leading to severe physical deformity.

of ionizing radiation. Consequently, it has found only limited application.

Non-invasive methods of postural assessment employ either scanning light beams or the projection of structured light patterns or infra-red projection techniques. The various techniques are accurate and offer the potential of fast acquisition and analysis of data when used in combination with a computer equipped with a frame grabber. Such techniques have been applied to the study of trunk shape, for example in scoliosis, and to the movement of joints such as the knee and shoulder.

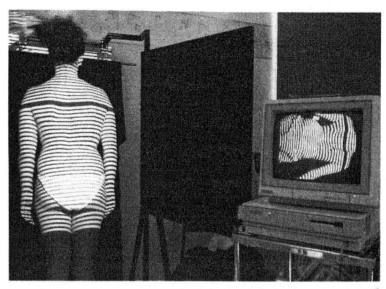

Figure 4.13 Grating projection system (SIPS: Spinal Image Processing System) used for clinical evaluation of trunk shape and scoliosis.

4.6.2 GRATING PROJECTION METHODS

Grating projection techniques are also well suited to research into posture, applied anatomy and body movement. These methods are subject to undergoing continual development (Hierholzer *et al.*, 1983; Hierholzer and Drerup, 1999; Dangerfield *et al.*, 1992). At present, it is possible to produce three-dimensional reconstructions of the trunk (Figure 4.13). The technique also allows automatic calculation of parameters of posture similar to those gathered using goniometers or flexicurves.

'Phase-measuring profilometry' also uses grating projection. This method employs algorithms for the phase function which are defined by the geometry of the system and the shape of the object (Halioua and Liu, 1989; Halioua *et al.*, 1990; Merolli *et al.*, 1999). The object's shape is converted into a phase distribution as in interferometry and is analysed by digital phase measuring techniques: accuracy to less than 1 mm is possible without the need for reference plane images. This technique has been used to measure the three-dimensional shape of the trunk, face and breasts and has obvious applications in plastic surgery. It is presently expensive for routine practical use as it employs precision optical components and high-speed computer image processing.

Laser imaging has the advantage of very accurate mapping of the entire torso, important if there is any indication of anatomical deviations from normal which may occur due to disease or injury. Generally, the techniques use four lasers and a bank of cameras to capture the images for computer processing and analysis. Examples include the Loughborough anthropometric shadow scanner and systems developed in Canada (Jones *et al.*, 1989; Poncet *et al.*, 1999). These scanners are used in the fields of ergonomics, clothing manufacture and medical assessment of back deformities including scoliosis.

The future of static measurements lies with further developments of these light-based systems. They offer the opportunity to develop accurate and fast recording of the three-dimensional shape of the trunk and legs.

4.6.3 RADIOGRAPHIC AND MAGNETIC RESONANCE IMAGES

In order to understand the interaction of the components of skeletal anatomy, invasive criterion techniques must be employed. These include conventional radiography, computer-aided tomography scans (CT) and magnetic resonance imaging (MRI). These methods are normally employed for the medical investigation of posture, especially if it is associated with injuries or deformities.

The radiographic approach has its attractions: it is widely employed in medical diagnostic investigations as it is relatively easy to interpret. With the introduction of a range of digitally based systems in the last decade, the dosage of radiation can be reduced by a factor of up to 10 times and the images presented on a computer rather than film. The quality of the images is also greatly improved over traditional radiographs. For the purposes of research, risks from ionizing radiation remain, raising ethical issues for anyone employing such methods as part of their protocols.

The employment of the latest generation of spiral CT scanners now permits the relatively easy creation of three-dimensional reconstruction of the skeletal, vascular and other soft tissue structures of the body and limbs. This has found important applications in the study of sports-related injury and a number of degenerative conditions. However, the presence of ionizing radiation excludes the use of CT in research rather than purely clinical medical investigations.

Magnetic resonance imaging (MRI) offers a far wider range of possibilities as it can be used to obtain highly detailed images of soft tissue such as muscles, nerves and blood vessels (Figure 4.3). It is less useful for bony tissue. The MRI method exploits the property of certain atoms, particularly hydrogen, to perform a precessing movement in a magnetic field when they are disturbed from a stationary state by application of a powerful magnetic field.

While it remains an expensive tool for use in research, scanners are now becoming more widely available in hospitals and specialist research centres. Scans are used in the investigation of sports-related injury and studies on body composition (see Chapter 1 by Hawes and Martin) as well as a wide range of medical conditions. Even the considerable cost of magnetic coils which require low temperature for their operation is likely to fall as newer conductive alloys are developed. Changes in the shape and working of the scanners themselves hold promise for their wider availability within the research community and thus their use as research tools will increase. The use of MRI to image vascular structures represents a development which will lead to newer designs less constrained by the shape and size of a scanner tube, and which will undoubtedly allow the procuring of static and dynamic images. Using contemporary advanced image processing methods, three-dimensional reconstruction of tissues in high detail is already commonplace. The water and other ionic contents of such tissue can be quantified using the decay times of molecular movement activated by the magnetic field (T1 and T2 images). It is expected that automation of these processes will benefit all fields of application, including acquiring geometric joint data from the spine in functional motion studies.

4.7 MEASUREMENTS IN A DYNAMIC PHASE OF POSTURE (MOVEMENT ANALYSIS)

When describing dynamic movement, it is necessary to consider qualitative and quantitative methods of biomechanical analysis. The former requires a careful, subjective description of movement while the latter requires detailed measurement and evaluation of the collected data. The guidelines of the British Association of Sport and Exercise Sciences provide the necessary detail for the conduct of biomechanical analysis of performance in sport (Bartlett, 1992).

Since the human rarely assumes static posture for more than a few seconds, analysis of dynamic posture will involve study of the range of motion of the joints of the spine. The relative position of the spine constantly varies throughout any movement such as during gait or in a sporting activity. Video recording of sports and other movements allows measurement of these changes in posture. Qualitative analysis of a movement or athletic technique within a sport is undertaken at a slow film speed with no disturbance to the subject. This film may subsequently be quantified by measuring movements such as spinal displacement or stride length. More complex kinematic quantitative analysis involves extensive digitization of data using a computer. Body landmarks are identified and marked on the subject, and co-ordinate digitization allows the undertaking of angular and linear measurement. Introduction of a time dimension permits longitudinal movement to be studied. Performance parameters, important in sporting applications, allow the identification of events within a movement to be compared between individuals. While the results are presented as outline and stick 'persons', infilling is possible. Currently, many solid-body modelling techniques are derived from computer software developed within the cinema and the computer games industry.

These techniques of quantification of movement in the lumbar spine are important when examining patients with low-back pain, a symptom frequently associated with sporting pastimes. Ranges of spinal mobility may be useful in studying athletic performance but allowance for age and sex should be made in interpreting observations.

Simple techniques can be employed which are frequently of low cost. Goniometers may be used to assess spinal range of motion (refer to the laboratory practical at the end of this chapter and also Chapter 5 by Borms and Van Roy). These measurements are useful in assessing spinal movement in patients with deformity or arthritic diseases. Techniques for marking the skin may also facilitate simple but accurate measurement of spinal flexion, and offer a useful measure of physical movement

(MacRae and Wright, 1969; Rae *et al.*, 1984). Although this technique requires only the use of a tape measure, it still has a value in assessing the contribution of lumbar flexion to body posture.

4.7.1 MOVEMENT ANALYSIS

Movement analysis is a complex specialist area but is increasingly available to researchers within a number of specialist laboratories. While the equipment required, such as force plates and multiple cameras, is expensive, the potential for collecting information relating to posture and axial skeletal movement is great. The current generation of computers are powerful and fast enough to address the issues of multiple channels of data input, while analysis in real time is possible.

The most common form of dynamic research involves gait and movement analysis. This applies to a wide range of sports and medical problems, which can be related to posture. The tracking and analysis of human movement commenced with the early application of still photography. With the advent of inexpensive video cameras, cinematography has been used in the analysis of performance of occupational and sports skills, with various models representing the human body as a mechanism consisting of segments or links and joints (Kippers and Parker, 1989; Vogelbach, 1990).

The application of this approach to the vertebral column overlooks its multi-unit nature, where the column and pelvis exhibit many varied movement patterns. The vertebral column has 25 mobile segments, corresponding to each intervertebral joint from the base of the skull to the lumbosacral junction and each has its own unique movement potential. This is the concept of spinal coupling, first described by Lovett in 1905 (Panjabi *et al.*, 1989). Posture affects the range of these coupled motions. In contrast, the pelvis moves about an axis through the hip joints. By separating these units, any overall appreciation of the complex movements of trunk flexion and muscle involvement in such flexion is impossible. This is important when considering movements in the context of posture and its application either in biological, clinical or athletic terms.

Three-dimensional measurement of movement is therefore important in advancing the understanding of athletic performance. The subject is complex, and only relatively recently has measurement become possible at an affordable cost. In all applications, the reproducibility and accuracy of the method must be established. Some methods have a poor record of reproducibility and offer little advantage over the use of low-cost goniometers (Dillard *et al.*, 1991).

Early methods for the three-dimensional analysis of motion included a system called CODA which was accurate, fast and non-invasive (Mitchelson, 1988). It consisted of three rapidly rotating scanning mirrors used to view fan-shaped beams of light which sweep rapidly across the region of the subject under study. The signals detected by the scanners permit triangulation and spatial measurement of markers placed on the subject and so are used to record movement of the subject in three dimensions. This system found application in clinical studies of Parkinsonian tremor, scoliosis and gait analysis programmes associated with fitting a prosthesis. Selspot optoelectronics and other video analysis systems have also been used for movement analysis (Thurston and Harris, 1983; Tani and Masuda, 1985; Thorstensson *et al.*, 1985) in addition to electrogoniometers which have also been employed to monitor dynamic movements of the lumbar spine (Paquet *et al.*, 1991) with a high degree of reliability and accuracy.

Existing biomechanical laboratory methods employ video sampling to record movement at a set frame rate; the number of such frames recorded per second is known as the sampling rate or frequency. The data collected require digitization of the film to generate results, and are often time-consuming and subject to inaccuracy. Opto-electronic systems which automatically track markers in real time allow 'real-time computer analysis' of the data. These systems are often combined with use of a forceplate which records dynamic changes in lower limb forces during walking or other movements. This is valuable data since it reveals much about the dynamics of the spine and upper body. Nevertheless, while the field of gait and movement analysis is large and growing, there are implications for the study of posture. Rapid progress in computer technology, with ever more powerful processors, cheaper memory and storage, is permitting the development of a number of different systems adapted to measure movement using multiple arrays of cameras or lasers. Consequently, the reader is encouraged to investigate developments in the field in specialist journals. (For a detailed review of the treatment of three-dimensional analysis methods, see Allard *et al.*, 1994).

Dynamic work is performed when any muscle changes its length (Pitman and Peterson, 1989). If the movement involves a constant angular velocity, it is called isokinetic, whereas, if the muscle acts on a constant inertial mass, it is termed isoinertial exertion. Isotonic exertion involves maintaining constant muscle tension throughout the range of motion (Rogers and Cavanagh, 1984). These terminologies are imprecise and refer to movements which are artificial. Attempts have been made to quantify such movements using dynamometers which act to control the range of motion and/or the resistance of muscles. Such devices have been applied to measuring trunk movement and thus can be used in assessment of posture. There are many different types of dynamometer available for investigations. These include cable tensiometers and strain-gauge dynamometers for the measurement of isometric forces and isokinetic devices for dynamic movements (Mayhew and Rothstein, 1985).

The Isostation B200 lumbar dynamometer (Isotechnologies Inc., Hillsborough, NC, USA) has been applied to the measurement of trunk motion, strength and velocity. Investigations have included the study of low-back pain and also normal lumbar spinal function (Gomez *et al.*, 1991; Dillard *et al.*, 1991). The application of dynamometers to study the wide range of muscle actions in the human body is a growing research field which has recently been extensively reviewed (Parnian-pour and Tan, 1993).

Three-dimensional analysis of movement using opto-electronic techniques permits sophisticated analysis of the dynamics of athletic performance, including the effects of an individual's posture on his or her athletic performance. An ideal method, which will become possible with further advances in electronics and computers, would be to link physiological investigations or metabolic functions, electromyographic recordings of muscle activity and analysis of movements in three dimensions so as to optimize performance to prevailing conditions and produce the best athletic performance from an individual.

Electromyography (EMG) employs surface electrodes applied to suitably prepared skin over appropriate muscle groups on the body's surface. Electrical activity generated by the underlying muscles can then be recorded using appropriate amplifiers and filters to process the signals. Muscle activity can be quantified using EMG, allowing investigation of the relationship between posture or body position and exercise response. The EMG technique is described in more detail by Gleeson (Chapter 2 Volume 2, Exercise Physiology). Within EMG, a sub-speciality has developed, called kinesiological EMG, with the aim of analysing the function and co-ordination of muscles in different movements and postures. These measurements are frequently combined with biomechanical analysis. However, the complexity of human movement in normal daily routines, sport or disability renders it impossible to sample all the muscles within the body during the performance of motor skills (Clarys, 1987). As many sports involve dynamic postural change, massive resources would be needed to record sport-specific movements using EMG and other methods.

The application of EMG to the study of sports has been reviewed by Clarys and Cabri (1993), who set down standards for the methodology and the limitations of the method due to its partly descriptive nature. There are also many applications to rehabilitation and other fields.

Electromyographic techniques have been applied to study the effect of posture and lifting on trunk musculature and, by inference, spinal loading (Hinz and Seidel, 1989; Mouton *et al.*, 1991).

There are large individual variations in spinal and trunk muscle activity in relation to load. Furthermore, inertial moments differ between standing and sitting positions. The relationship between EMG activity of abdominal muscles and intra-abdominal pressures has been studied in the context of lumbar spine support (Bartelink, 1957), lifting, and diaphragm and thoracic kinetics pertaining to sporting activities (Grassino *et al.*, 1978; Grillner *et al.*, 1978).

Accelerometers may be used to measure the transmission of vibrations through the body, particularly over joints such as the knee and the lumbar spine in patients with low-back pain (Wosak and Voloshin, 1981). Such devices have been used in volunteers where K-wires have been inserted through the skin into the spine or pelvis or, less invasively, piezoelectric surface electrodes have been mounted on the skin. These techniques have been used in conjunction with gait analysis research. The methods can be employed to examine spinal movements relating to posture in walking and running, provided that allowance is made for skin movement.

The study of human movement is developing rapidly as costs of high-powered and fast computer hardware fall. It has the potential to increase understanding of the problems of human posture and movement in sports and other occupations.

4.8 SPINAL LENGTH AND DIURNAL VARIATION

In anthropometry and ergonomics, stature is a fundamental variable. The vertebral column comprises about 40% of the total body length as measured in stature and has within it about 30% of its length occupied by the intervertebral discs. Spinal length and height vary through-out a 24-hour period. There is shrinking during daytime when the individual is normally active and walking about but lengthening at night when the individual is sleeping in bed. This change is due to compressive forces acting on the intervertebral discs, eliminating fluid from the nucleus pulposus. The degree of shrinkage is related to the magnitude of the compressive load on the spine and has been used as an index of spinal loading (Corlett *et al.*, 1987). Accurate measurement of spinal shrinkage has application in evaluating sports such as weight-training, running and jumping, and also in assessing procedures used to pre-vent back injury (Reilly *et al.*, 1991).

De Puky (1935), a pioneer investigator of spinal shrinkage, measured the change and found a daily oscillation of approximately 1% of total body height. This figure has subse-quently been confirmed (Reilly *et al.*, 1991). Wing *et al.* (1992) demonstrated that 40% of the change occurred in the lumbar spine, without any change in the lordosis depth and angle, and a further 40% occurred in the thoracic spine, associated with a reduction in the kyphotic angle. Most of the shrinkage appears to occur within an hour of assuming an upright posture, while this loss in height is regained rapidly in the prone position. Monitoring creep over 24 hours demonstrated that 71% of height gained during the night is achieved within the first half of the night and 80% is lost again within 3 hours of arising (Reilly *et al.*, 1984). The mechanism for these changes is that fluid dynamics within the intervertebral disc and vertebral body under compression forces fluid out of the disc, leading to the length vari-ation in the spine observed in the diurnal cycle. Intradiscal pressure is difficult to measure *in*

vivo so most studies have employed cadaveric material (Nachemson and Morris, 1964) although the magnitudes of such loads cannot be determined on this material. More recently, quantitative T2 magnetic resonance investiga-tions have been employed to image the dynamics of the lumbar spine, confirming the intervertebral disc fluid dynamic mechanism and indicating that the greatest amount of fluid is lost from the nucleus pulposus (Dangerfield *et al.*, 1995; Roberts *et al.*, 1998).

These changes are important in sport. Disc damage is more likely if it has a high water content (Adams *et al.*, 1987). The lumbar verte-brae have the highest fluid content. Further-more, the degree of lumbar flexion increases in the late afternoon, due to disc shrinkage. The clear message from these observations is that time of day is relevant in strategies to avoid straining and overloading the vertebral column. Weight training and lifting are influ-enced not only by the size of the forces involved but also in relation to the sleep pat-tern of the athlete. Avoiding such activities within the first few hours of rising reduces the risk of axial compression leading to disk damage through disc herniation and the sub-sequent onset of back pain.

4.9 DEVIATION FROM NORMAL POSTURE AND INJURY

Deviation from normal posture is common. While the human has adopted bipedalism, the underlying skeleton remains one which origi-nally evolved for quadrupedal gait, and sev-eral anatomical weaknesses remain which can give rise to problems. Sport and other stress-related activity can thus lead to problems affecting the feet, knees, spine and abdominal wall. The careful study of human anatomy is important to allow its application to the sport-ing and clinical fields and by implication the early detection of deviations from normality.

Low-back pain is probably the most common deviation from normal stability in humans and has received attention from researchers. For example, fin swimming has unique physiopathological features involving the low back which can lead to back pain (Verni *et al.*, 1999). Attention should also be paid to the design and type of equipment and the environment used for the activity. A review of the causative mechanisms of specific soccer injuries indicates that some soccer injuries may be attributable to the equipment used or the type of surface the sport is played on (Lees and Nolan, 1998). The effects on the individual of injury are therefore of considerable importance and need consideration in the context of effects on posture and performance.

Thus, posture is compromised by a range of problems that affect the normal anatomy of bipedalism. Injury to a bone, ligament or muscle will alter the normal anatomical framework and so interfere with the maintenance of the normal posture. Bad habits such as slouching in a chair can lead to changes in both muscle and bone which may develop into a permanent postural abnormality. The unequal loading of the spine can result in excessive strain and may eventually lead to an injury or pain. Asymmetries and skeletal imbalances are common, especially when they affect the lower limbs. A longer limb on one side of the body can lead to a pelvic tilt and consequently affect the hip joint and lumbar spine. Untreated, this may result in the development of scoliosis (lateral deviation of the spine). Nerve root compression or stretching of the sciatic nerve can also lead to the subject adopting an abnormal stance or posture (White and Panjabi, 1990). It also should be recognized that curvatures of the spine as a result of asymmetrical muscle function can also lead to postural and inertial abnormalities and may develop into acquired scoliosis.

Abnormal anatomical relationships, such as pes cavus (flat feet) and leg length asymmetry can rapidly result in injuries in sports such as running (Lorenzton, 1988). Early recognition of the defect by screening athletes is very important if the development of permanent anatomical deformity and eventual debilitation are to be avoided.

Traumatic injury to the body during any sporting activity can result in a wide range of different pathological outcomes. They depend on the posture adopted, the anatomical spinal position, the fitness of the individual and the degree of force sustained. It should be noted that these may be trivial in many cases but it still remains important to recognize them and initiate medical treatment as soon as possible to avoid potential permanent damage.

4.10 CONCLUSION

This chapter provides an overview of some of the techniques that have been employed to study posture. It is a field in which rapid advances in imaging technologies and computers can lead to the development of totally new equipment that can change the way a study may define posture and movement. The reader is guided to the appropriate scientific journals for these developments. It still remains important to remember the dynamic nature of the living human body and that at present, the study of movement is both complex, potentially expensive and little understood.

4.11 PRACTICAL 1: MEASUREMENT OF POSTURE AND BODY SHAPE

(a) Sagittal Plane

Erect spinal curvature is the basis of acceptable static posture. Expert opinion differs as what constitutes 'good' posture, a term relating to energy economy and cosmetic acceptability. Large variations can be seen in groups of healthy subjects. Significant individual variation can be seen between slumped/erect states and deep inhalation/exhalation and it is important to standardize the position for each subject as described in the method. Both 'flat back' and excessive curvature are considered problematic, having an association with subsequent back pain. Kyphosis of 20–45° and lordosis of 40–60° have been considered to indicate normal ranges (Roaf, 1960). Fon *et al.* (1980) suggested that these figures are inappropriate for children and teenagers since spinal curvature changes with age. This change is due to the reduction in elasticity of the spinal ligaments and alterations in bone mineral content.

The practicals detailed here are regularly used in back clinics and involve kyphometry and goniometry. These experiments will yield a range of values which describe back shape.

(b) Equipment

1. Debrunner's kyphometer. (Straumann Ltd., Welwyn Garden City, England or Protek AG, Bern, Switzerland).
2. Goniometer. For example, MIE hygrometer (see Figure 5.2: Medical Research Ltd., Leeds, UK) or Myrin Goniometer (LIC Rehab., Solna, Sweden).

(c) Method

The subject is instructed to stand barefoot, with the heels together, in an upright and relaxed position, looking straight ahead and breathing normally with the arms hanging loosely by the body. The shoulders should be relaxed.

Debrunner's kyphometer consists of two long arms where the angle between these arms is transmitted through parallel struts to a protractor (Figures 4.5 and 4.6). Spinal curvature should be assessed with the kyphometer with the subject both exhaling and inhaling maximally.

In order to measure thoracic kyphosis, one foot of the kyphometer should be located over the T1 & T2 and the other over the T11 & T12. The kyphosis angle is read directly from the protractor.

Lumbar curvature is measured between the T11 & T12 and the S1 & S2. The angle read directly from the protractor is lumbar lordosis.

A goniometer consists of a small dial that can be held to the patient's back (Figures 4.7, 4.8, 4.9 and 4.10). The difference between the back angle and the vertical is measured with a pointer which responds to gravity. The difference between the measurements at T1 and T12 indicates the degree of kyphosis and the deviation between the angles at T12 and S1 indicates the degree of lumbar lordosis. Other angles such as the proclive and declive angles can also be measured (Figure 4.7).

Use of the kyphometer or goniometer allows the quantification of the normal curvatures of the vertebral column. The angle of thoracic kyphosis and lumbar lordosis will yield useful information on individual and group posture.

4.12 PRACTICAL 2: ASSESSMENT OF SITTING POSTURE

Sitting posture may be assessed by first sitting the subject on a high stool. The knees should be flexed to 90° and the thighs 90° relative to the trunk. Most of the weight is taken by the ischial tuberosities, acting as a fulcrum within the buttocks. If the hip angle exceeds 60°, hamstring tension increases and the spine compensates by losing the lordosis concavity of the lumbar spine. A comfortable position therefore requires consideration of the lengths of the tibia and femur and the angles of the femur relative to the pelvis and the lordosis angle of the lumbar spine (maintaining lumbar lordosis is important in avoiding lumbar postural strain). To ascertain the appropriateness of a chair for an individual, an investigation of this usually can be easily undertaken using an anthropometer and goniometer.

The lateral flexibility of the spine can be assessed by placing the goniometer dial over the T1 vertebra and then asking the subject to flex to the right and to the left. Sagittal flexibility can be measured by goniometry. It more often quantified in field testing by the sit-and-reach test.

4.13 PRACTICAL 3: LATERAL DEVIATIONS

(a) Equipment

Scoliometer, e.g. Orthopedic Systems, Inc., Union City, CA, USA.

(b) Method

The scoliometer is employed to quantify lateral deviations of the spine expressed as an asymmetrical trunk deformity. Used in both the thoracic and lumbar regions, it has been found to be less sensitive for the identification of lumbar scoliosis. The reason for this is unclear since lateral spinal curvature and axial trunk rotation also occur in this region. Lateral deviations are found most commonly in scoliosis. Non-structural scoliosis may be formed by disparity in leg length and is usually non-progressive. Structural scoliosis is a serious condition with likelihood of progression throughout the growth period. If found, such cases should be referred for an urgent orthopaedic opinion.

The standing subject assumes a forward-bending posture with the trunk approximately parallel with the floor and feet together. The subject's hands are placed palms together and held between the knees. This position offers the most consistently reproducible results in clinical studies. The examiner places the scoliometer on the subject's back, with the centre of the device corresponding to the centre contour of the trunk, along the spinal column.

Starting where the neck joins the trunk, the scoliometer is moved down the spine to the sacrum, the maximum values for thoracic and lumbar areas being recorded.

Scoliometer readings in excess of 5–8° are taken to indicate significant scoliosis and should be referred to a general practitioner or scoliosis specialist for radiography examination.

Table 4.1 A sample of a data collection form

			Date	9.6.95
Subject Name	M			
Date of birth	1.1.80		Sex	Male
Height	1823.0 mm			
Body mass	73.6 kg			

	Test 1	Test 2
Kyphometer		
Kyphosis Angle T1–T12	34.0 degrees	32.4 degrees
Lordosis Angle T12–S1	23.5 degrees	24.5 degrees
Goniometer		
Upper Proclive Angle	37.0 degrees	35.0 degrees
Declive Angle	–11.0 degrees	–14.0 degrees
Lower Proclive Angle	–7.0 degrees	–10.0 degrees
Lordosis	–30.0 degrees	–35.0 degrees
Kyphosis	20.0 degrees	24.0 degrees
Flexibility		
Sit and Reach score	20.0 cm	20.5 cm
Scoliometer		
ATI	3.0 degrees	5.0 degrees
Lateral flexibility		
Right side	25.0 degrees	23.0 degrees
Left side	20.0 degrees	20.0 degrees
Leg length		
Supine		
Right leg	980.0 mm	980.0 mm
Left leg	970.0 mm	975.0 mm
Discrepancy	10.0 mm	5.0 mm
Standing		
Right leg	950.0 mm	955.0 mm
Left leg	945.0 mm	950.0 mm
Discrepancy	5.0 mm	5.0 mm

Data taken from P. H. Dangerfield (1995, unpublished data: Liverpool School Survey).

4.14 PRACTICAL 4: LEG-LENGTH DISCREPANCY

The subject lies on the floor (or suitable firm surface) with the feet approximately shoulder-width apart. A steel tape measure is used to measure the distance between the medial malleolus and the anterior superior iliac spine (this is an orthopaedic measurement of leg-length discrepancy). Although differences in leg length are found in many normal subjects, a difference greater than 10 mm may result in postural or adaptive scoliosis.

The subject should then stand bare-footed in a normal, relaxed stance. The distance between the floor by the subject's heel and the hip is measured. Any difference in the left and right side measurements may indicate that the hip is at an angle to the horizontal, indicating the presence of pelvic obliquity. If present, pelvic obliquity can also result in compensatory scoliosis. Pelvic obliquity can also be confirmed by placing the thumbs on each anterior superior iliac spines and 'eye-balling' their heights to check for horizontal alignment.

A specimen data collection form which could be adapted for use in a laboratory or field situation is shown in Table 4.1.

REFERENCES

Adams, M.A., Dolan, P. and Hutton, W.C. (1987). Diurnal variations in the stresses on the lumbar spine. *Spine*, **12**, 130–7.

Allard, P., Stokes, I.A.S. and Blanchi, J-P. (1994). *Three-Dimensional Analysis of Human Movement.* (Human Kinetics, Champaign, IL).

Alexander, M.J. (1985). Biomechanical aspects of lumbar spine injuries in athletes; a review. *Canadian Journal of Applied Sports Science*, **10**, 1–5.

Asazuma, T., Suzuki, N. and Hirabayashi, K. (1986). Analysis of human dynamic posture in normal and scoliotic patients. In *Surface Topography and Spinal Deformity* III. eds. J.D. Harris and A.R. Turner-Smith (Gustav Fischer Verlag, Stuttgart). pp. 223–34.

Bartelink, D.L. (1957). The role of abdominal pressure on the lumbar intervertebral discs. *Journal of Bone and Joint Surgery*, **39B**, 718–25.

Bartlett, R. ed. (1992). *Guidelines for the Biomechanical Analysis of Performance in Sport.* (British Association of Sport and Exercise Sciences, Leeds, U.K.)

Bloomfield, J., Ackland, T.R. and Elliot, B.C. (1994). *Applied Anatomy and Biomechanics in Sport.* (Blackwell Scientific Publications, Australia).

Burwell, R.G. and Dangerfield, P.H. (1992). Pathogenesis and assessment of scoliosis. In *Surgery of the Spine*. eds. G. Findlay and R. Owen (Blackwell Scientific Publications, Oxford), pp. 365–408.

Burwell, R.G. and Dangerfield, P.H. (2000). *Etiology of Adolescent Idiopathic Scoliosis.* State of the Art Reviews. eds. R.G. Burwell, P.H. Dangerfield,T.G. Lowe, and J.Y. Margulies. (Hanley and Belfus, Philadelphia), pp. 319-34.

Cameron, N. (1986). The methods of auxological anthropometry. In *Human Growth: A Comprehensive Treatise*, Vol. 3, 2nd edn. eds. F. Faulkner and J. M. Tanner (Plenum Press, New York and London), pp. 3–46.

Clarys, J. P. (1987). Application of EMG for the evaluation of performance in different sports. In *Muscular Function in Exercise and Training*. eds. P. Marconnet and P.V. Komi (Karger, Basel), pp. 200–23.

Clarys, J. P. and Cabri, J. (1993). Electromyography and the study of sports movements: a review. *Journal of Sports Sciences*, **11**, 379–448.

Cole, A.A., Burwell, R.G., and Dangerfield, P.H. (2000). *Etiology of Adolescent Idiopathic Scoliosis.* State of the Art Reviews. eds. R.G. Burwell, P.H. Dangerfield, T.G. Lowe and J.Y. Margulies (Hanley and Belfus, Philadelphia), pp. 411-22.

Corlett, E.N., Eklund, J.A.E., Reilly, T. and Troup, J.D.G. (1987). Assessment of work load from measurements of stature. *Applied Ergonomics*, **18**, 65–71.

Dangerfield, P.H. (1994). Asymmetry and growth. In *Anthropometry: The Individual and The Population.* eds. S.J. Ulijaszek and C.G.N. Mascie-Taylor (Cambridge University Press, Cambridge), pp. 7–29.

Dangerfield, P.H. and Denton, J.C. (1986). A longitudinal examination of the relationship between the rib-hump, spinal angle and vertebral rotation in idiopathic scoliosis. In *Proceedings of the 3rd International Symposium on Moiré Fringe Topography and Spinal Deformity*, Oxford. eds. J.D. Harris and A.R. Turner-Smith (Gustav Fischer Verlag, Stuttgart), pp. 213–21.

Dangerfield, P.H., Denton, J.C., Barnes, S.B. and Drake, N.D. (1987). The assessment of the rib-cage and spinal deformity in scoliosis. In *Proceedings of the 4th International Symposium on Moiré Fringe Topography and Spinal Deformity*, Oxford. eds. I.A.F. Stokes, J.R. Pekelsky and M.S. Moreland (Gustav Fischer Verlag, Stuttgart), pp. 53–66.

Dangerfield, P.H., Pearson, J.D., Atkinson, J.T., *et al.* (1992). Measurement of back surface topography using an automated imaging system. *Acta Orthopaedica Belgica*, **58**, 73–9.

Dangerfield, P.H., Walker, J., Roberts, N., *et al.* (1995). Investigation of the diurnal variation in the water content of the intervertebral disc using MRI. In *Proceedings of a 2nd Symposium on 3D Deformity and Scoliosis*, Pescara, Italy. eds. M. D´Amico, A. Merolli and G.C. Santambrogio (IOS Press, Amsterdam, The Netherlands), pp. 447–51.

Davis, P.R. (1959). The medial inclination of the human articular facets. *Journal of Anatomy*, **93**, 68–74.

De Puky, P. (1935). The physiological oscillation of the length of the body. *Acta Orthopaedica Scandinavica*, **6**, 338–47.

Dillard, J., Trafimow, J., Andersson, G.B.J. and Cronin, K. (1991). Motion of the lumbar spine; reliability of two measurement techniques. *Spine*, **16**, 321–4.

D´Orazio, B. ed. (1993). *Back Pain Rehabilitation.* (Andover Medical Publications, Oxford).

Fon, G.T., Pitt, M.J. and Thies, A.C. (1980). Thoracic kyphosis, range in normal subjects. *American Journal of Roentgenology*, **124**, 979–83.

Gomez, T., Beach, G., Cooke, C., *et al.* (1991). Normative database for trunk range of motion, strength, velocity and endurance with the Isostation B–200 lumbar dynamometer. *Spine*, **16**, 15–21.

Grassino, A., Goldman, M.D., Mead, J. and Sears, T.A. (1978). Mechanics of the human diaphragm during voluntary contraction. *Journal of Applied Physiology*, **44**, 829–39.

Grillner, S.J., Nilsson, J. and Thorstensson, A. (1978). Intra-abdominal pressure changes during natural

movements in man. *Acta Physiologica Scandinavica*, **104**, 275–83.

Halioua, M. and Liu, H-C. (1989). Optical three-dimensional sensing by phase measuring profilometry. *Optics and Lasers in Engineering*, **11**, 185–215.

Halioua, M., Liu, H-C., Chin, A. and Bowings, T.S. (1990). Automated topography of the human form by phase-measuring profilometry and model analysis. In *Proceedings of the Fifth International Symposium on Surface Topography and Body Deformity*. eds. H. Neugebauer and G. Windischbauer (Gustav Fischer Verlag, Stuttgart), pp. 91–100.

Hellsing, E., Reigo, T., McWilliam, J. and Spangfort, E. (1987). Cervical and lumbar lordosis and thoracic kyphosis in 8, 11 and 15-year-old children. *European Journal of Orthopaedics*, **9**, 129–30.

Hierholzer, E. and Drerup, B. (1999). Rasterstereographic functional examinations: precision measurement of kyphosis and lordosis. In *Research into Spinal Deformities* 2. ed. I.A.F. Stokes (IOS Press, Amsterdam, The Netherlands), pp. 101–4.

Hierholzer, E., Drerup, B. and Frobin, W. (1983). Computerized data acquisition and evaluation of moire topograms and rasterstereographs. In *Moiré Fringe Topography and Spinal Deformity*. eds. B. Drerup, W. Frobin and E. Hierholzer (Gustav Fisher Verlag, Stuttgart), pp. 233–40.

Hinz, B. and Seidel, H. (1989). On time relation between erector spinae muscle activity and force development during initial isometric stage of back lifts. *Clinical Biomechanics*, **4**, 5–10.

Hrdlicka, A. (1972). *Practical Anthropometry.* (AMS Press, New York (reprint)).

Jones, P.R.M., West, G.M., Harris, D.H. and Read, J.B. (1989). The Loughborough anthropometric shadow scanner (LASS). *Endeavor*, **13**, 162–8.

Kippers, V. and Parker, A. W. (1989). Validation of single-segment and three segment spinal models used to represent lumbar flexion. *Journal of Biomechanics*, **22**, 67–75.

Klausen, K. (1965). The form and function of the loaded human spine. *Acta Physiologica Scandinavica*, **65**, 176–90.

Lees, A. and Nolan, L. (1998). The biomechanics of soccer: a review. *Journal of Sports Sciences*, **16**, 211–34.

Lohman, T.G., Roche A.F. and Martorell, R. (1988). *Anthropometric Standardization Reference Manual.* (Human Kinetics, Champaign, IL).

Lorenzton, R. (1988). Causes of injuries: intrinsic

factors. In *Oxford Book of Sports Medicine I*. eds. A. Dirix, H.G. Knuttgen and K. Tittel (Blackwell Scientific Publications, Oxford).

MacRae, J.F. and Wright, V. (1969). Measurement of back movements. *Annals of Rheumatic Diseases*, **28**, 584–9.

Mayhew, T.P. and Rothstein, J.M. (1985). Measurement of muscle performance with instruments. *Clinics in Physical Therapy*, **7**, 57–102.

Merolli, A., Guidi, P., Kozlowski, J., *et al.* (1999). Clinical trial of CPT (Complex Phase Tracing) profilometry in scoliosis. *Research into Spinal Deformities 2*. ed. I.A.F Stokes (IOS Press, Amsterdam), pp. 57–60.

Mitchelson, D.L. (1988). Automated three dimensional movement analysis using the CODA-3 system. *Biomedical Technik*, **33**, 179–82.

Mouton, L.J., Hof, A.L., de Jongh, H.J. and Eisma, W.H. (1991). Influence of posture on the relation between surface electromyogram amplitude and back muscle moment: consequences for the use of surface electromyogram to measure back load. *Clinical Biomechanics*, **6**, 245–51.

Nachemson, A. and Morris, J.M. (1964). In vivo measurements of intradiscal pressure. *Journal of Bone and Joint Surgery*, **46**, 1077–81.

Ohlen, G., Sprangfort, E. and Tingwell, C. (1989). Measurement of spinal sagittal configuration and mobility with Debrunner's Kyphometer. *Spine*, **14**, 580–3.

Pal, G.P. and Routal, R.V. (1986). A study of weight transmission through the cervical and upper thoracic regions of the vertebral column in man. *Journal of Anatomy*, **148**, 245–61.

Panjabi, M., Yamamoto, I., Oxland, T. and Crisco, J. (1989). How does posture affect coupling in the lumbar spine? *Spine*, **14**, 1002–11.

Paquet, N., Malouin, F., Richards, C.L., *et al.* (1991). Validity and reliability of a new electrogoniometer for the measurement of sagittal dorso-lumbar movements. *Spine*, **16**, 516–19.

Parnianpour, M. and Tan, J.C. (1993). Objective quantification of trunk performance. In *Back Pain Rehabilitation*. ed. B. D'Orazio (Andover Medical Publications, Oxford).

Pheasant, S. (1986). *Bodyspace: Anthropometry, Ergonomics and Design*. (Taylor and Francis, London).

Pitman, M.I. and Peterson, L. (1989). Biomechanics of skeletal muscle. In *Basic Biomechanics of the Musculoskeletal System*. eds. M. Nordin and V. Fankel (Lea and Febiger, Philadelphia), pp. 89–111.

Poncet, P., Delorme, S., Dudley, R., *et al.* (1999). 3D reconstructions of the external and internal geometries of the trunk using laser and stereo-radiographic imaging techniques. In *Research into Spinal Deformities 2*. ed. I.A.F. Stokes (IOS Press, Amsterdam), pp. 21–28.

Rae, P.S., Waddell, G. and Venner, R.M. (1984). A simple technique for measuring lumber spinal flexion. *Journal of the Royal College of Surgeons of Edinburgh*, **29**, 281–4.

Reilly, T., Tyrrell, A. and Troup, J.D.G. (1984). Circadian variation in human stature. *Chronobiology International*, **1**, 121–6.

Reilly, T., Boocock, M.G., Garbutt, G., *et al.* (1991). Changes in stature during exercise and sports training. *Applied Ergonomics*, **22**, 308–11.

Roaf, R. (1960). The basic anatomy of scoliosis. *Journal of Bone and Joint Surgery*, **488**, 40–59.

Roaf, R. (1977). *Posture*. (Academic Press, London).

Roberts, N., Hogg, D., Whitehouse, G.H., *et al.* (1998). Quantitative analysis of diurnal variation in volume and water content of lumbar intervertebral discs. *Clinical Anatomy*, **11**, 1–8.

Rogers, M.M. and Cavanagh, P.R. (1984). A glossary of biomechanical terms, concepts and units. *Physical Therapy*, **64**, 1886–902.

Salisbury, P.J. and Porter, R.W. (1987). Measurement of lumbar sagittal mobility: a comparison of methods. *Spine*, **12**, 190–3.

Sarasate, H. and Ostman, A. (1986). Stereophotogrammetry in the evaluation of the treatment of scoliosis. *International Orthopaedics*, **10**, 63–7.

Suzuki, N., Yamaguchi, Y. and Armstrong, G.W.D. (1981). Measurement of posture using Moiré topography. In *Moiré Fringe Topography and Spinal Deformity*. eds. M.S. Moreland, M.H. Pope and G.W.D. Armstrong (Pergamon Press, New York), pp. 122–31.

Tani, K. and Masuda, T. (1985). A kinesiologic study of erector spinae activity during trunk flexion and extension. *Ergonomics*, **28**, 883–93.

Taylor, J. R. and Twomey, L. (1984). Sexual dimorphism in human vertebral body shape. *Journal of Anatomy*, **138**, 281–6.

Thorstensson, A., Oddsson, L. and Carlson, H. (1985). Motor control of voluntary trunk movements in standing. *Acta Physiologica Scandinavica*, **125**, 309–21.

Thurston, A.J. and Harris, J.D. (1983). Normal kinetics of the lumbar spine and pelvis. *Spine*, **8**, 199–205.

Tillotson, K.M. and Burton, A.K. (1991). Noninvasive measurement of lumbar sagittal mobility. An assessment of the flexicurve technique. *Spine*, **16**, 29–33.

Tsai, L. and Wredmark, T. (1993). Spinal posture, sagittal mobility and subjective rating of back problems in former female elite gymnasts. *Spine*, **18**, 872–975.

Ulijaszek, S.J. and Lourie, J.A. (1994). Intra- and inter-observer error in anthropometric measurement. In *Anthropometry: The Individual and The Population*. eds. S.J. Ulijaszek and C.G.N. Mascie-Taylor (Cambridge University Press, Cambridge), pp. 30–55.

Verni, E., Prosperi, L., Lucaccini, C., *et al.* (1999). Lumbar pain and fin swimming. *Journal of Sports Medicine and Physical Fitness*. **39**, 61–65.

Vogelbach, S.K. (1990). *Functional Kinetics*. (Springer Verlag, Stuttgart).

Weiner, J.S. (1982). The measurement of human workload. *Ergonomics*, **25**, 953–66.

Weiner, J.S. and Lourie, J.A. (1969). Anthropometry. In *Human Biology: A Guide to Field Methods*. International Biological Programme Handbook no 9. (Blackwell Scientific Publications, Oxford), pp. 3–42.

White, A.A. and Panjabi, M.M. (1990). *Clinical Biomechanics of the Spine*. 2nd edn. (Lippincott-Raven, Philadelphia).

Willner, S. (1979). Moiré topography for the diagnosis and documentation of scoliosis. *Acta Orthopaedica Scandinavica*, **50**, 295–302.

Willner, S. and Johnson, B. (1983). Thoracic kyphosis and lumbar lordosis during the growth period in children. *Acta Pediatrica Scandinavica*, **72**, 873–8.

Wing, P., Tsang, L., Gagnon, F., *et al.* (1992). Diurnal changes in the profile, shape and range of motion of the back. *Spine*, **17**, 761–5.

Wosak, J. and Voloshin, A. (1981). Wave attenuation in skeletons of young healthy persons. *Journal of Biomechanics*, **14**, 261–7.

FLEXIBILITY

5

Jan Borms and Peter van Roy

5.1 AIMS

The aims of this chapter are to:
- gain insight into the complexity of goniometric measurements of flexibility,
- gain insight into the need for test standardization,
- become acquainted with new measurement instruments, in particular goniometers,
- learn to mark certain anthropometric reference points,
- learn how to take several goniometric measurements of flexibility at both sides of the body,
- know how to interpret, compare and evaluate the results of goniometric measurements of flexibility,
- situate goniometry in a larger field of joint kinematics.

5.2 INTRODUCTION

Flexibility may be defined as the range of motion (ROM) at a single joint or a series of joints. The ROM reflects the kinematic possibilities of the joint(s) considered, which also depend on the ability of muscles and connective tissue surrounding the joint to be elongated within their structural limitations.

Measurements of flexibility are widely used in medicine, in sports, and in physical fitness. In the clinical practice, the improvement of the patient's flexibility is followed up by simple goniometric readings. In addition to anthropometric databases, normative data concerning ROM provide useful information for ergonomic design processes and improving the work area (Hsiao and Keyserling, 1990).

There is little doubt that good flexibility is needed, particularly in sports where maximum amplitude of movement is required for an optimal execution of technique. Testing this component has therefore been common practice in training situations as a means of evaluating progress in physical conditioning and of identifying problem areas associated with poor performance or possible injury (e.g. Cureton, 1941). Ever since this quality has been considered as a component of physical fitness, a test to express and evaluate it has been included in physical fitness test batteries (e.g. Larson, 1974; AAHPERD, 1984). These so-called field tests have been widely used to measure flexibility, specifically in trunk, hip and back flexion, such as Scott and French's (1950) Bobbing Test, Kraus and Hirschland's (1954) Floor Touch Test and finally the Sit-and-Reach Test of Wells and Dillon (1952). The latter test has been used worldwide in practice and is incorporated in the Eurofit test battery for European member states (Council of Europe, 1988).

In the 'sit-and-reach' test, the individual sits on the floor with the legs extended forward and feet pressed flat against a box that supports the measuring device. With the back of the knees pressed flat against the floor, the individual leans forward and extends the

Kinanthropometry and Exercise Physiology Laboratory Manual: Tests, Procedures and Data. 2nd Edition. Volume 1: Anthropometry
Edited by R.G. Eston and T. Reilly. Published by Routledge, London, August 2001

fingertips as far as possible. The distance reached is recorded and serves as an assessment of either the subject's flexibility at the hips, back muscle or hamstrings, or of the subject's general flexibility. It remains questionable which joints and muscles are being assessed because of the complexity of the movement. The test is used so widely, perhaps because the bending movement is popularly associated with being supple, and probably because many health problems associated with poor flexibility are related to the lower back.

In spite of the popularity the test enjoys, by virtue of its simple instructions, its low cost, its high reproducibility and its high loading on the flexibility factor in factor analysis studies, it has been subjected to criticism, as were other tests where linear instead of angular measurements were applied. The individual with long arms and short legs will tend to be advantaged compared to an individual with the opposite anthropometric characteristics (Broer and Galles, 1958; Borms, 1984). Because the question of bias for some individual extreme proportional arm/leg length differences persisted, Hopkins and Hoeger (1986) proposed the modified sit-and-reach test to negate the effects of shoulder girdle mobility and proportional differences between arms and leg.

Another criticism relates to the specificity of the test, which purports to assess the individual's general flexibility, whereas it is now generally considered as a specific trait. In non-performance-oriented testing, however, the indirect methods involving linear measurements can be suitable approximations of flexibility.

Direct methods of measuring angular displacements have been used in research and in clinical situations, unlike the case for mass screening. Direct methods of measurement are recommended because they are not affected by body segment proportions.

The success of these simple angular (two-dimensional goniometry) tests for evaluating flexibility is given by the combination of simplicity, low cost and standardization. From a mathematical perspective, joint motion or the movement of a particular region of the body (e.g. the cervical spine) results from the combination of rotation(s) and translation(s). Depending on the nature of movements, two-dimensional or three-dimensional analysis is appropriate.

In performance-oriented investigations of flexibility, complex three-dimensional motion patterns are often analysed in a broad field of view. Herein, velocity, acceleration, coordination and muscle function may be important parameters. In clinically oriented investigations of flexibility, however, joint kinematics are more focused on diagnostic purposes and on treatment of impairments, reduction of disabilities and increase in the patient's participation. Gross motion of body segments (main motion) and particular intra-articular movement mechanisms, like 'coupled motion' in the spine, and 'locking and unlocking mechanisms' in the joints of the extremities, are important issues in orthopaedics and rehabilitation. Here the field of view is rather reduced and particular attention may be given to joint-related features of intra-articular motion. With modern medical imaging techniques, the changes in orientation and position of helical axes may be registered simultaneously with contact areal analysis of the articulating joint surfaces.

5.3 MEASUREMENT INSTRUMENTS

Numerous research reports show the wide range of measuring equipment that can be adopted for the study of joint movement, ranging from simple two-dimensional measuring tools to several computerized systems for three-dimensional motion analysis. In particular, the development of equipment and methodology for three-dimensional motion analysis has undergone a remarkable evolution during the last decades of the twentieth-century (Allard *et al.*, 1995; Capozzo *et al.*, 1995; Capozzo *et al.*, 1996; Bull and Amis, 1998).

Standardization proposals concerning different aspects of three-dimensional methodology (reference frames, bony landmarks, Euler rotation sequences) reflect the need for communication and exchange about three-dimensional outcomes in a multidisciplinary context (Grood and Suntay, 1983; Benedetti *et al.*, 1994; Cappozzo and Della Croce, 1994). Different aims and circumstances of investigation, but also time and cost factors, influence the choice of an appropriate measuring tool, varying from a simple measuring device providing real-time readings in daily practice to a more complicated experimental set-up, used for expertise or research purposes.

For the context of this text, the focus of the following practical description involves two-dimensional goniometry. This can be used as an introduction to three-dimensional joint motion methodology with higher performance.

5.3.1 GONIOMETRY

Clinical goniometry is constrained within a mechanistic approach where the articulating surfaces are seen as 'solids of revolution', rotating around a fixed axis that coincides with the axis of the goniometer. Radii of curvature may vary substantially depending on the considered part of the articular surfaces. The degree of congruence between the articular surfaces may change greatly during joint motion. Movement capacities depend not only on the shape of the articulating surfaces, but also on capsular and ligamentous steering and muscular control.

The **protractor goniometer** is a simple but useful device consisting of two articulating arms, one of which contains a protractor made of Plexiglas or metal, constructed around the fulcrum of the apparatus, around which the second arm rotates (Figure 5.1). The arm with the protractor is named the stationary arm; the second arm is called the moving arm. Protractor goniometers were first introduced in the Grand Palais Hospital in Paris by Camus and Amar in 1915 (Fox, 1917).

The **inclinometer** is based on the principle that a joint movement is recorded as an angular change against the vector of the gravity force.

In **hygrometers**, angular values are recorded by moving a bubble of air or a fluid level relative to an initial zero position, using the fact that the bubble will always seek the highest position within a small fluid

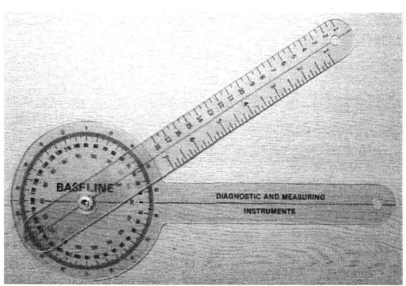

Figure 5.1 A protractor goniometer.

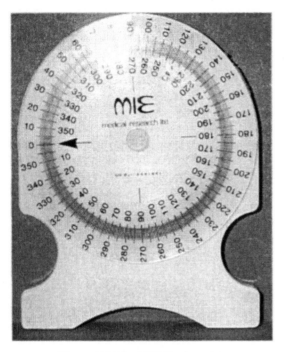

Figure 5.2 The MIE Hygrometer.

container, or using the principle that a fluid level will always tend to remain in a horizontal position (Figure 5.2).

The **pendulum goniometer** uses the effect of the force of gravity on the pointer (needle) of the goniometer, which is positioned in the centre of a protractor scale. The *Leighton Flexometer* (Leighton, 1966) contains a rotating circular dial marked off in degrees and a pointer counterbalanced to ensure it always points vertically. It is strapped on the appropriate body segment and the range of motion is determined with respect to this perpendicular (Figure 5.3). The length of limbs or segment does not influence this assessment, neither is the axis of the bone lever a disturbing factor. On the other hand, most movements must be made actively against gravity and the distinction between hip and back ROM measurement is questionable.

Other techniques include measurements of joint angles from arthrographs, photographs and radiographic images (Kottke and Mundale, 1959; Wright and Johns, 1960).

The **potentiometric electrogoniometer** is a device like a protractor which is used to measure the joint angle at both extremes of the total range of movement. The essence of the apparatus is that the protractor has been replaced by a potentiometer, which can modify a given voltage proportionally to the angle of the joint. This measuring system has been adopted in many configurations, from simple two-dimensional applications to computerized triaxial electrogoniometers and spatial linkages allowing registrations of up to six degrees of freedom.

The **strain gauge electrogoniometer** represents a valuable and easily applicable contemporary alternative to the potentiometric electrogoniometer (Nicol, 1987; Tesio *et al.*, 1995).

Unfortunately, the area of flexibility measurement is characterized by confusion in terminology and lack of standardization (e.g. units, warming-up or not, starting position, active or passive motion, detailed description of procedures). During the past two decades, however, renewed interest and efforts towards developing and/or improving measurement procedures are noticeable (Ekstrand *et al.*, 1982; Borms *et al.*, 1987).

5.3.2 TWO-DIMENSIONAL GONIOMETRY VERSUS THREE-DIMENSIONAL JOINT KINEMATICS

An increasing number of publications on three-dimensional analysis of joint motion in the field of biomechanics has been evident in the past two decades. For biomechanical engineers joint motion basically has to be described in terms of translation and rotation. In this respect, functional anatomical expressions like medial and lateral rotation may be rather confusing. A point of weakness of the biomechanical approach was related to the adoption of different reference frames and Euler rotation sequences for the calculation of the kinematic data, making it hard to compare results from different publications. This has been recognized by the International Society of Biomechanics (ISB). The ISB proposed the use of standardized orientations of reference

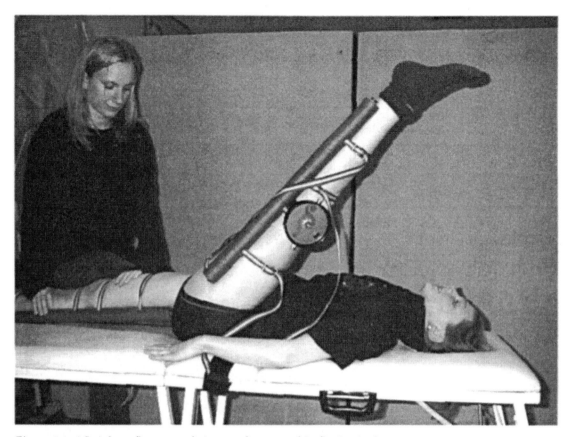

Figure 5.3 A Leighton flexometer being used to assess hip flexion in the supine position (straight leg).

frames (Grood and Suntay, 1983). The CAMARC II project (Computer Aided Motion Analysis in Rehabilitation Context) of the European Community (Benedetti *et al.*, 1994) provided a multidisciplinary effort to improve the communicability between clinical and experimental protocols. The call for standardization in definitions and identifications of anatomical landmarks must be seen in the context of data sharing for clinical and biomechanical research purposes.

Depending on the required level of accuracy and precision, several three-dimensional motion analysis systems may be adopted for *in vivo* registration of human joint movements. A number of these are commercially available and allow real-time recordings, such as computerized electrogoniometers and magnetic tracking devices. Depending on the time required for digitizing and analysis, video-based systems can be included in the group of instrumentation which can be used for clinical work. The efforts of Cappozzo and his team (Cappozzo *et al.*, 1995; 1996) to improve the methodology of working with clusters of markers or landmarks have helped to refine the applications of three-dimensional joint kinematics.

On the other hand, actual developments in radiological techniques are promising for further fundamental research in joint kinematics. It is regrettable that, in the past, more attention has been given to the precise steering of robots in industrial applications than to the precise measurement of human joint motion. Broadening the field of application of three-dimensional joint kinematics will call for new developments, meeting the particular needs of different disciplines. Bringing three-dimensional movement analysis closer to the daily practice of health science workers and sports medicine requires a willingness to learn and to accept some biomechanical principles and expressions with respect to the methodology of joint motion.

5.4 PRACTICAL: FLEXIBILITY MEASUREMENTS WITH GONIOMETRY

5.4.1 DEFINITIONS

(a) Goniometry

From a clinical point of view goniometry can be described as a technique for measuring human joint flexibility by expressing, in degrees, the range of motion, according to a given degree of freedom. Traditionally, degrees of freedom are assigned in relation to an anatomical reference frame. Hence, joint motion is an expression of functional anatomy. In most cases, clinical goniometry is restricted to the angular changes of peripheral pathways of limb segments, measured in a two-dimensional way. Although goniometry emphasizes relative angular changes between bony or body segments in joint motion, it should be mentioned that small amounts of translations simultaneously occur, and therefore are an essential part of the arthrokinematic mechanisms.

(b) Goniometers

A goniometer measures the angle between two bony segments. When maximal amplitude of a movement is reached, this maximal amplitude is then read and recorded. Figure 5.1 shows an example of a typical (short-armed) protractor goniometer.

The *Labrique goniometer* (1977) is a pendulum goniometer with a needle constructed within the protractor, and which maintains a vertical direction under the influence of

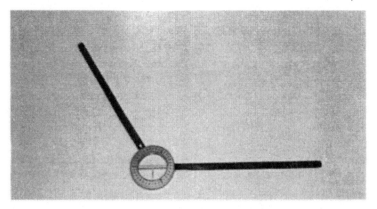

Figure 5.4 The Labrique goniometer.

gravity. This needle permits a rapid evaluation of the ROM of a joint, in relation to the vertical (or the horizontal if the scale on the reverse side of the apparatus is used) (Figure 5.4).

The *VUB goniometer* was developed at the Vrije Universiteit Brussel (VUB) (Van Roy *et al.*, 1985) and was applied in several projects to study the optimal duration of static stretching exercises (Borms *et al.*, 1987) and the maintenance of coxofemoral flexibility (Van Roy *et al.*, 1987). This goniometer differs from traditional protractor goniometers in that the graduated scale, the goniometer's fulcrum and the moving arm are mounted on a carriage, which slides along the stationary arm of the goniometer (Figure 5.5). This construction allows an easy orientation of the transparent 55 cm long arms of the goniometer along the longitudinal axes of the body segments. Joint range can then be measured without centring the fulcrum of the goniometer on the joint axis. In a previous study (Van Roy, 1981) indi-

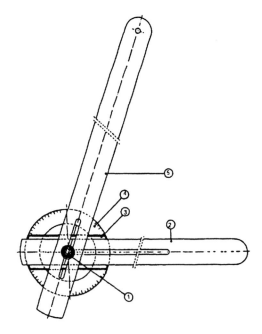

Figure 5.5 The VUB goniometer. Patent no 899964 (Belgium). 1. fulcrum; 2. stationary arm; 3. sliding carriage; 4. protractor scale; 5. moving arm.

cated that considering fixed joint axes as reference points introduces systematic errors in goniometry.

The rationale behind the development of such a goniometer was that goniometric measurements of hip motion (flexion) are not valid unless they account for the angular change between the pelvis and the femur (Mundale *et al.*, 1956; Clayson *et al.*, 1966). Straight leg raising indeed includes a posterior pelvic tilt and a reduction of lumbar lordosis.

(c) Possible interpretations of a range of motion

In Figure 5.6 OA always represents the segment which moves from position A_1 to position A_2 over an angle of 50° (Mundale *et al.*, 1956; Clayson *et al.*, 1966). As OA rotates around a point O, it changes the angular position in relation to OB, the stationary segment. This motion over an angle of 50° can be measured in four different ways (after Rocher and Rigaud, 1964):

1. The *true angle* between the skeletal segments in the end position of the motion: angle BOA_2 ($BOA_2 = BOA_1 - 50°$) (Figure 5.6a).
2. The *complementary angle* A_2OX (Figure 5.6b).
3. The *supplementary angle* A_2OY (Figure 5.6c).
4. The *range of motion angle* A_2OA_1 (Figure 5.6d).

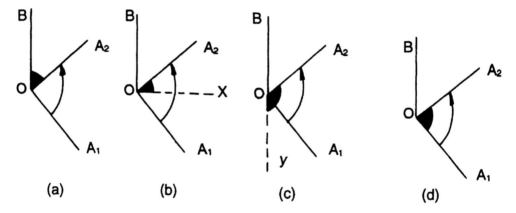

Figure 5.6 Four different ways to evaluate the angle in a joint (after Rocher & Rigaud, 1964). (a) true angle; (b) complementary angle; (c) supplementary angle; (d) ROM

From the above, it is clear that confusion can arise in the interpretation of the measurements obtained. If the measurement of the ROM is of interest, then it should also be specified from which reference point the range of motion has been measured. An important attempt to standardize goniometric techniques has been worked out by the American Academy of Orthopaedic Surgeons (1965). The standardization generalizes the 'Neutral Zero Method' of Cave and Roberts (1936). Herein, the ROM is measured from a specific reference position which, for every joint, is defined as the *zero starting position*. In this international convention, increasing ROM is always characterized by increasing angular values (which is not obvious in all manuals on goniometry). Moreover, rather than the anatomical position, an upright position with feet together, arms hanging alongside the body, and thumbs forwards, is the basis of a reference position for measurement.

5.4.2 ADAPTATION OF THE GONIOMETRIC TECHNIQUES TO RECENT KNOWLEDGE OF SYNOVIAL JOINTS' FLEXIBILITY

(a) Limitation of the validity of goniometry

Realising that real joint motion includes several angular components and small components of translation relative to different degrees of freedom, it is clear that two-dimensional goniometry is only a two-dimensional criterion to estimate the real flexibility, which in fact occurs three-dimensionally (Van Roy, 1981). Although the reliability and the objectivity of two-dimensional goniometry in standardized situations can be very high, the content validity therefore always remains restrained.

(b) Measurement without positioning of the goniometer's axis relative to the joint's axis

From the knowledge that motion does not occur around axes which remain constant, it is clear that attempts to let the goniometer's axis coincide with the axis of the motion are not only useless, but also generate a systematic measurement error (Van Roy, 1981). Therefore, the goniometer has to be positioned in such a way that the arms coincide with the longitudinal axes of the moving segments in the end position of the motion. When the angular position at that moment is measured with respect to the zero position, the relative ROM can be evaluated.

5.4.3 GENERAL GUIDELINES FOR GONIOMETRY

(a) Knowledge of anatomy of the motion apparatus

Measurements have to be carried out on the nude skin, whereby the examiner palpates two specific anthropometric reference points for each segment. These 'landmarks' can shift considerably under the skin as motion occurs. Therefore, all reference points should be marked in the end position of the segment.

(b) Knowledge of internal factors influencing flexibility

Understanding is required, as well as kinesiological knowledge, of the compensation movements which are to be expected in joints situated proximal and distal of the joint to be measured. It is therefore important that the starting position is described precisely and that compensatory movements are controlled. Lateroflexion of the spine can compensate for lack of arm abduction. On the other hand, a particular degree of hip abduction should theoretically represent pure coxofemoral abduction, but in most cases hip abduction results from a combination between pure coxofemoral abduction and lateral bending of the pelvis. One should differentiate between *osteokinematic* and *arthrokinematic* readings of flexibility, the former being an expression of angular changes in space in relation to an anatomical reference system, the latter being an expression of angular changes within a particular joint (starting from a zero position which of course can also be expressed in terms of an anatomical reference frame).

It is also very important to determine if the motion has been carried out actively or passively. A special point is the type of warm-up (see General Discussion).

(c) Knowledge of external factors influencing flexibility

Some external factors influencing flexibility are temperature, exercise, gender, age, race, professional flexibility needs, sports flexibility needs and pathology.

(d) Scientific rigour and precision in the choice and use of the goniometer

The following recommendations are made:

1. The goniometer needs to have long arms sufficient to reach two reference points.
2. The goniometer needs to have a protractor with a precision of one degree.
3. Esch and Lepley (1974) have pointed out the danger of creating parallax errors; therefore readings should be made at eye level.
4. The presence of a thin indicator line on the goniometer's arms can be helpful for increasing the goniometer's precision.
5. No loose articulation in the goniometer should be allowed.
6. Readings should be made prior to removing the goniometer from the segments.
7. The measurements should be recorded with three figures. If a recorder assists the examiner, the values should be dictated by the examiner as, for example, one-five-three rather than one hundred and fifty three. This should then be repeated and recorded on a pro forma by the recorder.
8. The pro forma (Figure 5.7) should contain personal details of the subject being measured (e.g. age, gender, profession, sport activities, daily habitual activity) as well as technical information regarding the measurements (starting position, room temperature).

(e) Replication of measurements

From experience, we know that data from a very large number of consecutive measurements are normally distributed around a value which very likely approaches the true amplitude. Thus, a difference of, for example, 5° with a later measurement is not necessarily an increase in amplitude but rather the result of a summation of small systematic errors and the absolute measurement error. Therefore, it is recommended to perform triple measurements with the median or the average of the two closest results as central value.

5.4.4 THE MEASUREMENTS

Considering the limitation of space in this book, only a selection of possible measurements is presented in the following pages. Special emphasis is given to a technique for measuring straight leg raising as a measurement of coxofemoral flexibility.

PROFORMA FOR GONIOMETRIC MEASUREMENTS

01. Subject .... ☐☐☐☐
    (Last name)   (First name)

02. Identity   Sex F=2 M=1   ☐
03. Date of observations year ☐☐ mo ☐☐ day ☐☐   ☐☐☐☐☐
04. Date of birth   year ☐☐ mo ☐☐ day ☐☐   ☐☐☐☐☐
05. Room t°   ☐☐☐

06. Body Mass (kg)   ☐☐☐☐
07. Stature (stretched/cm) ☐☐☐☐ ☐☐☐☐ ☐☐☐☐ ☐☐☐☐

08. Shoulder flexion   ☐☐☐ ☐☐☐ ☐☐☐ ☐☐☐
09. Shoulder extension   ☐☐☐ ☐☐☐ ☐☐☐ ☐☐☐
10. Shoulder lateral rotation   ☐☐☐ ☐☐☐ ☐☐☐ ☐☐☐
11. Shoulder medial rotation   ☐☐☐ ☐☐☐ ☐☐☐ ☐☐☐
12. Shoulder abduction   ☐☐☐ ☐☐☐ ☐☐☐ ☐☐☐
13. Shoulder horizontal adduction ☐☐☐ ☐☐☐ ☐☐☐ ☐☐☐
14. Elbow flexion   ☐☐☐ ☐☐☐ ☐☐☐ ☐☐☐
15. Elbow extension   ☐☐☐ ☐☐☐ ☐☐☐ ☐☐☐
16. Forearm pronation   ☐☐☐ ☐☐☐ ☐☐☐ ☐☐☐
17. Forearm supination   ☐☐☐ ☐☐☐ ☐☐☐ ☐☐☐
18. Wrist flexion   ☐☐☐ ☐☐☐ ☐☐☐ ☐☐☐
19. Wrist extension   ☐☐☐ ☐☐☐ ☐☐☐ ☐☐☐
20. Wrist radial deviation   ☐☐☐ ☐☐☐ ☐☐☐ ☐☐☐
21. Wrist ulnar deviation   ☐☐☐ ☐☐☐ ☐☐☐ ☐☐☐
22. Hip flexion (bent leg)   ☐☐☐ ☐☐☐ ☐☐☐ ☐☐☐
23. Hip flexion (straight leg)   ☐☐☐ ☐☐☐ ☐☐☐ ☐☐☐
24. Hip extension   ☐☐☐ ☐☐☐ ☐☐☐ ☐☐☐
25. Hip abduction   ☐☐☐ ☐☐☐ ☐☐☐ ☐☐☐
26. Hip adduction   ☐☐☐ ☐☐☐ ☐☐☐ ☐☐☐
27. Hip medial rotation   ☐☐☐ ☐☐☐ ☐☐☐ ☐☐☐
28. Hip lateral rotation   ☐☐☐ ☐☐☐ ☐☐☐ ☐☐☐
29. Knee flexion   ☐☐☐ ☐☐☐ ☐☐☐ ☐☐☐
30. Knee extension   ☐☐☐ ☐☐☐ ☐☐☐ ☐☐☐
31. Knee medial rotation   ☐☐☐ ☐☐☐ ☐☐☐ ☐☐☐
32. Knee lateral rotation   ☐☐☐ ☐☐☐ ☐☐☐ ☐☐☐
33. Ankle dorsiflexion   ☐☐☐ ☐☐☐ ☐☐☐ ☐☐☐
34. Ankle plantarflexion   ☐☐☐ ☐☐☐ ☐☐☐ ☐☐☐

WARM-UP :   YES ☐   NO ☐

     IF YES : HOW LONG, WHAT KIND ?
     ....
     ....

SPORT :
     ....

DAILY PHYSICAL ACTIVITY :
     ....

BODY TYPE :
     ....

INJURIES :
     ....

TESTING :   Passive ☐   Active ☐

Figure 5.7 Pro forma for goniometric measurements.

(a) Shoulder flexion

- A protractor or modified goniometer is recommended.
- The subject lies supine on a table, with legs bent, and the thorax fixed on the table with Velcro straps. The subject executes a bilateral shoulder flexion in a pure sagittal plane, with hand palms turned towards each other and elbows extended (Figure 5.8).
- Landmarks are made at the middle of the lateral side of the upper arm at the level of the deltoid tuberosity and of the lateral epicondyle of the humerus.

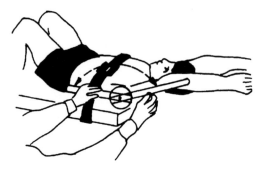

Figure 5.8 Measurement of shoulder flexion.

- The stationary arm of the goniometer is positioned along the thorax parallel to the board of the table, while the moving arm is in line with the longitudinal axis of the upper arm, oriented on both landmarks.

(b) Shoulder extension

- We recommend a protractor or modified goniometer.
- The subject lies prone on a table, with the head in neutral position (if possible), and with a small pillow under the abdomen to avoid hyperlordosis. A bilateral shoulder extension is executed in a sagittal plane, with elbows extended, and hand palms in the prolongation of the forearms turned towards each other (Figure 5.9).
- The landmarks are: the middle of the lateral side of the upper arm at the level of the deltoid tuberosity and the lateral epicondyle of the humerus.

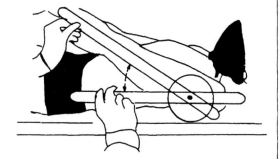

Figure 5.9 Measurement of shoulder extension.

- The stationary arm of the goniometer is positioned along the thorax parallel to the board of the table and the moving arm is in line with the longitudinal axis of the upper arm, oriented on both landmarks.

(c) Shoulder lateral (external) rotation

- We recommend the Labrique goniometer and the use of its blue scale.
- The subject lies prone on a table, with the shoulder in 90° abduction, the elbow flexed 90°, the wrist in neutral position (hand in prolongation of forearm, the palm towards the end of the table, thumb directed towards the medial axis of the body), the upper arm resting on the table, with the elbow free. The subject performs a maximal lateral rotation, fixing

the humerus in the same abduction angle on the table, with the shoulder in contact with the table, the head in neutral position (if possible) (Figure 5.10).

- The landmarks are the tip of the olecranon and the tip of the ulnar styloid process (this side is facing the end of the table).
- The goniometer is positioned in line with the longitudinal axis of the forearm, oriented on both landmarks.

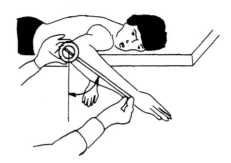

Figure 5.10 Measurement of shoulder lateral (external) rotation.

(d) Shoulder medial (internal) rotation

- We recommend the Labrique goniometer and the use of its blue scale.
- The subject lies prone on a table, with the shoulder in 90° abduction, the elbow flexed 90°, the wrist in neutral position (hand in prolongation of forearm), the palm towards the end of the table, thumb directed towards the medial axis of the body), the upper arm resting on the table, with the elbow free. The subject performs a maximal medial rotation, fixing the humerus in the same abduction angle on the table, with the shoulder in contact with the table, the head in neutral position (Figure 5.11).

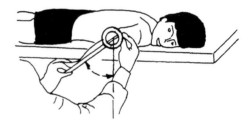

- The landmarks are the tip of the olecranon and the tip of the ulnar styloid process (this side is facing the end of the table).

Figure 5.11 Measurement of shoulder medial (internal) rotation.

- The goniometer is positioned in line with the longitudinal axis of the forearm, oriented on both landmarks.

(e) Shoulder abduction

- The protractor goniometer is recommended for this measurement.
- The subject sits on a chair, with feet on the floor, and hips and knees flexed 90°. The abduction is performed bilaterally in order to avoid compensatory movements within the spine (Figure 5.12). The palms are kept in a pure sagittal plane, with thumbs directed forwards, the elbows extended, and the wrists in neutral position (palms in prolongation of forearms).

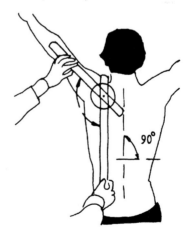

Figure 5.12 Measurement of shoulder abduction.

- Landmarks are indicated, when maximal abduction is reached, on the middle of the superior part of the upper arm and on the lateral epicondyle of the humerus. The angulus acromii and the deltoid tuberosity can be helpful in determining the middle of the upper part of the humerus.
- The stationary arm of the goniometer is positioned parallel with the spine, the moving arm is in line with the longitudinal axis of the humerus, oriented on both landmarks.

(f) Shoulder horizontal adduction

- The protractor goniometer is recommended for this measurement.
- The subject sits on a chair, with the feet on the floor, and hips and knees flexed 90°, with the back against a wall; the extended arm is kept at 90°, horizontally forwards, and the hand is in the prolongation of the forearm, palm facing the medial axis of the body. A maximal adduction of the arm is performed in a horizontal plane, while both shoulder blades remain in contact with the wall (Figure 5.13).
- When maximal horizontal adduction is reached, landmarks are indicated on the middle of the upper and the lower part of the humerus. The deltoid tuberosity and the most ventral aspect of the lateral epicondyle of the humerus can be helpful in determining these landmarks.
- The stationary arm of the goniometer is kept parallel with the wall, the moving arm is parallel with the longitudinal axis of the upper arm, oriented on both landmarks; it is important to read the ROM on the external (green) scale of the goniometer.

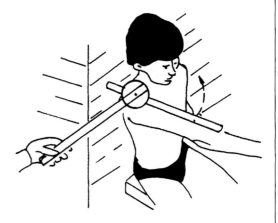

Figure 5.13 Measurement of shoulder horizontal adduction.

(g) Elbow flexion

- The protractor goniometer is recommended for this measurement.
- The subject lies supine on a table, with knees flexed and the feet on the table. The arm to be measured is held in a sagittal plane. The forearm is in a neutral position (palm directed toward the thigh). The subject performs a complete flexion of the elbow (Figure 5.14). The hand remains extended, in the prolongation of the forearm.
- The stationary arm of the goniometer is positioned parallel with the longitudinal axis of the humerus. The deltoid tuberosity and the ventral aspect of the lateral epicondyle of the humerus under the extensor carpi radialis longus and brevis muscles can be helpful in determining the midline of the humerus.
- The moving arm of the goniometer is aligned parallel with the longitudinal axis of the forearm. The middle of the radial head under the extensor carpi radialis longus and

brevis muscles, and the styloid process of the radius can be helpful in determining the reference points for the forearm.

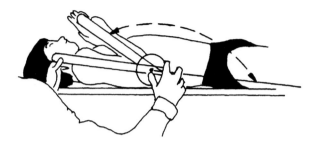

Figure 5.14 Measurement of elbow flexion.

(h) Elbow extension

- The protractor goniometer is recommended for this measurement.
- The subject lies supine on a table, with knees flexed, and feet on the table. The arm to be measured is situated in a sagittal plane, the elbow is flexed, and the forearm is in a position between pronation and supination.
- For the measurement of elbow hyperextension, the subject sits on a chair with the arm and forearm in the same base position as above. The subject extends (or eventually hyperextends) the elbow (Figure 5.15). The hand remains extended in the prolongation of the forearm. The thumb and fingers are kept together.

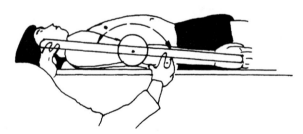

Figure 5.15 Measurement of elbow extension.

- Landmarks are indicated, at maximal ROM, on the acromiale, the tip of the lateral epicondyle of the humerus and on the head of the capitate bone.
- The stationary arm of the goniometer is positioned parallel with the longitudinal axis of the humerus. The deltoid tuberosity and the ventral aspect of the lateral epicondyle of the humerus under the extensor carpi radialis longus and brevis muscles can be helpful in determining the midline of the humerus.
- The moving arm of the goniometer is aligned parallel with the longitudinal axis of the forearm. The middle of the radial head under the extensor carpi radialis longus and brevis muscles, and the styloid process of the radius can be helpful in determining the reference points for the forearm.

(i) Forearm pronation

- The Labrique goniometer used in its holder is recommended.
- The subject sits on a chair. The upper arm of the side to be measured is held in a neutral position, the elbow is flexed 90°, and the forearm is kept in a neutral position between pronation and supination. The hand is extended, in the prolongation of the forearm with the fingers extended and kept together. The subject performs a complete pronation (Figure 5.16), taking care that the humerus remains in a pure vertical position and that no compensatory motion occurs in the shoulder girdle and/or the spine. (Should this occur, bilateral pronations should be carried out.)
- Eventually, landmarks could be indicated on the dorsal side of the head of the ulna and on the distal epiphysis of the radius.

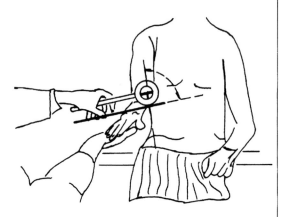

Figure 5.16 Measurement of forearm pronation.

- The flat side of the goniometer holder is placed against the dorsal side of the most distal part of the forearm, while the red scale is kept upwards and the pointer indicates zero degrees before pronation is performed.

(j) Forearm supination

- The Labrique goniometer used in its holder is recommended for this technique.
- The subject sits on a chair. The upper arm of the side to be measured is held in a neutral position, the elbow is flexed 90°, and the forearm is kept in a neutral position between pronation and supination. The hand is extended, in the prolongation of the forearm with the fingers extended and kept together. The subject performs a complete supination (Figure 5.17), taking care that the humerus remains in a pure vertical position and that no compensatory motion occurs in the shoulder girdle and/or the spine. (Should this occur bilateral supinations should be carried out.)
- Eventually, landmarks could be indicated on the dorsal side of the head of the ulna and on the distal epiphysis of the radius.

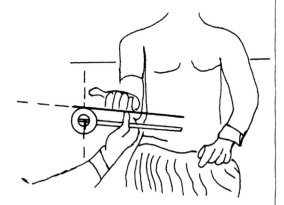

Figure 5.17 Measurement of forearm supination.

- The flat side of the goniometer holder is placed against the dorsal side of the most distal part of the forearm, while the blue scale is kept upwards and the pointer indicates zero degrees before supination is performed.

(k) Wrist flexion

- The protractor goniometer is recommended.
- The subject sits on a chair, the upper arm along the trunk, the elbow flexed 90°, the forearm in pronation, not in support, and the hand and fingers are aligned with the forearm. A maximal wrist flexion is executed, metacarpals and phalanges of fingers are kept in one line, and the thumb is kept in neutral position (Figure 5.18).
- A first line, reflecting the longitudinal axis of the third metacarpal bone between the base and the head of this metacarpal at the dorsal side, functions as one landmark. A second line, reflecting the longitudinal axis of the forearm which, for this purpose, can be drawn between the lateral epicondyle of the humerus and the tip of the styloid process of the ulna, serves as the other landmark.

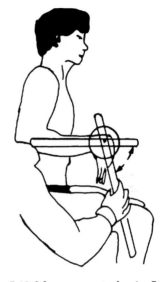

Figure 5.18 Measurement of wrist flexion.

- The stationary arm of the goniometer is positioned parallel with the longitudinal axis of the forearm, oriented on both landmarks.
- The moving arm is in line with the longitudinal axis of the third metacarpal bone, observed at the dorsal side.

(l) Wrist extension

- The protractor goniometer is recommended.
- The subject sits on a chair, the upper arm along the trunk, the elbow flexed 90°, the forearm in pronation, not in support, and the hand and fingers are aligned with the forearm. A maximal wrist extension is executed, fingers flexed to avoid passive insufficiency of the finger flexors, thumb fixed inside the closed fist (Figure 5.19).

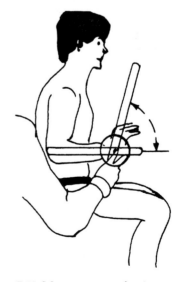

Figure 5.19 Measurement of wrist extension.

- A first line, reflecting the longitudinal axis of the third metacarpal bone, between the base and the head of this metacarpal at the dorsal side, functions as one landmark. A second line, reflecting the longitudinal axis of the forearm which, for this purpose, can be drawn between the lateral epicondyle of the humerus and the tip of the styloid process of the ulna, serves as the other landmark.
- The stationary arm of the goniometer is positioned parallel with the longitudinal axis of the forearm, oriented on both landmarks.
- The moving arm is in line with the longitudinal axis of the third metacarpal bone, observed at the dorsal side.

(m) Wrist radial deviation

- The protractor goniometer is recommended for this measurement which is alternatively indicated in the literature as radial abduction or radial inclination.
- The subject sits on a chair with the upper arms kept along the body. The elbow at the side to be measured is flexed 90°, the forearm is in pronation and in support on a table. The hand and fingers are in the prolongation of the forearm.
- The subject performs a radial deviation in the wrist (Figure 5.20) while the palm of the hand remains continuously in contact with the table. The fingers and thumbs are kept together. The humerus should not move.
- Landmarks are indicated at maximal radial deviation.

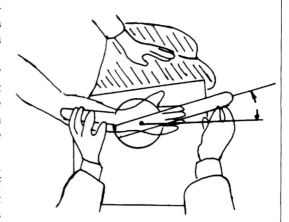

Figure 5.20 Measurement of wrist radial deviation.

- The stationary arm of the goniometer is parallel with the longitudinal axis of the forearm, held in pronation. To identify this line, it can be helpful to situate the middle of the upper part of the forearm between the brachioradialis muscle and the extensor carpi radialis muscle, and to localize the middle of the connection between the radial and the ulnar styloid processes in the lower part of the forearm.
- The moving arm of the goniometer is held parallel with the longitudinal axis of the third metacarpal, situated between the middle of the dorsal aspect of the basis and the middle of the dorsal aspect of the head of this metacarpal bone.

(n) Wrist ulnar deviation

- The protractor goniometer is recommended for this measurement which is alternatively indicated in the literature as ulnar abduction or ulnar inclination.
- The subject sits on a chair with upper arms kept along the body. The elbow at the side to be measured is flexed 90°, the forearm is in pronation and in support on a table. The hand and fingers are in the prolongation of the forearm.

- The subject performs ulnar deviation in the wrist (Figure 5.21) while the palm of the hand remains continuously in contact with the table. The fingers and thumbs are kept together. The humerus should not move.
- Landmarks are indicated at maximal ulnar deviation.
- The stationary arm of the goniometer is parallel with the longitudinal axis of the forearm, held in pronation. To identify this line, it can be helpful to situate the middle of the upper part of the forearm between the brachioradialis muscle and the extensor carpi radialis muscle, and to localize the middle of the connection between the radial and the ulnar styloid processes in the lower part of the forearm.

Figure 5.21 Measurement of wrist ulnar deviation.

- The moving arm of the goniometer is held parallel with the longitudinal axis of the third metacarpal, situated between the middle of the dorsal aspect of the basis and the middle of the dorsal aspect of the head of this metacarpal bone.

(o) Hip flexion (bent leg)

- We recommend the Labrique goniometer and use of its red scale.
- The subject lies supine on a table and carries out, in a pure sagittal plane, a complete flexion in the hip, with bent knee to avoid passive insufficiency of the hamstrings (Figure 5.22). When the opposite leg is beginning to lose contact with the table, a reading of the amplitude should be made, as this is a sign that the movement is continued in the spine. Therefore it is recommended to use a Velcro strap at the distal end of the opposite thigh or to call for assistance.
- The landmarks are the tip of the greater trochanter and the lateral femoral epicondyle.

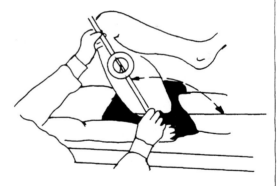

Figure 5.22 Measurement of hip flexion (bent leg).

- The goniometer is kept with the red scale left of the examiner (the needle is then at zero degrees at the start of the motion), in line with the longitudinal axis of the thigh oriented on both landmarks.

(p) Straight leg raising as a measurement of coxofemoral flexibility

- When the effect of hamstring stretches on coxofemoral flexibility (hip flexion with a straight leg) is measured by goniometry, the examiner should take into account the angular change between the pelvis and the femur (Mundale *et al.*, 1956; Clayson *et al.*, 1966). Straight leg raising indeed includes a posterior pelvic tilt and a reduction of lumbar lordosis.

- First a transverse line for the pelvis should be considered, connecting the anterior superior iliac spine with the posterior superior iliac spine (line *AB* in Figure 5.23). A line *CD* drawn perpendicular to this line in the direction of the most superior point of the greater trochanter serves as the longitudinal axis for the pelvis, and a line *DE* from the most superior point of the greater trochanter to the lateral epicondyle of the femur serves as the longitudinal axis of the femur. Between the lines *CD* and *DE*, an angle, α, can be measured in the resting position. An angle, β, is obtained between these reference lines in maximal flexion (Figure 5.24). Hence, in order to obtain the result of an isolated coxofemoral flexion, the value of α must be subtracted from that of β.

Figure 5.23 Reference lines for the measurement of hip extension described by Mundale *et al.* (1956).

- We recommend the VUB goniometer with a second carriage (Figure 5.25) which can slide along one of the arms and through which a very flexible piece of plastic can be inserted (based on previous work by Clayson *et al.*, 1966).

- The subject lies sideways with the trunk aligned with the posterior edge of a table (Figure 5.26 a, b). For reasons of stability the supporting leg is slightly bent at the hip and knee joints, with the sole of the foot parallel with the posterior edge of the table. Before starting the measurements, care must be taken to ensure that the acromiale, the superior point of the greater trochanter and the lateral epicondyle of the femur are well aligned. This position offers several advantages. The reference points on the pelvis and

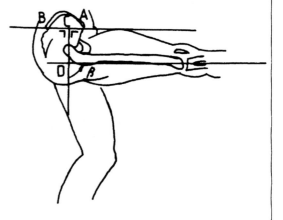

Figure 5.24 Angle β between the reference lines considered in the position of maximal hip flexion with the straight leg.

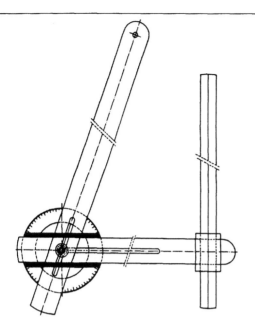

Figure 5.25 VUB goniometer with second carriage.

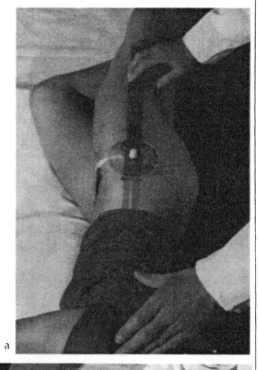

a

femur can be more easily reached. It also offers stability of the subject's body while moving, and hip flexion against gravity is avoided. In a pilot study (Van Roy *et al.*, 1987) a significant difference was obtained between the measurements of angle α in lying sideways and those of angle α in the normal standing position. Once angle α is determined, maximal hip flexion without bending the knee is performed. Abduction of the subject's leg can be eliminated by an

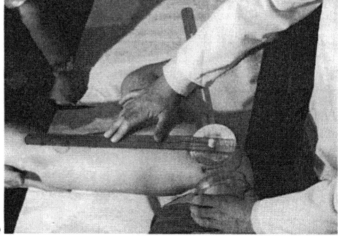

b

Figure 5.26 (a and b) Measurement of hip flexion (straight leg).

assistant who supports the leg during the movement. This assistant should not push the leg into passive hip flexion and should instruct the subject not to perform movements of the hip rotations, knee flexions or movements of the ankle joint during hamstring stretching. The angle β is determined. The final result is obtained by subtracting angle α from angle β.

(q) Hip extension

- The Labrique goniometer and its blue scale are used, or alternatively, another inclinometer with long arm(s) is recommended.
- The subject lies prone at the end of a table, with legs outside the table, the feet on the ground, with a small pillow under the abdomen; the opposite leg is in the greatest possible flexion at the hip; with the hands gripping the sides of the table. A maximal extension in the hip is performed while the opposite leg is kept bent (Figure 5.27).
- The landmarks are the tip of the greater trochanter and the lateral femoral condyle.
- The goniometer is kept with the blue scale left of the examiner (the needle is then at zero degrees at the start of the motion), in line with the longitudinal axis of the thigh oriented on both landmarks.

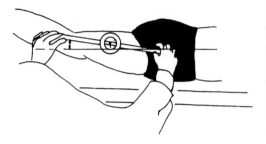

Figure 5.27 Measurement of hip extension.

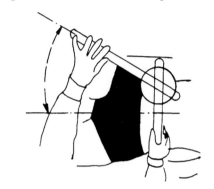

Figure 5.28 Measurement of hip abduction.

(r) Hip abduction

- The protractor (with long arms) or modified goniometer is recommended.
- The subject lies supine on a table with the opposite hip in slight abduction in order to allow the lower leg of the opposite leg to hang outside the table so that the hips can be stabilized. A maximal abduction is performed with a straight leg in the plane of the table, without lateral rotation of the foot point at the end of the movement (Figure 5.28).
- The landmarks are the left and right superior anterior iliac spines and the lateral board of the quadriceps tendon.
- The stationary arm of the goniometer is positioned on the line between both spines.
- The moving arm is in line with the longitudinal axis of the thigh, oriented on the spine of the side to be measured and the lateral board of the quadriceps tendon.

(s) Hip adduction

- The protractor goniometer (with long arms) is recommended.
- The subject lies supine on a table. A maximal adduction is performed with a

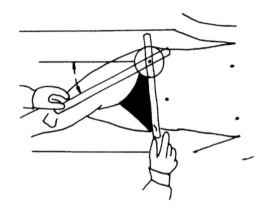

Figure 5.29 Measurement of hip adduction.

slightly elevated thigh (about 40° hip flexion), and an extended knee, without rotation in the hip (Figure 5.29).

- The landmarks are the left and right superior anterior iliac spines and lateral board of the quadriceps tendon.
- The stationary arm of the goniometer is positioned on the line between both spines; the moving arm is in line with the longitudinal axis of the thigh, oriented on the spine of the side to be measured and the lateral board of the quadriceps tendon.

(t) Hip medial (internal) rotation

- The Labrique goniometer with its blue scale is recommended for this measurement which is alternatively indicated in the literature as hip medial rotation.

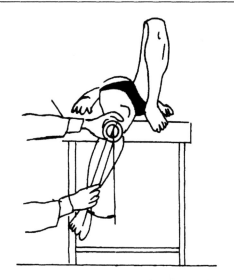

Figure 5.30 Measurement of hip medial (internal) rotation.

- The subject lies supine on a table with the contralateral leg bent at the knee and hip, and with the heel supported on the table. The hip at the side to be measured is in a neutral position relative to the trunk, the knee is flexed 90° and the lower leg hangs outside and at the end of the table. The pelvis is fixed on the table with a Velcro strap. The subject performs a maximal hip medial rotation (Figure 5.30). Compensatory motion such as pelvis tilt must be avoided.
- At maximum ROM, landmarks are indicated on the ventral margin of the tibia below the tuberosity of the tibia and on a point located about 5 cm above the tibiotarsal joint.
- The goniometer is kept so that the blue scale is positioned at the upper part of the tibia bone. The pointer now indicates zero degrees at the beginning of the movement. The goniometer is oriented on the landmarks.

(u) Hip lateral (external) rotation

- The Labrique goniometer with its blue scale is recommended for this measurement which is alternatively referred to in the literature as hip lateral rotation.
- The subject lies supine on a table with the contralateral leg bent at the knee and hip and with the heel supported on the table. The hip at the side to be measured is in a neutral position relative to the trunk, the knee is flexed 90° and the lower leg hangs outside and at the end of the table. The

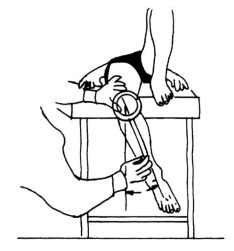

Figure 5.31 Measurement of hip lateral (external) rotation.

pelvis is fixed on the table with a Velcro strap. The subject performs a maximal hip lateral rotation (Figure 5.31). Compensatory motion such as pelvis tilt must be avoided.

- At maximum ROM, landmarks are indicated on the ventral margin of the tibia below the tuberosity of the tibia and on a point located about 5 cm above the tibiotarsal joint.
- The goniometer is kept so that the blue scale is positioned at the upper part of the tibia bone. The pointer now indicates zero degrees at the beginning of the movement. The goniometer is oriented on the landmarks.

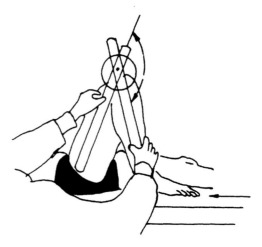

Figure 5.32 Measurement of knee flexion.

(v) Knee flexion

- The protractor goniometer (with long arms) is recommended.
- The subject lies supine on a table. A maximal flexion of the knee is performed, the sole of the foot gliding over the table in the direction of the heel (Figure 5.32).
- The landmarks are the tip of the greater trochanter, the lateral femoral epi- condyle, the tip of the fibular head and the middle of the inferior side of the lateral malleolus.
- The stationary arm of the goniometer is positioned in line with the longitudinal axis of the thigh, oriented on the tip of the greater trochanter and the lateral femoral epicondyle.
- The moving arm is in line with the longitudinal axis of the lower leg, oriented on both landmarks.

(w) Knee extension

- The protractor goniometer (with long arms) is recommended.
- The subject lies supine on a table, the leg to be measured flexed, the foot supported on the table, the opposite leg extended, and the arms alongside body. A maximal extension of the knee is performed, the sole of the foot gliding over the table in the direction of the end of the table (Figure 5.33).
- The landmarks are the tip of the greater trochanter, the lateral femoral epicondyle, the tip of the fibular head and

Figure 5.33 Measurement of knee extension.

the middle of the inferior side of the lateral malleolus.
- The stationary arm of the goniometer is positioned in line with the longitudinal axis of the thigh, oriented on both landmarks.
- The moving arm is in line with the longitudinal axis of the lower leg, oriented on both landmarks.

(x) Knee medial (internal) rotation

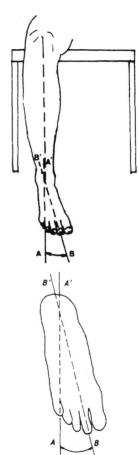

Figure 5.34 Measurement of knee medial (internal) rotation.

- A protractor goniometer is recommended.
- The subject sits on a chair with the hip and knee at the side to be measured flexed 90°. The foot is flat on a paper (size about 30 × 50 cm) fixed on the floor. The contralateral knee is a little more extended in order not to disturb the execution of the movement. The subject grasps, with both hands, the front side of the chair close to the knee to fix the lower limb. A maximal knee medial rotation is performed (Figure 5.34) without compensatory hip motion and knee flexion or extension.
- Landmarks are indicated on the projection of the middle of the calcaneus tuberosity at the bottom side of the heel. The landmarks must be localized on the paper when the foot is in neutral position (*AA'*); the same landmarks must then be indicated when the medial rotation of the knee is performed (*BB'*). Two lines *A–A'* and *B–B'* should be drawn and continued until they intersect.
- The angle between the two lines on the paper is subsequently read with the goniometer.

(y) Knee lateral (external) rotation

- A protractor goniometer is recommended.
- The subject sits on a chair with the hip and knee at the side to be measured flexed 90°. The foot is flat on a paper (size about 30 × 50 cm) fixed on the floor. The contralateral knee is a little more extended in order not to disturb the execution of the movement. The subject grasps, with both hands, the front side of the chair close to the knee to fix the lower limb. A maximal knee lateral rotation is performed (Figure 5.35) without compensatory hip motion and knee flexion or extension.

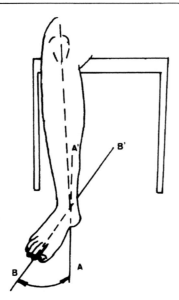

Figure 5.35 Measurement of knee lateral (external) rotation.

- Landmarks are indicated on the projection of the middle of the calcaneus tuberosity at the bottom side of the heel and at the longitudinal axis of the second metatarsal bone. The landmarks must be localized on the paper when the foot is in neutral position (*A–A'*); the same landmarks must then be indicated when the lateral rotation of the knee is performed (*B–B'*). Two lines *A–A'* and *B–B'* should be drawn and continued until they intersect.
- The angle between the two lines on the paper is subsequently read with the goniometer.

(z) Ankle dorsiflexion

- We recommend a modified or protractor goniometer with an extended stationary arm.
- The subject lies supine on a table, the lower legs hanging outside the table, the knees flexed 90° (to eliminate passive insufficiency of the gastrocnemius muscle. A maximal dorsiflexion is executed at the talocrural joint, making sure that the knee remains at 90° flexion (Figure 5.36).
- The landmarks are the tip of the fibular head at the lateral side of the lower leg and the middle of the inferior side of the lateral malleolus; a line parallel to the sole of the foot is drawn starting from the middle of the lateral side of the head of the fifth metatarsal.

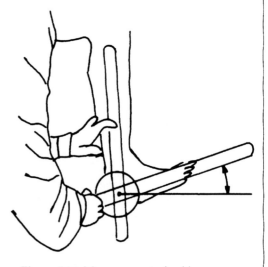

Figure 5.36 Measurement of ankle dorsiflexion.

- The stationary arm of the goniometer is in line with the longitudinal axis of the lower leg, oriented on both landmarks.
- The moving arm is in line with the longitudinal axis of the foot, oriented on the constructed reference line.

(aa) Ankle plantar flexion

- We recommend a modified or protractor goniometer with an extended stationary arm.
- The subject lies supine on a table, the lower legs hanging outside the table, with knees flexed 90°. A maximal plantar flexion is executed at the talocrural joint, making sure that the knee remains at 90° flexion. A flexion of the toes is normal with this movement (Figure 5.37).
- The landmarks are the tip of the fibular head at the lateral side of the lower leg and the middle of the inferior side of the lateral malleolus; a line parallel to the foot sole is drawn starting from the middle of the lateral side of the head of the fifth metatarsal.
- The stationary arm of the goniometer is in line with the longitudinal axis of the lower leg, oriented on both landmarks.
- The moving arm is in line with the longitudinal axis of the foot, oriented on the constructed reference line.

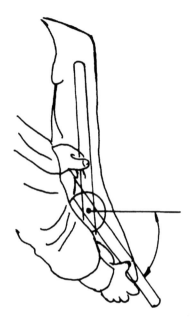

Figure 5.37 Measurement of ankle plantar flexion.

5.5 GENERAL DISCUSSION

From the detailed description of the measurements above, it should be clear that goniometry requires a good knowledge of anatomy and anthropometry. The goniometer is a reliable instrument when used by experienced individuals who follow carefully the standardized protocol.

When bony landmarks are visible or easy to determine, the goniometer usually provides an accurate and convenient clinical method of measuring joint motion. However, when the bony landmarks are not easy to locate, for

whatever reasons, the goniometer may not give accurate and satisfactory information.

Measurement precision will also improve when the examiner is assisted by a second examiner, checks and calibrates the equipment, explains the test procedures to the subject, adheres to triple measurements and notes on the pro forma those factors that may affect the test results such as age, gender, body type, certain pathologies or injuries, daily physical activities, room temperature and previous warm-up. Although most of these variables and their eventual causal relationship with flexibility have been reviewed elsewhere

(Borms, 1984; Hubley-Kozey, 1991), it is none-theless important to mention two factors among these, temperature and warm-up.

Although Wright (1973) demonstrated that stiffness increases with decreased temperature and vice versa and thus found a means of explaining the circadian variation in joint stiffness with lowest levels in the morning and late evening, others (Grobaker and Stull, 1975; Lakie *et al.*, 1979) could not entirely confirm these findings.

Research tends to indicate positive effects of warm-up (Skubic and Hodgkins, 1957; Atha and Wheatly, 1976). Most coaches and athletes believe that warm-up is essential to prevent injuries, but there is very little direct research

Table 5.1 Flexibility norms for men (physical education and physiotherapy students 20 years of age)

	Range	P_{25}	P_{50}	P_{75}
Shoulder flexion	154–195	170	177	188
Shoulder extension	25–80	43	49	59
Shoulder lateral rotation	43–93	56	72	79
Shoulder medial rotation	16–92	47	64	75
Shoulder abduction	110–199	143	156	181
Shoulder horizontal adduction	17–60	30	35	46
Elbow flexion	130–156	139	144	151
Elbow extension	168–191	175	179	181
Forearm pronation	40–98	78	85	91
Forearm supination	56–98	80	90	92
Wrist flexion	60–94	65	69	79
Wrist extension	45–88	58	67	75
Wrist radial deviation	12–38	20	27	30
Wrist ulnar deviation	19–59	33	44	50
Hip flexion (bent leg)	105–155	120	128	133
Hip flexion (straight leg)	—	—	—	—
Hip extension	9–29	18	21	26
Hip abduction	—	—	—	—
Hip adduction	9–68	16	29	31
Hip medial rotation	26–50	30	33	38
Hip lateral rotation	26–70	32	36	42
Knee flexion	130–155	136	142	146
Knee extension	160–187	175	178	181
Knee medial rotation	21–60	27	37	46
Knee lateral rotation	20–53	25	28	37
Ankle dorsiflexion	4–37	6	13	22
Ankle plantar flexion	18–78	47	57	70

Table 5.2   Flexibility norms for women (physical education and physiotherapy students 20 years of age)

	Range	P_{25}	P_{50}	P_{75}
Shoulder flexion	154–197	172	177	183
Shoulder extension	20–86	46	54	59
Shoulder lateral rotation	13–89	51	65	77
Shoulder medial rotation	24–89	52	66	74
Shoulder abduction	105–203	125	147	179
Shoulder horizontal adduction	11–55	27	36	40
Elbow flexion	128–161	136	144	151
Elbow extension	170–190	178	181	185
Forearm pronation	40–99	79	88	94
Forearm supination	51–99	80	88	91
Wrist flexion	62–95	68	70	79
Wrist extension	30–89	62	69	75
Wrist radial deviation	12–49	22	29	33
Wrist ulnar deviation	19–58	39	45	50
Hip flexion (bent leg)	103–155	115	126	130
Hip flexion (straight leg)	—	—	—	—
Hip extension	8–29	10	18	24
Hip abduction	—	—	—	—
Hip adduction	20–69	21	33	40
Hip medial rotation	24–65	29	32	37
Hip lateral rotation	23–62	27	30	35
Knee flexion	131–160	139	145	152
Knee extension	165–190	177	181	184
Knee medial rotation	20–69	38	48	56
Knee lateral rotation	22–54	26	34	43
Ankle dorsiflexion	1–31	12	14	20
Ankle plantar flexion	26–90	53	70	84

evidence to support their beliefs. Even though the scientific basis for recommending warm-up exercises is not conclusive, we advise a general warm-up prior to the main activity and prior to flexibility testing. A 5–10 minutes moderate intensity warm-up is suggested before testing, but should be standardized.

The interpretation of results can be done in different ways: pre-test and post-test comparisons (athletic season, before and after treatment and so on), carry-over effect, left-right comparisons and finally comparison with norms. The latter is difficult as few normative data exist for 'normal' populations (by age and gender) or for athletic groups. 'Normal' ROMs for athletes from different sports are not so well documented in the literature. Tables 5.1 and 5.2 give norms based on the measurements described in this chapter for a population of over 100 physical education and physiotherapy students, male and female (as separate groups). They were all tested in the period 1984–90. A typical pro forma, used by us, is displayed in Figure 5.7.

In general, there has been little appreciation that flexibility is more complex than one might think. Thus measurement procedures have remained relatively simple.

Although two-dimensional goniometry is very common in the daily practice of rehabilitation medicine and physiotherapy, it becomes clear that many shortcomings of two- dimensional joint motion analysis in general hamper its content validity. With an increasing interest in the different rotation and translation components of joint motion, many biomechanical studies on three-dimensional aspects of the joints of the extremities and the spine have been presented during the past decades.

In the search for standardization, attempts are developing to link biomechanical methodology and biomechanical language to the clinical needs and the traditional language of functional anatomy (Grood and Suntay, 1983; Benedetti *et al.*, 1994; Cappozzo and Della Croce, 1994; Bull and Amis, 1998). This will be particularly helpful in reducing the gap between fundamental research and applied technology in this field (Van Roy, 1988). This may lead to a more important implementation of real-time three-dimensional measuring techniques in the daily practice of several disciplines. Among other problems to solve, practical considerations deal with further study on the so-called neutral zero position of the joints and the clinical implications of alterations of the helical axes of joint motion.

REFERENCES

AAHPERD (1984). *Technical Manual, Health related Physical Fitness*. AAHPERD, Reston, VA.

Allard, P., Stokes, I.A.F. and Blanchi, J-P. (1995). eds. *Three-dimensional Analysis of Human Movement*. (Human Kinetics, Champaign, IL).

American Academy of Orthopaedic Surgeons (1965). *Joint Motion. Method of Measuring and Recording*. (Churchill Livingstone, Edinburgh, London and New York).

Atha, J. and Wheatly, D.W. (1976). The mobilizing effects of repeated measurement of hip flexion. *British Journal of Sports Medicine*, **10**, 22–5.

Benedetti, M.G., Cappozzo, A. and Leardini. A (1994). Anatomical landmark definition and identification. *CAMARC II Internal Report*, 15 May.

Borms, J. (1984). Importance of flexibility in overall physical fitness. *International Journal of Physical Education*, **XXI**, 15–26.

Borms, J., Van Roy, P., Santens, J.P. and Haentjens, A. (1987). Optimal duration of static stretching exercises for improvement of coxofemoral flexibility. *Journal of Sports Sciences*, **5**, 39–47.

Broer, M.H. and Galles, N.R.G. (1958). Importance of relationship between body measurements in performance of toe-touch test. *Research Quarterly*, **29**, 253–63.

Bull, A.M.J. and Amis, A.A. (1998). Knee joint motion: description and measurement. *Proceedings of the Institute of Mechanical Engineers*, **212**, 357–71.

Cappozzo, A. and Della Croce, U. (1994). The PGD Lexicon. *CAMARC II Internal Report*, 15 May.

Cappozzo A., Catani F., Della Croce U. and Leardini A. (1995). Position and orientation in space of bones during movement: anatomical frame definition and determination. *Clinical Biomechanics*, **10**, 171–8.

Cappozzo, A., Catani, F., Leardini, A., *et al.* (1996). Position and orientation in space of bones during movement: experimental artefacts. *Clinical Biomechanics*, **11**, 90–100.

Cave, E.F. and Roberts, S.M. (1936). A method of measuring and recording joint function. *The Journal of Bone and Joint Surgery*, **18**, 455–65.

Clayson, S., Mundale, M. and Kottke, F. (1966). Goniometer adaptation for measuring hip extension. *Archives of Physical Medicine and Rehabilitation*, **47**, 255–61.

Council of Europe, Committee for the Development of Sport, Eurofit (1988). *Handbook for the Eurofit Tests of Physical Fitness*. Committee of the Development of Sport within the Council of Europe, Rome, p. 72.

Cureton, T.K. (1941). Flexibility as an aspect of physical fitness. *Research Quarterly*, **12**, 381–90.

Ekstrand, J., Wiktorsson, M., Oberg, B. and Gillquist, J. (1982). Lower extremity goniometric measurements: A study to determine their reliability. *Archives of Physical Medicine and Rehabilitation*, **63**, 171–5.

Esch, D. and Lepley, M. (1974). *Evaluation of joint motion; methods of measurement and recording*. (University of Minnesota Press, Minneapolis). p. 33.

Fox, R.F. (1917). Demonstration of the mensuration apparatus in use at the Red Cross Clinic for the physical treatment of Officers. *Proceedings of the Royal Society of Medicine*, **10**, 63–9.

Grobaker, M.R. and Stull, G.A. (1975). Thermal applications as a determiner of joint flexibility. *American Corrective Therapy Journal*, **25**, 3–8.

Grood, E.S. and Suntay, W.J. (1983). A joint co-ordinate system for the clinical description of three-dimensional motions: application to the knee. *Journal of Biomechanical Engineering*, **105**, 136–44.

Hopkins, D.R. and Hoeger, W.W.K. (1986). The modified sit and reach test. In *Lifetime Physical Fitness and Wellness: A Personalised Program*. ed. W.W.K. Hoeger (Morton Pub. Co., Englewood, CO), p. 47.

Hsiao, H. and Keyserling, W.M. (1990). Three-dimensional ultrasonic system for posture measurement. *Ergonomics*, **33**, 1089–114.

Hubley-Kozey, C.L. (1991). Testing Flexibility, Chapter 7. In *Physiological Testing of the High-Performance Athlete*. eds. J.D. MacDougall, H.A. Wenger and H.J. Green (Human Kinetics, Champaign, IL), pp. 309–59.

Kottke, F.J. and Mundale, M.O. (1959). Range of mobility of the cervical spine. *Archives of Physical Medicine and Rehabilitation*, **47**, 379–82.

Kraus, H. and Hirschland, R.P. (1954). Minimum muscular fitness tests in school children. *Research Quarterly*, **25**, 178–88.

Labrique, Ph. (1977). *Le goniomètre de Labrique*. (Prodim, Brussels).

Lakie, M.I, Walsh, E.G. and Wright, G.W. (1979). Cooling and wrist compliance. *Journal of Physiology*, **296**, 47–8.

Larson, L.A. ed. (1974). *Fitness, Health and Work capacity: International Standards for Assessment*. (Macmillan Publishing Co. Inc., New York).

Leighton, J.R. (1966). The Leighton flexometer and flexibility test. *Journal of the Association for Physical and Mental Rehabilitation*, **20**, 86–93.

Mundale, M.O., Hislop, H.J., Rabideau, R.J. and Kottke, F.J. (1956). Evaluation of extension of the hip. *Archives of Physical Medicine*, **37**, 75–80.

Nicol, A.C. (1987). A new flexible electrogoniometer with widespread applications. In *Biomechanics X-B*. ed. B. Jonsson (Human Kinetics, Champaign, IL), pp. 1029–33.

Rocher, C. and Rigaud, A. (1964). Fonctions et bilans articulaires. *Kinésitherapie et Rééducation*. (Masson, Paris).

Scott, M.G. and French, E. (1950). *Evaluation in Physical Education*. (C.V. Mosby, St. Louis).

Skubic, V. and Hodgkins, J. (1957). Effect of warm-up activities on speed, strength and accuracy. *Research Quarterly*, **28**, 147–52.

Tesio, L., Monzani, M., Gatti, R. and Franchignoni, F. (1995). Flexible electrogoniometers: kinesiological advantages with respect to potentiometric goniometers. *Clinical Biomechanics*, **10**, 275–7.

Van Roy, P. (1981). *Investigation on the validity of goniometry as measuring technique to assess wrist flexibility* (in Dutch). Unpublished Licentiate thesis: Vrije Universiteit Brussel.

Van Roy, P. (1988). *Magnetic Resonance Imaging of the knee joint, with a special application: 3-D arthrokinematic investigation of the screw-home movement of the knee* (in Dutch). Unpublished Ph.D. thesis: Vrije Universiteit Brussel, 148–79.

Van Roy, P., Hebbelinck, M. and Borms, J. (1985). Introduction d'un goniomètre standard modifié avec la graduation et la branche pivotante montées sur un chariot déplacable. *Annales de Kinésitherapie*, **12**, 255–9.

Van Roy, P., Borms, J. and Haentjens, A. (1987). Goniometric study of the maintenance of hip flexibility resulting from hamstring stretches. *Physiotherapy Practice*, **3**, 52–9.

Wells, K.F. and Dillon, E.K. (1952). The sit and reach, a test of back and leg flexibility. *Research Quarterly*, **23**, 115–18.

Wright, V. (1973). Stiffness: a review of its measurement and physiological importance. *Physiotherapy*, **59**, 107–11.

Wright, V. and Johns, R.J. (1960). Physical factors concerned with the stiffness of normal and diseased joints. *John Hopkins Hospital Bulletin*, **106**, 215–31.

PART THREE

ASSESSMENT OF PHYSICAL ACTIVITY AND PERFORMANCE

FIELD METHODS OF ASSESSING PHYSICAL ACTIVITY AND ENERGY BALANCE

6

Ann V. Rowlands

6.1 AIMS

The aims of this chapter are:
- to demonstrate the importance of measuring physical activity accurately,
- to distinguish between physical activity and energy expenditure,
- to understand the options available to measure physical activity and the advantages and disadvantages associated with each,
- to consider the appropriateness of each method of assessing physical activity for any given question (taking into consideration the population involved, the accuracy of information required, cost restrictions, sample size and the type of physical activity that needs to be quantified).

6.2 PHYSICAL ACTIVITY AND HEALTH

6.2.1 ADULTS

The risks of an inactive lifestyle on the health of adults are well established. Sedentary living increases the risk of developing coronary heart disease, obesity, osteoporosis, hypertension and atherosclerosis (Bouchard *et al.*, 1994). Being physically active may also contribute to mental health; the incidence of depression is lower in habitually active people (Brown, 1990; McAuley, 1994).

6.2.2 CHILDREN

In children the relationship between physical activity and health is less clear than it is in adults. Risk factors for coronary artery disease have been found in children as young as three years old (Saris, 1986; Sallis *et al.*, 1988), but it is not known whether the presence or absence of risk factors are related to children's activity levels. There are several possible reasons for this: a relationship between activity levels and health may only be present in the adult; current methods of measuring activity in children may not be sensitive enough to assess the typical spontaneous bursts of activity typical in childhood; or activity levels in childhood may have a delayed effect and not be apparent until adult life (Blair *et al.*, 1989). Studies of the relationship between physical activity and levels of body fat have produced contrasting results. A meta-analysis of fifty studies identified a small to moderate negative relationship between current physical activity levels and body fat in children (Rowlands *et al.*, 2000).

6.3 TRACKING OF PHYSICAL ACTIVITY

It has been argued that physical activity should be promoted in childhood even if there is little evidence for a positive effect on the

Kinanthropometry and Exercise Physiology Laboratory Manual: Tests, Procedures and Data. 2nd Edition, Volume 1: Anthropometry
Edited by RG Eston and T Reilly. Published by Routledge, London, June 2001

cardiovascular health of children (Gutin and Owens, 1996). This is partly based on the assumption that an active child is more likely to be active in adult life, where the health-physical activity links have been proved. There is limited evidence for the tracking of physical activity from childhood to adulthood (Activity and Health Research, 1992). However, methodological difficulties may decrease the chances of identifying a link. Studies have relied on adults' recall of how active they were as children and on childhood participation in sports teams/clubs (Dishman and Dunn, 1988), and therefore have not used objective methods to assess childhood activity patterns. This method is confounded by problems relating to children's limited ability to recall activities (Sallis, 1991). This is naturally compounded when adults attempt to remember their childhood activities. Additionally, in longitudinal studies, the emotional and cognitive development of the child would be a confounding variable, affecting the accuracy of recall of physical activities.

If an active childhood can delay or prevent chronic diseases, either directly or by increasing the likelihood of maintaining activity during adult life, quality of life could be improved and chronic health care costs decreased. This is particularly important as the average lifespan is increasing with an increased ageing population (Spirduso, 1995, pp. 8–11). Together with the increase in sedentary lifestyles, there could be large increases in the number of people needing hospital and nursing care, hence leading to enormous health costs, just at a time when there are fewer young people to pay for them.

6.4 WHY ESTIMATE PHYSICAL ACTIVITY? THE NEED FOR A VALID MEASURE

Whether or not there are health benefits related to childhood physical activity, and whether or not these benefits come in childhood or adulthood, remains unresolved without valid and objective methods for assessing

children's physical activity. Whether or not a relationship is detected between physical activity and health may depend on the type of activity measure used (Rowlands et al., 1999; 2000). Similarly, the degree of tracking of physical activity from childhood to adulthood cannot be determined without an objective method for the measurement of activity levels throughout childhood and adulthood.

As mentioned earlier, in adults physical activity has been shown to reduce the risk of chronic disease (Bouchard et al., 1994). However, the effects of physical activity on the various forms of cancer are not understood. The strongest evidence is for a link between physical inactivity and colon cancer; approximately three-quarters of published studies have shown that physically active people have a lower incidence of colon cancer than inactive people (Nieman, 1998). An accurate, objective method of assessing activity may allow more insight into the effects, if any, of physical activity on the risk of this and other forms of cancer.

The lack of an accurate, objective, unobtrusive activity measure has been the major limiting factor in this type of research. Ideally, it is desirable to record the normal daily energy expenditure of an adult or child. This can require the subject to be burdened with equipment for measuring a number of physiological functions, for example oxygen uptake (Saris, 1986), which hinders normal daily activities.

Various methods have been employed in an attempt to solve this problem. The major shortcoming of all of the techniques is inadequate validation. This is the greatest obstacle in the assessment of daily physical activity. Without an adequate criterion by which techniques can be compared it is impossible to determine the true validity of any method (Montoye et al., 1996).

6.5 ENERGY EXPENDITURE AND PHYSICAL ACTIVITY

The terms energy expenditure and physical activity are not synonymous and cannot be used interchangeably. The same amount of energy may be expended in a short burst of strenuous exercise as in less intense endurance exercise of longer duration (Montoye *et al.*, 1996). However, the physiological effect of the two activities may be quite different.

6.5.1 EFFECT OF SIZE ON ENERGY EXPENDITURE MEASURES

Obese individuals have a higher total energy expenditure than non-obese individuals. When total energy expenditure is normalized for fat-free mass there appears to be no difference between obese and non-obese children (Goran, 1997). This indicates a lower level of actual activity in the obese children as any given movement will demand greater energy expenditure in the child with excess fat. Hence, energy expenditure is heavily dependent on body size. This highlights the importance of differentiating between physical activity and energy expenditure. It is unclear which aspects of physical activity are important in regulating body mass, so it is important to measure as many of these factors as possible. Goran (1997) has suggested that intensity, activity time, metabolic efficiency, overall energy cost, and the type of physical activity are relevant factors for consideration.

The ratio of total energy expenditure to basal metabolic rate (BMR) is known as physical activity level, which therefore expresses the physical activity level as a multiple of the BMR. Expressing energy expenditure as physical activity level removes the effect of body mass on energy expenditure (Black *et al.*, 1996). However, information is limited to a single number representing energy expended. No information regarding the physical activity pattern or intensity of individual activities is obtained.

6.6 METHODS OF ESTIMATING PHYSICAL ACTIVITY OR ENERGY EXPENDITURE

6.6.1 DOUBLY LABELLED WATER

Doubly labelled water (DLW) is considered the criterial standard for the assessment of daily energy expenditure in free-living subjects (Montoye *et al.*, 1996). It provides a measure of daily energy expenditure over approximately two weeks and has been demonstrated to have good precision in adults (Schoeller and Van Santen, 1982; Klein *et al.*, 1984; Prentice *et al.*, 1985) and in infants (Roberts *et al.*, 1986).

For human subjects, the measurement of energy expenditure using DLW is very simple. It does not interfere with their lifestyle and hence is relatively unlikely to affect their normal pattern of daily activity. All that is required is the consumption of a dose of isotope-enriched water followed by the collection of urine samples after 7 days and after 14 days (two-point method), or on a daily basis (multipoint method).

Subjects consume water containing a known concentration of isotopes of hydrogen ($^2H_2$) and oxygen (^{18}O). The concentration is higher than occurs naturally. After a few hours the isotopes have redistributed and are in equilibrium with body water (Montoye *et al.*, 1996). The method is based on the measurement of carbon dioxide production from the difference between the elimination rates of the isotopes of hydrogen (deuterium $^2H_2$) and oxygen (^{18}O) with which the water is labelled. This is possible as the labelled oxygen leaves the body in the form of water ($H_2^{18}O$) and in the form of carbon dioxide ($C^{18}O_2$). However, the labelled hydrogen only leaves the body in the form of water (^2H_2O). Hence from the difference in the elimination rates of the two isotopes it is possible to calculate the quantity of carbon dioxide produced. Together with an estimation of the respiratory quotient (RQ), the quantity of carbon dioxide produced allows the calculation of oxygen uptake for the time period. The RQ will be unknown when measuring energy expenditure in the field, hence the need for the estimation. There is some error in the calculation of oxygen consumption from carbon dioxide produced. In Western societies the RQ is usually estimated to be 0.85. A difference of 0.01 between the estimated and actual RQ would lead to an error of approximately 1% in calculated energy expenditure (Montoye *et al.*, 1996).

The main disadvantage of the DLW method is its high cost. This prevents its use in large-scale studies or as a standard physiological measure of physical activity. Additionally, it can only provide measures of total energy expenditure over a period of time. No information regarding the subject's activity pattern or the intensity of activity undertaken can be obtained. Nevertheless, it is accepted as the ideal criterial method for validating alternative measures of total daily energy expenditure (Montoye *et al.*, 1996). It has been used to validate measures of energy expenditure and physical activity, including triaxial accelerometers (Bouten *et al.*, 1996), heart rate monitoring (e.g. Livingstone *et al.*, 1990; Emons *et al.*, 1992) and questionnaires (e.g. Bratteby *et al.*, 1997).

6.6.2 SELF-REPORT – QUESTIONNAIRES

Self-report is probably the most common method used for assessing physical activity levels. This is due to low cost, ease of use and the ability to assess large numbers of people over a relatively short period of time (Sallis and Saelens, 2000). Questionnaires vary as to whether they assess activity over the previous few days (e.g. Ku *et al.*, 1981; Shapiro *et al.*, 1984), few weeks (e.g. Watson and O'Donovan, 1977) or more general 'typical' activity (e.g. Johnson *et al.*, 1956; Tell and Vellar, 1988; Woods *et al.*, 1992).

The types of activity assessed by questionnaire also vary. Several questionnaires for adults concentrate on leisure time physical activity alone or work time physical activity alone, others on total activity. Children's questionnaires usually concentrate on either sport participation and leisure time physical activity

or total physical activity. Memory aids are frequently used in an effort to make questionnaires more accurate. Partitioning the day into portions and providing lists of activities to choose from are two of the main strategies (e.g. Gazzaniga and Burns, 1993).

When assessing habitual physical activity in adults, questionnaires give a reasonably valid and reliable estimate, at least allowing the categorization of people into groups based on their levels of physical activity (Montoye *et al.*, 1996). In children there are limitations associated with the recall of activities. Cale (1994) highlighted the limited cognitive ability of children to recall activities. This problem is exacerbated when the child is also expected to remember duration and intensity of activities. Baranowski *et al.* (1984) showed that children can only recall 55–65% of their daily activities. This finding was supported in a later study where 11–13-year-olds were observed for seven days. In a subsequent recall of activities over this time period only 46% of observed activities were reported (Wallace *et al.*, 1985).

Different questionnaire styles can give quite different results. Detailed accounts of the previous seven days have shown no evidence of a relationship between activity levels and body fat ($r = -0.02$ in boys and $r = -0.09$ in girls, Sallis *et al.*, 1988). Conversely, a global rating of activity in the same sample had a stronger relationship with fat in boys ($r = -0.28$), though not in girls, ($r = -0.02$). The authors suggested that a global rating was more representative of typical activity whereas the last seven days may be atypical.

Great care needs to be taken when using questionnaires with children. For children younger than 10–12 years old, questionnaire methods appear to be inappropriate and more objective methods such as observation or motion counters are recommended (Montoye *et al.*, 1996).

A discussion of available questionnaires is beyond the scope of this chapter. For information pertaining to specific questionnaires, or diary methods, and their reliability and validity, the reader is referred to the text by Montoye *et al.* (1996).

6.6.3 OBSERVATION

The use of observation to determine level of physical activity is the logical solution to assessing physical activity. It has face validity. It allows the recording of additional information related to the activity, e.g. where it occurs and the social context that it occurs in. It may be possible to provide information regarding motivation toward being active and which environments are conducive to increased activity levels. However, it is very time-consuming and labour-intensive for the observer. Consequently, it is restricted to use with small groups. Observation techniques are rarely used with adults. Hence, the rest of this section concerns methods used to assess activity in children.

Observation techniques can capture intensity, duration and frequency of physical activity. The accuracy of the information differs according to the frequency of observations. An optimal frequency is high enough to capture activity changes and brief activities, yet long enough to allow an accurate record of the activity to be made. Children's activity is highly transitory (Welk *et al.*, 2000). Bailey *et al.* (1995) showed that the median duration of 6–10-year-old children's activity was 6 s for low-to-medium intensity activities and 3 s for high-intensity activities.

Potentially reactive behaviour could be a problem with observation techniques. Following one or two observation sessions, children appear to become habituated to the presence of the observer and reactivity is not a problem (Puhl *et al.*, 1990; Bailey *et al.*, 1995). Reactive behaviour may be more of a problem when using observation techniques with adults.

Protocols vary according to the frequency, duration of observation and the number of categories the activities can be assigned to. A comprehensive observation protocol was developed by Bailey *et al.* (1995) with fifteen children aged 6–10 years. The varying intervals between activities of different intensity and duration (tempo) were recorded, as well as the frequency and duration of activities. The protocol was very labour-intensive. Fourteen posture codes were used which allowed the observer to describe the child's behaviour without having to make judgements about energy expenditure. Each posture code was mutually exclusive of any other. Within each posture code there were three intensity levels (low, moderate and intense). The intensity level selected depended on factors such as speed, number of limbs, weight carried, incline and so on. Observation periods were four hours in duration and performed in whatever setting the subject happened to be in: school days, weekend days and summer holidays were included. Observers were cued every 3 s to record activity by an audible bleep from a microcassette recorder earphone. Observations every 3 s were determined as the highest frequency possible without losing accuracy. At the end of 24 minutes, observers had a 6 minute break during which they could review their records and turn over the tape.

More commonly, observation protocols code activities into just 4 or 5 categories (Epstein *et al.*, 1984; O'Hara *et al.*, 1989; Puhl *et al.*, 1990). The Children's Activity Rating Scale (CARS) (Puhl *et al.*, 1990) and the Children's Physical Activity Form (CPAF) (O'Hara *et al.*, 1989) utilize 5 and 4 activity categories, respectively. Instead of sampling activity at set time intervals a continuous minute-by-minute sampling method is employed in these protocols (Puhl *et al.*, 1990). The activity level is coded at the start of each minute and then any change in activity within that minute is recorded. The time and frequency of each activity within that minute is unavailable as each activity level can only be recorded once. This is the main limitation to this method as it is highly unlikely that each of the child's activities within that minute lasted an equal amount of time. However, Puhl *et al.* (1990) demonstrated that this method showed only a small discrepancy when compared with a method which weighted each category according to time spent.

Protocols also differ with respect to whether the outcome is a quantification of the amount of activity or whether this is converted to a prediction of energy expenditure. Energy expenditure may be predicted by taking a sub-sample of children into the laboratory and measuring the energy cost of some of the activities that could be coded (e.g. Puhl *et al.*, 1990; Bailey *et al.*, 1995). There is no realistic alternative for determining the energy cost of the typical activities. Doubly labelled water offers the only non-invasive method of measuring energy expenditure in the field, but it gives only an overall estimate of total energy expenditure and cannot be used to measure energy expenditure of individual activities. A portable respirometer can be used to measure oxygen consumption, and hence energy expenditure, in the field but this is very invasive, and requires the subject to carry a backpack and wear a mouthpiece and nose clip. The limitations of predicting energy expenditure based on laboratory simulations of activities should be noted. For example, the predictions will be based on steady-state activity. Children rarely reach steady-state in typical play activity. Several children's and adults' activities cannot be reproduced in the laboratory and hence an energy cost for these activities has to be estimated.

Observational data, analysed as low-, medium- or high-intensity activities, can be used together with the predictions of energy expenditure. This procedure gives an outcome that avoids the assumptions associated with prediction (e.g. Bailey *et al.*, 1995).

The CPAF was validated against heart rate, but the outcome variable was activity points not energy expenditure (O'Hara *et al.*, 1989). The CARS can be used as a measure of activity or a prediction of energy expenditure (Puhl *et al.*, 1990). It is important to remember that if the outcome variable is activity counts or points, this measure refers to quantity of movement and hence, is unaffected by body mass. If energy expenditure is used, a higher body mass leads to a higher energy expenditure for any given activity. The energy expenditure may be scaled for body mass. The method of scaling should be considered when interpreting the results of such studies (see Chapter 11 by Winter and Nevill).

When trying to capture an overall picture of a child's activity, the time spent observing the child and the variety of environments the child is observed in may be more important than the observation protocol used. Several studies have observed children during games/PE lessons (O'Hara *et al.*, 1989), or while at summer camp (Epstein *et al.*, 1984; Wallace *et al.*, 1985). This is fine for validation studies and studies assessing the activity content of PE lessons or camps. To obtain a full picture of a child's activity level the whole waking day needs to be accounted for, on several different days, at different times of the year, and during school term and holidays if possible. Logistically this is very difficult but organized games/PE lessons are far from ideal to show spontaneous activity differences between children. Activity decreases in all children, regardless of their activity level, as activities became more organized (Corbin and Fletcher, 1968).

6.6.4 HEART RATE

Heart rate is not a direct measure of physical activity, but does provide an indication of the relative stress placed upon the cardiopulmonary system by physical activity (Welsman and Armstrong, 1992). As it provides an objective measure, with no need for recall, heart rate monitoring has been commonly used to assess children's physical activity. Heart rate monitoring also allows the recording of values over time, which gives a picture of the pattern and intensity of activity. Due to its widespread use, and the quantity of information gleaned, heart rate is frequently used as a criterion against which new objective methods are compared (e.g. Janz, 1994; Welk and Corbin, 1995). Nevertheless, there are several limitations to the use of heart rate monitoring for assessing physical activity.

The rationale for using heart rate monitoring as a measure of physical activity or energy expenditure relies on the linear relationship between heart rate and oxygen uptake. This relationship differs between individuals. Ideally, individuals' heart rate:oxygen uptake regression lines should be produced prior to measuring activity. This permits the prediction of oxygen uptake, and hence the energy expenditure, from heart rate. This practice is time-consuming, expensive and labour-intensive. Hence, many authors do not carry out this calibration (Riddoch and Boreham, 1995). Additionally, even if this procedure is carried out, there are problems as the heart rate:oxygen uptake relationship of any individual is affected by the proportion of active muscle mass and whether the activity is continuous or intermittent (Klausen *et al.*, 1985). For example, heart rate is considerably higher at similar oxygen uptake values for exercise of a static nature, and also for dynamic exercise by the arms compared with the legs (Maas *et al.*, 1989). Thus, if a regression equation produced from a running or cycling task is used to predict the oxygen cost associated with the heart rate elicited during a task requiring upper body or static exercise, the oxygen uptake would be over-predicted.

Predictions of oxygen uptake from heart rate are dependent on the assumption that the relationship is linear. Although this tends to be true in the moderate activity range, increasing error is introduced at high and low intensities (McArdle *et al.*, 1991). This is a major problem in the assessment of daily physical activity in children as heart rates tend to be consistently low for the majority of the day (Armstrong *et al.*, 1991; Gilbey and Gilbey, 1995).

If an oxygen uptake:heart rate regression line is not produced there are a number of ways of interpreting heart rate data. Most commonly the time spent above pre-determined heart rate thresholds is recorded. Elevating the heart rate above these thresholds is considered to be indicative of activity beneficial to health. This method does not take into account any

individual differences in age, gender, weight, maturational level, resting heart rate or heart rate response (Riddoch and Boreham, 1995; Rowlands *et al.*, 1997). Some researchers have used net heart rate (Janz *et al.*, 1992; Rowlands *et al.*, 1999). This method controls inter-individual differences within resting heart rate. The resting heart rate is subtracted from each heart rate recorded to give an 'activity heart rate'. The 'activity heart rate' is then averaged for the day.

When assessing moderate to vigorous exercise, heart rate monitoring is accurate and hence is a good tool for measuring adherence to adult fitness guidelines such as 20 minutes of continuous vigorous exercise. However, children's natural activity pattern does not take this form. Children's physical activity is highly transitory (Saris, 1986; Bailey *et al.*, 1995). The delay in heart rate response relative to changes in movement suggests that heart rate monitors may mask potential information. Physical fitness levels are also a limiting factor when using heart rate monitoring to assess physical activity. A fitter individual has a higher stroke volume, and hence a lower heart rate, for any given activity (Saris *et al.*, 1980). Mean daily heart rates may, therefore, be more representative of fitness than activity level (Saris *et al.*, 1980). Hence, the use of heart rate to assess activity would confound any investigation into the relationship between fitness and activity levels. Additionally, physical activity is not the only behaviour that causes an elevation in heart rate. Heart rate can also be elevated by emotional stress, which is independent of any change in oxygen uptake.

The method chosen for analysing heart rate data needs careful consideration as it may affect the interpretation of the data. When activity level assessed by heart rate data is expressed as net heart rate, relationships with body fat differ from when threshold heart rates are used to assess activity. For example, Janz *et al.* (1992) found inverse correlations between total activity and percent fat in both boys and girls. However, correlations when thresholds were used were lower and not statistically significant. Rowlands *et al.* (1999) also found that results differed according to the method of analysis of the heart rate data. Low negative non-significant correlations were found between net heart rate and body fat, contrasting with relatively high significant positive correlations between time spent above heart rate thresholds and body fat in 8–10 year old girls.

Assessing heart rate requires the child or adult to wear electrodes for a day or longer. The electrodes are either attached to the chest by tape, or incorporated in a belt that is worn around the chest. Both methods are reported to be uncomfortable and itchy in hot weather. Compliance can be a problem, with some children complaining of discomfort or removing the monitors during the day (Janz *et al.*, 1992; Rowlands *et al.*, 1999).

A meta-analysis of fifty investigations of the relationship between activity and body fat in children and youth showed that the average effect size elicited from studies using heart rate to assess activity levels was significantly lower ($p < 0.05$) than the average effect size elicited from studies using a different method of activity assessment (questionnaire, observation, motion counter) (Rowlands *et al.*, 2000). This indicated that heart rate monitoring, a physiological measure, was not measuring the same thing as the other behavioural measures. Perhaps, heart rate monitoring does not capture the aspects of activity that are related to body fatness in children.

The above limitations question the suitability of heart rate telemetry for the validation of other methods that may have potential for population studies.

6.6.5 MOTION COUNTERS

Motion counters provide an objective assessment of activity levels that has minimal hindrance to the person wearing the monitor. They vary in cost and sophistication, from the simple, inexpensive pedometer invented 500 years ago (Gibbs-Smith, 1978) to the recently developed accelerometers. Pedometers provide one cumulative movement count representing total activity. In contrast, the new generation of accelerometers provide intensity, frequency and duration information of activity. Triaxial and uniaxial versions are available.

The main disadvantage of motion counters of any kind is their inability to measure static work, increased activity due to going up an incline or increased activity due to carrying a load. The contribution of static work to total daily energy expenditure has been observed to be trivial in adults (Meijer *et al.*, 1989). In children, the contribution of static work to a day's energy expenditure is likely to be less than in adults, so the inability of the pedometer to measure this type of work may not be a cause for concern when assessing the activity levels of most people. The inability to measure increased activity due to going up inclines or carrying loads may be more of a problem.

(a) Pedometers

Relatively early studies using mechanical pedometers have generally concluded that they are inaccurate at counting steps or measuring distance walked (Gayle *et al.*, 1977; Kemper and Verschuur, 1977; Saris and Binkhorst, 1977a; Washburn *et al.*, 1980). However, the newer, commercially available electronic pedometers provide a reasonably accurate estimate of distance walked and number of steps taken (Bassett *et al.*, 1996). Pedometers, therefore, have potential as a tool for the measurement of daily activity.

In a study on 493 adults, Sequeira *et al.* (1995) demonstrated that the pedometer could differentiate between varying levels of occupational activities (sitting, standing and moderate-effort occupational categories). However, the pedometer counts for the heavy work category did not differ from the counts for the moderate work category. The heavy work category was made up of a high proportion of static work, such as lifting heavy objects. As pedometers are unable to measure static work they underestimated the energy cost of the people in this occupational category.

Pedometer readings from children correlate highly with observation (Saris and Binkhorst, 1977b; Nishikido *et al.*, 1982). The pedometer differentiated between the most and least active 4–6-year-old children as predetermined by a supervisor's questionnaire ($p < 0.001$) and confirmed by observation ($p < 0.01$) (Saris and Binkhorst, 1977b). Pedometer readings have also been shown to correlate with running activity of kindergarten children as determined by observation (Nishikido *et al.*, 1982). In a study on 10–12-year-olds (Kilanowski *et al.*, 1999), pedometer counts (Yamax Digi-walker SW–200, Yamasa, Tokyo, Japan) also correlated significantly with both observation and triaxial accelerometry (TriTrac Professional Products, Reining International, Madison, WI, USA) counts during both high-intensity and low-intensity recreational activities. The correlation between pedometer counts and TriTrac counts was significantly lower during low-intensity activities than during high-intensity activities ($r = 0.50$ and 0.98 respectively, $N = 10$). However, the correlation between pedometer counts and observation did not differ significantly across the two situations ($r = 0.70$ and 0.94 for low intensity and high intensity activities, respectively, $N = 10$).

Eston *et al.* (1998) showed that using the Yamax Digi-walker SW–200 pedometer was as valid as heart rate monitoring and uniaxial accelerometry when assessing the energy cost of a variety of typical children's activities in the laboratory. Thirty 8–10-year-old children from North Wales wore the pedometer on their hips while playing catch, playing hopscotch, walking (2 speeds), running (2 speeds) and crayoning. No activities involving inclines or carrying loads were included in the protocol. The criterion was oxygen uptake scaled for body size. Additional pedometers worn on the wrist and ankle did not improve the estimation of energy cost. The pedometer used in this study is shown in Figure 6.1. Figure 6.2 shows one of the children taking part in this study. These results were replicated with twenty-one 8–10-year-old Hong Kong Chinese boys (Louie *et al.*, 1999).

Following these analyses a week-long field study was conducted with 34 boys and girls aged 8–10 years (Rowlands *et al.*, 1999). Activity measured by pedometry or the TriTrac correlated positively to fitness in the whole group (TriTrac $r = 0.66$; pedometer $r = 0.59$, $p < 0.01$) and boys and girls separately ($p < 0.05$) and negatively with fatness in the whole group (TriTrac $r = -0.42$; pedometer $r = -0.42$, $p < 0.05$).

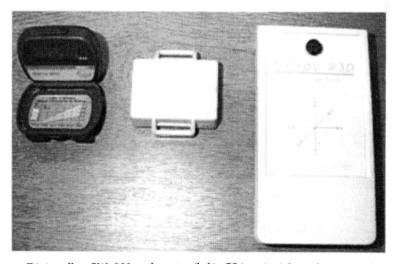

Figure 6.1 Yamax Digi-walker SW–200 pedometer (left), CSA uniaxial accelerometer (centre) and TriTrac triaxial accelerometer (right).

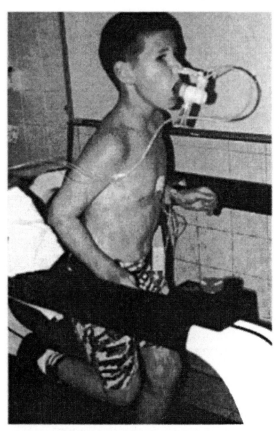

Figure 6.2 One of the children from the study by Eston et al. (1998). He is wearing the TriTrac on his left hip, the CSA accelerometer on his right hip, a heart rate monitor (BHL 6000 Medical) and three pedometers: one on his right hip, one on his left wrist and one on his right ankle.

It is very encouraging that the simple pedometer identified the same relationships with fitness and fatness as the sophisticated TriTrac. Evidence is accumulating that the pedometer may be a valid tool for the assessment of daily activity. The method is objective, cheap, unobtrusive and would be ideal for large population surveys, or any situation where only a measure of total activity is required. If information regarding the activity pattern is required, this would only be obtainable by recording the pedometer reading at set intervals. This is not ideal as doing so may interfere with the person's activity pattern and require the person to remember to record the pedometer counts at certain times. With adults and older children this procedure may be preferable and less intrusive or time-consuming than diaries or self-report.

Additionally, the pedometer can be used as a tool to self-regulate physical activity levels. Patients with chronic pain, for example, may benefit by using the pedometer as a pacing tool, allowing them to ensure they did not partake in more activity than they could cope with. Healthy people may benefit from using the pedometer to ensure they reach a target of total activity per day.

(b) Caltrac

The Caltrac (Muscle Dynamic Fitness Network, Torrance, CA) is a motion sensor, but unlike the pedometer, it estimates intensity of movement in addition to quantity. The output is in activity counts or calories (calculated from activity counts, age, gender, height and mass), a total output only being provided with no temporal information of movement counts. When the Caltrac is used with children, one of the obvious problems is the easy accessibility of buttons, which excite the child's curiosity!

The Caltrac has been used extensively to assess activity and/or energy expenditure in both children and adults. Reports on the validity of the Caltrac vary. Ballor *et al.* (1989) reported that the Caltrac accurately predicted energy expenditure during level walking. Conversely, the Caltrac has also been reported to overestimate energy expenditure at all walking speeds (Balogun *et al.*, 1989), to overestimate energy expenditure when walking fast and underestimate energy expenditure when walking slowly (Montoye *et al.*, 1983). The Caltrac is unable to account for increased energy expenditure due to treadmill inclines.

As the output of the Caltrac is based on vertical displacement, it has limited accuracy for activities such as cycling (Miller *et al.*, 1994). Because of this, the unit incorporates a cycle mode. Use of the cycle mode has been shown to underestimate the energy expenditure when cycling at both 60 rev min^{-1} and 90 rev min^{-1}, though the underestimation was less when cycling at 90 rev min^{-1} (Jensen *et al.*, 1997).

In a study using whole-room calorimetry to validate the Caltrac, Bray et al. (1994) observed a significant underestimation of energy expenditure in a variety of experimental conditions. However, the need to remain in a calorimeter for 24 hours restricts activity patterns. The only exercise was cycle ergometry, performed for 20 minutes twice a day. As mentioned above, the Caltrac has limited accuracy for activities not based on vertical displacement and has been shown to underestimate energy expenditure during cycling. Montoye *et al.* (1983) suggested that when the Caltrac was used in the field, the underestimation of sedentary activities, or activities where the torso is fairly stable, may be balanced by overestimation of level walking and running. This claim is not supported by results of a later study in which the Caltrac, although highly reliable, underestimated free-living energy expenditure by 34% in 21 adults (aged 19–45) when compared to self-report (Bray and Morrow, 1993). It is possible that the errors lie with an overestimation by self-report rather than an underestimation by the Caltrac.

(c) Time-sampling accelerometers

CSA accelerometer

Relatively recently, a new generation of accelerometers has become available. These have a time-sampling mechanism that allows them to store data for weeks at a time, allowing a temporal analysis. Frequency, intensity and duration measures of activity are recorded. Both uniaxial and triaxial units are commercially available. These units are initiated and downloaded via a computer interface and have no external controls or displays of activity levels.

The CSA accelerometer (Computer Science and Applications Inc., Shalimar, Florida. Also known as the 'WAM' and the 'Actigraph'.) is a uniaxial accelerometer (Figure 6.1). It can store data for 22 consecutive days compared with the maximum of 5.5 days of data storage of current heart rate monitors. It is very small and lightweight (5.1 cm × 3.8 cm × 1.5 cm, 43 g).

As with the Caltrac, the CSA accelerometer is based on vertical displacement. Hence, although the CSA accelerometer discriminates between changes in speed (Melanson and Freedson, 1995; Trost *et al.*, 1998), it does not discriminate between changes in grade during treadmill walking and running (Melanson and Freedson, 1995).

The CSA accelerometer has been validated against heart rate telemetry for use in assessing children's habitual daily activity (Janz, 1994). It was significantly correlated with heart rate telemetry (overall $r = 0.58$, $p < 0.05$), in 31 children aged 7–15 years, although the correlations between the CSA movement counts and heart rate were higher during the more vigorous activities (defined as greater than 60% of heart rate reserve, $r = 0.63$, $p < 0.05$) (Janz, 1994). The author suggested that the poorer relationship evident at low exercise intensities may reflect the weaknesses of heart rate telemetry in the evaluation of low exercise intensities.

There are inherent weaknesses in using heart rate telemetry, which is known to have limitations, to validate new methods such as the CSA accelerometer. To date there is no fully accepted and fully validated criterial standard of assessing physical activity or energy expenditure that can be used in the field.

When the CSA accelerometer is validated in laboratory settings, higher validity correlations are found than when it is validated in field settings (Janz *et al.*, 1995). Additionally, validity tends to be higher for adults compared with children (Janz, 1994). Laboratory studies may elicit higher validity coefficients because the criterial variable is more valid. Oxygen consumption is normally used as the criterion in a laboratory study, whereas less valid alternatives (heart rate, questionnaires) may be used in field studies. Hence, lower validity coefficients could reflect measurement error of the criterial variable as well as measurement error of the CSA accelerometer. Heart rate is sometimes used as the criterial variable in laboratory studies. However, activities used in laboratory validation studies are typically of moderate to high intensity, at which heart rate provides an accurate indication of energy expenditure. This is not the case when heart rate is used as a criterion in field studies, where low-intensity activities are predominantly encountered.

The size of validity coefficients can also be related to the variety of movement undertaken in the study. Movements are relatively ordered and controlled in laboratory studies, e.g. walking and running. Similarly, adults generally undertake a lower variety of movement than children. The uniaxial system of measurement employed by the CSA accelerometer may be more sensitive to common adult activities (walking/running) than children's activities (climbing/playing) (Janz, 1994). This suggests that a triaxial accelerometer may be more appropriate for the assessment of children's activity. This contention is supported by results of Eston *et al.* (1998) which indicated significantly lower correlations ($p < 0.001$) for the CSA accelerometer than a three-dimensional accelerometer (TriTrac, see below) with scaled oxygen uptake, when assessing a variety of typical children's activities in thirty 8–10-year-old children ($r = 0.780$ and 0.908 for the CSA accelerometer and the TriTrac respectively). The CSA accelerometer appears to be comfortable for children and adults alike. Importantly, it does not hinder their activities.

TriTrac-R3D accelerometer

The TriTrac-R3D (Professional Products, a division of Reining International, Madison, WI, USA) has all the benefits of the CSA accelerometer, but in addition measures activity in all three dimensions, for up to 30 days when using one minute sampling intervals (Figure 6.1). Studies on Welsh (Eston *et al.*, 1998) and Chinese (Louie *et al.*, 1999) children have confirmed that a triaxial accelerometer quantifies typical children's activities more accurately than a uniaxial accelerometer. The TriTrac

correlated more highly with scaled oxygen uptake than heart rate across a variety of play and treadmill activities in children aged 8–10 years.

The subject in Figure 6.2 is wearing a TriTrac on the left hip and a CSA accelerometer on the right hip. Figure 6.3 shows the TriTrac counts during walking, running, playing hopscotch, playing catch and crayoning. A similar validation study with adults also indicated that a triaxial accelerometer (the Tracmor unit) provided a more accurate estimate of a range of laboratory-based adult activities than uniaxial accelerometry alone (Bouten *et al.*, 1994). Triaxial accelerometry has been validated as a field measure of physical activity in children using heart rate as a criterial measure (Welk and Corbin, 1995), and in adults using indirect calorimetry as a criterial measure (Bouten *et al.*, 1996).

Jakicic *et al.* (1999) assessed the validity of the TriTrac to predict energy expenditure in adults performing treadmill walking and running, stepping, stationary cycling and slide-board activities. The TriTrac did not differentiate between increases in energy expenditure due to increases in grade during walking or running. Nichols *et al.* (1999) also found that the TriTrac differentiated between speeds of walking and running, but not increases in gradient. Increases in workload due to increased stepping rate, increased cycling speed or increased slides per minute were detected (Jakicic *et al.*, 1999). The computation of energy expenditure by the TriTrac software underestimated energy expenditure measured by indirect calorimetry during most activities, though correlated significantly for every activity except cycle ergometry. Increased energy expenditure due to carrying loads is also not detected by the TriTrac (Gotshall and DeVoe, 1997).

Hence, like other motion counters, the TriTrac cannot quantify increases in activity due to walking/running up inclines, carrying loads or isometric work. The contribution of static work to total daily energy expenditure has been observed to be trivial in adults

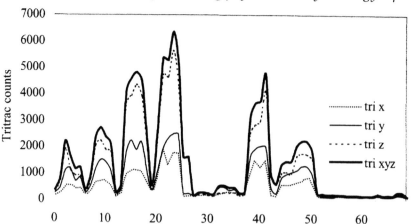

Figure 6.3 A typical plot of the TriTrac output during children's activities in the laboratory. Tri x = mediolateral plane, tri y = anteroposterior plane, tri z = vertical plane, tri xyz = vector magnitude). Reproduced from Eston *et al.* (1998) with the permission of the *Journal of Applied Physiology*.

(Meijer *et al.*, 1989) and is likely to be even less in children.

When predicting energy expenditure, as opposed to measuring activity levels, a more accurate prediction will be obtained by creating a sample-specific regression equation. This is particularly relevant if the subjects are children, older adults or represent a 'special' population.

Field study results have shown triaxial accelerometers to be superior to heart rate monitors for indicating physical activity (Meijer *et al.*, 1989). Accelerometer output correlated highly with energy intake ($r = 0.99, p < 0.025$), although the energy expenditure predicted from the accelerometer output was consistently 30% higher than that predicted by energy intake. When heart rate methods were used, individual differences were larger but the mean discrepancy was similar. Average daily energy expenditure (predicted from energy intake) was relatively low for these subjects. The apparent overestimation in energy expenditure by the accelerometers may have been due to energy intake being underestimated.

In contrast, energy expenditure is underestimated when using the TriTrac system, compared with self-report measures (Matthews and Freedson, 1995; Epstein *et al.*, 1996). Epstein *et al.* (1996) assessed the predictors of activity in obese children as measured by self-report and the TriTrac. Accelerometer-assessed activity was related to socio-economic status and parent activity levels (accounting for 14.8% of the variance in activity), whereas child self-reported activity was related to fitness (accounting for 23.5% of the variance). The authors concluded that self-report and accelerometry in children are not measuring the same activity construct. This study highlighted the potential error when using self-report as a criterial measure for objective methods and vice versa.

Activity counts, measured by means of the TriTrac system for up to 7 days, correlated positively with aerobic endurance and negatively with fatness in 8–10-year-old children (Rowlands *et al.*, 2000). This result indicates that the TriTrac measures those aspects of activity that relate to fatness and fitness.

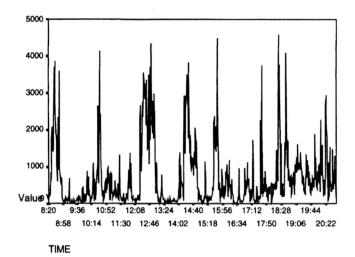

Figure 6.4 A typical TriTrac trace (vector magnitude) from a school day.

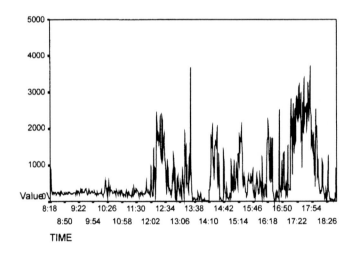

Figure 6.5 The same child as in Figure 6.4. All morning was spent travelling by car.

Typical graphs showing daily activity measured by the TriTrac during a typical school day and a day off school, are shown in Figures 6.4 and 6.5. With the exception of the morning spent in a car (Figure 6.5) the rapid transition in activities, typical of children, is quite evident from these time versus movement intensity graphs.

A limitation of the TriTrac used in the above studies is its size. It measures 12.0 × 6.5 × 2.2 cm, and weighs 168 g. It is supplied with a belt clip for attachment to the subject. This is an insecure method of attachment, particularly when worn by children. Indeed, in trials in our laboratory, even during treadmill activities, the TriTrac rattled around, which is not ideal for an accelerometer. During initial 'hopping' activities it was liable to fly off the subject! To rectify this it was necessary to tape the TriTrac securely to a belt worn by each subject. In comparison, the smaller CSA (5.1 × 3.8 × 1.5 cm, at 45 g) is supplied with a tightly fitting pouch which can be threaded onto a belt and therefore be held securely in position. This device does not hinder activities and is preferred for smaller children (Louie *et al.*, 1999).

Recently a company called 'Stayhealthy Inc' (Monrovia, CA, USA) purchased the technology and rights to the TriTrac-R3D from 'Reining International'. They have developed a smaller triaxial accelerometer called the RT3 (7.1 cm × 5.6 cm × 2.8 cm, 65 g). There is no published research using this device yet, but its validity is currently being assessed.

The relatively high cost of both CSA and TriTrac accelerometers may prohibit their use, particularly in large studies. Currently, the CSA accelerometer (Actigraph) costs US$400 per unit and US$929 for the starter pack (including one unit, computer interface, software, pouch, strap and belt). The new TriTrac (RT3) costs US$300 per unit and US$500 for the starter pack (including one unit, computer interface and software).

(d) Multiple measures

If cost is not an issue, the simultaneous measurement of heart rate and motion has been recommended by Freedson and Miller (2000). The assessment of motion would provide evidence that elevation of heart rate was due to increased physical activity and not other factors. The assessment of heart rate in addition to motion would improve estimates of hard activity involving carrying loads and walking/running up inclines.

6.7 PRACTICAL 1: WALKING AND RUNNING

6.7.1 PURPOSE

To assess the relationship between selected measures of physical activity and oxygen uptake during treadmill walking and running

6.7.2 METHODS

1. The TriTrac and CSA accelerometers are initialized. It is important to ensure that both units are set to the same clock, hence ensuring their internal clocks are temporally matched.
2. The subject rests for 10 minutes. Expired air is collected for 5 minutes and analysed for resting oxygen consumption. Heart rate at rest is recorded.
3. The subject wears the TriTrac accelerometer on one hip, the CSA accelerometer and a pedometer (set to zero) on the other hip. One pedometer (set to zero) is also attached to a strap worn on the ankle and one pedometer (set to zero) on a strap worn on the wrist. Heart rate is measured by radio telemetry.
4. The subject walks on the treadmill at 4 km h^{-1} for 4 minutes. During the final minute, heart rate is recorded and expired air is collected and analysed for oxygen consumption.
5. At the end of 4 minutes, the pedometer readings are taken. The reading is divided by 4 to give counts per minute.
6. The above is repeated with the subject walking at 6 km h^{-1}, and running at 10 km h^{-1} and 12 km h^{-1}.
7. The data from the TriTrac and CSA accelerometers are downloaded and the counts corresponding with the final minute of each activity recorded. For the TriTrac record the counts for each vector (x, y, z and vector magnitude).

6.7.3 ASSIGNMENTS

1. Correlate each of the activity measures (HR, ankle pedometer counts, wrist pedometer counts, ankle pedometer counts, x TriTrac counts, y TriTrac counts, z TriTrac counts, vector magnitude TriTrac counts, CSA counts) with $\dot{V}O_2$. Which activity measure has the highest correlation with $\dot{V}O_2$?
2. Compute the regression equation for the prediction of $\dot{V}O_2$ for each activity measure. What is the SEE associated with each regression equation?
3. Which TriTrac vector is the best predictor of oxygen uptake?
4. Calculate net heart rate for each activity and correlate this figure with $\dot{V}O_2$. Is the correlation between heart rate and oxygen uptake increased or decreased?
5. What would be the effect of increasing the treadmill gradient to manipulate workload, instead of changing treadmill speed, on the different correlations? Consider whether an increase or decrease in the correlation is expected.
6. What would be the effect of increasing the load carried to manipulate workload, instead of changing treadmill speed? Why do you think some of the correlations would increase or decrease?
7. Calculate the energy expenditure at rest and the energy expenditure during each activity. From these figures calculate the physical activity level associated with each activity.

6.8 PRACTICAL 2: MISCELLANEOUS ACTIVITIES

6.8.1 PURPOSE

To assess the relationship between miscellaneous activities and measures of physical activity

6.8.2 METHODS

Repeat the above methodology, but with different activities. The subject must reach steady state in each activity. Think of some appropriate activities, e.g. jumping, crayoning, sitting up and down at intervals, playing catch.

6.8.3 ASSIGNMENTS

1. Correlate each of the activity measures (HR, ankle pedometer counts, wrist pedometer counts, ankle pedometer counts, x TriTrac counts, y TriTrac counts, z TriTrac counts, vector magnitude TriTrac counts, CSA counts) with $\dot{V}O_2$. Which activity measure has the highest correlation with $\dot{V}O_2$?
2. Compute the regression equation for the prediction of $\dot{V}O_2$ for each activity measure. What is the SEE associated with each regression equation?
3. Compare the correlations and SEE values to the values obtained for treadmill activities. Comment on why any differences may occur.

4. Which TriTrac vector was the best predictor of oxygen uptake? Was this the same as when treadmill activities were assessed?
5. Explain why the data from the triaxial accelerometer are important for some activities.
6. Explain why certain activities may be better assessed by a heart rate monitor than an accelerometer.
7. How might the analysis of the heart rate data affect the results? For example, look at gross versus net heart rate.
8. Calculate the energy expenditure at rest and the energy expenditure during each activity. From these figures calculate the PAL associated with each activity.

REFERENCES

Activity and Health Research. (1992). *Allied Dunbar National Fitness Survey*, London: Health Education Authority/Sports Council.

Armstrong, N., Williams, J., Balding, J., *et al.* (1991). Cardiopulmonary fitness, physical activity patterns and selected coronary risk factors in 11–16 year olds. *Pediatric Exercise Science*, 3, 219–28.

Bailey, R.C., Olson, J., Pepper, S.L., *et al.* (1995). The level and tempo of children's physical activities: an observational study. *Medicine and Science in Sports and Exercise*, 27, 1033–41.

Ballor, D.L., Burke, L.M., Knudson, D.V., *et al.* (1989). Comparison of three methods of estimating energy expenditure: Caltrac, heart rate, and video analysis. *Research Quarterly for Exercise and Sport*, 60, 362–8.

Balogun, J.A., Martin, D.A. and Clendenin, M.A. (1989). Calorimetric validation of the Caltrac accelerometer during level walking. *Physical Therapy*, 69, 501–9.

Baranowski, T., Dworkin, R.J., Cieslik, C.J., *et al.* (1984). Reliability and validity of self-report of aerobic activity: Family health project. *Research Quarterly for Exercise and Sport*, 55, 309–17.

Bassett, D.R., Ainsworth, B.E., Leggett, S.R., *et al.* (1996). Accuracy of five electronic pedometers for measuring distance walked. *Medicine and Science in Sports and Exercise*, 28, 1071–7.

Black, A.E., Coward, W.A. and Prentice, A.M. (1996). Human energy expenditure in affluent societies: an analysis of 574 doubly-labelled water measurements. *European Journal of Clinical Nutrition*, 50, 72–92.

Blair, S.N., Clark, D.G., Cureton, K.J. and Powell, K.E. (1989). Exercise and fitness in childhood: Implications for a lifetime of health. In *Perspectives in Exercise Science and Sports Medicine. Vol. 2.*

Youth, Exercise and Sport. eds. C.V. Gisolfi and D.R. Lamb (Benchmark Press, Indianapolis), pp. 401–30.

Bouchard, C., Shephard, R.J. and Stephens, T. eds (1994). *Physical Activity, Fitness and Health: International Proceedings and Consensus Statement*. (Human Kinetics, Champaign, IL), pp. 61–3.

Bouten, C.V., Westerterp, K.R., Verduin, M. and Jansser, J.D. (1994). Assessment of energy expenditure for physical activity using a triaxial accelerometer. *Medicine and Science in Sports and Exercise*, 26, 1516–23.

Bouten, C.V.C., Verboeket-van de Venne, W.P.H.G., Westerterp, K.R., *et al.* (1996). Daily physical activity assessment: comparison between movement registration and doubly labelled water. *Journal of Applied Physiology*, 81, 1019–26.

Bratteby, L-E., Sandhagen, B., Fan, H. and Samuelson, G. (1997). A 7-day activity diary for the assessment of daily energy expenditure validated by the doubly labelled water method in adolescents. *European Journal of Clinical Nutrition*, 51, 585–91.

Bray, M.S. and Morrow, J.R. (1993). Accuracy and reliability of the Caltrac accelerometer in a field setting. *Research Quarterly for Exercise and Sport*, March supplement: A–69.

Bray, M.S., Wong, W.W., Morrow, J.R., *et al.*(1994). Caltrac versus calorimeter determination of 24-h energy expenditure in female children and adolescents. *Medicine and Science in Sports and Exercise*, 26, 1524–30.

Brown, D.R. (1990). Exercise, fitness, and mental health. In *Exercise, Fitness and Health: A Consensus of Current Knowledge*. eds. C. Bouchard, R.J. Shephard, T. Stephens, *et al.* (Human Kinetics, Champaign, IL), pp. 607–26.

Cale, L. (1994). Self-report measures of children's physical activity: recommendations for future development and a new alternative measure. *Health Education Journal*, **53**, 439–53.

Corbin, C.B. and Fletcher, P. (1968). Diet and physical activity patterns of obese and nonobese elementary school children. *Research Quarterly*, **39**, 922–8.

Dishman, R.K. and Dunn, A.L. (1988). Exercise adherence in children and youth. In *Exercise Adherence, Its Impact on Public Health*. ed. R. Dishman (Human Kinetics, Champaign, IL), pp. 155-200.

Emons, H.J.G., Groenenboom, D.C., Westerterp, K.R. and Saris, W.H.M. (1992). Comparison of heart rate monitoring combined with indirect calorimetry and the doubly labelled water ($^2H_2^{18}O$) method for the measurement of energy expenditure in children. *European Journal of Applied Physiology*, **65**, 99–103.

Epstein, L.H., McGowan, C. and Woodall, K. (1984). A behavioural observation system for free play activity in young overweight female children. *Research Quarterly for Exercise and Sport*, **55**, 180–3.

Epstein, L.H., Paluch, R.A., Coleman, K.J., et al. (1996). Determinants of physical activity in obese children assessed by accelerometer and self-report. *Medicine and Science in Sports and Exercise*, **28**, 1157–64.

Eston, R.G., Rowlands, A.V. and Ingledew, D.K. (1998). Validity of heart rate, pedometry and accelerometry for predicting the energy cost of children's activities. *Journal of Applied Physiology*, **84**, 362–71.

Freedson, P.S. and Miller, K. (2000). Objective monitoring of physical activity using motion sensors and heart rate. *Research Quarterly for Exercise and Sport*, **71**, 21–9.

Gayle, R., Montoye, H.J. and Philpot, J. (1977). Accuracy of pedometers for measuring distance walked. *Research Quarterly for Exercise and Sport*, **48**, 632–6.

Gazzaniga, J.M. and Burns, T.L. (1993). Relationship between diet composition and body fatness, with adjustment for resting energy expenditure and physical activity, in preadolescent children. *American Journal of Clinical Nutrition*, **58**, 21–8.

Gibbs-Smith C. (1978). *The Inventions of Leonardo da Vinci*. (Phaidon Press Ltd., London), pp. 31–43.

Gilbey, H. and Gilbey, M. (1995). The physical activity of Singapore primary school children as estimated by heart rate monitoring. *Pediatric Exercise Science*, **7**, 26–35.

Goran, M.I. (1997). Energy expenditure, body composition and disease risk in children and adolescents. *Proceedings of the Nutrition Society*, **56**, 195–209.

Gotshall, R.W. and DeVoe, D.E. (1997). Utility of the Tritrac-R3D accelerometer during backpacking. *Medicine and Science in Sports and Exercise*, **29**, S45.

Gutin, B. and Owens, S. (1996). Is there a scientific rationale supporting the value of exercise for the present and future cardiovascular health of children? The pro argument. *Pediatric Exercise Science*, **8**, 294–302.

Jakicic, J.M., Winters, C., Lagally, K., et al. (1999). The accuracy of the Tritrac-R3D accelerometer to estimate energy expenditure. *Medicine and Science in Sports and Exercise*, **31**, 747–54.

Janz, K.F. (1994). Validation of the CSA accelerometer for assessing children's physical activity. *Medicine and Science in Sports and Exercise*, **26**, 369–75.

Janz, K.F., Witt, J. and Mahoney, L.T. (1995). The stability of children's physical activity as measured by accelerometry and self-report. *Medicine and Science in Sports and Exercise*, **27**, 1326–32.

Janz, K.F., Golden, J.C., Hansen, J.R. and Mahoney, L.T. (1992). Heart rate monitoring of physical activity in children and adolescents: The Muscatine study. *Pediatrics*, **89**, 256–61.

Jensen, R.L., Daggett, M., Gallagher, P. and Wilkins, B. (1997). The reliability and validity of the Caltrac activity monitor during stationary cycling at 60 and 90 rpm. *Medicine and Science in Sports and Exercise*, **29**, 5: S45.

Johnson, M.L., Burke, B.S. and Mayer, J. (1956). Relative importance of inactivity and overeating in the energy balance of obese high school girls. *American Journal of Clinical Nutrition*, **4**, 37–44.

Kemper, H.C.G. and Verschuur, R. (1977). Validity and reliability of pedometers in habitual activity research. *European Journal of Applied Physiology*, **37**, 71–82.

Kilanowski, C.K., Consalvi, A.R. and Epstein, L.H. (1999). Validation of an electronic pedometer for measurement of physical activity in children. *Pediatric Exercise Science*, **11**, 63–8.

Klausen, K., Rasmussen, B., Glensgaard, L.K. and Jensen, O.V. (1985). Work efficiency during submaximal bicycle exercise. In *Children and Exercise XI*. eds. R.A. Binkhorst, H.C.G. Kemper, and W.H.M. Saris (Human Kinetics, Champaign, IL), pp. 210–17.

Klein, P.D., James, W.P.T., Wong, W.W., et al. (1984).

Calorimetric validation of the doubly labelled water method for determination of energy expenditure in man. *Human Nutrition: Clinical Nutrition,* **38C**, 95–106.

Ku, L.C., Shapiro, L.R., Crawford, P.B. and Huenemann, R.L. (1981). Body composition and physical activity in 8-year-old children. *American Journal of Clinical Nutrition,* **34**, 2770–5.

Livingstone, M.B.E., Prentice, A.M., Coward, W.A., *et al.* (1990). Simultaneous measurement of free-living energy expenditure by the doubly labeled water method and heart rate monitoring. *American Journal of Clinical Nutrition,* **52**, 59–65.

Louie, L., Eston, R.G., Rowlands, A.V., *et al.* (1999). Validity of heart rate, pedometry and accelerometry for estimating the energy cost of activity in Hong Kong Chinese boys. *Pediatric Exercise Science,* **11**, 229–39.

Maas, S., Kok, M.L.J., Westra, H.G. and Kemper, H.C. (1989). The validity of the use of heart rate in estimating oxygen consumption in static and in combined static/dynamic exercise. *Ergonomics,* **32**, 141–8.

McArdle, W.D., Katch, F.I. and Katch, V.L. (1991). *Exercise Physiology: Energy, Nutrition and Human Performance.* 3rd edn. (Lea and Febiger, Philadelphia), pp. 169–70.

McAuley, E. (1994). Physical activity and psychosocial outcomes. In *Physical Activity, Fitness, and Health: International Proceedings and Consensus Statement.* eds. C. Bouchard, R.J. Shephard and T. Stephens (Human Kinetics, Champaign, IL), pp. 851–67.

Matthews, C.E. and Freedson, P.S. (1995). Field trial of a three-dimensional activity monitor: comparison with self-report. *Medicine and Science in Sports and Exercise,* **27**, 1071–8.

Meijer, G.A., Westerterp, K.R., Koper, H. and ten Hoor, F. (1989). Assessment of energy expenditure by recording heart rate and body acceleration. *Medicine and Science in Sports and Exercise.* **221**, 343–7.

Melanson, E.L., and Freedson, P.S. (1995). Validity of the Computer Science and Applications, Inc. (CSA) activity monitor. *Medicine and Science in Sports and Exercise,* **27**, 934–40.

Miller, D.J., Freedson, P.S. and Kline, G.M. (1994). Comparison of activity levels using the Caltrac accelerometer and five questionnaires. *Medicine and Science in Sports and Exercise,* **26**, 376–82.

Montoye, H.J., Kemper, H.C.G., Saris, W.H.M. and

Washburn, R.A. (1996). *Measuring Physical Activity and Energy Expenditure.* (Human Kinetics, Champaign, IL).

Montoye, H.J., Washburn, R., Servais, R.S., *et al.* (1983). Estimation of energy expenditure by a portable accelerometer. *Medicine and Science in Sports and Exercise,* **15**, 403–7.

Nichols, J.F., Morgan, C.G., Sarkin, J.A., *et al.* (1999). Validity, reliability, and calibration of the Tritrac accelerometer as a measure of physical activity. *Medicine and Science in Sports and Exercise,* **31**, 908–12.

Nieman, D.C. (1998). *The Exercise-Health Connection. How to Reduce Your Risk of Disease and Other Illnesses by Making Exercise your Medicine.* (Human Kinetics, Champaign, IL).

Nishikido, N., Kashiwazaki, H. and Suzuki, T. (1982). Pre-school children's daily activities: direct observations, pedometry or questionnaire. *Journal of Human Ergology,* **11**, 214–8.

O'Hara, N.M., Baranowski, T., Simons-Morton, B.G., *et al.* (1989). Validity of the observation of children's physical activity. *Research Quarterly for Exercise and Sport,* **60**, 42–7.

Prentice, A.M., Coward, W.A., Davies, H.L. *et al.,* (1985). Unexpectedly low levels of energy expenditure in healthy women. *Lancet,* **1**, 1419–22.

Puhl, J., Greaves, K., Hoyt, M. and Baranowski, T. (1990). Children's activity rating scale (CARS): Description and calibration. *Research Quarterly for Exercise and Sport,* **61**, 26–36.

Riddoch, C.J. and Boreham, C.A.G. (1995). The health-related physical activity of children. *Sports Medicine,* **19**, 86–102.

Roberts, S.B., Coward, W.A., Schlingenseipen, K.H., *et al.* (1986). Comparison of the doubly labelled water ($^2H_2{}^{18}O$) method with indirect calorimetry and a nutrient-balance study for simultaneous determination of energy expenditure, water intake, and metabolizable energy intake in preterm infants. *American Journal of Clinical Nutrition,* **44**, 315–22.

Rowlands, A.V., Eston, R.G. and Ingledew, D.K. (1997). Measurement of physical activity in children with particular reference to the use of heart rate and pedometry. *Sports Medicine,* **24**, 258–72.

Rowlands, A.V., Eston, R.G. and Ingledew, D.K. (1999). The relationship between activity levels, aerobic fitness, and body fat in 8- to 10-year-old children. *Journal of Applied Physiology,* **86**, 1428–35.

Rowlands, A.V., Ingledew, D.K., and Eston, R.G.

(2000). The relationship between body fatness and habitual physical activity in children: A meta-analysis. *Annals of Human Biology*, **27**, 479–98.

Sallis, J.F. (1991). Self-report measures of children's physical activity. *Journal of School Health*, **61**, 215–19.

Sallis, J.F. and Saelens, B.E. (2000). Assessment of physical activity by self-report: Status, limitations and future directions. *Research Quarterly for Exercise and Sport*, **71**, 1–14.

Sallis, J.F., Patterson, T.L., Buono, J.J. and Nader, P.R. (1988). Relationship of physical fitness and physical activity to cardiovascular disease risk factors in children and adults. *American Journal of Epidemiology*, **127**, 933–41.

Saris, W.H.M. (1986). Habitual activity in children: methodology and findings in health and disease. *Medicine and Science in Sports and Exercise*, **18**, 253–63.

Saris, W.H.M. and Binkhorst, R.A. (1977a). The use of pedometer and actometer in studying daily physical activity in man. Part I. Reliability of pedometer and actometer. *European Journal of Applied Physiology*, **37**, 219–28.

Saris, W.H.M. and Binkhorst, R.A. (1977b). The use of pedometer and actometer in studying daily physical activity in man. Part II. Validity of pedometer and actometer measuring the daily physical activity. *European Journal of Applied Physiology*, **37**, 229–35.

Saris W.H.M., Binkhorst, R.A., Cramwinckel, A.B., *et al.* (1980). The relationship between working performance, daily physical activity, fatness, blood lipids and nutrition in schoolchildren. In *Children and Exercise IX*. eds. K. Berg and B.O. Eriksson (University Park Press, Baltimore), pp. 166–74.

Schoeller, D.A. and van Santen, E. (1982). Measurement of energy expenditure in humans by doubly labelled water method. *Journal of Applied Physiology*, **53**, 955–9.

Sequeira, M.M., Rickenbach, M., Wietlisbach, V., *et al.* (1995). Physical activity assessment using a pedometer and its comparison with a questionnaire in a large population survey. *American Journal of Epidemiology*, **142**, 989–99.

Shapiro, L.R., Crawford, P.B., Clark, M.J., *et al.* (1984). Obesity prognosis: A longitudinal study of children from the age of 6 months to 9 years. *American Journal of Public Health*, **74**, 968–72.

Spirduso, W.W. (1995). *Physical Dimensions of Ageing*. (Human Kinetics, Champaign, IL).

Tell, G.S. and Vellar, O.D. (1988). Physical fitness, physical activity and cardiovascular disease risk factors in adolescents. The Oslo Youth Study. *Preventive Medicine*, **17**, 12–24.

Trost, S.G., Ward, D.S., Moorehead, S.M., *et al.* (1998). Validity of the Computer Science and Applications (CSA) activity monitor in children. *Medicine and Science in Sports and Exercise*, **30**, 629–33.

Wallace, J.P., McKenzie, T.L. and Nader, P.R. (1985). Observed vs. recalled exercise behaviour: A validation of a seven day exercise recall for boys 11–13 year olds. *Research Quarterly for Exercise and Sport*, **56**, 161–5.

Washburn, R., Chin, M.K. and Montoye, H.J. (1980). Accuracy of pedometer in walking and running. *Research Quarterly for Exercise and Sport*, **51**, 695–702.

Watson, A.W.S. and O'Donovan, D.J. (1977). Influence of level of habitual activity on physical working capacity and body composition of post-pubertal school boys. *Quarterly Journal of Experimental Physiology*, **62**, 325–32.

Welk, G.J., and Corbin, C.B. (1995). The validity of the Tritrac-R3D activity monitor for the assessment of physical activity in children. *Research Quarterly for Exercise and Sport*, **66**, 202–9.

Welk, G.J., Corbin, C.B. and Dale, D. (2000). Measurement issues in the assessment of physical activity in children. *Research Quarterly for Exercise and Sport*, **71**, 59–73.

Welsman, J.R., and Armstrong, N. (1992). Daily physical activity and blood lactate indices of aerobic fitness in children. *British Journal of Sports Medicine*, **26**, 228–32.

Woods, J.A., Pate, R.R. and Burgess, M.L. (1992). Correlates to performance on field tests of muscular strength. *Pediatric Exercise Science*, **4**, 302–11.

Thomas Reilly

7.1 AIMS

The aims of this chapter are:
- to outline different means of analysing performance in field games,
- to describe field tests as used for fitness assessment in selected games,
- to exemplify two field tests for use in practical contexts.

7.2 INTRODUCTION

The ultimate goal of the athlete is to excel in performance of the sport in which he or she has specialized. In individual sports such as running, swimming or cycling, the level of performance is gauged by the time taken to reach a set distance. In horizontal or vertical jumping, the performance is indicated by the distance or height of the jump. Similarly, in throwing events competitive performance is measured by the distance the missile is propelled, and body mass is one determinant of performance along with the acceleration of the implement prior to its release. Anthropometric dimensions such as body mass are also relevant in events such as rowing, where propulsion of the shell or boat is a function of the absolute power which the athlete generates.

In these individual sports not only is performance easily assessed in the competitive environment but also it is highly related to individual characteristics. These factors may include anthropometric dimensions (e.g. body mass, body size, body composition, relative segmental lengths), physiological factors (e.g. muscle strength and power, anaerobic capacity, aerobic capacity or endurance, aerobic power as reflected in the maximal oxygen uptake) and biomechanical variables (e.g. mechanical efficiency) and so on. In sports in which complex skills and intricate teamwork are required, the link between individual characteristics and performance capability is not a parsimonious relationship. The relevance of kinanthropometry is obvious in games such as basketball and volleyball where stature provides an advantage but is less apparent in field hockey and Association Football, where there can be a great degree of variability between individuals within one team (see Reilly, 2000a).

In the field games, success in competition is achieved by scoring more goals (or points) than the opposition. The individual team members must harmonize into an effective unit. In such contexts the assessment of how well the team is playing and how much individuals contribute to team effort presents a challenge to the sports scientist. Furthermore, there is a need in such sports for test measures that will give a reasonable prediction of performance capability in applied contexts.

In this chapter various methods for describing performance in games contexts are outlined. Such methodologies include both notation analysis and motion analysis. The emphasis in

Kinanthropometry and Exercise Physiology Laboratory Manual: Tests, Procedures and Data. 2nd Edition, Volume 1: Anthropometry
Edited by RG Eston and T Reilly. Published by Routledge, London, June 2001

monitoring individual profiles is placed on field tests where measurements must have relevance to the sport in question and be socially convenient. For retaining scientific value such tests must be valid, reliable and objective. Examples of field tests for use with games teams are given later in the text.

7.3 METHOD OF ANALYSING TEAM PERFORMANCE

7.3.1 NOTATION ANALYSIS

Notation analysis represents a means of recording observations in an objective manner for the purpose of compiling statistical details of performance parameters. The objectives of notation systems include analysis of movements during play, technical and tactical evaluation and statistical compilation (Hughes, 1988). Principles of notation date back to the use of hieroglyphs by the ancient Egyptians to read dance, and primitive methods of the Romans to record gestures.

Initially, behavioural events were recorded manually, utilizing shorthand codes for notation. The more sophisticated systems entailed considerable learning time. By the mid-1980s computerized notation systems had evolved. These systems were used in conjunction with video recordings, either analysed post-event or in real time. The game may be represented digitally with data collected directly onto the computer, which can then be queried in a structured way. The game is represented in its entirety and contains a large database for manipulation. In this way, the performance of a team as a whole, or individual team members, can be analysed, as can particular aspects of performance such as attack or defence.

The minutiae of performance can be detailed using notation analysis. For every event, the action concerned, the player (or players) involved, and the location of the pitch can be entered into the computer. The method has been employed in a range of field games (Hughes, 1988), in squash (Hughes and Franks,

1994) and other racket sports (Hughes, 1998). Other uses have included the characteristics of the successful patterns of play by Manchester United during the 1998–9 football season and the changes in patterns of play between 1990 and 1999 (Grant and Williams, 1999).

The development of sports science support programmes hastened the acceptance of notation analysis by coaches. Olsen and Larsen (1997) described how notation analysis had benefited the national football team of Norway in competing with the best teams in the world. Currently its main use is in analysing team performance post-event. In conjunction with video-editing facilities it can provide interim feedback to players and coaches, for example in half-time team talks. Surveillance information may also be provided about the style of play of forthcoming opponents. Whilst largely a descriptive tool, notation analysis could be employed by sports scientists to address theory-driven questions. Such issues might include potential links between performance and individual variables characteristic of kinanthropometry.

7.3.2 MOTION ANALYSIS

The physiological demands of field games can be examined by making relevant observations during match-play or by monitoring physiological responses in real or in simulated games. The type, intensity and duration (or distance) of activities can be observed by means of motion analysis. Motion analysis entails establishing work-rate profiles of players within a team according to the intensity, duration and frequency of classified activities, e.g. walking, moving sideways or backwards, jogging, cruising and sprinting. The distribution of the distance covered in these activities over a whole game is illustrated in Figure 7.1.

The total distance covered during a game provides an overall index of work-rate, based on the assumption that energy expenditure is directly related to total work (distance covered) or power output (Reilly and Thomas,

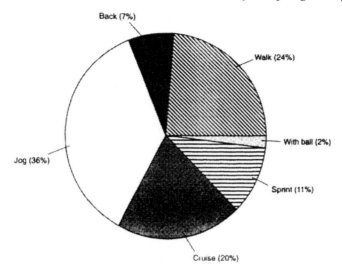

Figure 7.1 The percentages of the total distance covered in a soccer game for each of the categories of activity.

1976). Several methods have been employed in attempts to determine the distance covered during a soccer match. Early attempts focused on the use of hand notation systems for the recording of activity patterns. Such systems tracked players' movements on a scale plan of the pitch. Later systems made use of coded commentaries of activities recorded on audio tape, in conjunction with measurements based on stride characteristics taken from video recordings to evaluate the total distance covered during the 90 minutes of match-play. Other methods have included cine film taken from overhead views of the pitch for computer-linked analysis of the movements of the whole team, and synchronized cameras placed overlooking each half of the pitch to allow calculation of activities by means of trigonometry (Ohashi *et al.*, 1988; Drust *et al.*, 1998). The most sophisticated contemporary method employs 6 cameras, 3 placed high on the stand on each side, allowing observations to be made on all 22 players on the pitch.

Current practical methods favour the use of computerized notation systems to analyse previously recorded video footage of individual players. The total distance covered in each activity classification is estimated by determining stride frequencies on the playback of the video, provided the stride length for each activity is determined separately for the individual concerned. Alternatively, players' movement patterns around the pitch in each activity category can be plotted with estimations of the total distance covered being based on pre-determined pitch dimensions. Following the co-ordinates of the individual player's position on the representation of the pitch, the velocity (and acceleration) data can be computed and distance covered over time calculated. Irrespective of the specific details of the methods employed, all methodologies that are utilized for the measurement of distance should be reliable, objective and valid (Reilly, 1994).

Work-rate profiles in Association Football are influenced by factors such as positional role, the style of play, environmental factors and the level of competition (Reilly, 2000b). They are also influenced by physiological variables such as maximal oxygen uptake (Reilly and Thomas, 1976), endurance capacity (Bangsbo, 1994) and carbohydrate stores (Saltin, 1973). Anthropometric variables may dictate the optimal positions of players, tall players being favoured for central roles in defence and attack. The predisposition of players for positional roles according to their anthropometric characteristics is more pronounced in Rugby Union football (Reilly, 1997) than in Association Football or field hockey (Reilly and Borrie, 1992).

Anthropometric characteristics are more homogeneous in Rugby Sevens than in the 15-a-side version of the game, in view of the need for greater mobility around the pitch in the former. Players in a Rugby Sevens international tournament demonstrated muscular somatotypes (2.3–5.9–1.5), with forwards on average 15 kg heavier than the backs (Rienzi *et al.*, 1999). Anthropometric variables were reported to be significantly related to work-rate components, mesomorphy and muscle mass being negatively correlated with the amount of high-intensity activity during the game. Nevertheless, neither anthropometric profiles nor work-rate measures necessarily determine whether at this level of play a game is won or lost. The same conclusion applies to Association Football at international level (Rienzi *et al.*, 2000).

Notation and motion analysis techniques provide means of evaluating performances of athletes and are a valuable source of feedback in team games in particular. They yield data with respect to the demands that the game imposes on players. The performance capabilities of players are influenced by fitness factors and the demands which players are voluntarily prepared to impose on themselves. Whilst there has been a tradition of testing athletes in laboratory conditions for physiological functions such as maximal oxygen uptake ($\dot{V}O_2$ max) and 'anaerobic threshold' or responses of blood lactate to incremental exercise, the current trend is to use field tests of fitness where possible. The use of field measures increases the social acceptability of fitness testing, saves time when group members can be accommodated together and the sports-specific elements of the test battery are obvious to the practitioners.

7.4 'FIELD' TESTS

7.4.1 GENERIC TESTS

Field tests refer to measures that can be implemented in the typical training environment and do not necessarily require a visit to an institutional laboratory for assessment. An implication is that the test can be performed without recourse to complex monitoring equipment. The Eurofit test battery (EUROFIT, 1988) offers a range of fitness items for which norms are available to help in interpreting results. The Eurofit test battery is referred to in more detail by Beunen in Chapter 3, and by Boreham and Van Praagh in Chapter 8. Whilst the tests utilize performance measures such as runs, jumps, throws and so on, they are designed to assess physiological functions such as strength, power, muscle endurance and aerobic power, albeit indirectly.

The validation of the 20 m shuttle run test for estimation of maximal oxygen uptake (Léger and Lambert, 1982) marked a step forward for sports science support programmes. Athletes may be tested as a squad in a gymnasium or open ground such as a car park or synthetic sports surface. The pace of motion between two lines 20 m apart is dictated by signals from an audio tape-recorder, giving the name 'the bleep test' to the protocol. The pace is increased progressively, analogous to the determination of $\dot{V}O_2$ max on a motor-driven treadmill, until the athlete is forced to desist. The final stage reached is recorded and the $\dot{V}O_2$ max can be estimated using tables provided by the National Coaching Foundation (Ramsbottom *et al.*, 1988). For children, the prediction of $\dot{V}O_2$ max has been validated by Léger *et al.* (1988).

Alternative tests of aerobic fitness have employed runs, either distance run for a given period of time, such as the 12 minute run of Cooper (1968), or a set distance such as the 3 km run validated by Oja *et al.* (1989). The former has been used as a field test in games players whilst the latter has been used mainly for purposes of health-related fitness. The tests are essentially performance measures and have been validated against maximal oxygen uptake. The use of running tests for predicting $\dot{V}O_2$ max has been reviewed elsewhere (Eston and Brodie, 1985).

7.4.2 REPEATED SPRINT TESTS

The capability to reproduce high-intensity sprints may be examined by means of requiring the athlete to reproduce an all-out sprint after a short recovery period. A distance of 30 m is recommended. Timing gates may be set up at the start, after 10 m and at 30 m. There is then a 10 m deceleration zone for the athlete to slow down prior to jogging back to the start line. The recovery period is variable but 25 s is recommended (Williams et al., 1997). When the interval is reduced to 15 s, test performance is significantly related to the oxygen transport system (Reilly and Doran, 1999).

Seven sprints are recommended, from which peak acceleration (over 10 m) and speed (time over 30 m) can be ascertained. A fatigue index can be calculated both for acceleration and speed over 30 m, based on the drop-off in performance over the seven sprints. The mean time for the seven sprints is indicative of the ability to perform several short sprints within a short period of time within a game. Generally, the best performances are in the first and second sprints, the poorest over the sixth or seventh.

7.4.3 SPORTS-SPECIFIC TESTS

(a) The 'yo-yo' test

The 'yo-yo' tests were designed to test the capability to tolerate high-intensity activity for a sustained period. The test was designed by Bangsbo (1998) for relevance to field games. In the tests the player performs repeated 20 m shuttle runs interspersed with a short recovery period during which the player jogs. The time allowed for a shuttle is decreased progressively as dictated by audio bleeps from a tape recorder. The test ends when the athlete is unable to continue, the score recorded being the number of shuttles completed.

The 'yo-yo intermittent endurance' test evaluates the ability to perform intense exercise repeatedly after prolonged intermittent exercise. A 5 s rest period is allowed between each shuttle and the duration of the test in total is between 10 and 20 minutes.

The ability to recover from intense exercise is evaluated by means of the 'yo-yo intermittent recovery' test. The running speeds are higher than in the 'yo-yo intermittent endurance test' but a 10 s period of jogging is allowed between each shuttle. The total duration of the test is between 2 and 15 minutes.

Both tests have two levels, one for elite footballers and another for recreational players. It is recommended that the tests are conducted on a football field with the players wearing football boots. The tests can be completed in a relatively short period of time and a whole squad of up to 30 players can be tested at the same time. The 'yo-yo intermittent recovery test' is used as a compulsory test for football referees in Italy and Denmark, and both tests have been employed in professional teams in a number of European countries.

(b) Dribble tests for Association Football

The tests entail a run, as fast as possible, over a zigzag course whilst dribbling a football. They incorporate an agility component, calling for an ability to change direction quickly. The tests were part of a battery designed for testing young soccer players by Reilly and Holmes (1983) and employed in talent identification programmes (Reilly et al., 2000).

The slalom dribble is a test of total body movement requiring the subject to dribble a ball round a set obstacle course as quickly as possible. Plastic conical skittles 91 cm high and with a base of diameter 23 cm are used as obstacles. Two parallel lines are drawn as reference guides 1.57 m apart. Intervals of 1.83 m are marked along each line and diagonal connections of alternate marks 4.89 m long are made. Five cones are used on the course and a sixth is placed 7.3 m from the final cone, exactly opposite it and 9.14 m from the starting

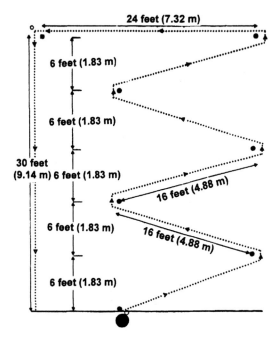

Figure 7.2 The slalom dribble test for soccer players (from Reilly and Holmes, 1983).

line (Figure 7.2). On the command 'go' each subject dribbles the ball from behind the starting line to the right of the first cone and continues to dribble alternately round the remainder in a zigzag fashion to the sixth where the ball is left and the subject sprints to the starting line. The time elapsed between leaving and returning past the starting line is recorded to the nearest one-tenth second and indicates the individual's score. Subjects are forced to renegotiate any displaced cones. A demonstration by the experimenter and a practice run by the subject is undertaken before four trials are performed, with a rest of 20 minutes between trials, the aggregate time representing the subject's score.

In the straight dribble five cones are placed in a straight line perpendicular to the start line, the first 2.74 m away, the middle two separated by 91 cm while the remainder are 1.83 m apart as shown in Figure 7.3. Subjects are required to dribble round alternate obstacles until the fifth is circled, and then to return down the course

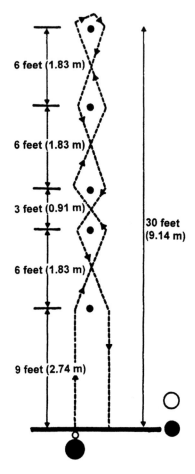

Figure 7.3 The straight dribble test for soccer players (from Reilly and Holmes, 1983).

in similar fashion. The ball has to be dribbled from the final obstacle to the start line, which now constitutes the finish. The aggregate score from four test trials constitutes the overall test score.

(c) Field test for field hockey

A battery of field tests was described by Reilly and Bretherton (1986) for use in assessing female hockey players. The tests consist of a sprint, a T-run dribbling test and a 'distance and accuracy' skill test.

The sprint over 50 yards (45.72 m) is timed to 0.01 s, the fastest of three trials being recorded.

The T-run is over 60 yards (54.86 m) while dribbling a leather hockey ball around skittles. The test involves as many circuits of the T-shaped course as possible in 2 minutes. All subjects are practised in the drill which excludes use of reversed sticks, and the best of the three trials is recorded. The distance and accuracy test involves a combination of dribbling a ball and hitting it at a target, a set sequence being repeated as often as possible within 2 minutes. Distance travelled is calculated to the nearest 2.5 yards (2.29 m) and relative accuracy is calculated by expressing the number of accurate shots as a percent of the number of hits. All subjects are familiarized with the drill before testing takes place.

(d) Field test for Rugby Union football

McLean (1993) described a functional field test for application to Rugby Union. The structure and content of the test were designed so as to relate to the effort and skill patterns a player is called upon to produce in the game. The test was used by the Scotland international squad in preparing for the 1991 Rugby World Cup.

The distance run is about 99 m. The course is run twice with a 45 s recovery which allows the drop-off in performance over the second run to be identified. Penalty points are applied for errors in the skills elements of the test.

The player starts the run with the ball in hand. Skills elements include passing the ball, running round flags, diving to win the ball on the ground, driving a crash pad, jumping and crash-tackling, a tackle bag, picking the ball from the ground. All of these are incorporated within the test. It was reported that players of different ability levels could be discriminated on the basis of performance in the test.

7.6 PRACTICAL 1: THE USE OF REPEATED SPRINT TESTS

7.6.1 AIMS

To determine the athlete's running speed over 10 m and 30 m sprints
To examine the ability to tolerate fatigue over repeated sprints

7.6.2 PROCEDURE

An open 40 m stretch is marked out in a series of zones. Starting gates are set up with electronic timing devices, the timer being activated when a beam of light is broken. Additional timing gates are set up at 10 m and 30 m, the time at each of these distances being recorded as the athlete's body breaks through the light beam. The athlete continues through a 10 m deceleration zone, then jogs back to the start line to perform the next sprint. Meanwhile the observers record the times for 10 m and 30 m and reactivate the telemetry recorder in time for the next sprint. A recovery of 25 s is permitted between sprints.

Verbal encouragement should be given to the athlete throughout the run. The athlete should also be reminded of the number of the forthcoming run and a countdown over 5 s prior to starting. It is important that the runner is stationary in the ready position when the recovery period has elapsed.

The data for two players are illustrated in Table 1. The first player's fastest times are 1.47 s for 10 m and 4.07 s for 30 m. Generally the fastest times are produced in the first two runs and the slowest in one of the last two runs. Thus the player's slowest times are 1.93 s and

4.65 s, respectively. A drop-off can be calculated by expressing the slowest over the fastest time, converting to a percentage and subtracting 100 as follows:

Drop-off (fatigue index)

$$10 \text{ m} = \text{(a) } (1.93/1.47) \times 100 = 131.3\%$$

$$\text{(b) } 131.3 - 100 = 31.3\%$$

$$30 \text{ m} = \text{(a) } (4.65/4.07) \times 100 = 114.3\%$$

$$\text{(b) } 114.3 - 100 = 14.3\%$$

The fatigue index is therefore 31.3% for 10 m and 14.3% for 30 m. In a similar way the drop-off rate can be calculated for the second player. The results are 17.5% and 12.6%, for 10 m and 30 m, respectively.

Table 7.1   Performance times for a games player in a repeated sprint test

		10 m (s)			30 m (s)	
		Player 1	*Player 2*		*Player 1*	*Player 2*
Sprints	1	1.47	1.71		4.09	4.28
	2	1.49	1.73		4.07	4.32
	3	1.60	1.82		4.20	4.41
	4	1.61	1.84		4.28	4.49
	5	1.69	1.90		4.38	4.61
	6	1.89	1.98		4.56	4.68
	7	1.93	2.01		4.65	4.82

7.5 OVERVIEW

There is a rich history of performance testing for particular sports, reflected in the various test and measurement texts (e.g. Kirkendall *et al.*, 1987). These tests have incorporated movements akin to patterns in the game, whether it be basketball (MacDougall *et al.*, 1991) or more recently badminton (Hughes and Fullerton, 1995). The latter test is performed on a regulation badminton court, the speed of movement around a marked course being dictated by a computer-generated sound tone. The test is incremental and consists of three stages, each of 3 minutes. Heart rate and blood lactate responses are recorded and used in the interpretation of results.

The application of scientific principles to field testing has progressed to a point where existing tests are refined and new tests designed. In such instances, one difficulty is that baseline and reference data become obsolete with use of new versions of the test. Applied sports scientists ultimately have to choose between protocols that allow direct physiological interpretations of results or have proven utility for determining game-related performance.

7.7 PRACTICAL 2: COOPER'S 12 MINUTE RUN TEST

7.7.1 AIMS

- To determine endurance capacity by means of recording distance run in 12 minutes
- To estimate maximal oxygen uptake from performance in the 12 minute test

7.7.2 PROCEDURE

A measured outdoor track is required. The ideal condition would be a running track with each lap being 400 m. Alternatively, a marked course around school playing fields can be used.

As the test entails a maximal effort, it is dependent on the motivation of the subject. For this reason the pacing of effort is a potential problem. Subjects can set off at designated intervals between one another and called to stop in turn as time is up.

The distance covered in 12 minutes should be recorded to the nearest 10 m for each individual. This distance is converted to miles, one mile being equivalent to 1609 m. For individual's of a high aerobic fitness level, the test tends to overestimate $\dot{V}O_2$ max and is more useful for health related purposes and recreational players than for serious games competitors. Maximal oxygen ($\dot{V}O_2$ max) can be predicted from the formula:

$$\dot{V}O_2 \ \text{max(ml kg}^{-1} \ \text{min}^{-1}) = \frac{(\text{Distance in miles}(D) - 0.3138)}{0.0278}$$

For example, two athletes, [A] and [B], cover distances of 2.82 km and 1.98 km, respectively in the time allowed. Calculations are as follows:

$$\text{A: } \dot{V}O_2 \ \text{max (ml kg}^{-1}\text{min}^{-1}) = ((2.82/1.609) - 0.3138)/0.0278$$

$$= (1.7526 - 0.3138)/0.0278$$

$$= 1.439/0.0278$$

$$= 52 \ \text{ml kg}^{-1}\text{min}^{-1}$$

$$\text{B: } \dot{V}O_2 \ \text{max (ml kg}^{-1}\text{min}^{-1}) = ((1.98/1.609) - 0.3138)/0.0278$$

$$= (1.2306 - 0.3138)/0.0278$$

$$= 0.9168/0.0278$$

$$= 33 \ \text{ml kg}^{-1}\text{min}^{-1}$$

REFERENCES

Bangsbo, J. (1994). Physiology of soccer – with specific reference to intense intermittent exercise. *Acta Physiologica Scandinavica*, **Suppl. 151**, 169.

Bangsbo, J. (1998). Performance testing in soccer. *Insight: The FA Coaches Association Journal*, **2 (2)**, 21–3.

Cooper, K.H. (1968). A means of assessing maximal oxygen intake correlating between field and treadmill running. *Journal of the American Medical Association*, **203**, 201–4.

Council of Europe, Committee for the Development of Sport, Eurofit (1988). *Handbook for the Eurofit Tests of Physical Fitness* . Committee of the

Development of Sport within the Council of Europe, Rome.

Drust, B., Reilly, T. and Rienzi, E. (1998). Analysis of work-rate in soccer. *Sports Exercise and Injury*, **4**, 151–5.

Eston, R.G. and Brodie, D.A. (1985). The assessment of maximal oxygen uptake from running tests. *Physical Education Review*, **8 (1)**, 26–34.

Grant, A. and Williams, M. (1999). Analysis of the final 20 matches played by Manchester United in the 1998–99 season. *Insight: The FA Coaches Association Journal*, **3 (1)**, 42–45.

Hughes, M. (1988). Computerised notation analysis in field games. *Ergonomics*, **31**, 1585–92.

Hughes, M. (1998). The application of notation analysis to racket sports. In *Science and Racket Sports II*. eds. A. Lees, I. Maynard, M. Hughes and T. Reilly (E. and F.N. Spon, London), pp. 211–20.

Hughes, M. and Franks, I.M. (1994). Dynamic patterns of movement in squash players of different standards in winning and losing matches. *Ergonomics*, **37**, 23–9.

Hughes, M.G. and Fullerton, F.M. (1995). Development of an on-court test for elite badminton players. In *Science and Racket Sports*. eds. T. Reilly, M.Hughes and A. Lees (E. and F.N. Spon, London), pp. 51–4.

Kirkendall, D., Gruber, J.J. and Johnson, R.E. (1987). *Measurement and Evaluation for Physical Education*. (Human Kinetics, Champaign, IL).

Léger, L. and Lambert, J. (1982). A maximal 20-m shuttle run test to predict $\dot{V}O_2$ max. *European Journal of Applied Physiology*, **49**, 1–12.

Léger, L.A., Mercier, D., Gadoury, C. and Lambert, J. (1988). The multistage 20 metre shuttle run test for aerobic fitness. *Journal of Sports Sciences*, **6**, 93–101.

MacDougall, J.D., Wenger, H.A. and Green, H.J. (1991). *Physiological Testing of the High-Performance Athlete*. (Human Kinetics, Champaign, IL).

McLean, D.A. (1993). Field testing in Rugby Union football. In *Intermittent High Intensity Exercise: Preparation, Stresses and Damage Limitation*. eds. D.A.D. Macleod, R.J. Maughan, C. Williams, *et al.* (E. and F.N. Spon, London), pp. 79–83.

Ohashi, J., Togari, H., Isokawa, M. and Suzaki, S. (1988). Measuring movement speeds and distances covered during soccer match-play. In *Science and Football*. eds. T. Reilly, A. Lees, K. Davids and W. Murphy (E. and F.N. Spon, London), pp. 320–3.

Oja, P., Laukkanen, R., Pasanen, M. and Vuori, I. (1989). A new fitness test for cardiovascular epidemiology and exercise promotion. *Annals of Medicine*, **21**, 249–50.

Olsen, E. and Larsen O. (1997). Use of match analysis by coaches. In *Science and Football III*. eds. T. Reilly, J. Bangsbo and M. Hughes (E. and F.N. Spon, London), pp. 209–20.

Ramsbottom, R., Brewer, T. and Williams, C. (1988). A progressive shuttle run test to estimate maximal oxygen uptake. *British Journal of Sports Medicine*, **22**, 141–44.

Reilly, T. (1994). Motion characteristics. In *Football (Soccer)*. ed. B. Ekblom (Blackwell Scientific Publications, Oxford), pp. 78–99.

Reilly, T. (1997). The physiology of Rugby Union football. *Biology of Sport*, **14**, 83–101.

Reilly, T. (2000a). Endurance aspects of soccer and other field games. In *Endurance in Sport*, 2nd edition. ed. R.J. Shephard (Blackwell Scientific Publications, Oxford), pp. 900-30.

Reilly, T. (2000b). The physiological demands of soccer. In *Soccer and Science: an Interdisciplinary Perspective*. ed. J. Bangsbo (Munksgaard, Copenhagen), pp. 91–105.

Reilly, T. and Thomas, V. (1976). A motion analysis of work-rate in different positional roles in professional football match-play. *Journal of Human Movement Studies*, **2**, 87–97.

Reilly, T. and Holmes, M. (1983). A preliminary analysis of selected soccer skills. *Physical Education Review*, **6**, 64–71.

Reilly, T. and Bretherton, S. (1986). Multivariate analysis of fitness in female field hockey players. In *Perspectives in Kinanthropometry*. ed. J.A.P. Day (Human Kinetics, Champaign, IL), pp. 135–42.

Reilly, T. and Borrie, A. (1992). Physiology applied to field hockey. *Sports Medicine*, **14**, 10–26.

Reilly, T. and Doran, D. (1999). Kinanthropometric and performance profiles of elite Gaelic footballers. *Journal of Sports Sciences*, **17**, 922.

Reilly, T., Williams, A.M., Nevill, A. and Franks, A. (2000). A multidisciplinary approach to talent identification in soccer. *Journal of Sports Sciences*, **18**, 695–702.

Rienzi, E., Reilly, T. and Malkin, C. (1999). Investigation of anthropometric and work-rate profiles of Rugby Sevens players. *Journal of Sports Medicine and Physical Fitness*, **39**, 160–64.

Rienzi, E., Drust, B., Reilly, T., *et al.* (2000). Investigation of anthropometric and work-rate profiles of elite South American international soccer players. *Journal of Sports Medicine and Physical Fitness*, **40**, 162–9.

Saltin, B. (1973). Metabolic fundamentals in exercise. *Medicine and Science in Sports*, **5**, 137–46.

Williams, M., Lees, D. and Reilly, T. (1999). *A quantitative analysis of matches played in the 1991–92 and 1997–98 seasons.* The Football Association, London.

Williams, M., Borrie, A., Cable, T., *et al.* (1997). *Umbro Conditioning for Football.* (Ebury, London).

SPECIAL CONSIDERATIONS FOR ASSESSING PERFORMANCE IN YOUNG CHILDREN

8

Colin Boreham and Emmanuel van Praagh

8.1 AIMS

The aims of this chapter are to:
- describe the physical performance of children in the context of growth and maturation,
- examine in detail concepts and practices associated with the testing of aerobic and anaerobic performance in children,
- provide normative tables to aid in the interpretation of EUROFIT field tests of fitness in children.

8.2 INTRODUCTION

Physiological testing of children's performance may be undertaken for a number of reasons, including:

1. *Performance Enhancement* – the regular monitoring of physiological function in young sportspersons may help in the identification of strengths and weaknesses, and as a motivation for training.
2. *Educational* – there is little doubt that fitness testing in the school setting is enjoyable and instructive for the vast majority of pupils, and can be used as an educational tool, particularly in relation to health-related aspects of exercise.
3. *Research* – there is a growing academic interest in paediatric exercise science, whether from the health, performance or growth

viewpoints. The measurement of physiological fitness and various anthropometric factors may shed light on important issues such as the effect of growth on sport performance.

4. *Clinical Diagnosis and Rehabilitation* – as with adults, the diagnosis and treatment of certain clinical conditions in children may be helped by exercise testing. This topic has been comprehensively covered by Bar-Or (1983) and Rowland (1993).

The diversity of approaches outlined above is matched by the variety of methods used to measure performance in children. These vary from sophisticated laboratory-based techniques (e.g. for measuring aerobic power and capacity, isokinetic strength, anaerobic power, and so on) to simple 'field' tests of fitness (e.g. sit-ups, jumping tests, timed distance runs and grip strength). The latter have often been grouped into 'batteries' of tests, which purportedly measure a variety of fitness variables in children. Such batteries include the North American 'AAHPERD' tests (1988) and the European 'EUROFIT' tests (1988) (See Chapter 3 by Beunen, Table 3.4). The limitations of such test batteries may include the high skill factor involved in performing individual test items (and hence the possibility of improvement merely reflecting the learning process) and difficulties in validation. Nevertheless, their

Kinanthropometry and Exercise Physiology Laboratory Manual: Tests, Procedures and Data. 2nd Edition, Volume 1: Anthropometry Edited by RG Eston and T Reilly. Published by Routledge, London, June 2001

usefulness, particularly in an educational setting or where large numbers of individuals need to be tested with limited resources, is often underestimated (Kemper, 1990).

Before examining specific areas of performance testing in children, it is important to review the processes of growth and maturation, and how these may influence test results. Without doubt, a basic understanding of the biological changes which occur throughout childhood, but most particularly at adolescence, is essential if test results are to be interpreted correctly. (For further information on the assessment of biological maturation, see pp. 74–8.)

8.3 GROWTH, MATURATION AND PERFORMANCE

Postnatal growth may be divided into four phases: *infancy* (from birth to one year), *early childhood* (pre-school), *middle childhood* (to adolescence) and *adolescence* (from 8 to 18 years for girls and 10 to 22 years for boys). As children younger than 8–9 years are seldom engaged in competitive sport, and may not possess the motor skills or the intellectual or emotional maturity required for successful fitness testing, the remainder of this chapter will deal primarily with the immediate pre-adolescent and adolescent phases of childhood. Important gender differences will be highlighted.

Generally speaking, sex differences which may influence performance are minimal before adolescence. Girls begin their adolescent growth spurt, on average, two years before boys (12 years vs. 14 years respectively), which can confer a temporary advantage of height and weight for girls around this time (see Figure 8.1). Boys eventually surpass girls in most dimensions during their adolescent growth spurt to attain, on average, a larger stature in adulthood. During the early part of the growth spurt, rapid growth in the lower extremities is evident, while an increased trunk length occurs later, and a greater muscle mass later still. There are also noticeable regional differences in growth during adolescence. Boys, for example, have only a slightly

greater increase in calf muscle mass than girls, but nearly twice the increase in muscle mass of the arm during the adolescent growth spurt (Malina and Bouchard, 1991).

Relatively minor somatic differences between boys and girls are magnified during adolescence. Following the growth spurt, girls generally display a broader pelvis and hips, with a proportionately greater trunk : leg ratio. Body composition also changes from approximately 20% body fat to 25% body fat over this period. Boys, in contrast, may actually become slightly leaner (from 16% to 15% body fat) over the adolescent growth period – a change that is accompanied by a dramatic rise in lean body mass, shoulder width (the shoulder : hip ratio is 1.40:1 in pre-pubertal children, but 1.45:1 in post-pubertal boys and 1.35:1 in mature girls), and leg length. Such differences between the sexes – the boys being generally leaner, more muscular, broader-shouldered and narrower-hipped with relatively straighter limbs and longer legs – have obvious implications for physical performance. Some examples of results from common field tests applied over the adolescent period illustrate these differences clearly (Figure 8.2a, b). It should be borne in mind when comparing physical performances of male and female adolescents, that other factors such as motivation and changes in social interests (Malina and Bouchard, 1991) and the documented fall-off in physical activity, particularly in girls (Boreham *et al.*, 1993) may also influence results. The disproportionate rise in strength of boys compared with girls over the adolescent growth spurt (see Figure 8.2a) has been largely attributed to increasing levels of testosterone in the former (Round *et al.*, 1999).

There is no such individual as the 'average adolescent' performer and confusion can arise as a result of the enormous individual variation inherent in the processes of biological maturation and sexual differentiation. While peak height velocity may, on average, be reached at 12 years for girls and 14 years for boys, there may be as much as five years difference in the

Figure 8.1 A group of 12 year-old schoolchildren illustrates typical variation in biological maturation at this age.

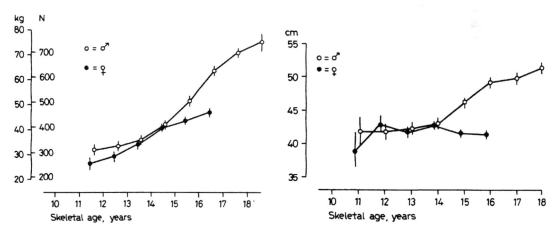

Figure 8.2 Mean and standard error for (left) static arm strength, and (right) vertical jump, in boys and girls versus skeletal age. (Reproduced from Kemper (1985) with the Permission of S Karger AG, Basel.)

timing of this phenomenon, and similar variation in the development of secondary sex characteristics, between any two individuals of the same sex. Thus, a child's chronological age may bear only a passing resemblance to its biological age – the latter being of greater significance to physical performance. This is illustrated in Figure 8.3 which shows that for most performance measures – the notable exception being maximal aerobic power – the early maturer is at a distinct advantage. This is particularly so for tasks requiring strength and power, possibly reflecting the tendency for early maturers to be more mesomorphic than late developers. Such biological variation may be accentuated by differences in chronological age. Within a single year group, a given child may be up to 11 months older than his or her peer. In the rapidly growing adolescent age group, this age difference may confer considerable physical advantages to the older child. A good example of this was provided by Brewer *et al.* (1992) who studied 59 members of the Swedish under-17 soccer squad. They discovered that the majority of the players were born in the first three months of the year, probably resulting in a slightly more advanced biological development. It is noteworthy that, possibly as a result of the relationship between adiposity and early maturity in girls, many of the physical advantages apparent in early maturing boys are absent in females (Malina and Bouchard, 1991).

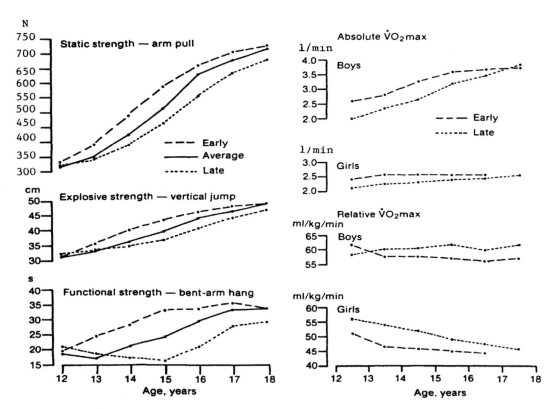

Figure 8.3 Mean motor performance scores of early-, average- and late-maturing boys in the Leuven Growth study of Belgian Boys. (Modified from *Growth, Maturation and Physical Activity* (p. 296) by R.M. Malina and C. Bouchard, 1991 (Champaign, IL: Human Kinetics. Copyright 1991 by Robert M. Malina and Claude Bouchard. Reprinted by permission).

Given the rapid rate of growth during the adolescent growth spurt (peak height velocity of 7–9 cm year^{-1}), it is perhaps not surprising that there is a common perception of 'adolescent awkwardness' during this period. The temporary disruption of motor function during the growth spurt, particularly relating to balance, may be due to a segmental disproportion arising from the period early in the growth spurt, when leg length increases in proportion to trunk length. Boys in particular, but amounting only to 10–30% of the adolescent male population, may be affected (Beunen and Malina, 1988). Furthermore, the effects are temporary, lasting approximately six months, and disappear by early adulthood. The above summary of events associated with growth and development, particularly over the period of adolescence, highlights the complexity of interpreting fitness test scores correctly in children of this age group. A 'poor' score may simply reflect a state of maturity, while an 'improved' score may reflect a change in maturity, irrespective of other factors such as training status.

8.4 PERFORMANCE TESTING OF CHILDREN

Although many of the protocols used for assessing performance in children are similar to those used with adults, there are several unique aspects which the investigator should be aware of. In brief these include the following:

- Although the risks associated with maximal testing of healthy children are low, the tester should take every reasonable precaution to ensure safety of the child. Such steps may include a carefully worded explanation of the test, adequate familiarization beforehand, extra testing staff (e.g. one standing behind a treadmill during testing) and a simple questionnaire relating to clinical contraindications, recent or current viral infections, asthma, and so on.
- Children will be less anxious if the right environment for testing is created. If groups of children are brought to the laboratory, some bright pictures, comics and even a

video will help occupy those who are not involved. Children recover very quickly from maximal effort, and should always be generously rewarded – at least verbally.
- Be aware of the sensitivities of children, particularly in the group situation. It is wise to underplay both extremes of performance.
- Approval for testing children must be sought from the appropriate authorities. For field testing in the school, it is normally sufficient to obtain the Principal's consent as well as that of the children themselves, and to liaise closely with the physical education staff. For laboratory testing, it would be normal practice to obtain consent from parents, children and an appropriate peer-review ethics committee. Children should be told that they are free to withdraw at any time from the test procedures.

8.5 ANTHROPOMETRIC TESTS (BODY COMPOSITION)

Techniques for the anthropometric measurements of stature commonly used with children are somewhat specialized, and are dealt with at length elsewhere (e.g. chapter 4 of Malina and Bouchard, 1991) and by Beunen in Chapter 3 of this text. Nevertheless, it is worth examining measures that may be used to gauge the body composition of children in some detail.

Possibly the simplest measure of assessing body composition in adults is the Body Mass Index (BMI). In growing children, particularly boys, the use of this index as a measure of relative obesity may be misleading, as a large proportion of weight gain during adolescence is lean rather than adipose tissue. Thus, the BMI may increase from 17.8 to 21.3 in 11- and 16-year-old boys respectively, while the sum of four skinfolds (biceps, triceps, subscapular and iliac crest) falls from 33.7 mm to 31.5 mm over the same period. The increase in BMI in girls from 11 to 16 years (from 8.6 to 21.5 respectively) may be a better indicator of increased adipose tissue (sum of four skinfolds rises from 37.2 to 43.1 mm; Riddoch *et al.*, 1991).

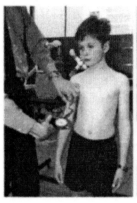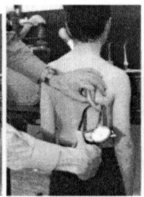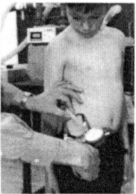

Figure 8.4 Skinfold thicknesses may be measured from (a) biceps, (b) triceps, (c) subscapular and (d) iliac sites.

By far the most common method of measuring body composition in children relies on the use of skinfold thicknesses (Figure 8.4). At least three options are open to the investigators:

1. The classic method published by Durnin and Rahaman (1967), in which the sum of four skinfold thicknesses (from the biceps, triceps, subscapular and iliac crest sites) measured with precision skinfold callipers is transformed into a measure of body fat percentage using Siri's equation (1956). This method is open to criticism, due to the relatively small number of boys and girls

Table 8.1 Prediction equations of percentage fat from triceps and subscapular skinfolds in children and youth for males and females[a]

Triceps and subscapular skinfolds > 35 mm
%Fat = 0.783 Σ SF + I Males
%Fat = 0.546 SF + 9.7 Females

Triceps and subscapular skinfolds (< 35 mm)[b]
%Fat = 1.21 (Σ SF) – 0.008 (Σ SF)^2 + I Males
%Fat = 1.33 (Σ SF) – 0.013 (Σ SF)^2 + 2.5 Females
(2.0 blacks, 3.0 whites)

I = Intercept; varies with maturation level and racial group for males as follows

Age	Black	White
Prepubescent	–3.5	–1.7
Pubescent	–5.2	–3.4
Postpubescent	–6.8	–5.5
Adult	–6.8	–5.5

Notes
[a] From Advances in Body Composition Assessment (p. 74) by T.G. Lohman (1992), Champaign, IL: Human Kinetics. Copyright 1992 by Timothy G. Lohman. Reprinted by permission.
Calculations were derived using the equation of Slaughter et al. (1988).
[b] Thus for a white pubescent male with a triceps of 15 mm and a subscapular of 12 mm, the % fat would be:
%Fat = 1.21 (27) – 0.008 (27)^2 – 3.4
= 23.4%

measured for the original study, and the potential error arising out of the changing body density of growing children (the water content of a child's fat-free mass decreases from 75.2% in a 10-year-old boy, to 73.6% at 18 years; Haschke, 1983). Bone density is also lower during childhood.

2. Because of the above reservations, some investigators choose simply to compare the sum of the four skinfold thicknesses.

3. The third option is to utilize more recently developed child-specific equations for two skinfolds only (Lohman, 1992). These are shown in Table 8.1.

8.6 AEROBIC ENDURANCE PERFORMANCE

If endurance performance is examined in children, a characteristic pattern emerges whereby boys improve continuously until late adolescence, but girls do not, and may even display a drop in performance in their late teens. Figure 8.5 shows the number of 20 m 'laps' completed on a multi-stage shuttle run test, plotted against age. What factors may account for these changes in performance?

It is generally accepted (Sjödin and Svedenhag, 1985) that endurance performance is governed by three factors; (i) aerobic power, or maximum oxygen uptake ($\dot{V}O_2$ max); (ii) aerobic capacity (or sustainable aerobic power), which is largely governed by the individual's 'anaerobic threshold', and (iii) movement economy.

8.6.1 MAXIMAL OXYGEN UPTAKE IN CHILDREN

During growth, $\dot{V}O_2$ max (expressed in litres of oxygen consumed per minute) increases steadily in boys and remains stable or increases only slightly in girls (Figure 8.6a). Such changes are thought to reflect proportional growth during childhood of the relevant structures involved in the transportation and utilization of oxygen during exercise (lungs, heart, muscle and mitochondrial mass). The notable exception is a disproportionate increase in

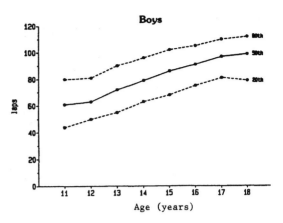

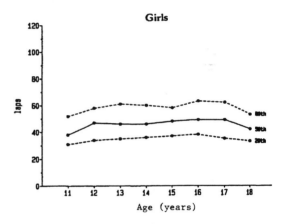

Figure 8.5 Endurance running ability, measured by 'laps' completed in the 20 metre endurance shuttle run. Mean scores and 20th and 80th percentiles are shown. (Reproduced from the Northern Ireland Fitness Survey 1990.)

haemoglobin concentration in boys (from 13 g 100 ml^{-1} blood to 16 g 100 ml^{-1} during adolescence) compared with girls (from 13g 100 ml^{-1} to 14g 100 ml^{-1}).

Maximal oxygen uptake ($\dot{V}O_2$ max) has been traditionally expressed (at least for ambulatory movement) relative to body weight. When viewed in this manner (Figure 8.6b) the $\dot{V}O_2$ max of boys remains relatively stable, while that of girls declines over the adolescent period (the latter largely as a result of changes in fat mass). While some argue convincingly that these changes in relative $\dot{V}O$ max may be

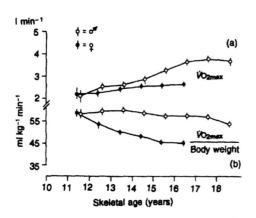

Figure 8.6 Mean and standard error of (a) absolute (l min⁻¹) and (b) relative (ml kg⁻¹ min⁻¹) of boys and girls. (Reproduced from Kemper (1985) with the permission of S. Karger AG, Basel.)

Table 8.2 Biochemical characteristics of m. vastus lateralis in 11–15-year-old boys and adults (Eriksson, 1972; Saltin and Gollnick, 1983)

Characteristic	Boys	Adults
Substrate concentration (mmol kg⁻¹ ww)		
ATP	4.3	5.0
CP	14.5	10.7
Glycogen (glucose units)	54.0	83.8
Enzyme activity (μmol g⁻¹ min⁻¹)		
Phosphofructokinase	8.4	25.2–25.3
Succinate dehydrogenase	4.7–5.8	3.6–4.4

influenced by the scaling method used (Nevill *et al.*, 1992; Winter, 1992) it seems, for the present, that changes in relative $\dot{V}O$ max cannot account for the observed development of endurance performance over childhood (Figure 8.6).

8.6.2 ANAEROBIC THRESHOLD IN CHILDREN

It is now well established that children's muscle is metabolically geared more to aerobic energy metabolism than to anaerobic energy metabolism (Table 8.2). This results in a reduced ability to produce lactic acid during exercise in younger children (Figure 8.7) and a consequent need to adjust the traditional concepts of the 'anaerobic threshold'. For example, the 4.00 mM blood lactate concentration (Heck *et al.*, 1985) which has often been used as a marker of running capacity, may occur at over 90% of $\dot{V}O$ max in 13–14-year-old children, compared with 77% $\dot{V}O$ max of in adults (Williams and Armstrong, 1991). Thus, these authors have suggested the use of 2.5 mM in children as a guide to running capacity, rather than 4.0 mM. Improvements over the adolescent period in the child's ability to produce energy anaerobically (Figure 8.7) may influence maximal running performance, particularly in boys.

8.6.3 MOVEMENT ECONOMY IN CHILDREN

Economy may be defined as the metabolic cost, measured by oxygen consumption, of exercising at a given submaximal workload. It is clear from Figure 8.8 that for running, pre-pubertal children are 10–15% less efficient than adults, and as they mature, they become progressively more economical in their movements. Such differences in efficiency are less apparent in cycle ergometry, leading to the conclusion that biomechanical rather than biochemical factors may be responsible. While various biomechanical differences between children and adults (gait, stretch-shortening cycle, and so on) have been postulated, it is likely that the simple observation of a relatively higher stride frequency at a given speed in children accounts for a large proportion of the observed differences in running efficiency (Unnithan and Eston, 1990). When body mass is used as the covariate (Eston *et al.*, 1993; Armstrong *et al.*, 1999), or when oxygen uptake is expressed as a power function of mass (e.g. 0.75) (Cooke *et al.*, 1991), the differences in oxygen uptake for a given running speed in children and adults disappears (see Volume 2, Chapter 7 by Cooke).

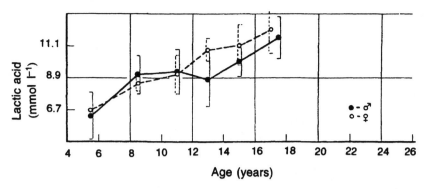

Figure 8.7 Maximal exercise blood lactate concentration in relation to age. (Reproduced from Åstrand (1952) with permission of Munksgaard International Publishers Ltd, Copenhagen.)

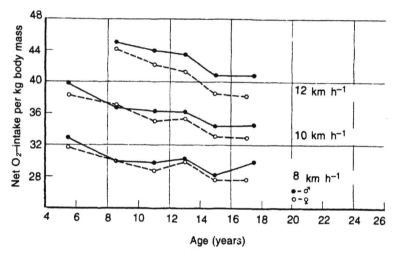

Figure 8.8 Changes in running efficiency with age. Values are mean net oxygen intakes for boys and girls while running at three different speeds. (Reproduced from Åstrand (1952) with permission of Munksgaard International Publishers Ltd, Copenhagen.)

From the above observations, it would appear that the improvement in running performance of growing children – particularly boys – observed in Figure 8.5 is more likely to be due to changes in 'anaerobic threshold' and running economy than to improvements in maximal oxygen uptake. While girls also appear to improve their 'anaerobic threshold' and running efficiency over the period of adolescence, these improvements may be counterbalanced by a decline in relative $\dot{V}O$ max.

8.7 AEROBIC ENDURANCE TESTING IN CHILDREN

Aerobic endurance is often measured in children, as it is in adults, using a progressive, incremental exercise test of some sort, during which oxygen uptake ($\dot{V}O$ max) is measured. While the recent development of sophisticated miniaturized gas analysers may permit measurement of $\dot{V}O$ max in 'free-living' exercise conditions, the bulk of such testing in children takes place using standard laboratory equipment (Figures 6.2 and 8.9).

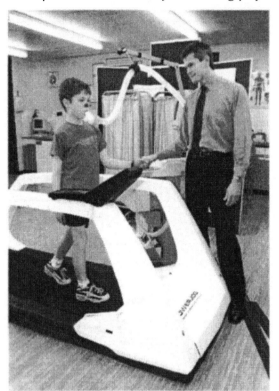

Figure 8.9 The measurement of oxygen uptake during treadmill exercise.

8.7.1 EQUIPMENT

Exercise tests are normally carried out using either a treadmill or cycle ergometer. In general, the treadmill is the preferred instrument with children who may find pedalling difficult, particularly if asked to maintain a set cadence on a mechanically-braked cycle. In addition, cycle ergometry may create local muscular fatigue in the legs of children at higher submaximal intensities, while specially built paediatric cycle ergometers may be required for exercise testing of very small children. Poorly motivated children may also respond better to exercise on a treadmill. On the other hand, the use of a treadmill can hinder procedures such as blood sampling and sphygmomanometry during exercise.

If a cycle ergometer is to be used, the seat height should be adjusted so that the extended leg is almost completely straight at the bottom of the pedal revolution (with the foot in the horizontal position). If a mechanically braked cycle is used, a metronome can provide an audible signal to guide the child's pedalling cadence. A familiarization period should always precede the test, and children should be instructed not to grip the handlebars too tightly.

If the treadmill is used, it may be advisable for the child to wear a safety harness, and for padding to be provided at the rear of the treadmill. Front and side rails may also need adjusting for small children. Before testing, the child should be familiarized with the sensation of walking and running on a moving belt, and with how to mount and dismount the treadmill. Non-verbal signals for stopping should be confirmed. During the test, the investigator should communicate in a positive, friendly manner continuously, and should avoid enquiring as to whether the child feels tired – invariably the answer will be 'yes'! Instead, signs of fatigue (both selective and objective) should be noted, and a heightened state of vigilance maintained towards the end of a test. Above intensities of approximately 85% of $\dot{V}O$ max, children may suddenly stop exercising without prior warning (Rowland, 1993). Anticipation of such an event by the investigator may be helped by the use of a perceived exertion rating scale during the exercise test (Williams *et al.*, 1994; Eston *et al.*, 2000).

After the test, a cool-down at walking speed of at least 5 minutes is recommended, to avoid peripheral venous pooling and syncope. The mouthpiece and nose clip should be removed as soon as possible, and a drink of water, or preferably juice, offered. In the unlikely event of prolonged or repeated exercise testing of pre-pubertal children, in whom thermoregulatory responses may not be fully developed (Sharp, 1991), frequent drinking by the subject should be encouraged if possible.

8.7.2 CRITERIA FOR $\dot{V}O_2$ MAX

Theoretically, the most objective criterion for determining whether a subject has reached $\dot{V}O_2$ max is a plateau in oxygen consumption despite an increase in workload. Most investigators, however, have found difficulty in identifying such a levelling-off in children (Zwiren, 1989). Thus, the term 'peak $\dot{V}O_2$' rather than 'maximum $\dot{V}O_2$' may be more appropriate for children, and the following criteria used to confirm attainment of peak $\dot{V}O_2$ during a test:

1. Heart rate that is 95% of age-related predicted maximum.
2. Respiratory exchange ratio (RER) greater than 1.0.
3. Extreme forced ventilation, or subjective signs of exhaustion.

In practice, it is often subjective exhaustion that terminates a paediatric exercise test. As mentioned above, the onset of this exhaustion may be rapid in the exercising child.

8.7.3 PROTOCOLS FOR MAXIMAL EXERCISE TESTING

Treadmill protocols for children generally involve either the Balke protocol, in which treadmill speed (usually 4.5 – 5.5 km h^{-1}) is held constant, while the slope is increased every minute by 2% (Rowland, 1993) or, more commonly, a modified Bruce protocol (Table 8.3). An appropriate cycle ergometer protocol is the McMaster protocol (Table 8.4). For further details, the reader is referred to Bar-Or (1983).

8.8 DETERMINATION OF THE ANAEROBIC THRESHOLD

Although there is some controversy over terminology, largely arising out of methodological differences, the term 'anaerobic threshold' is still widely used to describe the intensity of exercise at which the oxygen supply becomes insufficient to meet the energy demands of the active muscles. It is generally determined in one of three ways: (i) by blood sampling at various steady-state points of the incremental exercise test, and the determination of blood lactate concentrations in those samples. Lactate concentration may then be plotted against variables such as running speed or $\dot{V}O_2$ max, to denote the sudden changes in slope referred to as the 'onset of blood lactate accumulation' (OBLA). Alternatively, fixed blood concentrations of lactate (usually 2.0 and 4.0 mM in adults) may be used as reference points against which exercise intensity may be compared. This latter approach may be less prone to observer error, and is extremely useful for comparing states of training (Figure 8.10) or

Table 8.3 The Bruce treadmill protocol

Stage	Speed (km h^{-1})	Grade (%)	Duration (min)
1	2.7	10	3
2	4.0	12	3
3	5.5	14	3
4	6.8	16	3
5	8.0	18	3
6	8.8	20	3
7	9.7	22	3

Table 8.4 The McMaster continuous cycling protocol

Body height (cm)	Initial load (W)	Increments (W)	Duration of each load (min)
<119.9	12.5	12.5	2
120–139.9	12.5	25	2
140–159.9	25	25	2
>160	25	25 female	2
		50 male	

maturation. Care should be taken in specifying sampling sites and assay media in the interpretation of blood lactate concentrations (Williams *et al.*, 1992); (ii) the so-called ventilatory anaerobic threshold (T_{vent}). This non-invasive method may be particularly relevant to paediatric exercise testing, and relies upon the identification of an increased ventilatory drive (arising from increased CO_2 production associated with elevated blood lactate concentrations) during exercise. The point at which ventilation (V_E) rises out of proportion to $\dot{V}O$ max is known as the ventilatory anaerobic threshold (T_{vent}). This threshold has also been identified by non-linear increases in CO_2 production (Wasserman, 1984), and abrupt increases in the respiratory exchange ratio (Smith and O'Donnell, 1984), although a comparison of methods (Caiozzo *et al.*, 1982) favoured the use of $V_E/\dot{V}O$ max; (iii) by using the heart-rate deflection point, proposed by Conconi *et al.* (1982). If heart rate is plotted against a progressive workload, a downward deflection can be identified, which has been claimed to coincide with OBLA (Gaisl and Wiesspeiner, 1990) or T_{vent} (Mahon and Vaccaro, 1991). Much debate surrounds the use of the heart-rate deflection point to determine 'anaerobic threshold', and to date, relatively little research has been carried out on this topic with children.

8.9 FIELD TESTS OF AEROBIC ENDURANCE

Not all tests of aerobic endurance require laboratory facilities, and several field tests have been developed to cater for larger groups of children, or where time and equipment may be limited. Most of these tests, such as the 20 m multistage shuttle run (20-MST), and the timed one-mile run / walk, may involve maximal effort, while the cycle ergometer test of physical work capacity (PWC_{170}) does not, requiring only approximately 85% of maximum heart rate to be achieved. The PWC_{170} is, in effect, a compromise between laboratory and field, being restricted to one child at a time, and requiring some equipment (cycle ergometer, metronome, stopwatch) and expertise on the

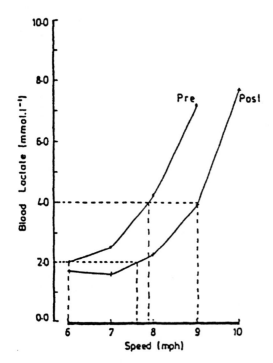

Figure 8.10 Blood lactate concentration during an incremental running test, pre and post one year's endurance training in an individual. (Reproduced with permission from the BASS Position Statement on the Physiological Assessment of the Elite Competitor, 1988).

Table 8.5 Criterion referenced health standards for the one mile run/walk test (min)

Age	FITNESSGRAM	AAHPERD
9	12.00	10.00
10	11.00	9.30
11	11.00	9.00
12	10.00	9.00
13	9.30	8.00
14	8.30	7.45
15	8.30	7.30
16	8.30	7.30

Table 8.6 Normscales for British children: selected EUROFIT test battery items (adapted from Northern Ireland Fitness Survey, 1990)

Percentile		Age 11	12	13	14	15	16	17
Height (mm)								
Boys	80	1502	1573	1630	1686	1744	1800	1817
	50	1441	1496	1560	1628	1690	1732	1756
	20	1389	1436	1498	1558	1642	1668	1703
	Mean	1449	1503	1566	1621	1689	1734	1760
	SD	69	76	82	84	68	70	67
Girls	80	1534	1573	1617	1642	1647	1670	1679
	50	1470	1510	1562	1595	1601	1617	1626
	20	1408	1443	1511	1546	1555	1566	1574
	Mean	1471	1511	1563	1594	1602	1620	1626
	SD	75	77	67	60	60	59	63
Body mass (kg)								
Boys	80	43.7	48.7	54.5	59.3	64.4	72.0	74.2
	50	36.3	41.1	44.7	50.4	57.1	63.5	66.0
	20	31.8	34.1	38.4	43.2	50.9	56.4	58.5
	Mean	37.7	42.1	46.5	51.7	58.0	64.2	66.5
	SD	7.2	8.8	9.9	10.1	9.5	9.6	9.0
Girls	80	47.7	50.3	54.9	59.1	60.1	61.9	62.6
	50	39.2	41.5	47.9	52.2	53.4	55.7	55.9
	20	32.9	36.3	41.2	46.8	48.2	49.8	50.6
	Mean	40.6	43.1	48.7	52.9	54.0	56.5	56.6
	SD	8.9	8.8	9.3	7.9	7.4	7.7	6.9
Skinfolds (sum of four sites: biceps, triceps, subscapular, suprailiac)								
Boys	80	41.9	45.9	41.4	39.0	36.7	38.8	35.7
	50	29.4	30.1	26.6	27.7	26.9	28.3	27.4
	20	22.8	23.3	21.2	21.9	22.7	22.8	22.8
	Mean	33.7	35.6	32.3	31.9	31.6	31.5	30.0
	SD	14.6	16.0	14.9	13.1	13.0	11.4	10.5
Girls	80	48.8	45.5	49.0	53.2	51.6	53.7	49.4
	50	33.1	33.5	34.6	40.2	40.3	41.5	40.1
	20	23.8	26.4	27.7	29.9	31.3	32.3	31.7
	Mean	37.2	36.6	39.2	42.1	42.4	43.1	43.3
	SD	17.0	13.0	14.4	13.8	12.7	12.5	11.7

continued on next page

Table 8.6 Normscales for British children: selected EUROFIT test battery items (adapted from Northern Ireland Fitness Survey, 1990) (cont.)

Percentile		Age 11	12	13	14	15	16	17
20 metre shuttle run (laps)								
Boys	80	80	81	90	96	102	105	110
	50	61	63	72	79	86	91	97
	20	44	50	55	63	68	75	81
	Mean	61	65	72	79	86	90	96
	SD	19	17	19	20	20	18	18
Girls	80	52	58	61	60	58	63	62
	50	38	47	46	46	48	49	49
	20	31	34	35	36	37	38	35
	Mean	41	47	48	49	49	50	50
	SD	13	14	15	16	14	15	16
Sit and reach (cm)								
Boys	80	21.5	21.0	22.5	22.5	26.5	28.0	30.5
	50	16.0	15.0	16.0	17.0	20.0	22.0	24.0
	20	11.5	9.5	10.0	11.5	13.5	15.0	17.0
	Mean	16.5	15.0	16.0	17.0	19.5	22.0	23.5
	SD	6.0	6.5	7.0	6.5	7.5	7.5	8.5
Girls	80	26.5	25.5	27.0	30.5	31.0	31.0	33.0
	50	21.0	21.0	22.0	25.0	25.5	25.5	26.5
	20	15.5	15.5	16.0	19.0	19.5	18.5	20.5
	Mean	20.5	20.5	21.5	24.5	25.0	25.0	26.0
	SD	6.5	6.0	6.5	6.5	6.5	7.0	7.5
Standing long jump (cm)								
Boys	80	162	166	180	188	204	214	218
	50	146	150	161	170	184	194	201
	20	129	133	138	149	162	173	183
	Mean	145	150	161	169	183	195	200
	SD	19	20	23	25	24	24	24
Girls	80	146	153	158	165	163	168	169
	50	130	136	138	143	143	147	148
	20	117	121	122	126	128	128	133
	Mean	131	136	140	144	459	147	151
	SD	19	19	21	22	21	22	22

continued on next page

Table 8.6 Normscales for British children: selected EUROFIT test battery items (adapted from Northern Ireland Fitness Survey, 1990) (cont.)

Percentile		Age 11	12	13	14	15	16	17
Sit-ups in 30 s **(number completed)**								
Boys	80	25	25	27	28	29	29	29
	50	22	23	24	25	25	26	26
	20	19	20	21	21	22	22	22
	Mean	22	23	24	25	25	26	26
	SD	4	4	4	4	4	4	4
Girls	80	22	23	23	23	23	23	23
	50	19	20	19	20	20	20	20
	20	16	17	16	17	17	17	16
	Mean	19	20	19	20	20	20	19
	SD	4	4	4	4	4	4	4
Handgrip strength (N)								
Boys	80	230	260	300	370	440	480	520
	50	190	220	260	290	370	420	460
	20	170	190	220	240	310	360	400
	Mean	200	230	260	300	370	420	460
	SD	40	50	60	70	80	70	70
Girls	80	220	240	270	300	310	320	320
	50	190	200	240	260	270	280	290
	20	150	160	200	230	240	240	250
	Mean	190	200	230	260	270	280	290
	SD	40	40	40	40	40	50	50
10 × 5 m shuttle sprint (s)								
Boys	80	23.3	23.2	21.9	21.5	20.9	20.3	20.0
	50	21.7	21.4	20.6	20.1	19.8	19.1	18.7
	20	20.4	20.1	19.4	18.9	18.6	17.9	17.6
	Mean	21.9	21.6	20.8	20.3	19.8	19.1	18.9
	SD	1.9	1.8	1.6	1.6	1.5	1.4	1.4
Girls	80	25.0	24.1	23.9	23.9	23.6	23.5	23.8
	50	23.3	22.5	22.5	22.4	22.1	21.9	21.9
	20	22.1	21.1	21.3	20.8	20.8	20.4	20.3
	Mean	23.5	22.6	22.7	22.4	22.1	22.0	22.0
	SD	1.8	2.0	1.7	1.9	2.2	1.9	2.0

part of the tester. For full details of the test protocol, the EUROFIT handbook should be consulted (EUROFIT, 1988).

The 20-MST and one-mile run / walk tests have been employed extensively by European and North American investigators, respectively. Both have shown variable but generally moderate correlations against laboratory-measured $\dot{V}O$ max (Van Mechelen *et al.*, 1986; Boreham *et al.*, 1990; Safrit, 1990) but this is not surprising given that endurance running performance is governed by other factors such as anaerobic threshold and running efficiency as well as $\dot{V}O$ max (see above).

The one-mile run / walk test has been incorporated into both the AAHPERD (1988) and FITNESSGRAM (1987) test batteries, and criterion-referenced standards for health developed. The standards adopted for AAHPERD are somewhat more stringent (Table 8.5).

The 20-MST, unlike the one-mile run / walk test, does not require a large, marked running area, and can conveniently be carried out indoors, provided that a hall at least 20 m long is available. Originally developed by Léger and Lambert (1982), the test consists of running to and fro between two lines, 20 m apart, in time with a pre-recorded audio signal from a cassette tape (Figure 8.11). Starting at a pace of 8.5 km h^{-1}, the speed progressively increases each minute until the child can no longer keep up with the required pace. A lap scoring protocol has been developed (Northern Ireland Fitness Survey, 1990) which may be particularly useful for testing children. Full details of the 20-MST are available in the EUROFIT manual (1988), and norms are also available (refer to Table 8.6 and Table 8.7).

Table 8.7 Normscales for Dutch children: EUROFIT test battery items (adapted from van Mechelen et al., 1992). Eurofit variable for boys aged 12 years

Scale	Low score	Below average	Average	Above average	High score
Test					
Standing long jump (cm)	<151	152–154	155–168	169–175	from 176
Bent arm hang (s)	<10.3	10.4–15	15.1–21.6	21.7–30.7	from 30.8
10 × 5 m run (s)	<20.8	20.0–20.7	19.4–19.9	18.7–19.3	18.6 and lower
Sit and reach (cm)	<12	13–15	16–18	19–22	from 23
Sit-ups (no. in 30)	<18	19–21	22–23	24–25	from 26
Body height (cm)	<152	153–156	157–160	161–165	from 166
Body mass (kg)	<39	40–43	44–47	48–51	from 52
Sum 4 skinfolds (mm)	<21	22–26	27–30	31–38	from 39
20 m shuttle (steps/paliers)	<5.0	5.5–6.5	7.0–7.5	8.0–9.0	from 9.5
Handgrip (kg)	<24	25–26	27–28	29–32	from 33

Table 8.7 (cont.) Eurofit variables for boys aged 13 years

Scale	Low score	Below average	Average	Above average	High score
Test					
Standing long jump (cm)	<152	153–162	163–172	173–184	from 185
Bent arm hang (s)	<8.6	8.7–15.2	15.3–22.0	22.1–31.3	from 31.4
10 × 5 m run (s)	<20.7	19.9–20.6	19.3–19.8	18.6–19.2	18.5 and lower
Sit and reach (cm)	<11	12–15	16–19	20–22	from 23
Sit-ups (no. in 30 s)	<18	19–21	22–23	24–25	from 26
Body height (cm)	<154	155–160	161–164	165–170	from 171
Body mass (kg)	<42	43–46	47–50	51–56	from 57
Sum 4 skinfolds (mm)	<21	22–25	26–31	32–42	from 43
20 m shuttle (steps/paliers)	<5.5	6.0–6.5	7.0–7.5	8.0–8.5	from 9.0

Eurofit variables for boys aged 14 years

Scale	Low score	Below average	Average	Above average	High score
Test					
Standing long jump (cm)	<157	158–170	171–181	182–194	from 195
Bent arm hang (s)	<10.5	10.6–17.6	17.7–25.4	25.5–38.5	from 38.6
10 × 5 m run (s)	<20.4	19.6–20.3	19.0–19.5	18.2–18.9	18.1 and lower
Sit and reach (cm)	<11	12–17	18–21	22–26	from 27
Sit-ups (no. in 30 s)	<19	20–21	22–23	24–25	from 26
Body height (cm)	<160	161–165	166–171	172–177	from 178
Body mass (kg)	<46	47–52	53–57	58–63	from 64
Sum 4 skinfolds (mm)	<21	22–25	26–29	30–40	from 41
20 m shuttle (steps/paliers)	<6.0	6.5–7.0	7.5–8.0	8.5–9.0	from 9.5

Table 8.7 (cont.)   Eurofit variables for boys aged 15 years

Scale	Low score	Below average	Average	Above average	High score
Test					
Standing long jump (cm)	<169	170–182	183–193	194–206	from 207
Bent arm hang (s)	<15.3	15.4–25.3	25.4–35.3	35.4–46.6	from 46.7
10 × 5 m run (s)	<19.9	19.0–19.8	18.2–18.9	17.7–18.1	17.6 and lower
Sit and reach (cm)	<12	13–18	19–23	24–27	from 38
Sit-ups (no. in 30 s)	<20	21–22	23–24	25–26	from 27
Body height (cm)	<168	169–173	174–177	178–181	from 182
Body mass (kg)	<53	54–58	59–62	63–69	from 70
Sum 4 skinfolds (mm)	<21	22–24	25–27	28–35	from 36
20 m shuttle (steps/paliers)	<6.5	7.0–7.5	8.0–9.0	9.5–9.5	from 10
Handgrips (kg)	<34	35–41	42–45	46–51	from 52

Eurofit variables for boys aged 16 years

Scale	Low score	Below average	Average	Above average	High score
Test					
Standing long jump (cm)	<181	182–193	194–201	202–211	from 212
Bent arm hang (s)	<19.5	19.6–32.4	32.5–42.8	42.9–51.4	from 51.5
10 × 5 m run (s)	<19.4	18.6–19.3	18.1–18.5	17.5–18.0	17.4 and lower
Sit and reach (cm)	<16	17–19	20–23	24–28	from 29
Sit-ups (no. in 30 s)	<20	21–22	23–24	25–26	from 27
Body height (cm)	<174	175–177	178–182	183–185	from 186
Body mass (kg)	<57	58–62	63–66	67–72	from 73
Sum 4 skinfolds (mm)	<19	20–22	23–26	27–32	from 33
20 m shuttle (steps/paliers)	<7.5	8.0–8.0	8.5–9.0	9.5–10.0	from 10.5
Handgrips (kg)	<42	43–47	48–51	52–56	from 57

Table 8.7 (cont.)   Eurofit variables for girls aged 12 years

Scale	Low score	Below average	Average	Above average	High score
Test					
Standing long jump (cm)	<139	140–149	150–157	158–165	from 166
Bent arm hang (s)	<3.8	3.9–7.5	7.6–12.6	12.7–22.0	from 22.1
10 × 5 m run (s)	<21.7	20.8–21.6	20.1–20.7	19.5–20.0	19.4 and lower
Sit and reach (cm)	<20	21–23	24–26	27–29	from 30
Sit-ups (no. in 30 s)	<17	18–18	18–20	21–22	from 23
Body height (cm)	<153	154–158	159–162	163–166	from 167
Body mass (kg)	<40	41–45	46–50	51–55	from 56
Sum 4 skinfolds (mm)	<26	27–34	35–42	43–51	from 52
20 m shuttle (steps/paliers)	<3.5	4.0–4.5	5.0–5.5	6.0–6.5	from 7.0
Handgrips (kg)	<21	22–24	25–26	27–30	from 31

Eurofit variables for girls aged 13 years

Scale	Low score	Below average	Average	Above average	High score
Test					
Standing long jump (cm)	<141	142–151	152–160	161–171	from 172
Bent arm hang (s)	<3.8	3.9–7.4	7.5–13.4	13.5–20.4	from 20.5
10 * 5 m run (s)	<21.8	20.9–21.7	20.3–20.8	19.4–20.2	19.3 and lower
Sit and reach (cm)	<20	21–24	25–28	29–32	from 33
Sit-ups (no. in 30 s)	<16	17–18	19–20	21–22	from 23
Body height (cm)	<156	157–160	161–164	165–168	from 169
Body mass (kg)	<44	45–48	49–52	53–57	from 58
Sum 4 skinfolds (mm)	<29	30–36	37–43	44–56	from 57
20 m shuttle (steps/paliers)	<4.0	4.5–4.5	5.0–5.5	6.0–6.5	from 7.0
Handgrips (kg)	<23	24–26	27–29	30–31	from 32

Table 8.7 (cont.)   Eurofit variables for girls aged 14 years

Scale	Low score	Below average	Average	Above average	High score
Test					
Standing long jump (cm)	<143	144–152	153–162	163–171	from 172
Bent arm hang (s)	<3.1	3.2–5.9	6.0–10.5	10.6–19.6	from 19.7
10 × 5 m run (s)	<21.7	20.7–21.6	20.0–20.6	19.2–19.9	19.1 and lower
Sit and reach (cm)	<20	21–24	25–28	29–32	from 33
Sit-ups (no. in 30 s)	<16	17–18	19–20	21–22	from 22
Body height (cm)	<161	162–164	165–168	169–171	from 172
Body mass (kg)	<49	50–52	53–56	57–62	from 63
Sum 4 skinfolds (mm)	<33	34–39	40–44	45–54	from 55
20 m shuttle (steps/paliers)	<4.0	4.5–5.0	5.5–5.5	6.0–6.5	from 7.0
Handgrips (kg)	<26	27–28	29–31	32–34	from 35

Eurofit variables for girls aged 15 years

Scale	Low score	Below average	Average	Above average	High score
Test					
Standing long jump (cm)	<142	143–151	152–161	162–171	from 172
Bent arm hang (s)	<3.4	3.5–6.3	6.4–10.8	10.9–17.2	from 17.3
10 × 5 m run (s)	<21.3	20.7–21.2	19.9–20.6	19.3–19.8	19.2 and lower
Sit and reach (cm)	<21	22–27	28–30	31–34	from 35
Sit-ups (no. in 30 s)	<16	17–17	18–19	20–21	from 22
Body height (cm)	<161	162–165	166–169	170–173	from 174
Body mass (kg)	<51	52–55	56–59	60–64	from 65
Sum 4 skinfolds (mm)	<36	37–43	44–50	51–62	from 63
20 m shuttle (steps/paliers)	<4.0	4.5–4.5	5.0–5.5	6.0–6.5	from 7.0
Handgrips (kg)	<27	28–30	31–33	34–37	from 38

Table 8.7 (cont.)   Eurofit variables for girls aged 16 years

Scale	Low score	Below average	Average	Above average	High score
Test					
Standing long jump (cm)	<145	146–153	154–162	163–171	from 172
Bent arm hang (s)	<3.0	3.1–6.8	6.9–12.2	12.3–20.1	from 20.2
10 × 5 m run (s)	<21.1	20.3–21.0	19.5–20.2	19.1–19.4	19.0 and lower
Sit and reach (cm)	<24	25–29	30–31	32–34	from 35
Sit-ups (no. in 30 s)	<16	17–18	19–20	21–23	from 24
Body height (cm)	<162	163–166	167–168	169–171	from 172
Body mass (kg)	<51	52–56	57–60	61–63	fom 64
Sum 4 skinfolds (mm)	<34	35–41	42–49	50–60	from 61
20 m shuttle (steps/paliers)	<4.0	4.5–5.0	5.5–5.5	6.0–6.5	from 7.0
Handgrips (kg)	<28	29–31	32–33	34–37	from 38

Figure 8.11 The 20 metre endurance shuttle run test (20-MST).

8.10 MUSCLE STRENGTH

Strength is the ability of muscle to generate force, and is determined both by myogenic factors (mainly muscle cross-sectional area) and neurogenic factors (e.g. skill, muscle fibre 'recruitment'; Sharp, 1991). Typical isometric strength gains during adolescence for boys and girls are illustrated in Figure 8.2a, and it is thought that the sudden and disproportionate increase in boys' strength in late adolescence is primarily due to the increases in muscle size resulting from rising testosterone concentrations (Round *et al.*, 1999). Thus, while girls may be 90% as strong as boys at 11–12 years, this drops to 85% by 13–14 years and 75% by 15–16 years (Israel, 1992). Strength may be measured in the laboratory, using sophisticated isokinetic dynamometers, or more usually with simple portable or hand-held dynamometers (Figure 8.12). The protocols are essentially the same for both adult and child subjects (McDougall *et al.*, 1982).

8.11 MEASUREMENT OF ANAEROBIC POWER IN CHILDREN

Human performance-related fitness may involve activities of extremely short duration (<1 s) and short-term activities over the first 10 s to 1 minute. The measurement of short-term power raises several theoretical questions. For instance, an individual's power output depends on the duration of the test (instantaneous power or mean power); on the muscle groups involved (legs, arms or both); on the type of muscle contraction or movement (concentric, eccentric, monoarticular, polyarticular); and on the joint range of motion. This section will focus on laboratory and field tests that assess mechanical power of children and adolescents.

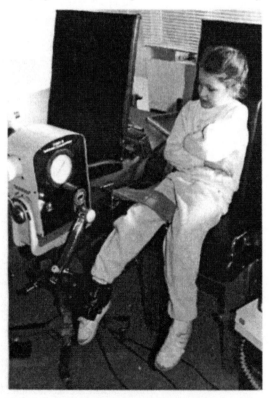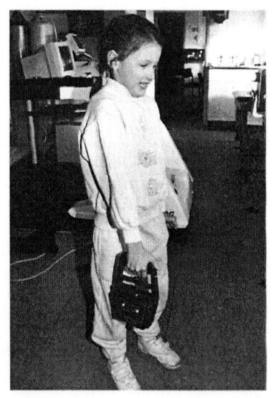

Figure 8.12 Strength may be tested (a) in the laboratory, using isokinetic apparatus, or (b) using a simple isometric hand dynamometer.

8.11.1 DEFINITION

Power refers to the ability of the neuromuscular system to produce the greatest possible impulse in a given time period. The time period depends on the resistance or the load against which the subject has to work and on the nature of the acceleration involved. In some physical activities and sports it is necessary to overcome resistance with the greatest possible speed of muscle action at the beginning of the movement (sprinting, jumping or throwing). In others, the maximal acceleration should be delayed to reach a maximal velocity for the body or parts of the body. Power production is therefore limited by the rate at which energy is supplied (adenosine triphosphate (ATP) production) for the muscle contraction (ATP utilization), or in other words the rate at which the myofilaments can convert chemical energy into mechanical work.

(a) ATP production

- *Anaerobic power*: is the maximal anaerobic ATP per second yield by the whole organism, during a specific type of short duration, maximal exercise (Green, 1994). Anaerobic power is characterized by the generation of very high power outputs (from about 1200 W in 11-year-old untrained children to about 6000 W in power athletes (Grassi *et al.*, 1991).
- *Anaerobic capacity*: is the maximal amount of ATP resynthesized via anaerobic metabolism (by the whole organism) during a specific type of short-duration, maximal exercise (Green, 1994). The anaerobic ATP yield during exercise can be estimated and provides a direct measure of anaerobic capacity. Short-term anaerobic muscle metabolism can also be investigated during exercise by the use of phosphorus magnetic resonance spectroscopy (^{31}P NMRS).

(b) Power output

Using work output to estimate or to reflect anaerobic capacity, is less difficult than attempting to quantify the ATP yield using 'direct methods' (e.g. needle biopsy, ^{31}P NMRS, or Accumulated Oxygen Deficit techniques). However, interpreting the physiological implications of work outputs is certainly more awkward. This is especially true as the mechanical work estimates reflect not only anaerobic ATP supply, but also the contribution of oxidative sources of ATP, as well as the various factors involved in the transduction of chemical to mechanical energy (or work done). Thus, factors which influence work estimates of anaerobic capacity may not be completely anaerobic in nature (Van Praagh *et al.*, 1991; Hebestreit *et al.*, 1993).

8.12 DEVELOPMENTAL ASPECTS OF ANAEROBIC PERFORMANCE

8.12.1 MUSCLE ENERGETICS

A few studies on muscle storage of phosphagens at rest have shown that the content of the peripheral energy-delivering substrates is the same for both children and adults (Eriksson *et al.*, 1971; Ferretti *et al.*, 1994). There are a limited number of reports of low glycolytic ability in pre-pubescent children when compared with adults. The exact underlying mechanism for relatively low anaerobic function is still unclear. In several textbooks and scientific reports, it is still assumed that the rate of anaerobic glycolysis is limited in children, because of their lower phosphofructokinase (PFK) activity. This assumption has been discussed only on the basis of the results of PFK activity at rest by Eriksson *et al.* (1973), who reported a 30% lower resting PFK activity in children compared with adults. In contrast to Eriksson's results, the pre-pubertal children studied by Berg *et al.* (1986) did not show the expected lower activities of glycolytic enzymes. The use of ^{31}P NMRS now provides safe and non-invasive means of monitoring intracellular inorganic phosphate (Pi), phosphocreatine (PCr), adenosine triphosphate (ATP) and pH at rest, during exercise and recovery (Zanconato *et al.*,

1993; Kuno *et al.*, 1995). These studies provide evidence of a reduced muscle glycolytic ability during exhaustive exercise and recovery in children compared with adults. These findings are consistent with the numerous reports of the relatively low muscle and blood lactates response to high-intensity exercise in children (for review see Cooper, 1995; Cooper and Barstow, 1996).

8.12.2 ANAEROBIC POWER

Many authors have reported an increase in anaerobic power with growth (Falk and Bar-Or, 1993; Fargeas, 1993; Fargeas *et al.*, 1993a, 1993b; Bar-Or, 1996; Van Praagh, 1996; Van Praagh and França, 1998; Doré *et al.*, 1999). Gender-related differences in anaerobic performance are apparent as early as 10–11 years of age. Boys have consistently higher average absolute cycling peak power (W) than girls between 13 and 21 years of age. Any gender differences are observed prior to the male pubertal growth spurt. Peak power continues to increase throughout childhood in males and up to puberty in females, even after normalizing for body mass (Doré *et al.*, 1999). The gender difference in relative anaerobic power (W kg^{-1}) before puberty is probably due partly to the higher proportion of fat mass in females during this period (Malina and Bouchard, 1991). The difference between sexes during puberty and adolescence may also be due to a greater absolute and proportional increase in fat mass in females and to a proportionately greater increase in muscle mass in males (Van Praagh *et al.*, 1990).

8.13 ANAEROBIC TESTING IN YOUNG PEOPLE

Although quantitative measurements of anaerobic energy supply during short-term exercise can be made by invasive techniques in adults, this kind of investigation is ethically questionable in the healthy child. Therefore, in this particular population some researchers have concentrated on measuring short-term

power generated during standardized tests (Bar-Or, 1996; Van Praagh, 1996; Van Praagh and França, 1998). Numerous daily activities and sports require a burst of muscular contractions of very short duration (<1 s). This instantaneous power reflects the ability to transform ATP into external power (Ferretti *et al.*, 1987). High muscle power output may also be sustained over a longer time period (>1 to 60 s). We may therefore consider:

* Instantaneous anaerobic performance (<1 s of duration) and
* Short-term anaerobic power (>1 to 60 s).

8.13.1 FUNDAMENTAL CONSIDERATIONS

Assessment of short-term power output raises several methodological problems:

* Since power is the product of force and velocity, the external load (for example, load on the cycle ergometer or body mass during jumping or running) must closely match the capability of the active muscles so that they operate at their optimal velocity (Wilkie, 1960). Clearly, this is a difficult condition to fulfil or to guarantee in freely accelerating or decelerating cycling or running sprint efforts. Several activities have been proposed for the measurement of short-term power output, including vertical jumping, running and cycle ergometry. Of these activities, only cycle ergometry allows precise measurement of power independent of body mass as the imposed load.
* If 'true' peak power output is to be measured, the duration of the test must be as short as possible, because power output decreases rapidly as a function of time (Wilkie, 1960; Van Praagh *et al.*, 1989). The measurement of 'true' peak power requires measurements of instantaneous values of force and velocity. This condition is only satisfied in monoarticular force–velocity tests (Wilkie, 1950), force platform tests (Davies and Rennie, 1968; Ferretti *et al.*, 1987), isokinetic cycle ergometry (Sargeant *et al.*, 1981), cycling power

tests including frictional force and flywheel inertia (Lakomy, 1986; Arsac *et al.*, 1996), and inertial-load cycling ergometry (Martin *et al.*, 1997). For example, the well-known 30 s Wingate test does not provide instantaneous measures and is, therefore, unable to elicit maximum power.

• Anaerobic glycolysis and aerobic contribution are limited during instantaneous power tests, although the aerobic fraction in pre-pubescent and adolescent boys is higher than in young men (Van Praagh *et al.*, 1991; Hebestreit *et al.*, 1993). Lactate production starts during the first seconds of a supra-maximal exercise. In adults (Saltin *et al.*, 1971), as in adolescents (Mercier *et al.*, 1991), glycolytic metabolism is already involved in exercise lasting less than 10 s. Therefore, only exercises lasting a few seconds can be considered as truly 'alactacid' (Ferretti *et al.*, 1987).

• Factors influencing peak power include whether: (1) instantaneous or mean power is measured; (2) the legs act simultaneously (vertical jumping) or successively (cycling); (3) total body mass or active muscle mass is taken into account (Van Praagh *et al.*, 1990); (4) peak power is measured at the beginning of exercise or after several seconds of a flying start (Vandewalle *et al.*, 1987). In all short-term power tests there are no objective criteria to confirm maximal peak power and thus the researcher or trainer must rely on the willing cooperation of the subject to work to his or her maximum.

8.13.2 TESTS OF INSTANTANEOUS ANAEROBIC PERFORMANCE

(a) **Monoarticular force-velocity tests**

Movement across a single joint (e.g. elbow or knee) can be measured with devices which control the force or the velocity of the movement. In adults, the first measurements were carried out with an isokinetic ergometer by means of mono-articular ballistic exercises such as elbow flexion or extension (Wilkie, 1950). For a comprehensive review see Vandewalle *et al.* (1987). This technique has some drawbacks. Firstly, isokinetic dynamometer recordings are rarely generated under true constant angular velocity (Murray and Harrison, 1986). Secondly, torque is measured throughout a range of motion at different limb velocities. Moreover, Sargeant (1989) reported the difficulty of voluntarily accelerating a limb to optimal velocity for peak power output. Thirdly, there is a need to standardize the torque–velocity relationship. Some authors report measured torque at slow (0.52 rad s^{-1}) and/or fast (5.23 rad s^{-1}) angular velocities. Finally, because isokinetic dynamometers are designed for adults, modification of the equipment is required to test children. Isokinetic strength methodology and results obtained during childhood and adolescence have been reviewed by Baltzopoulos and Kellis (1998).

(b) **Force platform vertical jump test**

Sophisticated instrumentation (force platform plus computer analysis) now enables the ground reaction forces and acceleration of the body's centre of mass to be recorded. Peak power output is calculated from the product of instantaneous force exerted by the subject on the force platform and the acceleration of the body's centre of mass. The use of the force platform technique improves the validity of the vertical jump test. Ferretti *et al.* (1994) measured maximal leg power in children aged 8–13 years. They used a method described by Davies and Rennie (1968), but the jump started from a squatting position, to minimize counter-movements. The velocity was obtained by time integration of the instantaneous acceleration, which is equal to the ratio of force to the subject's mass.

(c) **Cycling ergometry**

Isokinetic method

To obtain 'true' maximal power output, it is essential to match the external load to the capability of the active muscles to operate at their optimal velocity. As the velocity in anaerobic tests which employ a constant force is progressively reduced due to muscle fatigue, these conditions are hard to fulfil. To overcome the above shortcoming, Sargeant *et al.* (1981) developed an isokinetic cycle ergometer, where velocity is maintained constantly throughout the test. The level of peak force is inversely and linearly related to crank velocity over the range studied. In children, the intra-individual variation of the peak force was <6% (Sargeant *et al.*, 1984).

Force–velocity test (inertia included)

The inertia of the ergometer flywheel may induce errors in measurement of peak power of up to 30% (Lakomy, 1986). According to Martin and Malina (1998) the error may be even larger in children because the inertial load component represents a larger portion of total power for children than for adults. Cycle ergometry is performed on a friction-braked ergometer. Prior to the test, all subjects complete a habituation session. Each subject cycles submaximally for 2 minutes followed by a brief sprint. The test consists of three short 'all-out' sprints against different braking forces. During the acceleration of the flywheel the subject has to produce a total external force dependent on both a constant frictional force and an inertial force. The product of total external force multiplied by the pedalling rate allows the calculation of the instantaneous power of the subject (Doré *et al.*, 1999).

8.13.3 TESTS OF SHORT-TERM ANAEROBIC PERFORMANCE (INCLUDING FIELD TESTS)

(a) Cycling ergometry

External leg (or arm) power can be assessed on a cycle ergometer by measuring the velocity (v) of cycling for a given braking force (N). This method is used in the popular Wingate test (WAnT). Power can also be measured by determining the relationship between force and velocity, the so-called 'Force–Velocity Test' (FVT).

Arm cycling

Few data are available concerning children. Peak power and local muscle endurance determined during arm cranking (Wingate protocol) appears to increase for boys, but not for girls during the adolescent period (Blimkie *et al.*, 1988). More recently, Nindl *et al.* (1995) measured upper-body anaerobic power in male and female adolescent athletes. Peak power normalized for body mass, fat-free mass and cross-sectional area was significantly higher in boys than in girls.

Leg cycling

30 s Wingate Test

Cumming (1973) was the first to investigate short-term power on a cycle ergometer in 12–17-year-old children (the 30 s cycling test). The absolute braking force for the children to overcome in this supramaximal test was 4–4.5 kg (39.2–44.1 N) for girls and boys, respectively. This test was further developed by researchers of the Wingate Institute (Bar-Or, 1996). The test involves the subject pedalling on a cycle ergometer at a maximal velocity against a constant braking force (Table 8.8) for 30 s. This constant braking force is predetermined to produce mechanical power equivalent to between two and three times the metabolic power obtained during a $\dot{V}O$ max test. Peak power reflects the ability of the leg muscles to produce short-term mechanical power, whereas mean power or total work represents the local muscle endurance of the legs. For further information concerning the test protocol, the reader can consult recent reviews (Bar-Or, 1996; Van Praagh, 1996). The Wingate test has been examined more extensively than any other anaerobic performance test for several paediatric populations (abled, disabled, trained) and found to be highly valid and reliable. Test–retest reliability coefficients range from 0.89 to 0.97 (Tirosch *et al.*, 1990). Representative values in children are available (Bar-Or, 1996).

Table 8.8 Optimal resistance for the Wingate anaerobic test, by body-weight groups, using the Monark Cycle Ergometer

| Body mass (kg) | Resistance (kp[a]) | |
	Legs	Arms
20–24.9	1.75	1.25
25–29.9	2.13	1.50
30–34.9	2.50	1.75
35–39.9	2.83	2.00
40–44.9	3.25	2.25
45–49.9	3.63	2.50
50–54.9	4.00	2.75
55–59.9	4.50	3.00
60–64.9	5.00	3.35
65–69.9	5.50	3.70

(Reproduced from Bar-Or (1983) with the permission of Springer-Verlag.)

[a] 1 kp is the force acting on the mass of 1 kg at normal acceleration of gravity: 1 kp = 9.8066 N or approximately 10 N.

Force–Velocity Test (inertia not included)

With Wilkie's rationale (maximal power = optimal force × optimal velocity) in mind, i.e. it is not possible to measure maximal power with the same braking force, sprint cycling protocols which have used variable loads have been used (Maréchal *et al.*, 1979; Pirnay and Crielaard, 1979). In these studies, subjects performed several all-out sprints (5–7 s) on a Monark cycle ergometer at incremental loads from 3–7 kp, followed by a 3-minute recovery after each sprint. The highest value of peak power was assumed to correspond to peak power. Average peak power values of 7.6 W kg[-1] and 10.1 W kg[-1] were observed in 11-year-old boys and 19-year-old men, respectively. This test was the precursor of the load-optimization or force–velocity test (see Chapter 11, Volume 2, by Winter and MacLaren). In adults, both Pérès *et*

al. (1981) on a friction-loaded ergometer, and Sargeant *et al.* (1981) on a isokinetic-cycle ergometer, observed that cycling velocity decreased linearly as a function of increasing loads. In contrast to the *in vitro* studies, in which the relationship between force and velocity is exponential (Fenn and Marsh, 1935) or hyperbolic (Hill, 1938), a similar linear force–velocity and parabolic force–power relationship is generally observed in adults (Vandewalle *et al.*, 1987) and children (Van Praagh *et al.*, 1989) during cycling (See Figure 11.5, in Chapter 11, Volume 2, by Winter and MacLaren).

(b) Running ergometry

Sprinting upstairs

Margaria *et al.* (1966) were the first to have measured short-term power in boys and girls aged 10–15 years. They measured the vertical component of the maximum constant speed by having the subjects sprint up a staircase. Body mass (kg) of the subject represented the external force. To measure the power output, time was also recorded, with typical durations of about 400–500 ms. For additional information see also recent reviews (Bar-Or, 1996; Van Praagh, 1996). Absolute maximal anaerobic power (MAP) was higher in boys, although the difference disappeared when this was expressed relative to body mass. It was concluded that psychomotor, biomechanical and/or biochemical changes that occur in children at these ages contribute to fairly linear increases in absolute MAP up to approximately age 13 years. After that age the values for boys continue to increase, while those for girls level off (Davies *et al.*, 1972). The results may be influenced by factors such as skill of climbing at maximal velocity, leg length, stride pattern and body mass.

Acceleration in sprint running

A further test involves running as fast as possible over 10 m from a standing start (Nielsen *et al.*, 1980). Running velocity was measured by means of adjustable photocells placed at hip height. Accelerations were calculated using the time recordings from the cells placed at 0.2 m and 4 m from the starting line.

Motorized treadmill running

In a longitudinal study, Patterson and Cunningham (1985) measured 19 boys, aged 10–15 years, over a 5-year period. They utilized a treadmill run designed to estimate 'anaerobic capacity'. The boys ran on a 20% grade at speeds ranging from 7.8 km h^{-1} (age 10–11 years); to 11.9 km h^{-1} (age 14–15 years). Treadmill time to exhaustion (which ranged from 80 to 100 s according to the different age groups), post-exercise blood lactate levels and O$_2$ debt served as 'anaerobic capacity' indices. One drawback of this method is that only 'anaerobic' endurance performance can be measured. As only speed is recorded, without the force component, power cannot be calculated.

Non-motorized horizontal treadmill running

In adults, attempts have been made to measure maximal velocity and power output during maximal short-term running on a non-motorized treadmill (Lakomy, 1987).The same methodology has been used in order to examine short-term power output (< 10 s) in untrained and trained children (Van Praagh *et al.*, 1993). Fargeas *et al.* (1993b), studied the longitudinal running and cycling power of 38 girls and boys aged 8–14. The subject develops maximal velocity while connected to a belt at the waist. The belt, which is attached to a horizontal bar, is connected to a potentiometer (vertical displacement) and strain gauges (horizontal traction force). A constant torque motor installed in the rear wheel of the treadmill is not used to drive the treadmill, but to compensate for belt friction or to simulate different loads. Signals from the potentiometer, the transducers and from the treadmill (belt speed) allows

mechanical power (potential + kinetic power) to be calculated. This test seems promising for the measurement of running muscle power.

30–50 m sprints

Historically, physical educators and coaches have used a 30–50 m dash as a measure of running velocity. The test is easy to administer, can be done in- and outdoors, and paediatric populations can be assessed in a short time. This simple test enables categorization of subjects as: 'slow', 'medium slow' or 'rapid'. However, it cannot be considered as a 'real' power test, as the force component is not measured. Peak power (W kg^{-1}) measured by the cycle force–velocity test correlates quite well with a 30 m dash in a group of 7- and 12-year-old girls and boys ($r = 0.80$, $p < 0.001$), but it was significantly lower when only the girl's results were analysed (Van Praagh *et al.*, 1990).

30 s shuttle run

In this test, the child sprints to and fro (20 m for each lap). The average velocity is calculated from the distance covered in 30 s. There were no differences in peak blood lactate between the 30 s Wingate and the 30 s shuttle run test in 12-year-old girls and boys (Van Praagh *et al.*, 1990; Falgairette *et al.*, 1994). The reproducibility of this test has not yet been investigated.

(c) Jumping tests

Vertical jump test

Sargent (1921) developed the vertical jump test to measure maximal leg power in adults. Subjects are required to jump vertically as high as they can. The subject's ability to exert leg power is derived from the height of the jump. The best average value of the three jumps is generally taken as the test score. The vertical jump has been accepted as a valid measure of leg power and various vertical jump protocols have been derived from the Sargent test, e.g.

Jump-and-Reach test, Abalakov test (for review see Kirby, 1991). The objectivity and reliability coefficients are high. Reliability coefficients of 0.91–0.93 suggest high intra-individual consistency (Glencross, 1966). No test–retest reliability has been reported for paediatric populations. The validity of the test, compared with the sum of four power events in track and field, is rather low ($r = 0.78$, Safrit, 1990). The test does not involve high motor ability and can be easily learned by children. Norms are also available (Baumgartner and Jackson, 1991). A major weakness is the lack of standardization in test administration. For instance, a counter-movement increases the vertical jump performance by about 10% (Bosco *et al.*, 1983), probably due to the involvement of the stretch-shortening cycle. Moreover, a more rapid elevation of the arms also improves the height of a vertical jump. The Lewis nomogram test has been designed to be used concomitantly with the Sargent Jump. While the Sargent Jump has the dimension of work (force × distance), the aim of the Lewis nomogram (Baumgartner and Jackson, 1991) is to add 'velocity' to the body mass and the vertical distance jumped. This kind of 'artificial manipulation' cannot be taken into consideration for research purposes. Besides, Harman *et al.* (1991) conducted a validation study on male adults, and concluded that the Lewis formula does not provide an accurate estimate of muscle leg power.

Squat jump test

Bosco *et al.* (1983) presented a vertical jump test for measuring the muscular power of the leg extensors. They criticized the Margaria and the Wingate tests because of a failure to evaluate any functional-morphological characteristics of particular importance for the development of leg explosive power, such as the elastic properties of the muscle. The test comprises jumping vertically from a static squatting position with a knee angle of 90°. The subject keeps hands on hips throughout the entire test. For field purposes, it is easy to monitor leg power,

using a digital timer and a contact mat (Bosco and Komi, 1980). It was assumed that the 'stretch-shortening cycle' which occurs during this type of jump allows the stored elastic energy to be utilized during positive work and thus increases the vertical performance. Data are available for children (Bosco, 1992).

Hopping test

Power output measured during running or jumping events not only estimates the power of the chemomechanical conversion, but also gives information regarding the mechanical energy stored in the elastic elements of the muscles involved (Cavagna *et al.*, 1965). Moritani *et al.* (1989) investigated neural and biomechanical variables during fast and maximal hopping tasks on a force platform in 9-year-old boys. Hopping represents a cyclical motor task, with repeated stretch-shortening cycles of the leg extensor muscles. Children were asked to hop on both legs, with either the fastest possible frequency or the maximal height in each jump recorded for 10–15 s. A rest interval of 1–2 minutes was allowed between trials. Mechanical power (normalized for body mass) was higher in adults than in boys during maximal hopping (26 W kg^{-1} vs. 15.4 W kg^{-1}, $p < 0.01$). However, during fast hopping, boys generated significantly higher power than adults (4.3 W kg^{-1} vs. 2.3 W kg^{-1}, $p < 0.01$).

Standing long jump

Because of its easy execution and administration, this test is often used instead of the vertical jump as a measure of leg muscle power. The problem with all field-based assessments is that the tests do not reflect a single factor (leg power, in this particular case), but also learning, coordination and maturation. Thus, although the test appears to be objective as well as reliable, its validity is questionable. Coefficients of 0.79 between standing long jump and vertical jump assume that either can be used as a criterial measure for the other. Docherty (1996) asserted that the specific issue of validity for either test has not been examined. The test is feasible for girls and boys from 6 years on (EUROFIT, 1988). Normative data are available for both age and sex groups (see Tables 8.6 and 8.7 and American Alliance for Health, Physical Education and Recreation, 1975).

Counter-movement jump with added masses

Viitasalo *et al.* (1992) examined more than 300 male adolescent athletes aged 9–16 years old and representing six sports events. After a warm-up, each subject performed 3–5 maximal counter-movement jumps with each of four different barbell loads; for the smallest children, the loads were 2, 50, 100 and 150 N, while the older children had to overcome loads of 2, 100, 200 and 400 N. Jumping height (the height of rise of the body's centre of gravity = *hCG*) was calculated using the flight time (*t*) of the jump with the following formula:

$$hCG = (g \times t^2)/8$$

where *hCG* = the displacement of the centre of gravity; $g = 9.81$ m s^{-2}, *t* = flight time

The flight time was measured using a digital timer and a contact mat (Bosco *et al.*, 1983). In a previous study (Viitasalo, 1988), the coefficients of variation between determinations of the test decreased with age from 13% at 10 years old to 6% at 16 years old.

Drop jump

The subject drops from heights of 0.2–0.8 m onto a force platform with a subsequent upward jump. The young athlete should keep his or her hands on the hips throughout the entire jump. The tolerance to progressive dropping height increases from childhood up to the age of 20–25 years (Bosco and Komi, 1980). It is therefore strongly recommended that the young athlete is protected against high stretch loads.

Repeated rebound jumps

Bosco *et al.* (1983) proposed a 5–15 s vertical jump test in order to measure the mechanical leg power (W kg^{-1}). In children aged 5–10 years old, a 5 s test is recommended. In adolescents, the duration can be increased to 10–15 s. It was shown (Bosco, 1992) that the 5–15 repeated rebounds test is very relevant and sensitive to neuromuscular adaptations induced by training in relation to the individual characteristics and the specific sport activity practised (specifically all jump activities: basketball, volleyball, high jump, ice-hockey, alpine skiing, sprinting). The purpose is to assess mean leg power or total work of a subject during a series of vertical jumps on a force platform or a contact mat. The child stands on the contact mat and begins performing as many vertical jumps as possible in the time allotted. The performance is derived by plugging the total flight time and total number of jumps into a formula (Bosco *et al.*, 1983). A high degree of logical validity was found in athletic populations (basketball or volleyball players), but it lacks validity as a general power test. Even if the test is suitable for males from age 16 years, the reliability needs to be established for paediatric populations. Such assessments should include limits of agreement rather than test–retest correlations (see Chapter 10 by Nevill and Atkinson).

(d) Throwing tests

Throwing power has traditionally been measured in field conditions with throwing tests such as ball-throwing or medicine ball tests (see Kirby, 1991). In the latter 'power' tests, it is assumed that the best distance attained reflects anaerobic power of the arm.

Viitasalo (1988) developed a new test in order to measure throwing velocity of balls with different masses. In this test the subject threw balls of the same diameter, but of different masses (0.3–4.0 kg) through a photocell gate to a 0.4 × 0.4 m contact mat hanging on a wall.

The test was found to be reliable for 10–12-year-olds and had rather high correlations with their respective traditional field tests.

In summary, a universally accepted method which quantifies anaerobic energy supply in children is not available. The measurement of short-term external power is a suitable alternative, although it is important to consider the limitations of each power test.

8.14 FIELD TEST BATTERIES FOR CHILDREN

The use of laboratory tests to determine performance in children is not always appropriate or feasible, and several batteries of field tests have been proposed mainly to cater for large-scale population studies and/or the educational testing environment. Such test batteries include the American Alliance for Health, Physical Education, Recreation and Dance (AAHPERD) 'Physical Best' programme (1988) and the more comprehensive Council of Europe's EUROFIT test battery (Tables 8.6, 8.7 and Table 3.4 in Chapter 3 by Beunen). While the purpose (Pate, 1989), validity, reliability (Safrit, 1990) and interpretation (Plowman, 1992) of such tests have been the subject of intense debate, their expanding use, particularly in an educational setting, continues. It is likely that much of this debate is generated by an inability to (a) appreciate the limitation of the tests as scientific tools, (b) understand the underlying biological processes during growth which may contribute to a child's score on a particular test item, and (c) reach a consensus regarding criterion-referenced norms, particularly for health-related tests such as body composition and aerobic endurance.

REFERENCES

AAHPERD Physical Best Program (1988). American Alliance for Health, Physical Education, Recreation and Dance. Reston, VA.

American Alliance for Health, Physical Education and Recreation (1975). *Youth Fitness Test Manual*, Washington, DC.

Armstrong, N., Welsman, J.R. and Kirby, B.J. (1999). Submaximal exercise and maturation in 12-year-olds. *Journal of Sports Sciences*, **17**, 107–14.

Arsac, M.A., Belli, A. and Lacour, J-R. (1996). Muscle function during brief maximal exercise: accurate measurements on a friction-loaded cycle ergometer. *European Journal of Applied Physiology*, **74**, 100–6.

Baltzopoulos, V. and Kellis, E. (1998). Isokinetic strength during childhood and adolescence. In *Pediatric Anaerobic Performance*. ed. E. van Praagh (Human Kinetics, Champaign, IL), pp. 225–40.

Bar-Or, O. (1983). *Pediatric Sports Medicine for the Practitioner: from Physiologic Principles to Clinical Applications.* (Springer-Verlag, New York).

Bar-Or, O. (1996). Anaerobic Performance. In *Measurement In Pediatric Exercise Science*. ed. D. Docherty (Human Kinetics, Champaign, IL), pp. 161–82.

Baumgartner, T.A. and Jackson, A.S. (1991). *Measurement for Evaluation in Physical Education and Exercise Science*. (William C. Brown, Dubuque, IA).

Berg, A., Kim, S.S. and Keul, J. (1986). Skeletal muscle enzyme activities in healthy young subjects. *International Journal of Sports Medicine*, **7**, 236–9.

Beunen, G. and Malina, R.M. (1988). Growth and physical performance relative to the timing of the adolescent spurt. *Exercise and Sports Sciences Reviews*, **16**, 503–46.

Blimkie, C.J.R., Roache, P., Hay, J.T. and Bar-Or, O. (1988). Anaerobic power of arms in teenage boys and girls: relationship to lean tissue. *European Journal of Applied Physiology*, **57**, 677–83.

Boreham, C.A.G., Paliczka, V.J. and Nichols, A.K. (1990). A comparison of the PWC_{170} and 20-MST tests of aerobic fitness in adolescent schoolchildren. *Journal of Sports Medicine and Physical Fitness*, **30**, 19–23.

Boreham, C.A.G., Savage, J.M., Primrose, D., et al. (1993). Coronary risk in schoolchildren. *Archives of Disease in Childhood*, **68**, 182–6.

Bosco, C. (1992). *L'évaluation de la force par le test de Bosco*. (Force assessment by means of the Bosco test). Società Stampa Sportiva, Roma.

Bosco, C. and Komi, P.V. (1980). Influence of aging on the mechanical behaviour of leg extensor muscles. *European Journal of Applied Physiology*, **45**, 209–19.

Bosco, C., Luhtanen, P. and Komi, P.V. (1983). A simple method for measurement of mechanical power in jumping. *European Journal of Applied Physiology*, **50**, 273–82.

Brewer, J., Balsom, P.D., Davis, J.A. and Ekblom, B. (1992). The influence of birth date and physical development on the selection of a male junior international soccer squad. *Journal of Sports Sciences*, **10**, 561–2.

British Association of Sports Sciences (1988). *Position Statement on the Physiological Assessment of the Elite Competitor*. British Association of Sports Sciences, Leeds.

Cavagna, G.A., Saibene, P.F. and Margaria, R. (1965). Effect of negative work on the amount of positive work performed by an isolated muscle. *Journal of Applied Physiology*, **20**, 157–8.

Caiozzo, V.J., David, J., Ellis, *et al.* (1982). A comparison of gas exchange indices used to detect the anaerobic threshold. *Journal of Applied Physiology*, **53**, 1184–9.

Conconi, F., Ferrari, M., Ziglio, P.G., *et al.* (1982). Determination of the anaerobic threshold by a non-invasive field test in runners. *Journal of Applied Physiology*, **52**, 869–73.

Cooke, C.B, McDonagh, M.J.N., Neville, A.J. and Davies, C.T.M. (1991). Effects of load on oxygen intake in trained boys and men during treadmill running. *Journal of Applied Physiology*, **71**, 1237–44.

Cooper, D.M. (1995). New horizons in pediatric exercise research. In *New Horizons in Pediatric Exercise Science*. eds. C.J.R. Blimkie and O. Bar-Or (Human Kinetics, Champaign, IL), pp. 1–24.

Cooper, D.M. and Barstow, T.J. (1996). Magnetic resonance imaging and spectroscopy in studying exercise in children. In *Exercise and Sports Sciences Reviews*. ed. J.O. Holloszy (Williams and Wilkins, Baltimore, MD), Vol. 24, pp. 475–99.

Cumming G.R. (1973). Correlation of athletic performance and aerobic power in 12–17-year-old children with bone age, calf muscle, total body potassium, heart volume and two indices of anaerobic power. In *Pediatric Work Physiology*. ed. O. Bar-Or (Wingate Institute, Natanya), pp. 109–34.

Davies, C.T.M. and Rennie, R. (1968). Human power output. *Nature*, **217**, 770.

Davies, C.T.M., Barnes, C., Godfrey, S. (1972). Body composition and maximal exercise performance in children. *Human Biology*, **44**, 195–214.

Davis, J.A. (1985). Anaerobic threshold: review of the concept and directions for further research. *Medicine and Science in Sports and Exercise*, **17**, 6–18.

Docherty, D. ed. (1996). Measurement. In *Pediatric Exercise Science*. (Human Kinetics, Champaign, IL).

Doré, E., Bedu, M., França, N.M., *et al.* (1999). Testing peak cycling performance: effects of braking force during growth. *Medicine and Science in Sports and Exercise*, **32(2)**, 493–8.

Durnin, J.V.G.A. and Rahaman, M.M. (1967). The assessment of the amount of fat in the human body from measurements of skinfold thickness. *British Journal of Nutrition*, **21**, 681–9.

Eriksson, B.O. (1972). Physical training, oxygen supply and muscle metabolism in 11 to 15-year-old boys. *Acta Physiologica Scandinavica*, **Suppl.**, **384**, 1–48.

Eriksson, B.O., Karlsson, J. and Saltin B. (1971). Muscle metabolites during exercise in pubertal boys. *Acta Paediatrica Scandinavica*, **Suppl.**, **217**, 154–7.

Eriksson, B.O., Gollnick, P.B. and Saltin, B. (1973). Muscle metabolism and enzyme activity after training in boys 11–13 years old. *Acta Physiologica Scandinavica*, **87**, 485–7.

Eston, R.G. and Lamb, K.L. (2000) Effort perception. In *Paediatric Exercise Science and Medicine*. eds. N. Armstrong and W. Van Mecheler (Oxford University Press), pp. 85–91.

Eston, R.G., Robson, S. and Winter, E. (1993). A comparison of oxygen uptake during running in children and adults, in *Kinanthropometry IV*. eds. W. Duquet and J.A.P. Day (E. & F.N. Spon, London), pp. 236–41.

Eston, R.G., Parfitt, C.G., Campbell, L. and Lamb, K.L. (2000). Reliability of effort perception for regulating exercise intensity in children using the Cart and Load Effort Rating (CALER) Scale. *Pediatric Exercise Science*, **12**, 388–97.

EUROFIT: *European Test of Physical Fitness* (1988). Council of Europe, Committee for the Development of Sport (CDDS), Rome.

Falgairette, G., Bedu, M., Fellmann, N., *et al.* (1994). Evaluation of physical fitness from field tests at high altitude in circumpubertal boys: comparison with laboratory data. *European Journal of Applied Physiology*, **69**, 36–43.

Falk, B. and Bar-Or, O. (1993). Longitudinal changes in peak and anaerobic mechanical power of circumpubertal boys. *Pediatric Exercise Science*, **5**, 318–31.

Fargeas, M.A. (1993). *Mesure de la puissance mécanique externe chez l'enfant lors d'un exercice de courte durée sur ergocycle et tapis roulant (étude longitudinale)*. (Measurement of short-term external mechanical power in children, performed on a cycle ergometer and a 'power' treadmill). Université

Blaise Pascal, Clermont-Ferrand (unpublished doctoral thesis).

Fargeas, M.A., Lauron, B., Léger, L. and Van Praagh, E. (1993a). A computerized treadmill ergometer to measure short-term power output. *Proceedings of the Fourteenth International Congress of Biomechanics*, Paris: pp. 394–5.

Fargeas, M.A., Van Praagh, E., Léger. L., *et al.* (1993b). Comparison of cycling and running power outputs in trained children. *Pediatric Exercise Science*, 5, p. 415.

Fenn, W.O. and Marsh, B. S. (1935). Muscular force at different speeds of shortening. *Journal of Physiology*, 85, 277–97.

Ferretti, G., Gussoni, M., di Prampero, P.E. and Cerretelli, P. (1987). Effects of exercise on maximal instantaneous muscular power of humans. *Journal of Applied Physiology*, 62, 2288–94.

Ferretti, G., Narici, M.V., Binzoni, T., *et al.* (1994). Determinants of peak muscle power: effects of age and physical conditioning. *European Journal of Applied Physiology*, 68, 111–15.

FITNESSGRAM Users Manual (1987). Institute for Aerobics Research, Dallas, TX.

Gaisl, G. and Wiesspeiner, G. (1990). A non-invasive method of determining the anaerobic threshold in children. *Pediatric Exercise Science*, 2, 29–36.

Glencross, D.J. (1966). The nature of the vertical jump test and the standing broad jump. *Research Quarterly*, 37, 353–9.

Grassi, B., Cerretelli, P., Narici, M.V. and Marconi, C. (1991). Peak anaerobic power in master athletes. *European Journal of Applied Physiology*, 62, 394–9.

Green, S. (1994). A definition and systems view of anaerobic capacity. *European Journal of Applied Physiology*, 69, 168–73.

Harman, E.A., Rosenstein, M.T., Frykman, P.N., *et al.* (1991). Estimation of human power output from vertical jump. *Journal of Applied Sport Science Research*, 5(3), 116–20.

Haschke, F. (1983). Body composition of adolescent males. Part 2. Body composition of male reference adolescents. *Acta Paediatrica Scandinavica*, 307 Suppl., 1–12.

Hebestreit, H., Mimura, K. and Bar-Or, O. (1993). Recovery of anaerobic muscle power following 30-s supramaximal exercise: Comparison between boys and men. *Journal of Applied Physiology*, 74, 2875–80.

Heck, H., Mader, A., Hess, G. and Hollman, W. (1985) Justification of the 4-mmol/lactate

threshold. *International Journal of Sports Medicine*, 6, 117–30.

Hill, A.V. (1938). The heat of shortening and the dynamic constraints of muscle. *Proceedings of the Royal Society*, B, 126, 136–95.

Israel, S. (1992). Age-related changes in strength and special groups. In *Strength and Power in Sport*. ed. P.V. Komi (Blackwell Scientific Publications, Oxford), pp. 319–28.

Kemper, H.C.G. ed. (1985.) *Medicine and Sports Science*, Vol. 20, *Growth, Health and Fitness of Teenagers*. (Karger, Basel).

Kemper, H.C.G. (1990). Physical fitness testing in children: is it a worthwhile activity? *Proceedings of the European EUROFIT Research Seminar*, Ismir. Council of Europe, pp. 7–27.

Kirby, R.F. (1991). *Kirby's Guide for Fitness and Motor Performance Tests*. (BenOak, Cape Girardeau, MO).

Kuno, S., Takahashi, H., Fujimoto, K., *et al.* (1995). Muscle metabolism during exercise using phosphorus–31 nuclear magnetic resonance spectroscopy in adolescents. *European Journal of Applied Physiology*, 70, 301–4.

Lakomy, H.K.A. (1986). Measurement of work and power output using friction loaded cycle ergometers. *Ergonomics*, 29, 509–17.

Lakomy, H.K.A. (1987). The use of a non-motorized treadmill for analysing sprint performance. *Ergonomics*, 30, 627–38.

Léger, L. and Lambert, J. (1982). A maximal 20 metre shuttle run test to predict O_2max. *European Journal of Applied Physiology*, 49, 1–12.

Lohman, T. (1992). Advances in body composition assessment. *Current Issues in Exercise Science Series*, (Monograph Number 3). (Human Kinetics, Champaign, IL).

MacDougall, J.D., Wenger, H.A. and Green, H.J, (1982). *Physiological Testing of the Elite Athlete*. (Published by the Canadian Association Sports Sciences, in collaboration with the Sports Medicine Council of Canada, Mutual Press, Ottawa).

Mahon, A.D. and Vaccaro, P. (1991). Can the point of deflection from linearity of heart rate determine ventilatory threshold in children? *Pediatric Exercise Science*, 3, 256–62.

Malina, R.M. and Bouchard, C. (1991). *Growth, Maturation and Physical Activity*. (Human Kinetics, Champaign, IL).

Maréchal, R., Pirnay, F., Crielaard, J.M. and Petit, J.M. (1979). Influence de l'âge sur la puissance anaerobie. (Influence of age on anaerobic power). *Economica*, Paris.

Margaria, R., Aghemo, P. and Rovelli, E. (1966). Measurement of muscular power (anaerobic) in man. *Journal of Applied Physiology*, 21, 1662–4.

Martin, J.C. and Malina, R.M. (1998). Developmental variations in anaerobic performance associated with age and sex. In *Pediatric Anaerobic Performance*. ed. E. Van Praagh (Human Kinetics, Champaign, IL), pp. 155–89.

Martin, J.C., Wagner, B.M. and Coyle, E.F. (1997). Inertial-load method determines maximal cycling power in a single exercise bout. *Medicine and Science in Sports and Exercise*, 11, 1505–12.

Mercier, J., Mercier, B. and Préfaut, C. (1991). Blood lactate increase during the force velocity exercise test. *International Journal of Sports Medicine*, 12, 17–20.

Moritani, T., Oddsson, L., Thorstensson, A. and Astrand, P. O. (1989). Neural and biomechanical differences between men and young boys during a variety of motor tasks. *Acta Physiologica Scandinavica*, 137, 147–55.

Murray, D.A. and Harrison, E. (1986). Constant velocity dynamometer: an appraisal using mechanical loading. *Medicine and Science in Sports and Exercise*, 6, 612–24.

Nevill, A.M., Ramsbottom, R. and Williams, C. (1992). Scaling measurements in physiology and medicine for individuals of different size. *European Journal of Applied Physiology*, 65, 110–17.

Nielsen, B., Nielsen, K., Behrendt Hansen, M. and Asmussen, E. (1980). Training of 'functional muscle strength' in girls 7–19-years-old. In *Children and Exercise IX*. eds. K. Bergh and B.O. Eriksson (University Park Press, Baltimore, MD), pp. 69–78.

Nindl, B.C., Mahar, M.T., Harman, E.A. and Patton, J.F. (1995). Lower and upper body anaerobic performance in male and female adolescent athletes. *Medicine and Science in Sports and Exercise*, 27, 235–41.

Northern Ireland Fitness Survey (1990). *The Fitness, Physical Activity, Attitudes and Lifestyles of N. Ireland Post-primary Schoolchildren*. Division of Physical and Health Education, The Queen's University of Belfast.

Pate, R.R. (1989). The case for large-scale physical fitness testing in American youth. *Pediatric Exercise Science*, 1, 290–4.

Patterson, D.H. and Cunningham, D.A. (1985). Development of anaerobic capacity in early and late maturing boys. In *Children and Exercise XI*. eds. R.A. Binkhorst, H.C.G. Kemper, and W.H. Saris (Human Kinetics, Champaign, IL), pp. 119–28.

Pérès, G., Vandewalle, H. and Monod, H. (1981). Aspect particulier de la relation charge-vitesse lors du pédalage sur cycloergomètre. (Particular aspect of the load-velocity relationship during pedalling on the cycle ergometer). *Journal of Physiology* (Paris) 77, 10A.

Pirnay, F. and Crielaard, J.M. (1979). Mesure de la puissance anaérobie alactique (Measurement of alactic anaerobic power). *Medicine and Sport*, 53, 13–16.

Plowman, S. A. (1992). Criterion-referenced standards for neuromuscular physical fitness tests: an analysis. *Pediatric Exercise Science*, 4, 10–19.

Riddoch, C., Savage, J.M., Murphy, N., *et al.* (1991). Long term health implications of fitness and physical activity patterns. *Archives of Disease in Childhood*, 66, 1426–33.

Round, J., Jones, D.A., Honour, J.W. and Nevill, A.M. (1999). Hormonal factors in the development of differences between boys and girls during adolescence: a longitudinal study. *Annals of Human Biology*, 26(i), 49–62.

Rowland, T.W. ed. (1993). *Pediatric Laboratory Exercise Testing: Clinical Guidelines*. (Human Kinetics, Champaign, IL).

Safrit, M.J. (1990). The validity and reliability of fitness tests for children: a review. *Pediatric Exercise Science*, 2, 9–28.

Saltin, B. and Gollnick, P.D. (1983). Skeletal muscle adaptability: significance for metabolism and performance. In *Handbook of Physiology; Skeletal Muscle*, Section 10. eds. L.D. Peachey *et al.* (American Physiological Society, Williams and Wilkins, Baltimore, MD), pp. 555–631.

Saltin, B., Gollnick, P.D., Eriksson, B.O. and Piehl, K. (1971). Metabolic and circulatory adjustments at onset of work. In *Proceedings from Meeting on Physiological Changes at Onset of Work*. eds. A. Gilbert and P Guille (Toulouse), pp. 46–58.

Sargeant, A.J. (1989). Short-term muscle power in children and adolescents. In *Advances in Pediatric Sports Sciences, Vol. 3, Biological Issues*. ed. O. Bar-Or. (Human Kinetics, Champaign, IL), pp. 41–63.

Sargeant, A.J., Dolan, P. and Thorne, A. (1984). Isokinetic measurement of maximal leg force and anaerobic power output in children. In *Children and Sport XII*. eds. J. Ilmarinen and I. Välimäki (Springer-Verlag, Berlin), pp. 93–8.

Sargeant, A.J., Hoinville, E. and Young, A. (1981). Maximum leg force and power output during short-term dynamic exercise. *Journal of Applied Physiology*, **51**, 1175–82.

Sargent, D.A. (1921). The physical test of a man. *American Physical Education Review*, **26**, 188–94.

Sharp, N.C.C. (1991). The exercise physiology of children. In *Children and Sport*. ed. V. Grisogono. (W.H. Murray, London), pp. 32–71.

Siri, W.E. (1956). The gross composition of the body. *Advances in Biological and Medical Physics*, **4**, 239–80.

Sjödin, B. and Svedenhag, J. (1985). Applied physiology of marathon running. *Sports Medicine*, **2**, 83–99.

Slaughter, M.H., Lohman, T.G., Boileau, R.A., *et al.* (1988), Skinfold equations for estimation of body fatness in children and youth. *Human Biology*, **60**, 709–23.

Smith, D.A. and O'Donnell, T.V. (1984). The time course during 36 weeks endurance training of changes in O₂max and anaerobic threshold as determined with a new computerised method. *Clinical Science*, **67**, 229–36.

Tirosch, E., Rosenbaum, P. and Bar-Or, O. (1990). A new muscle power test in neuromuscular disease: feasibility and reliability. *American Journal of Disease in Childhood*, **144**, 1083–7.

Unnithan, V.B. and Eston, R.G. (1990). Stride frequency and submaximal treadmill running economy in adults and children. *Pediatric Exercise Science*, **2**, 149–55.

Van Mechelen, W., Hlobil, H. and Kemper, H.C.G. (1986). Validation of two running tests as estimates of maximal aerobic power in children. *European Journal of Applied Physiology*, **55**, 503–6.

Van Mechelen, W., Van Lier, W.H., Hlobil, H., *et al.* (1992). Dutch Eurofit reference scales for boys and girls aged 12–16. In *Children and Exercise XVI – Pediatric Work Physiology. Methodological, Physiological and Pathological Aspects*. eds. J. Coudert and E. van Praagh. (Masson, Paris), pp. 123–7.

Van Praagh, E. (1996). Testing of anaerobic performance. In *The Encyclopaedia of Sports Medicine: The Child and Adolescent Athlete*. International Olympic Committee. ed. O.Bar-Or. (Blackwell Science, London), pp. 602–16.

Van Praagh, E. and França, N.M. (1998). Measuring maximal short-term power output during growth. In *Pediatric Anaerobic Performance*. ed. E. van Praagh. (Human Kinetics, Champaign, IL), pp. 155–89.

Van Praagh, E., Falgairette, G., Bedu, M., *et al.* (1989). Laboratory and field tests in 7-year-old boys. In *Children and Exercise XIII*. eds. S. Oseid and K-H. Carlsen. (Human Kinetics, Champaign, IL), pp. 11–17.

Van Praagh, E., Fellmann, N., Bedu, M. *et al.*, (1990). Gender difference in the relationship of anaerobic power output to body composition in children. *Pediatric Exercise Science*, **2**, 336–48.

Van Praagh, E., Bedu, M., Falgairette, G., *et al.* (1991). Oxygen uptake during a 30-s supramaximal exercise in 7–15-year-old boys. In *Children and Exercise XV*. eds. R. Frenkl and I. Szmodis. (Nevi, Budapest), pp. 281–7.

Van Praagh, E., Fargeas, M.A., Léger, L., *et al.* (1993). Short-term power output in children measured on a computerized treadmill ergometer. *Pediatric Exercise Science*, **5**, 482 (abstract).

Vandewalle, H., Pérès, G. and Monod, H. (1987). Standard anaerobic exercise tests. *Sports Medicine*, **4**, 268–89.

Viitasalo, J.T. (1988). Evaluation of explosive strength for young and adult athletes. *Research Quarterly for Exercise and Sport*, **59**, 9–13.

Viitasalo, J.T., Rahkila, P., Österback, L. and Alén, M. (1992). Vertical jumping height and horizontal overhead throwing velocity in young male athletes. *Journal of Sports Sciences*, **10**, 401–13.

Washington, R.L. (1989). Anaerobic threshold in children. *Pediatric Exercise Science*, **1**, 244–56.

Wasserman, K. (1984). The anaerobic threshold measurement to evaluate exercise performance. *American Review of Respiratory Disease*, **129**, S35–40.

Wilkie, D.R. (1950). The relation between force and velocity in human muscle. *Journal of Physiology*, **110**, 249–80.

Wilkie, D.R. (1960). Man as a source of mechanical power. *Ergonomics*, **3**, 1–8.

Williams, J.R. and Armstrong, N. (1991). Relationship of maximal lactate steady state to performance at fixed blood lactate reference values in children. *Pediatric Exercise Science*, **3**, 333–41.

Williams, J.R., Armstrong, N. and Kirby, B.J. (1992). The influence of the site of sampling and assay medium upon the measurement and interpretation of blood lactate responses to exercise. *Journal of Sports Sciences*, **10**, 95–107.

Williams, J.R., Eston, R. and Furlong, B.A.F. (1994). CERT: a perceived exertion scale for young children. *Perceptual and Motor Skills*, **79**, 1451–8.

Winter, E.M. (1992). Scaling: partitioning out differences in size. *Pediatric Exercise Science*, **4**, 296–301.

Zanconato, S., Buchtal, S., Barstow, T.J. and Cooper, D.M. (1993). ^{31}P-magnetic resonance spectroscopy of leg muscle metabolism during exercise in children and adults. *Journal of Applied Physiology*, **74**, 2214–18.

Zwiren, L.D. (1989). Anaerobic and aerobic capacities of children. *Pediatric Exercise Science*, **1**, 31–44.

PART FOUR
SPECIAL CONSIDERATIONS

Tim S. Olds

9.1 AIMS

The main aims in this chapter are to:

- consider the anthropometric aspects of body image,
- address the question of what makes a person physically attractive or beautiful.

There are four laboratory experiences, each illustrating

- an aspect of recent theoretical developments in the study of body image,
- conceptual and practical aspects of anthropometry, and
- statistical and analytical techniques.

9.2 INTRODUCTION

The study of body image can be thought of as the intersection of anthropometry and psychology. It involves an understanding of the ways we perceive our own bodies, and the bodies of others (often ideal bodies, such as those of models, movie stars and sportspeople), and how those perceptions drive body-related behaviours such as eating, sex and exercise. It is therefore of great interest to the exercise specialist.

People often ask: 'What makes a body beautiful or sexually attractive?' Some theorists (e.g. Wolf, 1992) have argued that beauty is variable and driven by local social and economic forces. They point to shifting ideals of female beauty, often contrasting the highly endomorphic forms of Rubens' women (estimated somatotype

7.5–3–0.5) and the highly ectomorphic forms of 1960s' models and their 1990s' analogue. Much recent research (for a summary, see Etcoff, 1999) suggests that at a structural level there is a universal grammar or geometry of beauty. In other words, there are simple anthropometric characteristics that are common to all (female) bodies generally considered to be beautiful. These characteristics include symmetry, an hourglass shape, and slimness.

Why is it that these characteristics may be universally desired? One attempt to answer this question uses a sociobiological or evolutionary approach, arguing that characteristics which are desired are markers or 'honest advertisements' of reproductive potential (Symons, 1995). Slimness, for example, is a marker of youth and fitness, while a low waist–hip ratio (WHR) is a marker of health, reproductive maturity and nulliparity (i.e. not yet having borne children) (Singh & Young, 1995). In one study of women attending an *in vitro* fertilization clinic, for example, those with a WHR below 0.8 had a twice greater chance of a live birth than those with a WHR above 0.8 (Zaadstra *et al.*, 1993).

One area that has attracted a considerable amount of recent scientific attention has been the effect of symmetry. A particular type of asymmetry is of interest here – 'fluctuating' asymmetry, where the differences between the left and right sides of the body are normally distributed about a mean of zero. A series of animal studies have shown that both males and females are more attracted to symmetrical

Kinanthropometry and Exercise Physiology Laboratory Manual: Tests, Procedures and Data. 2nd Edition, Volume 1: Anthropometry
Edited by RG Eston and T Reilly. Published by Routledge, London, June 2001

partners, and that symmetrical animals have greater reproductive success (Møller, 1997). In humans, both males and females prefer partners with greater facial and body symmetry. Symmetrical males become sexually active three years before non-symmetrical males and enjoy more sexual success (Thornhill and Gangestad, 1994). Males also prefer women with symmetrical breasts (Møller *et al.*, 1995). Soft-tissue symmetry in women actually increases on the day of ovulation (Manning *et al.*, 1996). Symmetrical racehorses run faster (Manning and Ockenden, 1994) and there is some evidence that athletes with greater non-functional (e.g. facial) symmetry perform better than their lopsided peers (Manning and Pickup, 1998).

Why should symmetry be a desired characteristic? Evolutionary biologists argue that symmetry is an 'honest advertisement' of the ability of the organism to resist environmental insults which disrupt growth, such as parasite infections and illness. The symmetrical person is supposedly indicating to a potential mate: 'I have such good genes that I can resist these challenges unscathed. You should mate with me!' This argument has been supported by a number of studies in animals and humans (Palmer and Strobeck, 1992).

9.3 THE ANTHROPOMETRIC CHARACTERISTICS OF BEAUTIFUL FEMALE BODIES

When the anthropometric characteristics, such as stature, mass and muscularity are examined in elite sports people, their mean values are found to deviate greatly from those of the general population, and the scatter of scores is much less. For example, only 1 in 1000 women would be tall enough to play as a centre in the Women's National Basketball Association (Norton and Olds, 1999). In other words, specific sportspeople form distinct and homogeneous subgroups. On moving up the ladder of ability, from novice competitors to Olympians, the deviations become greater and the scatters

become less (Norton and Olds, 1999). Similar patterns are found in other groups of elite 'performers', including the 'ideal' bodies of fashion models.

If the universalist theory is correct, we should find that the mean values for desirable characteristics – slimness, an hourglass shape – are more extreme in the 'ideal' bodies of regional, international and 'super' models, and in the 'hyperideal' bodies of shop mannequins, than in the general population. We should also find that there are well-defined and consistent gradients as we move from average young women to 'hyperideal' figures. In the following pages, different groups of women of varying levels of perceived beauty are considered and their anthropometric characteristics contrasted.

Consider the following five groups, chosen to represent a range of beauty:

- Women aged 18–34 years from the third National Health and Nutrition Examination Survey (NHANES III) (U.S. Department of Health and Human Services, 1996), an American survey conducted between 1988 and 1994. This group will form the reference population.
- Regional models (*n* = 11; Norton *et al.*, 1996).
- International models (*n* = 48), using data provided by the Elite Modeling Agency (http://www.models-online.com).
- 'Supermodels' (models earning more than $US2,000,000 in 1999), using data provided by their respective agencies (http://www.newfaces.com/supermodels, February 1999).
- Female shop mannequins (*n* = 22) from an Australian mannequin warehouse (Tomkinson *et al.*, 1999).

Height and mass were estimated from regression equations based on segmental lengths and height-corrected girths using data from the Australian Anthropometric Database (AADBase; Norton and Olds, 1996, pp. 395–411).

The data on mass, height, body mass index (BMI), height-adjusted waist girth, and WHR

Table 9.1 Mean (SD) values for the six datasets

	Reference population n = 3084	Regional models n = 11	International models n = 22-48*	Supermodels n = 12-21**	Mannequins n = 22
Height (cm)	166.1 (7.1)	169.6 (4.1)	171.9 (7.2)	177.3 (3.3)	172.5 (3.8)
ln(mass) (kg)	4.188 [65.9] (0.240)	4.031 [56.3] (0.104)	3.958 [52.4] (0.090)	3.985 [53.8] (0.094)	3.914 [50.1] (0.062)
ln(BMI)	3.230 [25.3] (0.227)	2.974 [19.6] (0.089)	2.876 [17.7] (0.101)	2.832 [17.0] (0.084)	2.824 [16.8] (0.065)
Waist/height	0.527 (0.095)	0.391 (0.018)	0.361 (0.017)	0.341 (0.015)	0.347 (0.014)
WHR	0.841 (0.073)	0.714 (0.037)	0.705 (0.017)	0.687 (0.028)	0.680 (0.020)

BMI = Body Mass Index; WHR = waist–hip ratio.
The figures in square brackets are the antilogged values for mass and BMI.
*n = 12 for ln(mass) and ln(BMI), n = 21 elsewhere.
**n = 22 for waist/height and WHR, n = 48 elsewhere.

for each of the groups are shown in Table 9.1. The natural log of mass and BMI – ln(mass) and ln(BMI) – have been analysed, because both of these characteristics show very skewed distributions, and log-transformation normalizes them.

Fashion models are characterized by significantly ($p < 0.0001$) lower WHR and BMI values than women of a comparable age in the reference population. These lumped variables are powerful discriminators between fashion models and young women in the general population. For example, only 31 of 3084 women from the reference population have both WHRs and BMIs within 2 SDs of the average values for supermodels. This means that 99% of women would be highly unlikely to be supermodels based on these two characteristics alone.

Another interesting way of looking at these data is to situate each of the groups in a bivariate anthropometric space. By this it is meant that two variables are used conjointly –

WHR and BMI. Figure 9.1 represents this space. The groups are represented as 'density ellipses' – in this case, 67% density ellipses, meaning that two thirds of all individuals within each group will fall within the boundaries of the ellipse. The figures at each corner of the graph depict what women located in those zones look like. At the bottom left-hand corner are women with a low WHR and a low BMI – i.e. women who are both thin and shapely. At the top left-hand corner are women with a low BMI but a moderate WHR – these are the very thin women with a 'straight up and down' shape. At the bottom right-hand corner are women with a moderate BMI but a low WHR – curvaceous or voluptuous women. Finally, the top right-hand corner represents women with a high BMI and a high WHR – women with a block or balloon shape.

Figure 9.1 also shows the changes in BMI and WHR in the general population as women age. BMI and WHR have been calculated for

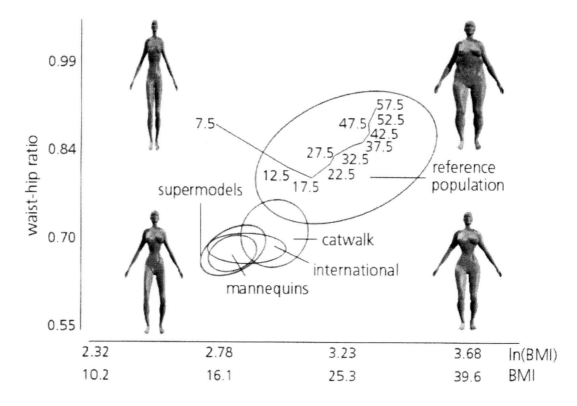

Figure 9.1 Bivariate location of each of the groups. The outline figures represent iconically the shapes of women located at the different extreme points of the anthropometric space. The ellipses are the 90% density ellipses, meaning that 90% of women in each group fall within the boundaries of the ellipse. The continuous line represents the evolution of mean ln(BMI) and WHR throughout the life cycle, in 5-year age groups with midpoints from 7.5 to 57.5 years (data from U.S. Department of Health and Human Services, 1990).

women from the Australian population in age bands from 5–10 to 55–60 years. The median age in each group (from 7.5 to 57.5 years) is shown at each point on the continuous line. As women age, BMI increases, rapidly at first and then more slowly. In fact, BMI is one of the main factors people use in assessing how old a woman is. Singh and Young (1995) found that when figures with identical faces are shown to people, they judge the heavier figures to be up to 10 years older than the slimmer ones. The WHR decreases until adolescence and then starts to increase. The 'turning point' for these two variables, with the lowest WHR and lowest post-pubertal BMI, is during late adolescence and early adulthood, an age where reproductive potential is greatest. Younger

women, models and 'hyperideal' bodies are located progressively closer to the bottom left-hand corner of the graph.

9.4 SOMATOTYPE AND BODY IMAGE IN MEN

Somatotype is a way of quantifying the shape of the human body, independently of size (See Chapter 2 by Duquet and Carter). Somatotype is nowadays usually assessed anthropometrically, i.e. by taking measurements. However, the criterial method is a combination of both visual inspection ('photoscopic' somatotyping) and measurement. Skilled anthropometrists can visually assess somatotype with surprising precision and accuracy. This has made it possible to rate figures from art and popular culture, including dolls, shop mannequins, sculptures and figures from the great painters.

In the 1940s, Sheldon developed his theory of 'constitutional psychology' (Sheldon, 1944), arguing that psychological characteristics were reflected in physical conformation. He identified three major personality types, corresponding to the extreme somatotypes:

- *Endotonia*: governed by the viscera – indolent and hedonistic
- *Mesotonia*: governed by the active muscles – dynamic, outgoing, aggressive
- *Ectotonia*: withdrawn, inhibited, quiet

Psychological health was seen as a balance between the three. Those with too little endotonia suffered from endopaenia (no sense of relaxation or pleasure). Those with too little mesotonia suffered from mesopaenia (lack of ambition or drive). Those with too little ectotonia suffered from ectopaenia (a lack of inhibition, compulsive disorders).

Sheldon's theory built on a long tradition of pseudo-scientific and popular beliefs relating outward appearance to inner characteristics. In many cases, these attributions turned out to be self-fulfilling prophecies. For example, fat people saw themselves as lazy because everyone else saw them as lazy. Traditionally, the ideal male has been considered to be very mesomorphic, close to due north or north-north-east on the somatochart. Tucker (1984) found not only that the mesomorphic shape was preferred by both men and women, but also that men who perceived themselves as mesomorphic were more extroverted, less neurotic and had a higher self-concept. Another research group found that chest–waist ratio in men was directly related to men's satisfaction with their own body shape, and with female preferences for male body shapes (Furnham *et al.*, 1990) – the higher the chest–waist ratio, the greater the satisfaction (Figure 9.2).

Concern with body image has usually been associated mainly with women; however, there is now increasing concern among men,

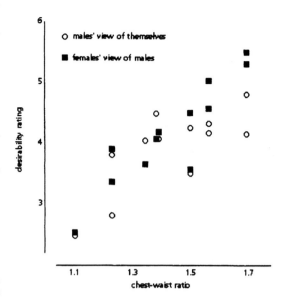

Figure 9.2 The relationship between desirability (rated on a 1–7 scale) and chest-waist ratio in men. The open circles represent men's view of themselves, and the closed squares women's view of men (plotted from data in Furnham, et al., 1990).

probably as they become more and more exposed to images of ideal male bodies. In response to a *Psychology Today* survey in 1972, 15% of men expressed overall dissatisfaction with their bodies. By 1997, this had risen to almost 45%. The percentage of men unhappy with their waist girths had risen from 36% to 63%. Unhappiness was so great that 17% of men said they would give up 3 years of their lives to be at their ideal weight, and 11% would give up 5 years of life (Cash *et al.*, 1986). Recent work by Pope and his colleagues at Harvard (1993) has shown that some male bodybuilders may suffer from 'reverse anorexia' – a feeling that they are not big enough, in spite of very high muscularity. Increasing exposure to extremely lean and muscular ideals is probably behind the increase in the recreational use of steroids in young men. There has also been an increase in the number of males choosing to have cosmetic surgery, including chest and calf implants. About 10% of the estimated one million people having cosmetic surgery in the US in 1998 were males (Etcoff, 1999, p. 111).

9.5 THE ANTHROPOMETRY OF 'KEN' AND 'BARBIE'

Barbie is the biggest-selling doll of all time, with over one billion dollars' worth of sales each year. To many people, Barbie represents a 'hyperideal' female shape. Her makers, Mattel, have been criticized for imposing unrealistic expectations of thinness on young girls. Barbie has even borne the brunt of political action. In the early 1990s a group calling itself the Barbie Liberation Organization stole talking Barbie and GI Joe dolls from toy store shelves, swapped their voice boxes, and replaced the dolls. When little girls opened their Christmas Barbies, they would come out with phrases like 'Vengeance is mine' and 'Eat lead, cobra!'. The little boys' GI Joes, on the other hand, would say things like 'Shopping is such fun!' or 'Let's plan a dream wedding!'

Ideal bodies have often been represented as being almost impossible for most women to achieve. One famous Body Shop advertisement stated that 'there are 3 billion women who don't look like supermodels and only 8 who do'. Once we know the key anthropometric characteristics of ideal bodies, we can calculate the probability of someone randomly chosen from the reference population having characteristics as extreme as these groups. For the regional models described in Table 9.1, the values range from about 2 to 11% for any single characteristic; for international models, from about 4 to 11%; for supermodels, from 0.5 to 8%; and for mannequins, from 0.5 to 6%. Unless characteristics are perfectly correlated, the chances of sharing two or more characteristics are smaller. About 1 in 25 individuals from the reference population will have both a WHR and ln(BMI) as extreme as a catwalk model, about 1 in 100 as extreme as a supermodel, and 1 in 200 as extreme as a mannequin. In the NHANES III database, only 20 of 3084 woman aged 18–34 had a BMI less than that of the average supermodel.

'Blowing up' Barbie or Ken to life size involves a number of practical and theoretical difficulties. Let us imagine for a moment that we know Ken's or Barbie's dimensions at life size. How can we make judgments about how probable or improbable their proportions are? Fortunately, many anthropometric characteristics are normally distributed. This means the likelihood of a measurement can be calculated by expressing it as a z-score relative to a reference population. Consider Barbie's upper leg length (trochanterion–tibiale laterale length). People often think that Barbie has improbably long upper legs. Is this true? At average height, Barbie would have an upper leg length of 45.5 cm (Norton *et al.*, 1996). In the population of Australian women aged 18–34, the average upper leg length is 42.6 cm, with a standard deviation of 3.57 cm. How unlikely is an upper leg length of 45.5 cm? Barbie's value is 2.9 cm above the mean, which is $(45.5 - 42.6) / 3.57 = 0.8$ SDs above the mean (i.e. a z-score of 0.8). Looking up z-tables, it is clear this is greater than about 79% of the population. So Barbie has a long, but not an improbably long, upper leg. This ratio can be compared to Barbie's chest–waist ratio (CWR; the ratio of the chest girth taken at the level of the mesosternale, and the minimum waist girth). It is 2.0, compared to a population mean of 1.3 ± 0.06. This is $(2.0 - 1.3) / 0.06 = 11.7$ SDs above the mean! This is biologically impossible, however desirable it may seem.

Similar considerations apply to Ken. Ken's dimensions, however, are nowhere as extreme as Barbie's (Norton *et al.*, 1996). Ken represents a much less 'hypermesomorphic' figure than some of the 'action figures' such as GI Joe. His slim ectomorphic shape is probably designed to appeal to girls rather than to boys. A number of studies (e.g. Fallon and Rozin, 1985) have shown that while men prefer mesomorphic male bodies, women favour ectomorphic body shapes in men.

The claims about Barbie's unrealistic thinness would certainly seem appropriate from a visual inspection. How can we make a scientific judgment about her proportions when she is just 27.5 cm tall? How can we 'blow up' Barbie to life size and compare her to young women in the general population? Measuring Ken and Barbie poses special problems for the anthropometrist, but also illustrates some key principles in anthropometry, including scaling and the logic of hydrostatic weighing. Practical 3 provides experience in solving these problems.

9.6 THE ANTHROPOMETRY OF THE IDEAL FACE

People tend to be judged by their faces. We attribute personality traits – dominance, honesty, intelligence – based on facial traits alone. In one study, the success of male army cadets later in their career was strongly correlated with judgments of how dominant they looked in graduation photos (Mazur *et al.*, 1984). A substantial body of anthropometric research has tried to establish correlations between the anthropometry of the face and the characteristics we ascribe to the person (e.g. Secord and Bevan, 1956). Some recent work using digital manipulation has uncovered what appear to be elements of a transcultural geometry of facial beauty.

One study conducted in England and Japan (Perrett *et al.*, 1994) identified key points on the faces of 60 young women, and then digitized and averaged them, thereby constructing a 'mean face'. The faces of the 15 women who were subjectively rated as the most attractive were then digitized using the same key points. The differences between the two faces were calculated. There were six main areas of difference. In the beautiful face the cheekbones were higher, the mouth-chin spacing was smaller, the nose–mouth spacing was smaller, the jawline was less square, the eyebrows were more arched, and the pupils were larger. These differences were consistent in both Japan and England. The beautiful face was more neotenous or 'baby-like'.

Consider the faces shown in Figures 9.3 and 9.4. The original image of a shop mannequin's face (Figure 9.4) has been digitally edited to increase jaw width and nose–lip and lip–chin spacing. The eyes have been made smaller and the eyebrows less arched, and the cheekbones

Figure 9.3 Face of a shop mannequin before digital manipulation.

Figure 9.4 Face of the same mannequin as in Figure 9.3, with the following manipulations: nose–lip spacing and lip–chin spacing increased; jaw widened; eye area reduced; eyebrow arching reduced; cheekbones lowered.

have been lowered (Figure 9.3). Although the altered face is still very attractive to middle-aged males, it is not as pretty as the neotenous pouting of the original face. Women often use cosmetics to highlight exactly the characteristics identified in this study: mascara to enlarge the eyes, blusher to highlight cheek bones, lipstick to increase lip area.

Other research groups have used digital techniques to scale and superimpose photographs of different people, and then average them on a pixel-by-pixel basis, thus producing a 'composite portrait'. This was a technique performed photographically by Galton (1879) over a century ago. Galton noticed that the composite or averaged faces appeared to be more attractive. Creating composite faces has the effect of evening out differences and asymmetries. Composite faces are well-balanced and have clear skin tone, because local blemishes are washed out in the averaging process.

9.7 PRACTICAL 1: THE ANTHROPOMETRIC CHARACTERISTICS OF BEAUTIFUL FEMALE BODIES

9.7.1 RATIONALE AND PURPOSE

In this practical, females can compare the size and shape of their bodies, quantified using the Body Mass Index (BMI) and waist–hip ratio (WHR), to those of supermodels and shop mannequins. This experience illustrates the sociobiological theory of physical attractiveness, and gives students practice in calculating BMI and WHR, as well as introducing statistical procedures such as log-transformation to normalize skewed distributions and bivariate probability spaces.

9.7.2 PROCEDURES

Step 1 All subjects must be female. Weigh each participant in light indoor clothing, and measure their stretch stature without shoes. From these data, calculate the Body Mass Index (= mass (kg)/height^2 (m)). Take the natural log of BMI. This is the X value. Example: height = 165 cm, mass = 65 kg, BMI = 65 / 1.652 = 23.9 kg m^{-2}, ln(BMI) = 3.1739.

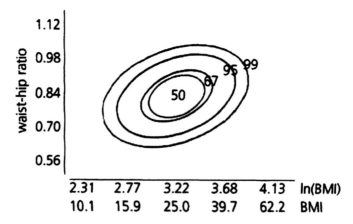

Figure 9.5 Ln(BMI) is shown on the X-axis, and waist–hip ratio on the Y-axis. The ellipses represent the 99, 95, 67 and 50% density ellipses for the US population.

Step 2 Next, measure the minimum waist girth and gluteal girth. See Chapter 1 for the exact location of these sites. From these data, calculate the WHR – this will be the Y value. Example: waist girth = 77 cm, hip girth = 97 cm, waist-hip ratio = 77 / 97 = 0.79.
Step 3 Plot the position on the chart provided (Figure 9.5).
Step 4 Follow Steps 1–4 for other females in your group.

9.7.3 ASSIGNMENT

Using Figure 9.2, plot the position of the following celebrities:
  Kate Moss: height = 168.9 cm, mass = 47.5 kg, waist = 58.4 cm, hip = 88.9 cm;
  Twiggy: height = 166 cm, mass = 40.7 kg, waist = 58.4 cm, hip = 80 cm;
  Marilyn Monroe: height = 166.4 cm, mass = 53.4 kg, waist = 61 cm, hip = 91.4 cm;
  Elle MacPherson: height = 183 cm, mass = 57.9 kg, waist = 60.2 cm, hip = 88.9 cm;
  Centrefolds: height = 169 cm, mass = 51.7 kg, waist girth = 61 cm, hip = 90 cm (Tovée *et al.*, 1997).

  Others are available at the following website, where you might do some research: http://www.playboy.com

9.8 PRACTICAL 2: THE ANTHROPOMETRY OF THE 'IDEAL' MALE BODY

9.8.1 RATIONALE AND PURPOSE

Using the somatotype procedures explained by Duquet and Carter in Chapter 2, males can calculate and plot their own somatotypes, and quantify how far away they are from 'ideal' figures in somatotype space. This experience outlines recent research into male body image, and gives students practice in calculating and plotting somatotypes, and using basic somatotype statistics. The 'ideal' male figures are taken from art and popular culture.

9.8.2 PROCEDURES

Step 1 Presented below are some somatotype ratings of figures from Renaissance and Baroque art, rated by the Czech anthropometrists Bok (1976) and Stepnicka (1983):

  Michelangelo's *David*: 1–7.5–2
  Bernini's *David*: 1–7–1
  El Greco's *Laokoon*: 2–6–1
  Adam (Sistine Chapel): 1.5–8–1
  Titian's *Adam*: 1.5–6.5–1
  Tintoretto's *Adam*: 1.5–6–2

Plot each of these on the somatochart provided in Chapter 2. You can also plot:

  competitive bodybuilders (Borms *et al.*, 1986): 1.6–8.7–1.2
  male shop mannequins (Tomkinson *et al.*, 1999): 2.5–4.7–3.5

Step 2 Calculate your own somatotype and plot yourself on the graph.

Step 3 To see how well your own somatotype compares to these ideals, calculate the mean somatotype of those mentioned above. The mean somatotype is simply the average of each of the components calculated separately. Then calculate the somatotype attitudinal distance (SAD) between your own somatotype and the mean. The SAD is the three-dimensional distance between two somatotypes. You will find the equation in Table 2.3, Chapter 2. The greater the SAD, the further the example is from the 'ideal' male body.

9.8.3 ASSIGNMENT

Table 9.2 shows the mean somatotypes of national-level athletes from a number of sports (Olds and Norton, 1999). Plot each on the somatochart and calculate the SAD of each from the mean of the 'ideal' bodies. Which is closest to the 'ideal' body?

Table 9.2 The mean somatotypes of national-level athletes (Olds and Norton, 1999).

basketball	2.4–4.4–3.7	rugby union – forwards	3.4–7.0–1.0
cycling – road	1.6–4.5–3.0	running – middle distance	1.5–4.0–3.8
gymnastics	1.8–6.2–2.3	soccer	2.5–4.6–2.7
kayak – sprint	2.0–5.4–2.3	table tennis	3.5–3.9–2.5
orienteering	2.0–4.7–3.5	tennis	2.2–4.5–3.1
power lifting	2.7–7.9–0.6	triathlon	1.7–4.3–3.1
rugby union – backs	2.5–5.8–1.9	volleyball	2.3–4.4–3.3

9.9 PRACTICAL 3: THE ANTHROPOMETRY OF 'KEN' AND 'BARBIE'

Students measure the dolls Ken and Barbie using vernier callipers and dental floss, scale them to life size, and compare them to real-life people. This experience introduces novel measurement techniques, and raises theoretical issues concerning the logic of scaling and underwater weighing. Use is made of z-scores to compare Ken and Barbie to a reference population of young people.

9.9.1 PROCEDURES

To measure Ken and Barbie you will need: a roll of dental floss; a set of vernier callipers; a basin or bucket at least 20 cm deep and 30 cm in diameter; a flat dish with a diameter greater than 30 cm; a small pair of scissors; electrical tape and a fine-tipped felt pen.

The following dimensions will be measured: height, girths: waist (minimum); gluteal or hips (maximum posterior protuberance); chest (mesosternale); chest (nipple); ankle (minimum), breadths and lengths: biacromial; biiliocristal; foot length.

Step 1 Cut off all of Barbie's hair as close to the scalp as possible. This will be important when we estimate Barbie's mass. Warning: do not do this in the presence of small children.
Step 2 Take off Barbie's clothes.
Step 3 With a felt pen, mark as nearly as you can the following landmarks: mesosternale, acromiale (left and right), biiliocristale (left and right).

Step 4 Cut off a length of dental floss about 10 cm long. Using it as a 'tape measure', measure the following sites: waist (minimum), gluteal or hips (maximum posterior protuberance), chest (mesosternale), chest (nipple) and ankle (minimum). Locate landmarks as nearly as you can using the descriptions in Chapters 1 and 2 as a guide.

Step 5 Using vernier callipers, measure Barbie's biacromial and biiliocristal breadths, and foot length. Repeat each of the measurements in Steps 4 and 5. If the second measurement deviates by more than 5% from the first, take a third measurement. Use the mean of two and median of three measurements as your final value.

Step 6 Measure Barbie's height from vertex to heel. Enter all girths, heights and lengths in the 'Barbie (raw)' column in Table 9.3.

Step 7 Tape over any gaps in Barbie's articulations to make her watertight. Fill the basin to the very brim, and put it inside the larger flat dish. Submerge Barbie completely, so that the overflow falls into the large flat dish below. Measure the volume of water (ml) Barbie displaces either by weighing or by using a measuring cup. (If an object is used to hold Barbie down to prevent her floating, be sure to place the object in the water before filling the container to the top.)

Step 8 Scale each of the linear measurements in Steps 4 and 5 by dividing them by height, and then multiplying by 166.1 (which is the height in cm of active young women in the reference population). For example, if Barbie's measured waist girth is 6.5 cm, and her height is 27.5 cm, the scaled value will be (6.5 / 27.5) × 166.1 = 39.3 cm. This represents what Barbie's waist girth would be if she were 166.1 cm tall. Also calculate Barbie's chest

Table 9.3   Datasheet for entering measurements of Barbie

Measurement	Pop. mean*	Pop. SD	Barbie (raw)	Barbie (adj.)	z-score
Chest girth (mesosternale)	87.5	5.64			
Waist girth	72.2	9.59			
Gluteal girth	95.5	6.67			
Biacromial breadth	36.2	1.86			
Biiliocristal breadth	27.4	1.67			
Foot length	24.1	1.35			
Ankle girth	21.4	1.30			
CWR (mesosternale)	1.27	0.057			
CWR (nipple)	n/a	n/a			
WHR	0.76	0.092			
ln(mass)	4.089	0.142			
ln(BMI)	3.077	0.118			

CWR = chest–waist ratio; WHR = waist–hip ratio.
The population means and SDs are from a reference population of active 18–34-year-old Australian females (*n* = 475; AADBase, 1996).
* Girths, breadths and lengths are in cm.

(mesosternale)–waist ratio, and her waist–hip ratio, and also her chest (nipple)–waist ratio. No scaling is necessary when calculating ratios. Enter these values in the 'Barbie (adj.)' column in Table 9.3.

Step 9 Now estimate Barbie's mass. Assuming she has 15% body fat (an error of even 10% either way in this assumption will affect the final estimate of mass by less than 5%). Using the Siri equation (see Chapter 1 by Hawes and Martin), percent body fat = (495 / BD) – 450 where BD is body density in g ml^{-1}, we can calculate body density if we know percentage body fat. At 15% body fat, BD = 1.0645. Multiply Barbie's measured volume (ml) by 1.0645 to estimate her mass (mass = volume × density).

Step 10 These values must be scaled. 'Blow up' Barbie to the reference height (166.1 cm). When objects are scaled geometrically, mass is proportional to the cube of height. Let Barbie's height be *H* cm. Multiply her estimated mass from Step 9 by (166.1 / *H*)^3 to arrive at what Barbie would weigh were she the same height as the reference population. For example, if Barbie's estimated mass from Step 9 were 200 g, and her measured height 28 cm, her estimated mass at life size would be 200 × (166.1 / 28)^3 = 41750 g or 41.75 kg. We can now calculate her BMI (continuing to assume that her height is 166.1 cm), ln(mass) and ln(BMI) and enter those values into Table 9.3.

Step 11 Finally, situate Barbie relative to the reference population by calculating z-scores. The population means and SDs are given in Table 9.3. The z-scores can be converted into probability values by consulting tables in any standard statistical text.

Step 12 Repeat Steps 1–11 for Ken, entering data into Table 9.4. Population means and SDs are provided in Table 9.4. Ken should be standardized to a height of 179.2 cm.

Table 9.4 Datasheet for entering measurements of Ken

Measurement	Pop. mean*	Pop. SD	Ken (raw)	Ken (adj.)	z-score
Chest girth (mesosternale)	97.6	7.41			
Waist girth	81.1	7.20			
Gluteal girth	96.7	6.72			
Biacromial breadth	40.0	2.29			
Biiliocristal breadth	28.3	2.09			
Foot length	26.7	1.71			
Ankle girth	22.9	1.93			
CWR (mesosternale)	1.23	0.057			
CWR (nipple)	n/a	n/a			
WHR	0.85	0.051			
ln(mass)	4.336	0.142			
ln(BMI)	3.171	0.116			

CWR = chest–waist ratio; WHR = waist–hip ratio.
The population means and SDs are from a reference population of active 18–40-year-old Australian males
(*n* = 677; AADBase, 1996). *Girths, breadths and lengths are in cm.

9.10 PRACTICAL 4: THE ANTHROPOMETRY OF THE IDEAL FACE

9.10.1 PURPOSE

Students measure individual female faces to see how well they embody a 'geometry of beauty'. This experience is based on recent work into digital manipulation of facial features. It introduces measurement techniques using images rather than real bodies, and touches upon the techniques of scaling. It is important that this Practical is approved by the local institution's Human Ethics Committee.

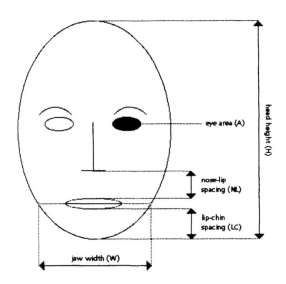

Figure 9.6 Measurement dimensions for facial characteristics.

9.10.2 PROCEDURES

Step 1 Take a photograph of a female volunteer. Because all members of the group will be rating the attractiveness of each subject, it is probably best that the volunteers not be part of the group. The photograph can be a developed print, or taken using a digital camera. The image can then be downloaded onto a computer for digital analysis, or enlarged by photocopying for manual analysis. For the photograph, the subject should be facing the camera directly, with hair drawn back, and should assume a neutral pose.

Step 2 On the image, measure the vertical distance between the bottom of the nose and the top of the upper lip (*NL* on Figure 9.6).

Step 3 Measure the vertical distance between the bottom of the lower lip and the tip of the chin (*LC*).

Step 4 Measure the width of the jaw at the level of the middle of the lips (*W*).

Step 5 Measure the eye area (*A*). This can be done with a planimeter, if it is available, or you can calculate an area index by multiplying eye height by eye width. The eye area should include the pupil, iris and white of the eye, plus the eyelid.

Step 6 These four measures have to be standardized for facial size. Divide *NL, LC* and *W* by the height of the face (*H*) from the vertex to the tip of the chin. Divide the eye area (or eye area index) by the area of the whole face (determined by planimetry) or the square of the height of the face (*H²*).

We now have four indices of facial attractiveness: NL / H, LC / H, W / H and A / H^2.

Step 7 Repeat Steps 1–6 for a further 9 female volunteers.

9.10.3 ASSIGNMENTS

1. Get each member of the group to rate the attractiveness of each face on a scale of 0 (extremely unattractive) to 10 (extremely beautiful). Calculate the average score for each face. This is their overall 'subjective attractiveness rating'.
2. For each of these four indices, calculate the mean and standard deviation, and convert each individual score to a z-score. Add up the z-scores for each of the 10 subjects. This is their overall 'objective attractiveness rating'.
3. We now have two attractiveness ratings – subjective and objective. To quantify the agreement between them, use Pearson's product-moment correlation coefficient. Most studies have shown strong associations between the two sets of ratings.

REFERENCES

Bok, V. (1976). A comparison of selected illustrations of creative works from the point of view of constitutional typology. *Acta Universitatis Carolinae (Gymnica)*, **10**, 79–91.

Borms, J., Ross, W.D., Duquet, W., and Carter, J.E.L. (1986). Somatotypes of world class bodybuilders. In *Perspectives in Kinanthropometry*. ed. J.A.P. Day (Human Kinetics, Champaign, IL), pp. 81–90.

Cash, T., Winstead, B. and Janda, L. (1986). The great American shape-up. *Psychology Today*, **April**, 30-7.

Etcoff, N. (1999). *Survival of the Prettiest: the Science of Beauty*. (Doubleday, New York).

Fallon, A.E. and Rozin, P. (1985). Sex differences in perceptions of desirable body shape. *Journal of Abnormal Psychology*, **94**, 102–5.

Furnham, A., Hester, C., and Weir, C. (1990). Sex differences in the preferences for specific female body shapes. *Sex Roles*, **22**, 743–54.

Galton, F. (1879). Composite portraits, made by combining those of many different persons in a single figure. *Nature*, **8**, 132–44.

Manning, J.T. and Ockenden, L. (1994). Fluctuating asymmetry in racehorses. *Nature*, **370**, 185–6.

Manning, J.T. and Pickup, L.J. (1998). Symmetry and performance in middle-distance runners. *International Journal of Sports Medicine*, **19**, 205–9.

Manning, J.T., Scutt, D., Whitehouse, G.H., *et al.* (1996). Asymmetry and the menstrual cycle in women. *Ethology and Sociobiology*, **17**, 1–15.

Mazur, A., Mazur, J. and Keating, C. (1984). Military rank attainment of a West Point class: effects of cadets' physical features. *American Journal of Sociology*, **90(1)**, 125-50.

Møller, A.P. (1997). Developmental stability and fitness: a review. *American Naturalist*, **149**, 916–32.

Møller, A.P., Soler, M. and Thornhill, R. (1995). Breast asymmetry, sexual selection and human reproductive success. *Ethology and Sociobiology*, **16**, 207–19.

Norton, K.I. and Olds, T.S. eds. (1996). *Anthropometrica*. (UNSW Press, Sydney).

Norton, K.I. and Olds, T.S. (2000). Evolution of the size and shape of athletes: causes and consequences. In *Kinanthropometry VI*. eds. T.S. Olds, J. Dollman and K.I. Norton (International Society for the Advancement of Kinanthropometry, Adelaide). pp. 3–36.

Norton, K.I., Olds, T.S., Dank, S. and Olive, S.C. (1996). Ken and Barbie at life size. *Sex Roles*, **34** (3/4), 1996.

Olds, T.S. and Norton, K.I. (1999). *LifeSize* (software). (Human Kinetics, Champaign, IL).

Palmer, R.A. and Strobeck, C. (1992). Fluctuating asymmetry as a measure of developmental stability: implications of non-normal distributions and power of statistical tests. *Acta Zoologica Fennica*, **191**, 57–72.

Perrett, D.I., May, K.A. and Yoshikawa, S. (1994). Facial shape and judgements of female attractiveness. *Nature*, **368**, 239–42.

Pope, H.R., Katz, D.L. and Hudson, J.I. (1993). Anorexia nervosa and reverse anorexia among 108 male bodybuilders. *Comprehensive Psychiatry*, **34**, 406–9.

Secord, P. and Bevan, W. (1956). Personality in faces: III. A cross-cultural comparison of impressions of physiognomy of personality in Faces. *Journal of Social Psychology*, **43**, 283–8.

Sheldon, W.H. (1944). Constitutional factors in personality. In *Personality and Behavior Disorders*. ed. J.M. Hunt. (Ronald Press, New York), pp. 526–49.

Singh, D. and Young, R.K. (1995). Body weight, waist-to-hip ratio, breasts, and hips: role in judgements of female attractiveness and desirability for relationships. *Ethology and Sociobiology*, **16**, 483–507.

Stepnicka, J. (1983). The comparison of Adam's and Eve's depiction in selected style periods from the point of view of somatotype (in Czech). *Acta Universitatis Carolinae*, **19 (1)**, 73–83.

Symons, D. (1995). Beauty is in the adaptations of the beholder: the evolutionary psychology of human female sexual attractiveness. In *Sexual Nature, Sexual Culture*. eds. P.R. Abramson and S.D. Pinkerton (University of Chicago Press, Chicago), pp. 80–118.

Thornhill, R. and Gangestad, S.W. (1994). Human fluctuating asymmetry and sexual behavior. *Psychological Science*, **5**, 297–302.

Tomkinson, G.R. and Olds, T.S. (1999). The size and shape of male shop mannequins. *Proceedings of The Body Culture Conference*, Melbourne, Australia, 27–28 July.

Tomkinson, G.R., Olds, T.S. and Carter, J.E.L. (2000). The anthropometry of desire: the body size and shape of female shop mannequins. In *Kinanthropometry VI*. eds. T.S. Olds, J. Dollman and K.I. Norton (International Society for the Advancement of Kinanthropometry, Adelaide). pp. 233–52.

Tovée, M.J., Mason, S.M., Emery, J.L., *et al.* (1997). Supermodels: stick-insects or hourglasses? *Lancet*, **350**, 1474–5.

Tucker, L.A. (1984). Physical attractiveness, somatotype and the male personality: a dynamic interactional perspective. *Journal of Clinical Psychology*, **40**, 1226–34.

U.S. Department of Health and Human Services (1996). National Centre for Health Statistics. *NHANES III Reference Manuals and Reports* (CD-ROM), Centers of Disease Control and Prevention, Hyattsville, MD.

Wolf, N. (1992). *The Beauty Myth: How Images of Beauty are used against Women*. (Anchor Press, New York).

Zaadstra, B.M., Seidell, J.C., van Noord, P.A.H., *et al.* (1993). Fat and female fecundity: prospective study of effect of body fat distribution on conception rates. *British Medical Journal*, **306**, 484–7.

STATISTICAL METHODS IN KINANTHROPOMETRY AND EXERCISE PHYSIOLOGY

10

Alan M. Nevill and Greg Atkinson

10.1 AIMS

The aims of this chapter are:
- to outline the most commonly used statistical methods that are used to describe and analyse the results of research work in exercise physiology and kinanthropometry,
- to show how such methods are applied to real examples from these disciplines,
- to show the command syntax for each respective test that is relevant to the popular statistical package 'MINITAB'. Although this software can now be used with pull-down menus, command syntax can be typed into the 'session window' in MINITAB version 12.1 (1998). In the following examples, this is also useful to illustrate the logic of the statistical procedures.

10.2 ORGANIZING AND DESCRIBING DATA IN KINANTHROPOMETRY AND EXERCISE PHYSIOLOGY

Kinanthropometry is a relatively new branch of science that is concerned with measuring the physical characteristics of human beings and the movements they perform. In our attempt to further our understanding of 'the human in motion', there is a clear need for laboratory-based tests or experiments that will frequently involve the collection of one or more measurements or variables on a group(s) of subjects.

10.2.1 VARIABLES IN KINANTHROPOMETRY AND EXERCISE PHYSIOLOGY

A variable is any characteristic or measurement that can take on different values. When planning or designing a laboratory-based experiment, the researcher will be able to identify those measurements that can be regarded as either independent or dependent variables. A variable that is under the control of the researcher is referred to as the independent variable. The resulting measurements that are recorded on each subject as a response to the independent variable are known as the dependent variables. For example, in an experiment investigating the oxygen cost of treadmill running, the independent variable is the running speed, set by the researcher, and the recorded oxygen cost is the resulting dependent variable.

(a) Classifying measurements in kinanthropometry and exercise physiology

Measurements in kinanthropometry and exercise physiology can be classified as either (i) categorical or (ii) numerical (quantitative) data.

Categorical data

The simplest type of measurement is called the nominal scale, where observations are allocated to one of various categories. Examples of

Kinanthropometry and Exercise Physiology Laboratory Manual: Tests, Procedures and Data. 2nd Edition, Volume 1: Anthropometry Edited by RG Eston and T Reilly. Published by Routledge, London, June 2001

nominal data with only two categories (binary) are: male / female, winners / losers or presence / absence of a disease. Examples of nominal data with more than two unordered categories are: country of birth, favourite sport, team supported and different equipment manufacturers. As long as the categories are exhaustive (include all cases) and non-overlapping or mutually exclusive (no case is in more than one category), we have the minimal conditions necessary for the application of statistical procedures on observations catagorized on a nominal scale.

Suppose that we retain the idea of grouping from the nominal scale and add the restriction that the variable that we are measuring has an underlying continuum so that we may speak of a person having 'more than' or 'less than' another person of the variable in question. This would be an ordinal scale or rank order scale of measurement. Level of achievement at a particular sport would be an example of this type of measurement, i.e. beginner, recreational participant, club standard, county representative, national or international standard.

Numerical data

Numerical data, often referred to as either interval or ratio scales of measurement, are the highest level of measurement. The distinction between interval and ratio scales (the latter has a fixed zero, the former does not) is not very useful, since most data collected in kinanthropometry and exercise physiology are measured using the ratio scale, e.g. one of the few examples of an interval scale of measurement in kinanthropometry would be the results from a sit-and-reach flexibility test. An interval or ratio scale variable can be either a discrete count or a 'continuous' variable. A discrete count can only take on specific values. The number of heart beats per minute and the number of people in a team are examples of discrete variables. A 'continuous' variable may take any value within a defined range of values. Height, weight and time are examples of continuous variables. Quotation marks are used around 'continuous' because all such variables are in practice measured to a finite precision, so they are actually discrete variables with a large number of numerical values. For example, height may be measured to the nearest centimetre and the time to run 100 m may be recorded to the nearest one-hundredth of a second.

10.2.2 FREQUENCY TABLES OR DISTRIBUTIONS

The first step necessary to investigate and understand the results of experiments is to discover how the experimental results vary over the range of responses. Are the scores evenly spread over the entire range of responses or do they tend to be more frequent in a particular section of the range, i.e. are the scores symmetric over the range or are they skewed with one or two atypical results or outlyers? The scores, often referred to as the *raw data*, need to be

Table 10.1 The maximal oxygen uptake $\dot{V}O_{2max}$ results of 30 recreationally active male subjects (Nevill *et al.*, 1992a)

$\dot{V}O_{2\,max}$	*(ml kg^{-1} min^{-1})*				
60.9	59.3	59.2	58.9	58.3	58.1
55.7	53.4	53.0	51.8	50.6	54.4
63.0	60.3	59.5	57.3	57.1	57.0
56.1	55.1	55.0	54.4	54.0	53.0
52.9	52.8	52.4	51.2	48.5	53.6

Table 10.2   Frequency table for the maximal oxygen uptake results in Table 10.1

Class intervals	Mid-points (M_j)	Tally	Frequency (f_j)
47.0–48.9	47.95	I	1
49.0–50.9	49.95	I	1
51.0–52.9	51.95	IIIII	5
53.0–54.9	53.95	II IIIII	7
55.0–56.9	55.95	IIII	4
57.0–58.9	57.95	I IIIII	6
59.0–60.9	59.95	IIIII	5
61.0–62.9	61.95		0
63.0–64.9	63.95	I	1

Note: the class intervals do not overlap (there are no points in common), and do not exclude scores in the gaps between class intervals.

arranged in the form of a *frequency table* to discover the distribution of measurements over the range of subjects' responses. Consider the following maximal oxygen uptake ($\dot{V}O$ max) results given in Table 10.1 (Nevill *et al.*, 1992a).

The first step in calculating a frequency table is to obtain the *range* of scores, i.e.

$$\text{Range} = \text{highest score} - \text{lowest score}$$
$$= 63.0 - 48.5 = 14.5 \ (\text{ml kg}^{-1} \text{min}^{-1})$$

The next step is to divide the range into a convenient number of *class intervals* of equal size. Since the number of intervals should lie between 5 and 15, depending on the number of observations, we can obtain a rough estimate of the interval size. In this example, a reasonable number of intervals would be about 8 or 9 that would require an interval size of 2 (ml kg^{-1} min^{-1}). Hence Table 10.2 might be the result.

10.2.3 HISTOGRAMS AND FREQUENCY POLYGONS

A histogram or frequency polygon is a graphical representation of a frequency table. A histogram is a set of adjacent rectangles with the class intervals forming the base of the rectangles and the areas proportional to the class frequencies. If the class intervals are all of equal size, it is usual to take the height of the rectangles as the class frequencies. If the class intervals are not of equal size, the height of the rectangles must be adjusted accordingly, e.g. if one of the class intervals is twice the size of all the other intervals, then the height of this rectangle should be the frequency score divided by 2. The histogram describing the maximal oxygen uptake results from Table 10.2 is given in Figure 10.1.

A frequency polygon is a broken-line graph of frequencies plotted against their class intervals. It can be obtained by simply joining the mid-points of the rectangles in the histogram. In order to preserve the area representation of the frequencies, the end points of the polygon have been positioned on the base line at the mid-points of the intervals on either side of the two extreme intervals, see Figure 10.1. If the class intervals are made smaller and smaller while at the same time the number of measurements or counts further increase, the frequency polygon may approach a smooth curve, called a

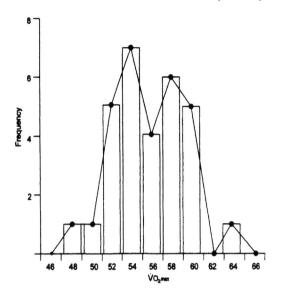

Figure 10.1 Frequency histogram of 30 male maximal oxygen uptake results (ml kg^{-1} min^{-1}). (From Nevill *et al.*, 1992a.)

frequency distribution. An important example of a frequency distribution that is symmetrical and bell-shaped is the normal distribution. The results of tests and experiments in kinanthropometry and exercise physiology are often found to take on the form of a normal distribution. However, the normal distribution is not the only type of frequency distribution obtained when results of such tests and experiments come to be investigated. Other asymmetric or skewed frequency distributions are also obtained. An asymmetric or skewed frequency distribution has a longer tail to one side of the central maximum than the other. If the longer tail is found to the right hand side of the distribution, the data are described as positively skewed, while if the longer tail is found on the left side of the distribution, the data are described as negatively skewed. Certain transformations can be used to overcome the problems of skewed data that correct the asymmetry in the frequency distribution, e.g. a logarithmic transformation will frequently correct positively skewed data such as body mass (kg) or maximal oxygen uptake (l min^{-1}) that have a 'log-normal' distribution.

10.2.4 THE NORMAL PLOT

With a small number of observations, it is often difficult to examine the underlying distribution with a histogram. This is because the frequency in each class interval will be small, so the appearance of the histogram will change markedly in response to small fluctuations in frequencies. An alternative graphical method of exploring data which works better with small samples is the Normal plot. The exact calculations for this plot are beyond the scope of this book, but are covered by Altman (1991). Suffice to say that the normal plot is based on relative cumulative frequencies plotted on non-linear axes, so that a normal distribution is judged by the points on the plot lying in a

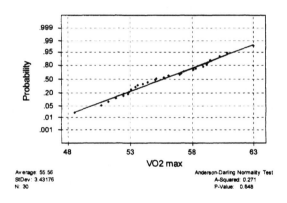

Figure 10.2 A Normal plot for the example data. On a Normal plot the normal probabilities are plotted against the data. The data depart from the fitted line most evidently in the extremes or distribution tails. This would indicate departure from the normal distribution. MINITAB also provides the results of a statistical test which examines the null hypothesis that the data are not normally distributed. The Anderson-Darling test in this example has provided a *p* value of 0.648 which indicates that there is little evidence that the data do not follow a normal distribution. A normal plot can also be used to assess which population percentiles individual athletes fit into (e.g. a person with a maximal oxygen uptake of 63 ml kg^{-1}min^{-1} would lie in the top 5th percentile of scores for that population).

straight line. A departure from normality usually shows up as an s-shaped curve on the plot. An example of a Normal plot using the maximal oxygen uptake data is shown in Figure 10.2

10.2.5 MEASURES OF LOCATION OR CENTRAL TENDENCY (AVERAGES)

(a) Arithmetic Mean

The arithmetic mean of a set of measurements is defined as the sum of all the scores divided by the total number of measurements. When using the raw data such as the maximal oxygen uptake measurements from Table 10.1, we need to calculate,

$$\overline{X} = \frac{\Sigma X_i}{n} = \frac{(X_1 + X_2 + X_3 \quad + X_n)}{n}$$

$$= \frac{(60.9 + 59.3 + 59.2 + \quad + 48.5 + 53.6)}{30}$$

$$= \frac{1666.8}{30}$$

$$= 55.560$$

where X_i refers to the individual scores and Σ is the usual 'sigma' summation notation.

If the data are available only in the form of a frequency table (secondary data), an estimate of the arithmetic mean can be obtained by assuming all the scores of each class interval are approximated by its mid-point (M_i). The estimated arithmetic mean for the maximal oxygen uptake results given in Table 10.2 is given by,

$$\overline{X} = \frac{\Sigma(f_i M_i)}{n} = \frac{(f_1 M_1 + f_2 M_2 + \quad + f_k M_k)}{n}$$

$$= \frac{(1 \times 47.95 + 1 \times 49.95 + 5 \times 52.95 + \quad + 1 \times 63.95)}{30}$$

$$= \frac{1670.5}{30}$$

$$= 55.68$$

where k equals the number of class intervals and M_i and f_i are the mid-point and frequency of the ith class interval, respectively.

(b) Median

The median is the middle score of the ranked data. If there are an odd number of scores, the median is unique. However, if the number of scores is even, we simply take the arithmetic mean of the two middle values. To obtain the median of the maximal oxygen uptake results of Table 10.1 we need to arrange the scores in order of magnitude as follows,

48.5 50.6 51.2 51.8 52.4 52.8 52.9 53.0 53.0
53.4 53.6 54.0 54.4 54.4 55.0 55.1 55.7 56.1
57.0 57.1 57.3 58.1 58.3 58.9 59.2 59.3 59.5
60.3 60.9 63.0.

Hence, the median (M) becomes,

$$M = (55.0 + 55.1) / 2 = 55.05$$

(c) Mode

The mode is the most frequent observation. In small data sets, the mode is not always unique. In the case of grouped or secondary data where a frequency table has been constructed, the mode can be obtained as follows,

$$\text{Mode} = L_1 + c \, (d_1 / (d_1 + d_2))$$

where:

L_1 = lower class boundary of the modal class (i.e. the most frequent class interval)

c = size of the modal class interval

d_1 = excess of the modal frequency over frequency of the next lower class

d_2 = excess of the modal frequency over frequency of the next higher class

The mode for the maximal oxygen uptake results taken from Table 10.2 becomes

$$\text{Mode} = L_1 + c \left(\frac{d_1}{(d_1 + d_2)} \right)$$

$$= 52.9 + 2 \left(\frac{2}{(2+3)} \right)$$

$$= 52.9 + \frac{4}{5} = 52.9 + 0.8$$

$$= 53.7$$

In summary, if the data are numerical (interval and ratio scales) and symmetric, the mean, median, and mode will all tend to coincide at the centre of the frequency distribution. As such, the arithmetic mean provides the simplest and best measure of central tendency. If, however, the numerical data have a skewed frequency distribution, the arithmetic mean will be distorted towards the longer tail of the distribution and the median would become a more representative average. If the observed information on a group of subjects is categorical, the calculation of the arithmetic mean is impossible. When the observed data are recorded as an ordered categorical (ordinal) scale, the median and mode are available as measures of central tendency. However, if the observed information on a group of subjects is simply a nominal scale, the mode is the only measure of central tendency that remains available, e.g. the most popular sports footwear manufacturer.

10.2.6 MEASURES OF VARIATION OR DISPERSION

Although the arithmetic mean provides a satisfactory measure of location or central tendency, it fails to indicate the way the data are spread about this central point. Are all the observed measurements very similar, demonstrating little variation among the scores, or are the measurements spread over a wide range of observations? The degree to which the numerical data are spread out is called the variation or dispersion in the data. A number of measures of variation or dispersion are available, the most common being the range, mean deviation, the variance and the standard deviation (the standard deviation = $\sqrt{\text{variance}}$).

(a) Range

The range = highest score – lowest score, has already been introduced in Section 10.2.2, is the simplest measure of variation and has the advantage of being quick and simple to calculate. Its limitation is that it fails to represent the variation in all the data since it is obtained from just the two extreme scores.

(b) Mean deviation

The mean deviation is the sum of the deviations of a set of scores from their mean.

$$Mean\ Deviation = MD = \sum \frac{\left| X_i - \overline{X} \right|}{n}$$

where the notation $\left| X_i - \overline{X} \right|$ denotes the absolute value of $X_i - \overline{X}$, without regard to its sign. The mean deviation of the maximal oxygen uptake results from Table 10.1 becomes,

$MD =$

$$= \frac{\left(\left| 60.9 - 55.56 \right| + \left| 59.3 - 55.56 \right| + \quad + \left| 53.6 - 55.56 \right| \right)}{30}$$

$$= \frac{\left(5.34 + 3.74 + \quad + 1.96 \right)}{30}$$

$$= \frac{85.71}{30}$$

$$= 2.9 (\text{ml kg}^{-1} \text{min}^{-1})$$

The advantages of the mean deviation are that it includes all the scores, is easy to define, and is easy to compute. Its disadvantage is its unsuitability for algebraic manipulations, since signs must be adjusted (ignored) in its definition, e.g. if the mean and mean deviations of two sets of scores are known, there is no formula allowing the calculations of the mean deviations of the combined set without going back to the original data.

(c) Variance

The variance of a set of data, denoted by s^2, is defined as the average of the squared deviations from the mean.

$$s^2 = \sum \frac{\left(X_i - \overline{X} \right)^2}{n} = \sum \frac{(x_i)^2}{n}$$

where $x_i = X_i - \overline{X}$.

The variance overcomes the problem of converting positive and negative deviations into quantities that are all positive by the process of squaring. Unfortunately, whatever the units of the original data, the variance has to be described in these units 'squared'. For this reason the standard deviation = $\sqrt{\text{variance}}$, is more frequently reported. An alternative method of defining the variance is to divide the sum of squared deviations by $n-1$ rather than n. When we divide the sum of square deviations by n, the variance will show a systematic tendency to under-estimate the variance of the entire population of scores, denoted by the Greek letter sigma (σ^2). When we divide the sum of squared deviations by $n-1$, however, we obtain an unbiased estimate of σ^2. Hence, the unbiased estimate of σ^2 is $s^2 = \Sigma(X_i - \overline{X})^2 / (n-1)$ where the variance estimate, s^2, has $n-1$ 'degrees of freedom', i.e. the maximum number of variates that can be freely assigned before the rest of the variates are completely determined.

(d) Standard deviation

The standard deviation, denoted by s, is the square root of the variance.

$$s = \sqrt{\Sigma_i \frac{(X_i - \overline{X})^2}{n}}$$

The standard deviation of the maximal oxygen uptake results from Table 10.1 can be found as follows,

$$s = \sqrt{\frac{(60.9 - 55.56)^2 + (59.3 - 55.56)^2 + \ +(53.6 - 55.56)^2}{30}}$$

$$= \sqrt{\frac{(28.52 + 13.99 + \ + 3.84)}{30}}$$

$$= \sqrt{11.38}$$

$$= 3.373$$

However, the calculation above requires a lot of computation. For many reasons it is more convenient to calculate the standard deviation using the alternative 'short method' formula:

$$s = \sqrt{\Sigma \frac{X^2}{n} - \left(\Sigma \frac{X}{n}\right)^2}$$

$$= \sqrt{\frac{92949}{30} - \left(\frac{1666.8}{30}\right)^2}$$

$$= \sqrt{3098.3 - (55.56)^2}$$

$$= \sqrt{3098.3 - 3086.9}$$

$$= \sqrt{11.4}$$

$$= 3.376$$

The variance and standard deviation have a number of advantages over the mean deviation. In particular, they are more suitable for algebraic manipulation as demonstrated by the more convenient 'short method' formula given above.

10.2.7 RELATIVE MEASURE OF PERFORMANCE OR THE 'Z' STANDARD SCORE

A 'z' standard score is the difference between a particular score X_i and the mean X, relative to the standard deviation s, i.e.

$$z_i = \frac{(X_i - \overline{X})}{s}$$

An important characteristic of a standard score is that it provides a meaningful way of comparing scores from different distributions that have different means and standard deviations. To illustrate the value of standard scores, suppose we wished to compare a decathlete's performance in two events relative to the other competitors, e.g. 1500 m and 100 m run times, at a certain competition. Suppose the athlete ran the 1500 m in 4 minutes 20 seconds and the 100 m in 10.2 seconds. Clearly, a direct comparison of the two performances is impossible. However, if the mean performance (and standard deviation) of all the competing athletes at the two events were 4 minutes 30 (10) seconds and 10.5 (0.2) seconds respectively, the decathlete's standard scores at each event, recorded in seconds, are given by:

$z\ (1500\ m) = (260 - 270) / 10 = 10 / 10 = -1.0$

$z\ (100\ m) = (10.2 - 10.5) / 0.2 = -0.3 / 0.2 = -1.5$

Clearly, the greater standard score, $z = -1.5$, indicates that the athlete performed better at the 100 m than the 1500 m relative to the other competitors. Note that standard scores also play an essential role when carrying out parametric tests of significance, discussed in Section 10.4.

10.2.8 REFERENCE INTERVALS AND DESCRIPTION OF MEASUREMENT ERROR

Another advantage of the standard deviation statistic is that it can be used to estimate the likely range that includes a certain percentage of values for the population of interest. Such 'reference intervals' are used in classical ergonomics to ensure that a piece of equipment is designed to fit a specified range of individual sizes. Reference intervals can also be used in normative studies of athletic ability to assess the population percentiles (e.g. the top 2.5%) that individual athletes fit into. About 68% of observations from a normal distribution will be within the mean ±1 standard deviation(s). A popular reference interval covers the central 95% of observations (excludes the upper and lower 2.5% of people) and is calculated from mean ±1.96 multiplied by s (about 2 times s above and below the mean). Interested readers are directed to Wright and Royston (1999) for a fuller discussion of how to calculate reference intervals and how to apply them to laboratory measurements.

Reference intervals can also be used to describe the error in taking measurements on a particular variable with a particular population, and can be much more informative than the conventional analysis of calculating a test–retest correlation (Atkinson and Nevill, 1998). For one type of measurement error description (Bland and Altman, 1999), the reference interval is calculated from the standard deviation of the test–retest differences. If this standard deviation is multiplied by 1.96 and added to and subtracted from the mean difference between test and retest, it would be expected that the majority (95%) of individuals in the population would show test–retest differences, purely due to measurement error, of no greater than this calculated reference range. It is also useful to examine the mean difference between test and retest on its own as an indicator of the degree to which measurements were affected by systematic errors (e.g. learning effects leading to an increased score).

The above '95% limits of agreement' (Bland and Altman, 1999) are useful for estimating the likelihood that a change in an individual athlete's test scores are 'real' or merely due to measurement error on the test. For example, if the 95% limits of agreement for a maximal oxygen uptake test on a population of athletes are –5 to +5 ml kg^{-1} min^{-1}, then it is likely that a change in maximal oxygen uptake of >5 ml kg^{-1} min^{-1} for an individual athlete from the same population is a 'true' change and not due merely to measurement error on the test (Harvill, 1991). In other words, only 2.5% of the population would show test-retest differences greater than 5 ml kg^{-1} min^{-1} that could be attributed to random measurement error. Limits of agreement can also be employed for assessing the likelihood that different methods of measurement give similar scores for individual athletes (Bland and Altman, 1999). Reference intervals should not be confused with confidence intervals, which involve the likelihood of a population mean being within a range of sample means. Most reference intervals for measurement error assume that the data are normally distributed, the errors are homoscedastic (constant throughout the range of measured values) and that the sample size is large enough to provide a precise assessment of the population interval. The first two assumptions can be explored and corrected for by logarithmic transformation (Bland and Altman, 1999). The latter assumption should be controlled a priori by employing an adequate sample size (preferably >40). In addition, the researcher can estimate the precision of the limits of agreement by calculating the confidence intervals according to the methods of Bland and Altman (1999).

Anthropometrists may wish to calculate the 'technical error of measurement' (TEM) which is purported to represent 'the typical magnitude of measurement error that one can expect to occur' (Knapp, 1992; p. 253). In reality, this statistic is similar to the standard error of measurement (Harvill, 1991) in that it represents the range above and below the observed value for which there is a 68% chance of a hypothetical 'true value' existing in the 'average' subject. Whether this reference range for measurement error is considered as 'typical' is up to the researcher. It may be better to extrapolate the described measurement error to what it means for actual uses of the measurement tool. For example, researchers may be more interested in describing the measurement error so that they are more confident that the true value is within the stated reference range. This could be done by multiplying the TEM by 1.96 which gives a 95% reference range for the 'true' value (Harvill, 1991). One can also estimate how the described measurement error impacts upon statistical power and estimated sample size in experiments (Atkinson *et al.*, 1999; Atkinson and Nevill, 2001). TEM is calculated by summing the squared differences (d_i) between test and retest for each person (i), dividing the sample size (n) by 2 and taking the square root (Knapp, 1992):

$$TEM = \sqrt{\frac{\sum d_i^2}{2n}}$$

It is stressed that the individual differences between test and retest are involved in the calculation, rather than the individual differences from the sample mean, as is the case for the standard deviation of the differences. Practically, this would mean that TEM assumes that all error is random instrument error and that no systematic learning influences are present. Kinanthropometrists should be aware that some measurements are prone to learning effects from both the subject and the tester. The TEM also assumes that the measurement error is the same, irrespective of the general magnitude

of the measured variable (homoscedasticity). This is so, even though it is known that the measurement error of some anthropometric variables is greater for subjects with higher values in general (Atkinson and Nevill, 1998). This characteristic, called heteroscedasticity, can be controlled for by a certain extent by expressing the TEM as a percentage of the mean measured value for the sample:

$$'Relative'\ TEM\,(\%) = \frac{TEM}{Sample\ mean\ score} \times 100$$

We maintain that a much more informative reference range for measurement error is the 95% limits of agreement, especially for assessing individual variability, and a more thorough analysis and exploration of measurement error is through the associated methods of Bland and Altman (1999).

10.2.9 THE MINITAB COMMANDS TO ILLUSTRATE THE METHODS OF SECTION 10.2

Data in MINITAB are stored in columns. To enter the data we can use either the READ or SET command, e.g. the maximal oxygen uptake data in Table 10.1 could be entered or SET into column 1 (C1) by

```
MTB > SET C1
    DATA> 60.9 59.3 59.2 58.9 58.3 58.1
    55.7 53.4 53.0 51.8
    DATA> 50.6 54.4 63.0 60.3 59.5 57.3
    57.1 57.0 56.1 55.1
    DATA> 55.0 54.4 54.0 53.0 52.9 52.8
    52.4 51.2 48.5 53.6
    DATA> END
```

To help identification, the data in column C1 can now be named as follows;

```
MTB > NAME C1 'VO2 MAX'
```

The frequency table and distribution can be displayed with the histogram command, i.e.

```
MTB > HISTOGRAM C1
    HISTOGRAM OF VO2 MAX N = 30
```

```
MIDPOINT COUNT
48  1 *
50  1 *
52  5 *****
54  7 *******
56  4 ****
58  6 ******
60  5 *****
62  0
64  1 *
```

Note: When using the MINITAB histogram command, observations falling on a class boundary are put into the interval with the larger midpoint. Hence, in the above example, a score of 49 would be put into the class interval with midpoint 50. In reality, this decision rule will result in precisely the same frequency table and distribution given in Table 10.2 derived in Section 10.2.2.

If the data are typed in C1, a normal plot can be obtained by typing the following in the session window of MINITAB:

MTB > %NormPlot C1.

The simplest method to obtain most of the descriptive statistics given in Sections 10.2.5 and 10.2.6 is to use the DESCRIBE command as follows,

MTB > DESCRIBE C1

from the smallest to the largest scores. As described in Section 10.2.5, the median or second quartile (Q2), is the middle score or the 50th percentile. The Q1 and Q3 values are simply the 25th and 75th percentiles respectively. Note that the STDEV is calculated using the unbiased definition for the population variance σ^2, i.e. by dividing the sum of squared deviations by $n - 1$.

10.3 INVESTIGATING RELATIONSHIPS IN KINANTHROPOMETRY AND EXERCISE PHYSIOLOGY

10.3.1 CORRELATION

The first and most important step when investigating relationships between variables in kinanthropometry and exercise physiology is to plot the data in the form of a scatter diagram. The eye can still identify patterns or relationships in data better than any statistical tests. If X and Y denote the independent and dependent variables respectively of our experiment, a scatter diagram describes the location of points (X, Y) on a rectangular coordinate system. The term 'correlation' is used to describe the degree of relationship that exists between the dependent and independent variables.

	N	MEAN	MEDIAN	TRMEAN	STDEV	SEMEAN
$\dot{V}O_2$ max	30	55.560	55.050	55.531	3.432	0.627
	MIN	MAX	Q1	Q3		
$\dot{V}O_2$ max	48.500	63.000	52.975	58.450		

The term TRMEAN represents a trimmed mean, averaged from the middle 90% of the data, where 5% of the smallest and largest values are ignored. The standard error of the mean, SEMEAN, is defined as $s / \sqrt{n}$. The first and third quartiles are denoted by Q1 and Q3. Quartiles are obtained by ranking the data

(a) Positive correlation

Example 1 An example of a positive correlation is the relationship between the mean power output (W) of 16 subjects, recorded on a non-motorized treadmill, and their body mass (kg), see Figure 10.3. (Nevill *et al.*, 1992b).

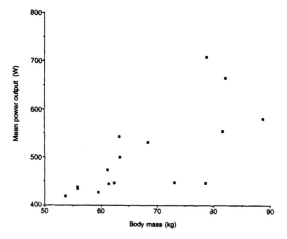

Figure 10.3 Mean power output (W) versus body mass (kg) of 16 male subjects, recorded on a non-motorized treadmill (Nevill *et al.*, 1992b).

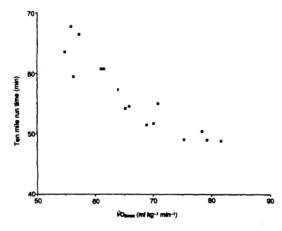

Figure 10.4 Ten-mile run times (min) versus maximal oxygen uptake (ml kg⁻¹ min⁻¹) of 16 male subjects (Costill *et al.*, 1973).

The scatter diagram demonstrates a positive correlation since the subjects with a greater body mass (X) are able to record a higher mean power output (Y), i.e. as X increases, Y also increases.

(b) Negative correlation

Example 2 In contrast, an example of a negative correlation is seen in Figure 10.4 between maximal oxygen uptake (ml kg⁻¹ min⁻¹) and ten mile (16.1 km) run times (minutes) of 16 male subjects, representing a wide range of distance running abilities (adapted from Costill *et al.*, 1973).

The figure describes a negative correlation because the subjects with lower 10 mile run times (X) are found to have recorded higher maximal oxygen uptake measurements (Y), i.e. as X increases Y is found to decrease.

(c) No correlation

If a scatter diagram indicates no obvious pattern or relationship between the two variables, then the variables are said to have no correlation, i.e. they are uncorrelated.

10.3.2 MEASURES OF CORRELATION

Although a scatter diagram gives a clear indication of the degree of relationship between two variables, a single numerical statistic or correlation coefficient would summarize the relationship and facilitate the comparison of several different correlations.

(a) Pearson's product-moment correlation coefficient

The most appropriate correlation coefficient for numerical variables was introduced by Karl Pearson and hence is often referred to as Pearson's product-moment correlation coefficient. The definition of the product-moment correlation coefficient requires a new measure of variation similar to the variance introduced in Section 10.2.6, known as the covariance, i.e.

$$s_{xy} = \frac{(X_i - \overline{X})(Y_i - \overline{Y})}{n} \quad (10.1)$$

The covariance is a measure of the joint variation in X and Y, but its magnitude will depend on the variation in both variables. Hence, the product-moment correlation coefficient is defined as the ratio of the covariance to the product of the standard deviations of X and Y, given by

Table 10.3   Data required to calculate the correlation coefficient between mean power output (W) and body mass (kg) for example 1 (Nevill *et al.*, 1992b)

Mean power (Y)	Body mass (X)	Y^2	X^2	YX
499.6	63.4	249 600.2	4 019.56	31 674.6
473.7	61.2	224 391.7	3 745.44	28 990.4
444.5	61.4	197 580.2	3 769.96	27 292.3
438.0	55.8	191 844.0	3 113.64	24 440.4
446.2	78.7	199 094.5	6 193.69	35 115.9
665.8	82.1	443 289.7	6 740.41	54 662.2
709.2	78.8	502 964.7	6 209.44	55 885.0
542.5	63.3	294 306.3	4 006.89	34 340.2
581.0	88.7	337 561.0	7 867.69	51 534.7
434.1	55.8	188 442.8	3 113.64	24 222.8
554.7	81.7	307 692.1	6 674.89	45 319.0
418.3	53.7	174 974.9	2 883.69	22 462.7
530.8	68.4	281 748.6	4 678.56	36 306.7
446.8	62.4	199 630.2	3 893.76	27 880.3
447.4	73.1	200 166.8	5 343.61	32 704.9
426.6	59.5	181 987.6	3 540.25	25 382.7
Total 8 059.2	1 088.0	4 175 275.3	75 795.12	558 214.8

$$r = \frac{\sum(X_i - \bar{X})(Y_i - \bar{Y})}{\sqrt{\left[\sum(X_i - \bar{X})^2\right]\left[\sum(Y_i - \bar{Y})^2\right]}} \quad (10.2)$$

Note that the divisor (*n*) cancels in both the numerator and denominator terms in the ratio.

A more convenient formula to calculate the product-moment correlation coefficient 10.1 is given by

$$r = \frac{n\sum X_i Y_i - (\sum X)(\sum Y)}{\sqrt{\left[n\sum X_i^2 - (\sum X)^2\right]\left[n\sum Y_i^2 - (\sum Y)^2\right]}}$$

The correlation coefficient in Example from Nevill *et al.* (1992b), between mean power output (W) and body mass (kg) can be obtained as follows. From the two columns 'mean power (Y)' and 'body mass (X)', three further columns are required, i.e. Y^2, X^2 and YX, given in Table 10.3.

The only additional information required to calculate the correlation coefficient, given by equation (10.2), is the number of subjects, *n* = 16. Hence, the correlation coefficient becomes

$$r = \frac{16(558214.8)-(1088.0)(80592)}{\sqrt{[16(75795.12)-(1088)^2][16(4175275.3)-(80592)^2]}}$$

$$= \frac{8931436.8-8768409.6}{\sqrt{[1212721.9-1183744][66804405-64950705]}}$$

$$= \frac{1630272}{\sqrt{[28977.9][1853699.8]}}$$

$$= \frac{1630272}{231767.8}$$

$$= 0.703$$

The obtained value of +0.703 indicates that for this group of subjects, there was a high positive correlation between the two variables. The correlation coefficient can take any value between +1.00 and –1.00, with values of r close to zero indicating no linear relationship between the two variables. The above calculations are somewhat complex due to the size or scale of the variables X and Y. However, the correlation coefficient is unaffected by adding or subtracting a constant value to or from either column. Hence, in Example 2 from Costill *et al.* (1973), by subtracting convenient constants, say 40 from the Y column, i.e. $y = (Y - 40)$, and

Table 10.4 Data required to calculate the correlation coefficient between 10-mile run time (min) and maximal oxygen uptake (ml kg^{-1} min^{-1}) for Example 2 (Costill *et al.*, 1973)

Run time (Y)	$\dot{V}O_{2max}$ (X)	$y = (Y - 40)$	$x = (X - 50)$	x^2	y^2	xy
48.9	81.6	8.9	31.6	79.21	998.56	281.24
49.0	79.2	9.0	29.2	81.00	852.64	262.80
49.1	75.2	9.1	25.2	82.81	635.04	229.32
50.5	78.4	10.5	28.4	110.25	806.56	298.20
51.6	68.9	11.6	18.9	134.56	357.21	219.24
51.8	70.1	11.8	20.1	139.24	404.01	237.18
54.3	65.2	14.3	15.2	204.49	231.04	217.36
54.6	65.9	14.6	15.9	213.16	252.81	232.14
55.1	70.8	15.1	20.8	228.01	432.64	314.08
57.4	63.9	17.4	13.9	302.76	193.21	241.86
59.5	56.3	19.5	6.3	380.25	39.69	122.85
60.8	61.0	20.8	11.0	432.64	121.00	228.80
60.8	61.5	20.8	11.5	432.64	132.25	239.20
63.6	54.8	23.6	4.8	556.96	23.04	113.28
66.6	57.2	26.6	7.2	707.56	51.84	191.52
67.8	55.9	27.8	5.9	772.84	34.81	164.02
Total 901.4	1 065.9	261.4	265.9	4 858.4	5 566.3	3 593.1

50 from the X column, i.e. $x = (X - 50)$, in the data in Table 10.4, an alternative 'short method' of calculating the correlation coefficient, between ten mile run times (minutes) and maximal oxygen uptake or $\dot{V}O_2$ max (ml kg^{-1} min^{-1}) can be used to simplify the arithmetic.

Hence, the correlation coefficient for this example becomes

$$r = \frac{16(3593.1)-(261.4)(265.9)}{\sqrt{[16(4858.4)-(261.4)^2][16(5566.3)-(265.9)^2]}}$$

$$= \frac{57489.6-69506.26}{\sqrt{[77734.4-68329.96][89060.8-70702.8]}}$$

$$= \frac{-12016.7}{13139.48}$$

$$= -0.9145$$

In this example, the value of $r = -0.91$ indicates that for this group of subjects, there was a high negative correlation between the two variables. Pearson's product-moment correlation coefficient is an appropriate statistic to describe the relationship between two variables provided the data are approximately linear and numerical (interval or ratio scales of measurement). However, Pearson's correlation coefficient is not the only method of measuring the relationship between two variables.

(b) Spearman's rank correlation coefficient

The ranks given by two independent judges to a group of six gymnasts are given in Table 10.5. Are the two judges in agreement?

The most frequently used statistic to describe the relationship between ranks is Spearman's rank correlation coefficient r_s, given by

$$r_s = 1 - \left(\frac{6 \times \sum D^2}{N(N^2 -1)}\right)$$

where D is the difference between paired ranks and N is the number of pairs. For the ranks given in Table 10.5, the Spearman's rank correlation becomes

$$r_s = 1 - \frac{6 \times 24}{6(6^2 -1)}$$

$$= 1 - \frac{24}{25}$$

$$= 0.314$$

Table 10.5 Six gymnasts ranked on performance by two independent judges

| Gymnast | Ranks given by | | $D = R_1 - R_2$ | D^2 |
	Judge 1 (R_1)	Judge 2 (R_2)		
1	5	6	−1	1
2	2	5	−3	9
3	1	1	0	0
4	6	3	3	9
5	3	4	−1	1
6	4	2	2	4
Totals			0	$\sum D^2 = 24$

As with the Pearson's correlation coefficient, the value of r_s lies between +1.0 and E−1.0. Suppose Judge 1 decided that gymnast 2 and gymnast 3 were equally good in their performances and should share first place. This can be incorporated into the calculation by averaging the two shared ranks in question. In this example the two gymnasts were sharing ranks 1 and 2, so the average 1.5 would be given to both performers. Note that the next best gymnast would receive the rank of 3.

As with the Pearson's correlation coefficient, the value of r_s lies between +1.0 and –1.0. Negative correlations are of course highly unlikely in any examinations of agreement. A correlation of 0.314 is low to moderate, so agreement between observers could be questionable in this case. Suppose judge 1 decided that gymnast 2 and gymnast 3 were equally good in their performances and should share first place. This can be incorporated into the calculation by averaging the two shared ranks in question. In this example the two gymnasts were sharing ranks 1 and 2, so the average 1.5 would be given to both performers. Note that the next best gymnast would receive the rank of 3.

10.3.3 PREDICTION AND LINEAR REGRESSION

Suppose we wish to predict a male endurance athlete's 10-mile (16.1 km) run time having previously recorded his maximal oxygen uptake. If we assume that our athlete is of a similar standard as the subjects used by Costill *et al.* (1973), we could use these data to predict the 10-mile run time of such an athlete. Nevill *et al.* (1990) were able to show that since maximal oxygen uptake is a rate of using oxygen per minute, i.e. ml kg^{-1} min^{-1}, running

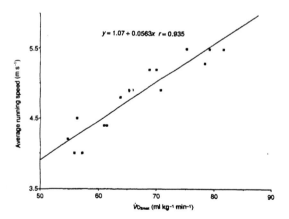

Figure 10.5 Ten mile run times, recalculated as average run speeds (m s^{-1}), versus maximal oxygen uptake results (ml kg^{-1} min^{-1}) (Costill et al., 1973).

performance is also better recorded as a rate, e.g. average run speed in metres per second (m s^{-1}). Hence, when the 10-mile run times of the athletes studied by Costill *et al.* (1973) were recalculated as average run speeds (m s^{-1}) and correlated with their results for maximal oxygen uptake results, the relationship appeared more linear, Figure 10.5, and the correlation increased from $r = -0.91$ to $r = 0.935$.

Let us assume that we wish to predict the average running speed (Y) of an athlete from the maximal oxygen uptake (X). The predicted variable Y, is often described as the dependent variable and the variable X that provides the information on which the predictions are based is referred to as the independent variable. If we accept that the relationship in Figure 10.5 between running speed and maximal oxygen uptake is a straight line, we can write the equation of a line as follows,

$$Y = a + b.X$$

where a, the Y-intercept, and b, the slope of the line, are both constants.

The simplest method of estimating the constants a and b is to use 'the method of least squares'. If we denote the predicted or estimated value of the dependent variable Y as $Y_e = a + b.X$, the 'method of least squares' is the method that minimizes the squared differences, $d^2 = \Sigma(Y - Y_e)^2$. The equation of the line, often referred to as the '*least squares regression line of Y on X*', fitted to n points (X,Y) by the method of least squares is given by,

$$Y_e = a + b \cdot X$$

where

$$b = \frac{n\Sigma X_i Y_i - (\Sigma X)(\Sigma Y)}{n\Sigma X_i^2 - (\Sigma X)^2} \quad (10.3)$$

and

$$a = \Sigma\frac{Y_i}{n} - b\Sigma\frac{Y_i}{n} \quad (10.4)$$

The regression line to predict the average 10-mile run speed from an athlete's maximal

Table 10.6 Data required to calculate the regression line between average 10 mile (16.1 km) run speed (m s^{-1}) and maximal oxygen uptake (ml kg^{-1} min^{-1}) for example 2 (Costill *et al.*, 1973)

$\dot{V}O_{2max}$ (X)	Speed (Y)	X^2	Y^2	XY
81.6	5.5	6 658.56	30.25	448.80
79.2	5.5	6 272.64	30.25	435.60
75.2	5.5	5 655.04	30.25	413.60
78.4	5.3	6 146.56	28.09	415.52
68.9	5.2	4 747.21	27.04	358.28
70.1	5.2	4 914.01	27.04	364.52
65.2	4.9	4 251.04	24.01	319.48
65.9	4.9	4 342.81	24.01	322.91
70.8	4.9	5 012.64	24.01	346.92
63.9	4.7	4 083.21	22.09	300.33
56.3	4.5	3 169.69	20.25	253.35
61.0	4.4	3 721.00	19.36	268.40
61.5	4.4	3 782.25	19.36	270.60
54.8	4.2	3 003.04	17.64	230.16
57.2	4.0	3 271.84	16.00	228.80
55.9	4.0	3 124.81	16.00	223.60
Totals 1 065.9	77.1	72 156.35	375.65	5 200.87

oxygen uptake measurements can be obtained from the quantities in Table 10.6.

Using equation (10.3), the slope of the line becomes

$$b = \frac{16 \times 5200.87 - (1065.9)(77.1)}{16 \times 72156.35 - (165.9)^2}$$

$$= \frac{83213.92 - 82180.89}{1154501.6 - 1136142.8}$$

$$= \frac{1033.03}{18358.8}$$

$$= 0.05627$$

and the intercept a becomes,

$$a = (77.1/16) - (0.05627 \times 1065.9)/16$$

$$= 4.82 - 3.75$$

$$= 1.07$$

Hence, the least squares regression line, required to predict the average 10-mile run speed from maximal oxygen uptake, is given by

$$Y_e = a + b.X$$

$$Y_e = 1.07 + 0.05627.X$$

An athlete who recorded a maximal oxygen uptake of 80 ml kg^{-1} min^{-1} would expect to run 10 miles at an average speed of 1.07 + 0.05627 × (80) = 5.57 m s^{-1}, i.e. he would expect to complete the 10 mile distance in 48.14 minutes.

10.3.4 MULTIPLE LINEAR REGRESSION

In the previous section, we were able to predict the average running speed (Y) of an athlete from the maximal oxygen uptake (X) using linear regression, assuming the relationship between running speed and maximal oxygen uptake was linear.

Suppose we wish to predict running performance using *more* than just one independent variable. Multiple linear regression allows the researcher to predict values of a dependent variable from a collection of k independent variables. The multiple linear regression equation becomes,

$$Y = a + b_1.X_1 + b_2.X_2 + \ldots + b_k.X_k$$

where $X_1, X_2, \ldots X_k$, are the independent (or predictor) variables and $b_1, b_2, \ldots b_k$ are the unknown slope parameters. These slope parameters can be calculated using 'the method of least-squares' as described above. In practice, statistical software such as MINITAB can estimate these unknown parameters quickly, accurately and efficiently. The MINITAB commands necessary to perform such multiple regression will be described at the end of this section.

When predicting variables in kinanthropometry and exercise physiology, however, there may be certain instances when the dependent variable can be predicted, more than adequately, using a subset of the independent variables, i.e. a 'reduced model'. There are a number of useful methods available for choosing good reduced models. These fall into two categories: best subset selection methods and stepwise regression methods.

Cockerill *et al.* (1991) used multiple linear regression to identify which of the six 'Profile of Mood States' (POMS) (Morgan, 1985) were best able to predict the cross-country race times of 81 runners competing in the 1990 British Students Cross-country Championships. When all six POMS factors were entered into MINITAB's 'BREG' multiple regression routine as possible predictors of run time, the best subset of mood factors was found to be:

$$\text{Time (min)} = 62.6 - 0.266 \, Ten$$
$$+ 0.246 \, Dep - 0.317 \, Ang \qquad (10.5)$$

where *Time* (min) = race time, *Ten* = tension, *Dep* = depression and *Ang* = anger. Evaluating all possible combinations of subset models is the most comprehensive and thorough way to proceed in variable selection. Unfortunately, the computational demands of evaluating every possible 'subset' model can be prohibitive, especially when more than 15 predictor variables are available. A more computationally efficient method of identifying a reduced subset model is to use stepwise regression.

Stepwise regression methods either remove or add variables for the purpose of identifying a reduced model. The three commonly used procedures are: standard stepwise regression (adds and removes variables), forward selection (adds variables), and backwards elimination (removes variables). The *best* of these methods, backward elimination, begins with a full or saturated model and the least important variables can then be eliminated sequentially (based on the size of the *t* statistic for dropping the variable from the model). When backward elimination stepwise regression was applied to the cross-country running results of Cockerill *et al.* (1991), the same solution as that chosen from the 'BREG' output (Equation 10.5) was obtained. Note that when both standard and forward stepwise regression methods were employed to predict the athletes' run times, only the factor 'Tension' was selected. The preferred solution (see Equation 10.5) suggests that a linear combination of three mood states provides the researcher with a valuable insight into the complex interaction between moods that is likely to result in successful cross-country running performance.

10.3.5 THE MINITAB COMMANDS TO ILLUSTRATE THE METHODS OF SECTION 10.3

One of the most important and useful statistical tools used to explore relationships is the scatter diagram. This can be easily obtained using the MINITAB 'PLOT' command as follows,

MTB > PLOT C1 C2

The Pearson product-moment correlation coefficient can be obtained using the MINITAB 'CORRELATION' command as follows,

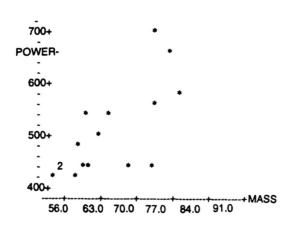

Figure 10.6 Example of MINITAB scatterplot.

MTB > CORRELATION C1 C2
CORRELATION OF POWER AND
  MASS = 0.703

Similarly, the correlation between the 10 mile run times and maximal oxygen uptake can be obtained as,

MTB > CORRELATION C3 C4
CORRELATION OF RUNTIME AND
  VO2MAX = −0.915

However, when the 10 mile run times were recalculated as an average speed (m s^{-1}) using the 'LET' command, the magnitude of the correlation is improved, as follows (there are 1609.35 metres in a mile),

MTB > LET C5=10*1609.35/(C3*60)
MTB > NAME C5 'SPEED'
MTB > CORRELATION C5 C4
CORRELATION OF SPEED AND
  VO2MAX = 0.935

Finally, the least squares linear regression line to predict average 10 mile run speed from maximal oxygen uptake, can be obtained as follows,

MTB > REGRESSION C5 1 C4
THE REGRESSION EQUATION IS SPEED =
  1.07 + 0.0563 VO2MAX

PREDICTOR	COEF	STDEV	T-RATIO	P
CONSTANT	1.0702	0.3714	2.88	0.012
VO2MAX	0.056269	0.005531	10.17	0.000

s = 0.1874   R-SQ = 88.1%   R-SQ(ADJ) = 87.2%
ANALYSIS OF VARIANCE

SOURCE	DF	SS	MS	F	P
REGRESSION	1	3.6330	3.6330	103.50	0.000
ERROR	14	0.4914	0.0351		
TOTAL	15	4.1244			

The first table in the above output gives the estimated values of the coefficients, the intercept a (CONSTANT) and the slope b (VO2MAX), along with their standard deviations, t values for testing if the coefficients are 0, and the p value for this test. Below this table, the estimated standard deviation about the regression line, s = 0.1874 is given. This is followed by the coefficient of determination, R^2 = 88.1 and the $R^2(adj)$ = 87.2, adjusted for the degrees of freedom.

The Analysis of Variance table contains the component sums of squares. The total variation of the dependent variable (SPEED) is partitioned into that explained by the regression line (REGRESSION) and the remaining unexplained variation (ERROR). Note that the estimated variance about the regression line MS ERROR = s^2 = $(0.1874)^2$ = 0.0351.

The multiple regression command is precisely the same as the regression command described above. For example, suppose we wished to predict the cross-country run times (labelled 'TIME') described in Cockerill *et al.* (1991), using all six 'POMS' mood state factors (labelled 'TEN' 'DEP' 'ANG' 'VIG' 'FAT' and 'CON'). The MINITAB command is

MTB > REGRESSION 'TIME' 6 'TEN'
  'DEP' 'ANG' 'VIG' 'FAT' 'CON'

The dependent variable 'TIME' is followed by the number 6, indicating that six independent variables are to be used to predict 'TIME'.

The best subsets multiple regression command 'BREG' is given by,

MTB > BREG 'TIME' 'TEN' 'DEP' 'ANG'
    'VIG' 'FAT' 'CON';
SUBC> NVARS 1 6;
SUBC> BEST 2;
SUBC> Constant.

where the subcommand 'NVARS' confirms the number of dependent and independent variables, 'BEST' confirms that the best two models with the largest R^2 will be selected and displayed, and the subcommand 'CONSTANT' indicates that an intercept will be included in the model.

The stepwise multiple regression command 'STEPWISE', is given by,

MTB > STEPWISE 'TIME' 'TEN' 'DEP' 'ANG'
    'VIG' 'FAT' 'CON';
SUBC> ENTER 'TEN'-'CON';
SUBC> FENTER 1000;
SUBC> FREMOVE 4.0;
SUBC> CONSTANT.

where the subcommand 'ENTER' confirms that all possible independent or predictor variables will be included. The program removes the variables one at a time and ends when no other variable in the model has an F value (see Section 10.4.1a; Step 2) less than 'FREMOVE'. The subcommand 'FENTER', in this example set at 10000, prevents any of the independent variables from being re-entered. As before, the subcommand 'CONSTANT' indicates that an intercept will be included in the model.

10.4 COMPARING EXPERIMENTAL DATA IN KINANTHROPOMETRY

Laboratory-based experiments are not conducted simply to describe the results of the experiment as outlined in Sections 10.2 and 10.3. The researcher will often wish to 'test' whether the experimental results (dependent variable) have been truly affected by different experimental conditions (the independent variable) or if the findings can be merely attributed to chance influences. This important step is the function of *inferential statistics*. For further reading in the methods of inferential statistics, see Snedecor and Cochran (1989).

10.4.1 DRAWING INFERENCES FROM EXPERIMENTAL DATA; INDEPENDENT SUBJECTS

The simplest experiment to design involves a group of subjects that require to be divided into two or more groups on a random basis. We shall describe the three most frequently used tests that adopt this design:

- The t test for independent samples
- One-way analysis of variance (ANOVA) for independent samples
- The Mann–Whitney test for independent samples

These tests will be introduced together with some general points about inferential statistics with examples from kinanthropometry and exercise physiology.

(a) The t test for independent samples

Example 3 A group of 13 male subjects was divided into two groups at random. One group of 6 subjects were given an exercise training programme for 6 months whilst the remaining 7 subjects acted as a control group. The blood lactate concentrations (mM) were measured whilst running at 70% of VO_2 max and are given in Table 10.7.

The requirements of the independent t test are as follows:

1. That the samples are drawn from a normal population with equal variance.
2. The variable is measured in the interval scale.

Clearly the blood lactate measurements can take any value within a certain range of

Table 10.7   Blood lactate concentrations recorded at 70% of $\dot{V}O_{2max}$

Lactate conc. (mmol 1^{-1})

Untrained subjects	Trained subjects
2.5	1.8
2.9	2.6
1.9	2.4
3.6	1.5
2.9	2.4
3.7	2.0
2.6	

observations and hence we can assume the measurements are recorded on an interval scale. Also by simply producing a frequency table, the two sets of data can be checked to demonstrate an approximate normal distribution, i.e. symmetric and bell-shaped. All these characteristics are described in Section 10.2.

The steps required to implement the *t* test for independent samples are as follows.

Step 1   Calculate the mean, standard deviation and variance for both samples.

	Untrained subjects ($n^1 = 7$)	Trained subjects ($n^2 = 6$)
Mean	$X_1 = 2.87$	$X_2 = 2.12$
Standard deviation	$s_1 = 0.63$	$s_2 = 0.42$

Step 2   The assumption of equal variances can be confirmed using the F-ratio test. For this test we need to calculate the ratio of variances, taking care to put the largest variance on top, i.e.

$$F = \frac{(s_1)^2}{(s_2)^2} = \frac{0.3969}{0.1764} = 2.25$$

The value of the *F* ratio has two 'degrees of freedom' parameters. The degrees of freedom associated with the numerator variance is $n_1 - 1 = 6$, whilst the degrees of freedom associated with the denominator variance is $n_2 - 1 = 5$.

If the two variances are similar, the value of *F* would be expected to be near unity. If a very large value of *F* (a small *F* ratio, less than unity, has been precluded by always requiring the largest variance to be the numerator term) is obtained, the assumption of equal variances should be rejected. From the *F* tables (Table 10.A.2) we find that the critical value of *F* is given by $F_{0.025}$ (6,5) = 6.98. Hence, we conclude that the two variances are not significantly different (5% level of significance).

Step 3   Since the population variances are assumed to be the same, the variances of the two samples can now be combined to produce a single (pooled) estimate for the population variance σ^2. As in our example the sample sizes are not equal. Hence, a weighted average must be used to obtain the *pooled estimate of the variance s^2*, i.e.

$$s^2 = \frac{(n_1 - 1)(s_1)^2 + (n_2 - 1)(s_2)^2}{n_1 + n_2 - 2}$$

$$= \frac{(6)(0.3969) + (5)(0.1764)}{7 + 6 - 2}$$

$$= \frac{2.38 + 0.882}{11}$$

$$= \frac{3.262}{11}$$

$$= 0.297$$

Step 4   We can now proceed to test for differences between the sample means. Provided the population means are normally distributed with a common variance, the distribution of differences between means is known as the *t* distribution. Under the assumption that no difference exists between the two population mean (commonly referred to as the null hypothesis), the standard score *t* value (and therefore a probability value) can be found for any difference, as follows:

$$t = \frac{\overline{X}_1 - \overline{X}_2}{\sqrt{\dfrac{s^2}{n_1} + \dfrac{s^2}{n_2}}}$$

$$= \frac{2.87 - 2.12}{\sqrt{\dfrac{0.297}{7} + \dfrac{0.297}{6}}}$$

$$= \frac{0.75}{\sqrt{0.0424 + 0.0494}}$$

$$= \frac{0.75}{\sqrt{0.0918}}$$

$$= \frac{0.75}{0.303} = 2.48$$

The degrees of freedom associated with this value of t is determined from the estimate of the population variance in Step 3 above, i.e. $df = n_1 + n_2 - 2 = 11$. If the two sample means are similar, the value of t would be expected to be near zero. If a large value of t is obtained, the assumption of equal means should be rejected. From the t tables (Table 10.A.1) we find that the critical value of t is given by $t_{0.025}(11) = 2.201$. Hence, we conclude that the two means are significantly different (5% level of significance), i.e. there is evidence to suggest that there is a significant difference in blood lactate concentrations between trained and untrained subjects whilst running at 70% of $\dot{V}O_2$ max.

The above t test is called a *two-tailed* test of significance. The assumption of equal means would have been rejected if the t value was either greater than the critical $t_{0.025}(df)$ value *or* less than $-t_{0.025}(df)$. On the other hand, if we suspect that a difference between the mean blood concentrations *does* exist, the trained subjects would have lower scores than the untrained subjects, a *one-tailed* test can be used. For this one-tailed test, the critical value of t is given by $t_{0.05}(11) = 1.796$, allowing the 5% level of significance to remain in one tail of the t distribution . In our example, the observed t value of 2.48 still exceeds this critical value of 1.796 and the conclusion remains the same.

(b) One-way analysis of variance (ANOVA) for k independent samples

One-way analysis of variance, a natural extension to the t test for two independent samples, is used to test the significance of the differences between the means from two or more (k) populations.

Example 4 The maximal oxygen uptake results of five groups of six elite Olympic sportsmen ($n = 6$) are given in Table 10.8 (Johnson *et al.*, 1998).

The analysis of variance is based on the supposition (or null hypothesis) that all $N = 30$ observations are distributed about the same mean population μ, with the same variance σ^2. Based on this assumption, we can make three different estimates of the population variance, σ^2, using the data in Table 10.8. The first is based on the total sum of squared deviations (TSS) from a common mean, given by

$$TSS = \sum (X - \overline{X})^2$$

$$= \sum X^2 - \frac{\left(\sum X\right)^2}{N}$$

$$= \sum X^2 - \frac{T^2}{N}$$

$$= 73.8^2 + 79.9^2 + 75.5^2 + \quad + 68.8^2 + 63.2^2 - \frac{2180.8^2}{30}$$

$$= 159617.1 - 158530$$

$$= 1087.1$$

This sum of squares has 29 degrees of freedom (df). The mean square (MS), $1087 / 29 = 37.48$, is the first estimate of the population variance σ^2.

The second estimate is based on the pooled within-group variance, similar to the pooled estimate of the population variance used in the independent t-test above. For each group (j), we can estimate the within-group sum of squares as follows,

$$\Sigma (X - X_j)^2 = \Sigma X^2 - (\Sigma X)^2 / n = \Sigma X^2 - (T_j)^2 / n$$

For example (see Table 10.8), the middle-distance runners' within-group sum-of-squares is $35674.7 - 35604.8 = 69.9$. Since we can

Table 10.8. The maximal oxygen uptake results (ml kg^{-1} min^{-1}) of five groups of elite Olympic sportsmen (n = 6), results from Johnson *et al.,* (1998)

Groups (j)	Middle distance runners	Long distance runners	Heavy-weight rowers	Light-weight rowers	Triathletes	Total
	73.8	79.5	65.1	71.1	76.6	
	79.9	76.7	67.7	67.9	69.9	
	75.5	80.4	69.1	67.1	69.3	
	72.5	82.3	61.5	73.8	73.6	
	82.2	81.8	63.1	75.7	68.8	
	78.3	75.9	64.1	74.4	63.2	
$T_j = S X$	462.2	476.6	390.6	430.0	421.4	T = 2 180.8
Mean X_j	77.03	79.43	65.10	71.67	70.23	72.69
ΣX_j^2	35 674.7	37 892.6	25 468.8	30 880.3	29 700.7	159 617
$(T_j)^2/n$	35 604.8	37 857.9	25 428.1	30 816.7	29 596.3	158 530

assume that all the variances within each group are the same, the sum of squared deviations within each group can be added, to give a quantity known as the within sum of squares (WSS),

$$WSS = 69.9 + 34.7 + 40.7 + 63.6 + 104.4 = 313.3,$$

and subsequently divided by its degrees of freedom, $k \times (n - 1) = 5 \times 5 = 25$, to give the mean square within-groups (MS), 313.3 / 25 = 12.53, to estimate of the population variance.

The third estimate for σ^2 is based on the variance between the k group means X_j (77.03, 79.43, ..., 70.23). The between groups' sum-of-squares (BSS) is estimated as

$$BSS = \sum (X_j - X)^2$$

$$= \sum \left(\frac{(T_j)^2}{n} - \frac{T^2}{N} \right)$$

$$= \frac{462.2^2 + 476.6^2 + 390.6^2 + 430.0^2 + 421.4^2}{6} - \frac{2180.8^2}{30}$$

$$= 159303.8 - 158530$$

$$= 773.8$$

where

$$N = k \times n = 5 \times 6 = 30 \quad \text{(for } n = 6\text{)}$$

The 'between sum of squares' has $k - 1 = 4$ *df* and hence the third estimate of the population variance σ^2 or mean square (MS) is

$$\frac{773.8}{4} = 193.45$$

Clearly, these three estimates of the population variance σ^2, based on the TSS ($\sigma^2 = 37.48$), WSS ($\sigma^2 = 12.53$) and BSS ($\sigma^2 = 193.45$), would lead us to question the original supposition that the population variances were the same. We can formally test this assumption in precisely the same way that we were able to test the assumption of equal variances, prior to performing an independent t-test described in part (i), using the F-ratio test. In this example, we would compare the variance estimate between-groups with the variance estimate within-groups, i.e. calculate the F-ratio $F = 193.45/12.53 = 15.44$. Traditionally, this is set out in a standard table, known as the Analysis of Variance or ANOVA table (Table 10.9), given below.

Table 10.9 Analysis of variance to compare the maximal oxygen uptake results (ml kg^{-1} min^{-1}) of five groups of elite Olympic sportsmen

Source of variation	df	SS	MS	F	p
BSS	4	773.8	193.45	15.44	<0.05
WSS	25	313.3	12.53		
TSS	29	1 087.1			

where p is the probability, taken from the F Tables (Table 10.A.2).

As with the independent t test, the value of the F ratio, $F = 15.44$, has two degrees of freedom (df) parameters. The degrees of freedom associated with the between groups (BSS) variance is the number of groups $k - 1 = 4$, whilst the degrees of freedom associated with the within groups (WSS) variance is $k (n - 1) = 25$. From the F tables (Table 10.A.2) we find that the critical values of F are given by $F_{0.05} (4,25) = 2.76$ and $F_{0.025} (4,25) = 3.35$. Hence, we conclude that the two variances are significantly different (using both 5% and 2.5% levels of significance) and we must reject the supposition that the variances are the same and conclude that the mean maximal oxygen uptake results differ significantly between the five groups of elite Olympic sportsmen.

(c) The Mann–Whitney test for independent samples

If any of the requirements of the independent t test or ANOVA are not satisfied, the Mann–Whitney test will provide a similar test but does not make any assumptions about the level of measurement or the shape and size of the population distributions.

Example 5 The calf muscle's time-to-peak-tension (TPT) of 8 male sprint-trained athletes and 8 male endurance-trained athletes are given in Table 10.10. (A muscle's TPT is thought to be an indicator of its fibre type).

These steps are required to implement the Mann–Whitney test for independent samples.

Step 1 Let n_1 be the size of the smaller group of scores, and n_2 be the size of the larger group. In

Table 10.10 The calf muscle's time-to-peak tension recorded in milliseconds (ms) of five groups of elite Olympic sportsmen

Sprint-trained athletes ($n_1 = 8$)		Endurance-trained athletes ($n_2 = 8$)	
TPT	Rank	TPT	Rank
110	4	118	12.5
117	10	109	3
111	5	122	15
112	6	114	8
117	10	117	10
113	7	120	14
106	1	124	16
108	2	118	12.5
Total	45		91

our example, the sample sizes are equal. Hence, either group can be arbitrarily assigned as the group with n_1 scores.

Step 2 Rank the combined set of $n_1 + n_2$ results. Use rank 1 for the lowest, 2 for the next lowest, and so on (if two or more scores have the value, give each score the arithmetic mean of the shared ranks).

Step 3 Sum the ranks of the group with n_1 scores. Let this sum be called R_1. For our example, the sprint trained athletes ranks sum to $R_1 = 45$.

Step 4 Calculate the Mann–Whitney U statistic as follows,

$$U = n_1 n_2 + \frac{n_1(n_1 + 1)}{2} - R_1$$

$$= 8.8 + \frac{8(8+1)}{2} - 45$$

$$= 84 + 36 - 45$$

$$= 55$$

Step 5 Calculate U' statistic, given by

$$U' = n_1 n_2 - U$$

$$= 64 - 55$$

$$= 9$$

Step 6 Using the tables for the Mann–Whitney U statistic (Table 10.A.4), assuming a two-tailed test (5% level of significance), we find the critical value is 13. If the observed value of U or U' (whichever is the smaller) is *less than or equal to* the critical value of U, the assumption that the two samples have identical distributions can be rejected.

In our example, $U' = 9$ (the smaller of 55 and 9) is less than the critical value 13. Hence, there is a significant difference between the sprint-trained and endurance-trained athletes' time-to-peak-tension of the calf muscle.

10.4.2 DRAWING INFERENCES FROM EXPERIMENTAL DATA; CORRELATED SAMPLES

In the previous section, we considered experiments that use independent groups of subjects. The problem with this type of design is that subjects can vary dramatically in their response to the task, i.e. the differences between subjects tend to obscure the experimental effect. Fortunately 'correlated samples' experimental designs will overcome these problems of large variations between subjects. For example, between-subject variation can be 'partitioned out' by adopting a *repeated measures design*, where the same subject performs both experimental conditions. Alternatively, subjects can be paired off on the basis of relevant characteristics and the subjects from each pair are then allocated at random to one or the other experimental condition. This type of experimental design is known as the *paired subjects design*.

Three of the most frequently used tests to investigate correlated sample experimental designs are:

- The *t* test for correlated samples
- One-way analysis of variance (ANOVA) with repeated measures
- The Wilcoxon test for correlated samples

As in Section 10.4.1, these tests will be introduced using examples from kinanthropometry and exercise physiology.

(a) The *t* test for correlated samples

Example 6 Ten subjects were randomly selected to take part in an experiment to determine if isometric training can increase leg strength. The results are given in Table 10.11.

The requirements of the correlated *t* test are as follows,

1. That the differences between each pair of scores are drawn from a normal population.

Table 10.11 Leg strength in newtons (N) before and after isometric training

Before training (X_i)	After training (Y_i)	Differences ($D_i = Y_i - X_i$)
480	484	4
669	676	7
351	355	4
450	447	−3
373	372	−1
320	322	2
612	625	13
510	517	7
480	485	5
492	502	10

2. That these differences are measured in the interval scale.

Clearly, the differences in the strength measurements can take any value within a continuous range, confirming an interval scale. A simple frequency table can be used to check the differences have an approximate normal distribution, i.e. symmetric and bell-shaped (in particular, no obvious outlyers). Again, all these characteristics are described in Section 10.2.

The steps required to implement the *t* test for correlated samples are as follows.

Step 1 Calculate the differences between each pair of scores, i.e. $D_i = X_i - Y_i$. Care should be taken to subtract consistently, recording any negative differences.

Step 2 Calculate the mean and standard deviation of the differences D_i using the unbiased estimate for the population standard deviation, i.e. $s = \sqrt{\Sigma (D_i - D)^2 / (n-1)}$. In our example the mean and standard deviation is $D = 4.8$ and $s = 4.8$.

Step 3 Calculate the *t* standard score given by

$$t = \frac{D}{\left(\dfrac{s}{\sqrt{n}}\right)}$$

$$= \frac{4.8}{\left(\dfrac{4.8}{\sqrt{10}}\right)}$$

$$= \frac{4.8}{\left(\dfrac{4.8}{3.16}\right)}$$

$$= \frac{4.8}{1.52}$$

$$= 3.16$$

Step 4 The degrees of freedom associated with this value of *t* is determined from the estimate of the population variance in Step 3 above, i.e. $df = n - 1 = 9$. If the two experimental conditions produce a similar response to the given task, the differences D_i will be relatively small and the value of *t* would be expected to be near zero. If a large value of *t* is obtained, the assumption of equal differences should be

rejected. From the *t* tables (Table 10.A.1) we find that the critical value of *t* is given by $t_{0.025}(9) = 2.262$. Hence, we conclude that the two experimental conditions are significantly different (5% level of significance), i.e. it would appear that leg strength measurements before and after isometric training are significantly different. Clearly, by observing the differences in Table 10.11, the leg strength had improved, on average, by 4.8 (*N*).

As with the tests for independent samples, if we assume that isometric training will improve leg strength, a one-tailed test can be used. For this one-tailed test, the critical value of *t* is given by $t_{0.05}(9) = 1.833$, allowing the 5% level of significance to remain in one tail of the *t* distribution. In this case, the observed *t* value of 3.16 still exceeds this critical value of 1.833 and our conclusion remains the same.

(b) One-way analysis of variance (ANOVA) with repeated measures

Many experiments in kinanthropometry and exercise physiology require more than two repeated measurements to be taken from the same subjects.

Example 7 Eight volunteers take part in a study to assess the effect of a six-month recreational cycling programme on weight control. Estimates of percentage body fat were determined at the beginning of the study (baseline), after 3 months and at the end of the study, (after 6 months). The results are given in Table 10.12.

The rows are the eight subjects ($n = 8$), denoted by the subscript *i*, and columns are treatments or time points ($k = 3$), denoted by the subscript *j*. Note that the total number of observations (*N*) is 24. In effect, the one-way analysis of variance with repeated measures is a two-way analysis of variance with three sources of variation / variance and associated sums of squares. These are the sums of squares due to the subjects (rows), treatments (columns) and an interaction (or error). These can be calculated as follows,

Rows effects (subjects)

Columns effects (treatments or time)

$$\frac{\sum T_i^2}{k} - \frac{T^2}{N} = \frac{90.2^2 + 77.8^2 + \ +105.8^2}{3} - \frac{774.4^2}{24}$$

$$= \frac{77143.74}{3} - \frac{599695.36}{24}$$

$$= 25714.58 - 24987.3$$

$$= 727.28$$

$$\frac{\sum T_j^2}{n} - \frac{T^2}{N} = \frac{264.7^2 + 257.8^2 + 251.9^2}{8} - \frac{774.4^2}{24}$$

$$= \frac{199980.54}{8} - \frac{599695.36}{24}$$

$$= 24997.57 - 24987.3$$

$$= 10.27$$

Table 10.12 Estimates of percentage (%) body fat at baseline, 3 months and 6 months into the cycling programme.

	Baseline	3 months	6 months	Mean (X_i)	Total (T_i)
Subject 1	31.6	30.5	28.1	30.07	90.2
Subject 2	26.5	25.8	25.5	25.93	77.8
Subject 3	35.9	34.0	32.1	34.00	102.0
Subject 4	35.1	34.6	34.9	34.87	104.6
Subject 5	43.2	40.9	41.0	41.70	125.1
Subject 6	33.8	33.1	33.4	33.43	100.3
Subject 7	22.5	23.8	22.3	22.87	68.6
Subject 8	36.1	35.1	34.6	35.27	105.8
Mean (X_j)	33.09	32.23	31.49	32.27	
Total (T_j)	264.7	257.8	251.9		$T = 774.4$

Table 10.13 Analysis of variance table to compare the estimates of percentage body fat (%) recorded during the cycling programme.

Source of variation	df	SS	MS	F	P
Treatments or time	2	10.27	5.135	7.08	<0.05
Subjects	7	727.28	103.897		
Interaction/error	14	10.15	0.725		
Total	23	747.70			

where *p* is the probability, taken from the *F* Tables (Table 10.A.2).

Interaction (error)

$$\sum X^2 - \frac{\sum T_i^2}{k} - \frac{\sum T_j^2}{n} + \frac{T^2}{N} = \left(31.6^2 + 26.5^2 + \cdots + 35.27^2\right) - 25714.58 - 24997.57 + 24987.3$$

$$= 25735.0 - 25714.58 - 24997.57 + 24987.3$$

$$= 10.15$$

As with the one-way ANOVA for k independent samples, these results can be summarized in an ANOVA table (Table 10.13).

The data from this study are presumed to represent a random sample of subjects observed under three different treatment conditions or time points. The term used to describe such a study with repeated measurements is known as a mixed model, i.e. the treatments are thought to be a fixed effect whilst the subjects are thought to be a random effect. The F ratio for the treatment or time effects is $F = 7.08$. From the F tables (Table 10.A.2) we find that the critical values of F are given by $F_{0.05}(2,14) = 3.74$ and $F_{0.025}(2,14) = 4.86$. Clearly, the time effect F ratio (7.08) exceeds both these critical values. Hence, we can conclude that the mean estimated percentage body fat of the subjects has declined significantly during the 6 months recreational cycling programme (from 33.09%

at baseline, to 32.23% at 3 months, and 31.49% at the end of the study). Note that since the subjects constitute a random factor, there is no meaningful test of row (subject) effects.

An additional assumption associated with repeated measures analysis of variance is that of compound symmetry or 'sphericity' of the covariance matrix. Discussion of this topic is beyond the scope of this book, but interested readers are directed towards the guidelines provided by Field (2000) for exploring and correcting for violations of this assumption. For cases in which this assumption is extremely violated, readers may be interested in adopting the 'analysis of summary statistics' approach (Mathews *et al.*, 1991), which involves the recording of statistics that describe the nature of the repeated measures factor and analysing these separately. For example, rather than treating 10 measurements over time as a repeated measures factor in an

Table 10.14 The percentage body fat, before and after an aerobics course, and the corresponding differences and ranked differences (ignoring signs)

Subject	Before (X_i)	After (Y_i)	Differences ($D_i = Y_i - X_i$)	Ranks
1	34.4	33.5	−0.9	4
2	37.9	34.7	−3.2	10
3	35.2	35.3	0.1	1
4	37.2	34.2	−3.0	9
5	45.1	43.9	−1.2	5
6	34.1	35.7	1.6	6
7	36.0	34.2	−1.8	7
8	38.9	36.2	−2.7	8
9	36.1	35.9	−0.2	2
10	28.3	27.8	−0.5	3

ANOVA model, the researcher could record the peak value, mean and time of peak value to describe the time factor. These statistics could then be compared between groups with a two-sample *t* test for example.

(c) The Wilcoxon test for correlated samples

If some of the requirements of the correlated *t* test were not satisfied, the Wilcoxon matched-pairs sign-ranks test will provide the same function as the correlated *t* test but would make no assumptions about the shape of the population distributions.

Example 8 A study was designed to investigate the effects of an aerobics class on reducing percentage body fat. The percentage body fat measurements of ten subjects, before and after the aerobics course, are given in Table 10.14.

The steps required to implement the Wilcoxon test for correlated samples are as follows.

Step 1 Calculate the differences between each pair of scores, i.e. $D_i = X_i - Y_i$. As with the correlated *t* test, care should be taken to subtract consistently, recording any negative differences.

Step 2 *Ignoring* the sign, rank the differences using rank 1 for the lowest, 2 for the next lowest, and so on. If two or more differences have the same value, give each score the arithmetic mean of the shared ranks. Any pairs with differences equal to zero are eliminated from the test.

Step 3 Sum the ranks of the less frequent sign and call this sum *T*. For our example, the positive ranks are less frequent and $T = 1 + 6 = 7$.

Step 4 Using the critical tables for the Wilcoxon *T* statistic (Table 10.A.5), assuming a two-tailed test (5% level of significance), we find the critical value ($n = 10$) is 8. If the observed value of *T* is *less than or equal to* the critical value of *T*, the assumption that the experimental conditions are the same can be rejected.

In our example, the observed $T = 7$ value is less than the critical value 8. Hence, there is a significant reduction in percentage body fat during the aerobics course.

10.4.3 MULTIFACTORIAL ANALYSIS OF EXPERIMENTAL DATA

Sometimes an experimenter wishes to examine the influence of a number of independent variables on the dependent variable(s). For example, a researcher may wish to assess the changes of a kinanthropometric variable (e.g. maximal oxygen uptake) over time in response to a specific training regime (compared to not doing that type of training). Such a design would be defined as a two-factor experiment, since there is one factor of *time* and another factor of *training*. The time factor is a 'within-subjects' or 'repeated measures' factor, since all subjects are tested more than once. The training factor would be a 'between-subjects' factor, if the subjects were allocated to either a training group or a control group. If the experimental design was 'crossover' in nature, i.e. all subjects undertook a period of training and a period of no training, ideally administered in a 'counter-balanced' order, the training factor becomes a 'within-subjects' factor. Similarly, the training factor could be treated as correlated if the subjects were initially pair-matched on the dependent variable (Altman, 1991).

The number of possible alternatives within an experimental factor is called 'levels'. In the above example, the group factor contains two levels – a training group and a control group. Four levels within the time factor would mean that all the subjects are tested on four occasions. It is common to pre-test both groups before any influence of another factor has taken place to ensure the groups are matched.

In a multifactorial experiment, the experimenter is interested in the 'main effect' of each factor together with 'interactions' between factors. These are given as part of the results of a multifactorial analysis of variance (general linear model). A significant main effect infers that the factor in question has a significant influence on the dependent variable, irrespective of the influence of any other factors in the experiment. For example, a 'time main effect' in the above study implies that maximal oxygen uptake has changed significantly across time. An interaction between factors describes the combined influence of the independent variables. Main effects and interactions should be examined together to arrive at conclusions. A graphical method of interpreting the results of multifactorial analyses is the 'interaction plot' (Figure 10.7). In the above example, there was a significant interaction of training type and time on maximal oxygen uptake. Examination of the interaction plot reveals that training caused an increase in maximal oxygen uptake over time, whilst no such increase occurred in the control group. Some interaction effects may be more complicated than this example, and therefore may need multiple comparisons to unravel the results (Kinnear and Gray, 1997). It is stressed that, ideally, such comparisons should be decided a priori with a specific research question in mind. We recommend that researchers attempt their first multifactorial ANOVA with the statistical package SPSS (SPSS, 2000) and

the excellent guide published by Kinnear and Gray (1997).

10.4.4 THE MINITAB COMMANDS TO ILLUSTRATE THE METHODS OF SECTION 10.4

The *t* test for independent samples is obtained in MINITAB as follows. First, the two groups of data are SET into two separate columns C1 and C2. Then by typing the command TWOSAMPLE C1 C2, we get the following output.

```
MTB > TWOSAMPLE C1 C2;
SUBC> POOLED
TWOSAMPLE T FOR UNTRAIN VS TRAINED
          N   MEAN  STDEV  SE MEAN
UNTRAIN  7   2.871  0.629   0.24
TRAINED  6   2.117  0.422   0.17
95 PCT CI FOR MU UNTRAIN - MU
    TRAINED: (0.09, 1.42)
TTEST MU UNTRAIN = MU TRAINED
    (VS NE): T = 2.49 P = 0.030 DF = 11
POOLED STDEV = 0.545
```

The subcommand POOLED will provide the solution that assumes the two populations have equal variances. By default, the 95% confidence interval is given, followed by the two-sample (independent) *t* test. A two-tailed test is provided automatically with the standard score t-value, associated probability and appropriate degrees of freedom. If a one-tailed *t* test is required, the subcommand ALTERNATIVE = +1 or −1 gives the alternative test C1 > C2 or C1 < C2 respectively.

In example 4, if the five groups of Olympic sportsmen's maximal oxygen uptake data are SET in 5 separate columns C1, C2, C3, C4 and C5, then by typing the command

```
MTB > AOVO C1–C5
```

we obtain the results describe in the ANOVA table (Table 10.9).

The MINITAB command to implement the

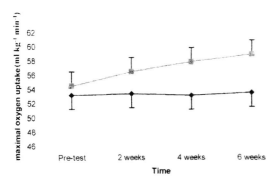

Figure 10.7 Interaction plot of time x training on maximal oxygen uptake (training group (■); control group (◆). In this example, a significant interaction between group (training and no training) and test time is likely, since the gradients of the two lines are not parallel. Note that the presence of an interaction does not necessarily mean that the lines have to cross at some point, only that the magnitude of the effect of one independent variable depends on another independent variable.

Mann–Whitney test for independent samples, stored in C3 (SPRINT) and C4 (ENDURE), is given as follows,

MTB > MANN-WHITNEY C3 C4
MANN-WHITNEY CONFIDENCE
   INTERVAL AND TEST

SPRINT   N = 8   MEDIAN = 111.50

ENDURE   N = 8   MEDIAN = 118.00

POINT ESTIMATE FOR ETA1-ETA2 IS –6.50
95.9 PCT C.I. FOR ETA1-ETA2 IS (–11.00,–1.00)
W = 45.0
TEST OF ETA1 = ETA2 VS ETA1 N.E.
   ETA2 IS SIGNIFICANT AT 0.0181
THE TEST IS SIGNIFICANT AT 0.0177
   (ADJUSTED FOR TIES)

The median values are given for both samples followed by the 95% confidence intervals for the difference between population medians ETA1 – ETA2. Note that the confidence interval does not contain the value zero. Next the sum of ranks W (R_i in our notation) is given followed by the Mann–Whitney (two-tailed) test of significance. As with the TWOSAMPLE independent *t* test, if a one-tailed Mann–Whitney test is required, the subcommand ALTERNATIVE = +1 or –1 gives the alternative test C3 > C4 or C3< C4 respectively.

The MINITAB commands to implement the *t* test for correlated samples, stored in columns C5 (AFTER1) and C6 (BEFORE1), are as follows,

Firstly, the differences between the leg strength before and after training need to be calculated. This is achieved using the LET command.

MTB > LET C7=C5–C6
MTB > NAME C7 'DIFF1'

The *t* test for correlated samples is obtained using the TTEST command.

MTB > TTEST C7
TEST OF MU = 0.00 VS MU N.E. 0.00

	N	MEAN	STDEV	SE MEAN	T	P-VALUE
DIFF1	10	4.80	4.80	1.52	3.16	0.012

The resulting table provides the mean differences, the standard deviation (using the unbiased estimate for the population mean $s = \sqrt{\Sigma(X_i - X)^2 / (n-1)}$, the standard error of the mean $s / \sqrt{n}$, followed by the *t* standard score and its associated probability.

The MINITAB commands for the WILCOXON test are similar to the *t* test for correlated samples. Once again, the differences between the percentage body fat measurements before and after the aerobics course, in C8 (AFTER2) and C9 (BEFORE2), need to be calculated. This is achieved using the LET command.

MTB > LET C10=C8–C9
MTB > NAME C10 'DIFF2'

The Wilcoxon test for correlated samples is obtained using the WTEST command.

MTB > WTEST C10
TEST OF MEDIAN = 0.000000
   VERSUS MEDIAN N.E. 0.000000

	N	N FOR TEST	WILCOXON STATISTIC	P-VALUE	ESTIMATED MEDIAN
DIFF2	10	10	7.0	0.041	–1.200

This syntax conducts a Wilcoxon signed-rank test assuming the median value of the differences is zero, using two-tailed significance. The number of differences is stated. This is followed by the sum of ranks corresponding to the positive differences together with its associated probability. Finally, the estimated median is provided, indicating the nature of the differences. In our example, the majority of differences were negative. Hence, the estimated median was also negative, confirming the findings of the Wilcoxon test, i.e. the aerobics course resulted in a significant reduction in the participants' percentage body fat.

Finally, the one-way ANOVA with repeated measures, requires all 24 observation of the percentage body fat (%) to be stored (or stacked) into a single column, labelled 'PCFAT'. A second column is used to identify the three time-points, labelled 'TIME', whilst the eight subjects are identified by a third column, labelled 'SUBJ' (the numbers 1, 2, to 8, repeated three times).

The data would appear in the MINITAB spreadsheet as follows;

pcfat	time	subj
31.6000	1	1
26.5000	1	2
35.9000	1	3
.	.	.
.	.	.
22.3000	3	7
34.6000	3	8

The MINITAB commands to conduct the repeated measures ANOVA described in Table 10.13 are given below.

```
MTB > ANOVA 'PCFAT' = TIME SUBJ;
    SUBC> RANDOM 'SUBJ';
    SUBC> RESTRICT.
```

The subcommands RANDOM and RESTRICT simply indicates that the subjects 'SUBJ' are a random factor in the mixed model and, as such, no appropriate F statistic exists.

SUMMARY

This chapter has illustrated some of the basic procedures which are frequently adopted to describe and interpret data from exercise physiology and kinanthropometry studies. For additional information on some of the issues associated with studies involving multiple regression and experimental designs in exercise physiology and kinanthropometry research, you are referred to Eston and Rowlands, (2000), Winter *et al.*, (2001) and Atkinson and Nevill, (2001).

Appendix A: Critical values

Table 10.A.1 The critical values of the t distribution

df	*Level of significance for one-tailed test*					
	0.10	*0.05*	*0.025*	*0.01*	*0.005*	*0.0005*
	Level of significance for two-tailed test					
	0.20	*0.10*	*0.05*	*0.02*	*0.01*	*0.001*
1	3.078	6.314	12.706	31.821	63.657	636.619
2	1.886	2.920	4.303	6.965	9.925	31.598
3	1.638	2.353	3.182	4.541	5.841	12.941
4	1.533	2.132	2.776	3.747	4.604	8.610
5	1.476	2.015	2.571	3.365	4.032	6.859
6	1.440	1.943	2.447	3.143	3.707	5.959
7	1.415	1.895	2.365	2.998	3.499	5.405
8	1.397	1.860	2.306	2.896	3.355	5.041
9	1.383	1.833	2.262	2.821	3.250	4.781
10	1.372	1.812	2.228	2.764	3.169	4.587
11	1.363	1.796	2.201	2.718	3.106	4.437
12	1.356	1.782	2.179	2.681	3.055	4.318
13	1.350	1.771	2.160	2.650	3.012	4.221
14	1.345	1.761	2.145	2.624	2.977	4.140
15	1.341	1.753	2.131	2.602	2.947	4.073
16	1.337	1.746	2.120	2.583	2.921	4.015
17	1.333	1.740	2.110	2.567	2.898	3.965
18	1.330	1.734	2.101	2.552	2.878	3.922
19	1.328	1.729	2.093	2.539	2.861	3.883
20	1.325	1.725	2.086	2.528	2.845	3.850
21	1.323	1.721	2.080	2.518	2.831	3.819
22	1.321	1.717	2.074	2.508	2.819	3.792
23	1.319	1.714	2.069	2.500	2.807	3.767

continued on next page

df	Level of significance for one-tailed test					
	0.10	0.05	0.025	0.01	0.005	0.0005
	Level of significance for two-tailed test					
	0.20	0.10	0.05	0.02	0.01	0.001
24	1.318	1.711	2.064	2.492	2.797	3.745
25	1.316	1.708	2.060	2.485	2.787	3.725
26	1.315	1.706	2.056	2.479	2.779	3.707
27	1.314	1.703	2.052	2.473	2.771	3.690
28	1.313	1.701	2.048	2.467	2.763	3.674
29	1.311	1.699	2.045	2.462	2.756	3.659
30	1.310	1.697	2.042	2.457	2.750	3.646
40	1.303	1.684	2.021	2.423	2.704	3.551
60	1.296	1.671	2.000	2.390	2.660	3.460
120	1.289	1.658	1.980	2.358	2.617	3.373
∞	1.282	1.645	1.960	2.326	2.576	3.291

Adapted from Table III of R.A. Fisher and F. Yates, *Statistical Tables for Biological, Agricultural and Medical Research* (1948 ed.), Oliver and Boyd, Edinburgh and London, by permission of the authors and publishers.

Table 10.A.2 The critical values of the F distribution at the 5% level of significance (one-tailed)

Degrees of freedom for numerator

df[a]	1	2	3	4	5	6	7	8	9	10	12	15	20	24	30	40	60	120	∞
1	161	200	216	225	230	234	237	239	241	242	244	246	248	249	250	251	252	253	254
2	18.5	19.0	19.2	19.3	19.3	19.4	19.4	19.4	19.4	19.4	19.4	19.4	19.4	19.5	19.5	19.5	19.5	19.5	19.5
3	10.1	9.55	9.28	9.12	9.01	8.94	8.89	8.85	8.81	8.79	8.74	8.70	8.66	8.64	8.62	8.59	8.57	8.55	8.53
4	7.71	6.94	6.59	6.39	6.26	6.16	6.09	6.04	6.00	5.96	5.91	5.86	5.80	5.77	5.75	5.72	5.69	5.66	5.63
5	6.61	5.79	5.41	5.19	5.05	4.95	4.88	4.82	4.77	4.74	4.68	4.62	4.56	4.53	4.50	4.46	4.43	4.40	4.37
6	5.99	5.14	4.76	4.53	4.39	4.28	4.21	4.15	4.10	4.06	4.00	3.94	3.87	3.84	3.81	3.77	3.74	3.70	3.67
7	5.59	4.74	4.35	4.12	3.97	3.87	3.79	3.73	3.68	3.64	3.57	3.51	3.44	3.41	3.38	3.34	3.30	3.27	3.23
8	5.32	4.46	4.07	3.84	3.69	3.58	3.50	3.44	3.39	3.35	3.28	3.22	3.15	3.12	3.08	3.04	3.01	2.97	2.93
9	5.12	4.26	3.86	3.63	3.48	3.37	3.29	3.23	3.18	3.14	3.07	3.01	2.94	2.90	2.86	2.83	2.79	2.75	2.71
10	4.96	4.10	3.71	3.48	3.33	3.22	3.14	3.07	3.02	2.98	2.91	2.85	2.77	2.74	2.70	2.66	2.62	2.58	2.54
11	4.84	3.98	3.59	3.36	3.20	3.09	3.01	2.95	2.90	2.85	2.79	2.72	2.65	2.61	2.57	2.53	2.49	2.45	2.40
12	4.75	3.89	3.49	3.26	3.11	3.00	2.91	2.85	2.80	2.75	2.69	2.62	2.54	2.51	2.47	2.43	2.38	2.34	2.30
13	4.67	3.81	3.41	3.18	3.03	2.92	2.83	2.77	2.71	2.67	2.60	2.53	2.46	2.42	2.38	2.34	2.30	2.25	2.21
14	4.60	3.74	3.34	3.11	2.96	2.85	2.76	2.70	2.65	2.60	2.53	2.46	2.39	2.35	2.31	2.27	2.22	2.18	2.13
15	4.54	3.68	3.29	3.06	2.90	2.79	2.71	2.64	2.59	2.54	2.48	2.40	2.33	2.29	2.25	2.20	2.16	2.11	2.07
16	4.49	3.63	3.24	3.01	2.85	2.74	2.66	2.59	2.54	2.49	2.42	2.35	2.28	2.24	2.19	2.15	2.11	2.06	2.01
17	4.45	3.59	3.20	2.96	2.81	2.70	2.61	2.55	2.49	2.45	2.38	2.31	2.23	2.19	2.15	2.10	2.06	2.01	1.96
18	4.41	3.55	3.16	2.93	2.77	2.66	2.58	2.51	2.46	2.41	2.34	2.27	2.19	2.15	2.11	2.06	2.02	1.97	1.92
19	4.38	3.52	3.13	2.90	2.74	2.63	2.54	2.48	2.42	2.38	2.31	2.23	2.16	2.11	2.07	2.03	1.98	1.93	1.88
20	4.35	3.49	3.10	2.87	2.71	2.60	2.51	2.45	2.39	2.35	2.28	2.20	2.12	2.08	2.04	1.99	1.95	1.90	1.84
21	4.32	3.47	3.07	2.84	2.68	2.57	2.49	2.42	2.37	2.32	2.25	2.18	2.10	2.05	2.01	1.96	1.92	1.87	1.81
22	4.30	3.44	3.05	2.82	2.66	2.55	2.46	2.40	2.34	2.30	2.23	2.15	2.07	2.03	1.98	1.94	1.89	1.84	1.78
23	4.28	3.42	3.03	2.80	2.64	2.53	2.44	2.37	2.32	2.27	2.20	2.13	2.05	2.01	1.96	1.91	1.86	1.81	1.76
24	4.26	3.40	3.01	2.78	2.62	2.51	2.42	2.36	2.30	2.25	2.18	2.11	2.03	1.98	1.94	1.89	1.84	1.79	1.73
25	4.24	3.39	2.99	2.76	2.60	2.49	2.40	2.34	2.28	2.24	2.16	2.09	2.01	1.96	1.92	1.87	1.82	1.77	1.71
30	4.17	3.32	2.92	2.69	2.53	2.42	2.33	2.27	2.21	2.16	2.09	2.01	1.93	1.89	1.84	1.79	1.74	1.68	1.62
40	4.08	3.23	2.84	2.61	2.45	2.34	2.25	2.18	2.12	2.08	2.00	1.92	1.84	1.79	1.74	1.69	1.64	1.58	1.51
60	4.00	3.15	2.76	2.53	2.37	2.25	2.17	2.10	2.04	1.99	1.92	1.84	1.75	1.70	1.65	1.59	1.53	1.47	1.39
120	3.92	3.07	2.68	2.45	2.29	2.18	2.09	2.02	1.96	1.91	1.83	1.75	1.66	1.61	1.55	1.50	1.43	1.35	1.25
∞	3.84	3.00	2.60	2.37	2.21	2.10	2.01	1.94	1.88	1.83	1.75	1.67	1.57	1.52	1.46	1.39	1.32	1.22	1.00

Adapted from Table V of R.A. Fisher and F. Yates, *Statistical Tables for Biological, Agricultural and Medical Research* (1948), Oliver and Boyd, Edinburgh and London, by permission of the authors and publishers.

[a] Degrees of freedom for denominator

Table 10.A.3 The critical values of the F distribution at the 2.5% level of significance (one tailed) or 5% level of significance for a two-tailed test

Degrees of freedom for numerator

df^a	1	2	3	4	5	6	7	8	9	10	12	15	20	24	30	40	60	120	∞
1	648	800	864	900	922	937	948	957	963	969	977	985	993	997	1001	1006	1010	1014	1018
2	38.5	39.0	39.2	39.2	39.3	39.3	39.4	39.4	39.4	39.4	39.4	39.4	39.4	39.5	39.5	39.5	39.5	39.5	39.5
3	17.4	16.0	15.4	15.1	14.9	14.7	14.6	14.5	14.5	14.4	14.3	14.3	14.2	14.1	14.1	14.0	14.0	13.9	13.9
4	12.2	10.6	9.98	9.60	9.36	9.20	9.07	8.98	8.90	8.84	8.75	8.66	8.56	8.51	8.46	8.41	8.36	8.31	8.26
5	10.0	8.43	7.76	7.39	7.15	6.98	6.85	6.76	6.68	6.62	6.52	6.43	6.33	6.28	6.23	6.18	6.12	6.07	6.02
6	8.81	7.26	6.60	6.23	5.99	5.82	5.70	5.60	5.52	5.46	5.37	5.27	5.17	5.12	5.07	5.01	4.96	4.90	4.85
7	8.07	6.54	5.89	5.52	5.29	5.12	4.99	4.90	4.82	4.76	4.67	4.57	4.47	4.42	4.36	4.31	4.25	4.20	4.14
8	7.57	6.06	5.42	5.05	4.82	4.65	4.53	4.43	4.36	4.30	4.20	4.10	4.00	3.95	3.89	3.84	3.78	3.73	3.67
9	7.21	5.71	5.08	4.72	4.48	4.32	4.20	4.10	4.03	3.96	3.87	3.77	3.67	3.61	3.56	3.51	3.45	3.39	3.33
10	6.94	5.46	4.83	4.47	4.24	4.07	3.95	3.85	3.78	3.72	3.62	3.52	3.42	3.37	3.31	3.26	3.20	3.14	3.08
11	6.72	5.26	4.63	4.28	4.04	3.88	3.76	3.66	3.59	3.53	3.43	3.33	3.23	3.17	3.12	3.06	3.00	2.94	2.88
12	6.55	5.10	4.47	4.12	3.89	3.73	3.61	3.51	3.44	3.37	3.28	3.18	3.07	3.02	2.96	2.91	2.85	2.79	2.72
13	6.41	4.97	4.35	4.00	3.77	3.60	3.48	3.39	3.31	3.25	3.15	3.05	2.95	2.89	2.84	2.78	2.72	2.66	2.60
14	6.30	4.86	4.24	3.89	3.66	3.50	3.38	3.28	3.21	3.15	3.05	2.95	2.84	2.79	2.73	2.67	2.61	2.55	2.49
15	6.20	4.77	4.15	3.80	3.58	3.41	3.29	3.20	3.12	3.06	2.96	2.86	2.76	2.70	2.64	2.59	2.52	2.46	2.40
16	6.12	4.69	4.08	3.73	3.50	3.34	3.22	3.12	3.05	2.99	2.89	2.79	2.68	2.63	2.57	2.51	2.45	2.38	2.32
17	6.04	4.62	4.01	3.66	3.44	3.28	3.16	3.06	2.98	2.92	2.82	2.72	2.62	2.56	2.50	2.44	2.38	2.32	2.25
18	5.98	4.56	3.95	3.61	3.38	3.22	3.10	3.01	2.93	2.87	2.77	2.67	2.56	2.50	2.44	2.38	2.32	2.26	2.19
19	5.92	4.51	3.90	3.56	3.33	3.17	3.05	2.96	2.88	2.82	2.72	2.62	2.51	2.45	2.39	2.33	2.27	2.20	2.13
20	5.87	4.46	3.86	3.51	3.29	3.13	3.01	2.91	2.84	2.77	2.68	2.57	2.46	2.41	2.35	2.29	2.22	2.16	2.09
21	5.83	4.42	3.82	3.48	3.25	3.09	2.97	2.87	2.80	2.73	2.64	2.53	2.42	2.37	2.31	2.25	2.18	2.11	2.04
22	5.79	4.38	3.78	3.44	3.22	3.05	2.93	2.84	2.76	2.70	2.60	2.50	2.39	2.33	2.27	2.21	2.14	2.08	2.00
23	5.75	4.35	3.75	3.41	3.18	3.02	2.90	2.81	2.73	2.67	2.57	2.47	2.36	2.30	2.24	2.18	2.11	2.04	1.97
24	5.72	4.32	3.72	3.38	3.15	2.99	2.87	2.78	2.70	2.64	2.54	2.44	2.33	2.27	2.21	2.15	2.08	2.01	1.94
25	5.69	4.29	3.69	3.35	3.13	2.97	2.85	2.75	2.68	2.61	2.51	2.41	2.30	2.24	2.18	2.12	2.05	1.98	1.91
30	5.57	4.18	3.59	3.25	3.03	2.87	2.75	2.65	2.57	2.51	2.41	2.31	2.20	2.14	2.07	2.01	1.94	1.87	1.79
40	5.42	4.05	3.46	3.13	2.90	2.74	2.62	2.53	2.45	2.39	2.29	2.18	2.07	2.01	1.94	1.88	1.80	1.72	1.64
60	5.29	3.93	3.34	3.01	2.79	2.63	2.51	2.41	2.33	2.27	2.17	2.06	1.94	1.88	1.82	1.74	1.67	1.58	1.48
120	5.15	3.80	3.23	2.89	2.67	2.52	2.39	2.30	2.22	2.16	2.05	1.95	1.82	1.76	1.69	1.61	1.53	1.43	1.31
∞	5.02	3.69	3.12	2.79	2.57	2.41	2.29	2.19	2.11	2.05	1.94	1.83	1.71	1.64	1.57	1.48	1.39	1.27	1.00

Adapted from Table V of R.A. Fisher and F. Yates, *Statistical Tables for Biological, Agricultural and Medical Research* (1948 ed.), Oliver and Boyd, Edinburgh and London, by permission of the authors and publishers.
^{a} Degrees of freedom for denominator

Table 10.A.4   The critical values of the Mann–Whitney U statistic at the 5% level of significance (two-tailed)

N_s	\ $N2$ \ 5	6	7	8	9	10	11	12	13	14	15	16	17	18	19	20
5	2	3	5	6	7	8	9	11	12	13	14	15	17	18	19	20
6		5	6	8	10	11	13	14	16	17	19	21	22	24	25	27
7			8	10	12	14	16	18	20	22	24	26	28	30	32	34
8				13	15	17	19	22	24	26	29	31	34	36	38	41
9					17	20	23	26	28	31	34	37	39	42	45	48
10						23	26	29	33	36	39	42	45	48	52	55
11							30	33	37	40	44	47	51	55	58	62
12								37	41	45	49	53	57	61	65	69
13									45	50	54	59	63	67	72	76
14										55	59	64	67	74	78	83
15											64	70	75	80	85	90
16												75	81	86	92	98
17													87	93	99	105
18														99	106	112
19															113	119
20																127

REFERENCES

Altman, D.G. (1991). *Practical Statistics for Medical Research*. (Chapman and Hall, London).

Atkinson G. and Nevill A.M. (1998). Statistical methods for assessing measurement error (reliability) in variables relevant to sports medicine. *Sports Medicine*, **26**, 217–38.

Atkinson, G. and Nevill, A.M. (2001). Research methods and statistics in the assessment of sports performance. *Journal of Sports Sciences*. In press.

Atkinson, G., Nevill, A. and Edwards, B. (1999). What is an acceptable amount of measurement error? The application of meaningful 'analytical goals' to the reliability analysis of sports science measurements made on a ratio scale. *Journal of Sports Sciences*, **17**, 18.

Bland J.M. and Altman D.G. (1999). Measuring agreement in method comparison studies. *Statistical Methods in Medical Research*, **8**, 135–60.

Cockerill, I.M., Nevill, A.M. and Lyons N. (1991). Modelling mood states in athletic performance. *Journal of Sports Sciences*, **9**, 205–12.

Costill, D. L., Thomason, H. and Roberts, E. (1973). Fractional utilization of the aerobic capacity during distance running. *Medicine and Science in Sports*, **5**, 248–52.

Eston, R.G. and Rowlands, A.V. (2000). Stages in the development of a research project: putting the idea together. *British Journal of Sports Medicine*, **34**, 59–64.

Field, A. (2000). *Discovering statistics using SPSS for Windows*. (Sage, London).

Harvill, L.M. (1991). An NCME instructional module on standard error of measurement. *Educational Measurement: Issues and Practice*, **10**, 33–41.

Johnson, P.J., Godfrey, R., Moore, J., *et al.* (1998). Scaling maximal oxygen uptake of elite endurance sportsmen. *Journal of Sports Sciences*, **16**, 27–8.

Table 10.A.5 The critical values of the Wilcoxon T statistic for correlated samples (two tailed)

	Level of significance		
	0.05	*0.02*	*0.01*
6	0	—	—
7	2	0	—
8	4	2	0
9	6	3	2
10	8	5	3
11	11	7	5
12	14	10	7
13	17	13	10
14	21	16	13
15	25	20	16
16	30	24	20
17	35	28	23
18	40	33	28
19	46	38	32
20	52	43	38
21	59	49	43
22	66	56	49
23	73	62	55
24	81	69	61
25	89	77	68

Adapted from Table 1 of F. Wilcoxon (1949) *Some Rapid Approximate Statistical Procedures*, The American Cyanamid Company, New York, by permission of the authors and publishers.

Kinnear, P.R and Gray, C.D (1997). *SPSS for Windows Made Simple.* (Psychology Press, London).

Knapp, T.R. (1992). Technical error of measurement: a methodological critique. *American Journal of Physical Anthropometry*, **87**, 235–6.

MINITAB (1998). *Reference Manual.* Minitab Inc., 3081 Enterprise Drive, State College, PA 16801, USA.

Mathews, J.N.S., Altman, D.G., Campbell, M.J. and Royston, P. (1990). Analysis of serial measurements in medical research. *British Medical Journal*, **300**, 230–5.

Morgan, W.B. (1985). Selected psychological factors limiting performance: A mental health model. In *Limits of Human Performance.* eds. D.H. Clarke and H.M. Eckert (Human Kinetics, Champaign, IL). pp. 70–80.

Nevill, A. M., Ramsbottom, R. and Williams, C. (1990). The relationship between athletic performance and maximal oxygen uptake. *Journal of Sports Sciences*, **8**, 290–2.

Nevill, A.M., Cooke, C.B., Holder, R.L., *et al.* (1992a). Modelling linear relationships between two variables when repeated measurements are made on more than one subject. *European Journal of Applied Physiology*, **64**, 419–25.

Nevill, A.M., Ramsbottom, R. and Williams, C. (1992b). Scaling physiological measurements for individuals of different body size. *European Journal of Applied Physiology*, **65**, 110–7.

Snedecor, G. W. and Cochran, W. G. (1989). *Statistical Methods*, 8th edn. (Iowa State University Press, Ames, IA).

SPSS (2000). SPSS Inc., Chicago, IL. (www.spss.com).

Winter, E., Eston, R.G. and Lamb, K.L. (2001). Statistical techniques for physiology research, *Journal of Sports Sciences*, **19** (10). In press.

Wright, E.M. and Royston, P. (1999). Calculating reference intervals for laboratory measurements. *Statistical Methods in Medical Research*, **8**, 93–112.

Edward M. Winter and Alan M. Nevill

11.1 AIMS

The aims of this chapter are to develop knowledge and understanding of how performance and physiological measures can be adjusted for differences in body size as a whole or the size of its exercising segments. Specifically, the chapter aims to:
- describe the historical background to scaling,
- outline the imperfections of ratio standards,
- explain the principles that underlie allometric modelling,
- select and apply statistical analyses that compare physiological and performance measures in groups adjusted for differences in size,
- evaluate techniques for use in cross-sectional and longitudinal studies.

11.2 INTRODUCTION

Physiological and performance variables are frequently influenced by body size. For instance, the performance capabilities of children are less than those of adults. Similarly, there are track and field events such as hammer, discus and shot in which high values of body mass are especially influential. Furthermore, oxygen uptake (O_2) during a particular task in a large person will probably be greater than in a small person. These observations give rise to a simple question: to what extent are performance differences attributable to differences in size or to differences in qualitative characteristics of the body's tissues and structures?

To help answer this question, differences in body size have to be partitioned out. This partitioning is called *scaling* (Schmidt-Nielsen, 1984) and is a key issue in kinanthropometry. There are four main uses (Winter, 1992):

1. To compare an individual against standards for the purpose of assessment.
2. To compare groups.
3. In longitudinal studies that investigate the effects of growth or training.
4. To explore possible relationships between physiological characteristics and performance.

11.3 HISTORICAL BACKGROUND

Scaling has become an area of particular interest in kinanthropometry and the physiology of exercise (Nevill *et al.*, 1992a; Jakeman *et al.*, 1994; Nevill, 1994; Nevill and Holder, 1994; Winter, 1996) although it is by no means a new area of interest and is well established in biological science. One of the earliest scientific papers on the subject was by Sarrus and Rameaux (1838) but even that was pre-dated by Jonathan Swift's *Gulliver's Travels* published in 1726. Lilliputian mathematicians were faced with a challenge: they had to calculate how much food their captive would require each day. Because Gulliver

Kinanthropometry and Exercise Physiology Laboratory Manual: Tests, Procedures and Data. 2nd Edition, Volume 1: Anthropometry
Edited by RG Eston and T Reilly. Published by Routledge, London, June 2001

was twelve times taller than Lilliputians, they surmised, not unreasonably, that he would need 1728 times (i.e. 12^3) the amount they consumed each day.

In 1917 D'Arcy Wentworth Thompson's *Growth and Form* was published and fifteen years later so too was Huxley's (1932) *Problems of Relative Growth*. These texts made a significant contribution to the development of our understanding of the ways in which the size and function of living organisms are intimately related. Also noteworthy are the works of Sholl (1948), Tanner (1949) and Tanner (1964). The area was revisited in the early 1970s (Katch, 1973) but it was some twenty years later before concerted interest in applications of scaling to exercise science was revived.

This revival was partly attributable to advances in microcomputing that made otherwise complex and unwieldy analyses much quicker and easier to perform. Established debate about model specifications (Kermack and Haldane, 1950; Ricker, 1973; Rayner, 1985) continued enthusiastically (Sokal and Rohlf, 1995; Nevill, 1994; Batterham *et al.*, 1997). It is now generally recognized that scaling has an important role in the development of our understanding of how the body responds and adapts to exercise.

11.4 THE RATIO STANDARD – THE TRADITIONAL METHOD

The most commonly used scaling technique is termed a *ratio standard* (Tanner, 1949) in which a performance or physiological variable is divided by an anthropometric characteristic such as body mass. A well-known ratio standard is O_2 expressed in ml kg^{-1} min^{-1}. This is used to compare groups using t tests or analysis of variance as appropriate, to explore relationships between aerobic capabilities and performance and to evaluate the physiological status of subjects.

More than forty years ago, Tanner (1949) warned against the use of these standards for evaluative purposes and demonstrated that

they were, '... theoretically fallacious and, unless in exceptional circumstances, misleading' (Tanner, 1949, p. 1). Furthermore, he later stated (Tanner, 1964) that comparisons of groups based on mean values of ratio standards were also misleading because they, '... involve some statistical difficulties and are neither as simple nor as informative as they seem' (Tanner, 1949, p. 65). What is the problem?

A ratio standard is valid only when:

$$\frac{\varepsilon_x}{\varepsilon_y} = r$$

where:

ε_x = coefficient of variation of x, i.e.
$(SDx / \bar{x}) \times 100$

ε_y = coefficient of variation of y, i.e.
$(SDy / \bar{y}) \times 100$

r = Pearson's product-moment correlation coefficient

This expression is Tanner's (1949) 'exceptional circumstance' and is equivalent to the regression standard with an intercept of 0 and a slope the same as the ratio standard. If it is not satisfied, a distortion is introduced. Figure 11.1 illustrates the principle. The solid line represents the ratio standard whereas the other lines represent regression lines of O_2 on body mass for various values of r. The only point through which all the lines pass – the intersection point – is where the mean values for x and y occur. As r increases, the ratio standard and regression line get closer but they will be coincident only when the special circumstance is satisfied. Rarely, if ever, is this test made and, arguably, rarer still is it actually fulfilled. In fact there are numerous instances where it simply cannot be satisfied. As the value of r reduces, the regression line rotates clockwise. The further data points are from the intersection, the more the ratio standard distorts the 'true' relationship.

If the ratio standard is used for evaluative purposes, those with body mass values below

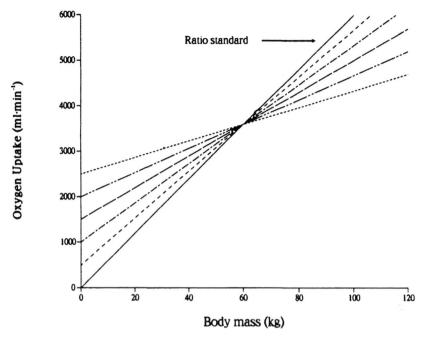

Figure 11.1 The effect of departures from Tanner's (1949) 'special circumstance' on the difference between regression standards and the ratio standard.

the mean will be ascribed high aerobic capability, whereas those whose body mass is greater than the mean will tend to be ascribed low aerobic capability. In other words, little people receive an artefactual arithmetic advantage whereas large people are similarly disadvantaged. The greater the distance of the point from the mean, the greater the distortion will be. Later, Packard and Boardman (1987) provided support for this principle and elaborated on the theme.

Because of the artefacts that ratio standards can introduce, Tanner (1964) suggested that *regression standards* should be used for evaluation and that groups should be compared by means of the comparison of regression lines through the statistical technique *analysis of covariance* (ANCOVA) (Snedecor and Cochran, 1989).

11.5 REGRESSION STANDARDS AND ANCOVA

For the purposes of evaluation, a regression standard is straightforward. If an individual is above the regression line, he or she is above average; if below the line, he or she is below average. Norms can be established on the basis of how far above and how far below particular values lie. Comparisons of regression lines by means of ANCOVA in order to compare groups is more involved although the principles are actually simple. See Appendix A to carry out the appropriate statistical analysis using SPSS (Norusis, 1992). Texts such as Snedecor and Cochran (1989) and Tabachnick and Fidell (1996) provide a useful theoretical background.

Figure 11.2a illustrates the basis for comparing two groups, 1 and 2. Regression lines for each group identify the linear relationship between variables. The x variable – the independent variable – is called a *covariate* because as x increases, so too does y – the dependent variable. The effect of x is partitioned out and the, so-called, *adjusted means* are calculated. In the comparison of regression lines, three tests are made:

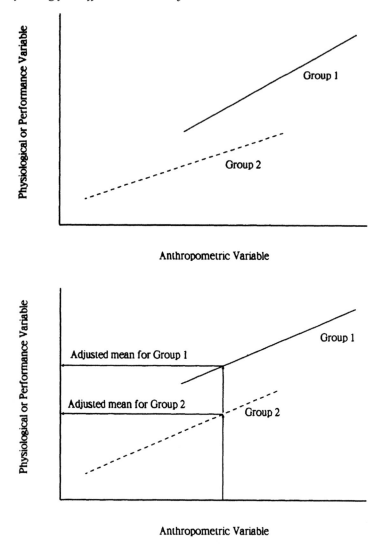

Figure 11.2 The identification of 'adjusted means'. Actual slopes and slopes constrained to be parallel.

1. Variance about regression.
2. Equality of slopes.
3. Comparison of elevations of the lines.

Ideally there should be *homogeneity* of variance about regression, i.e. the variance about regression should be the same in both (or all) groups. (*Heterogeneity* means that the variances are not the same.) If this test is satisfied, the slopes are compared. If there are no statistical differences between the slopes, the lines are recast and constrained to be parallel. If the slopes of the lines are different, the analysis stops; the groups are qualitatively different. The parallel slopes are used to calculate the adjusted means (Figure 11.2b). For the overall mean value of x, equivalent values of y for each group are calculated. The error term for each group is the standard error of the estimate (SEE).

Table 11.1 Absolute and natural logarithm values (ln) for lean leg volume (LLV) and optimized peak power output (OPP) in men and women

Men				Women			
LLV	lnLLV	OPP	lnOPP	LLV	lnLLV	OPP	lnOPP
(l)	(lnl)	(W)	(lnW)	(l)	(lnl)	(W)	(lnW)
7.03	1.950	928	6.833	4.79	1.567	658	6.489
7.47	2.011	825	6.715	4.55	1.515	490	6.194
8.80	2.175	1 113	7.015	4.94	1.597	596	6.390
7.44	2.007	950	6.856	5.26	1.660	491	6.196
7.16	1.969	1 231	7.116	5.54	1.712	717	6.575
7.69	2.040	942	6.848	4.95	1.599	467	6.146
7.50	2.015	889	6.790	4.50	1.504	534	6.280
6.43	1.861	904	6.807	7.32	1.991	769	6.645
8.41	2.129	1 235	7.119	5.09	1.627	644	6.468
7.73	2.045	889	6.790	3.57	1.273	427	6.057
6.70	1.902	917	6.821	4.63	1.533	664	6.498
6.72	1.905	850	6.745	4.93	1.595	624	6.436
6.41	1.858	997	6.905	4.33	1.466	573	6.351
8.26	2.111	1 003	6.911	7.89	2.066	821	6.711
7.97	2.076	1 205	7.094	6.82	1.920	733	6.597
8.46	2.135	1 211	7.099	5.46	1.697	800	6.685
8.47	2.137	978	6.886	4.54	1.513	672	6.510
6.91	1.933	1 087	6.991	5.85	1.766	590	6.380
8.50	2.140	1 082	6.987	5.38	1.683	679	6.521
7.82	2.057	1 026	6.933	5.68	1.737	607	6.409
7.45	2.008	970	6.877	5.09	1.627	714	6.571
7.74	2.046	1 131	7.031	4.66	1.539	755	6.627
6.83	1.921	902	6.805	5.97	1.787	755	6.627
7.72	2.044	1 129	7.029	4.95	1.599	561	6.330
6.04	1.798	832	6.724	5.10	1.629	518	6.250
8.29	2.115	1 242	7.124	5.91	1.777	680	6.522
6.08	1.805	938	6.844	4.19	1.433	634	6.452
6.36	1.850	856	6.752	5.00	1.609	734	6.599
7.43	2.006	939	6.845	4.35	1.470	784	6.664
5.83	1.763	801	6.686	4.62	1.530	632	6.449
6.64	1.893	919	6.823	5.76	1.751	709	6.564
8.87	2.183	1 091	6.995	5.35	1.677	712	6.568

continued on next page

Table 11.1 Absolute and natural logarithm values (ln) for lean leg volume (LLV) and optimized peak power output (OPP) in men and women (cont.)

Men					Women			
LLV	*lnLLV*	*OPP*	*lnOPP*		*LLV*	*lnLLV*	*OPP*	*lnOPP*
(l)	*(lnl)*	*(W)*	*(lnW)*		*(l)*	*(lnl)*	*(W)*	*(lnW)*
7.46	2.010	977	6.884		4.75	1.558	639	6.460
7.48	2.012	1 248	7.129		5.58	1.719	726	6.588
					5.60	1.723	815	6.703
					5.70	1.740	847	6.742
					5.45	1.696	701	6.553
					3.92	1.366	653	6.482
					4.09	1.409	550	6.310
					5.22	1.653	835	6.727
					4.89	1.587	893	6.795
					5.13	1.635	760	6.633
					4.40	1.482	564	6.335
					5.70	1.740	758	6.631
					4.60	1.526	630	6.446
					4.90	1.589	657	6.488
					7.06	1.954	841	6.735

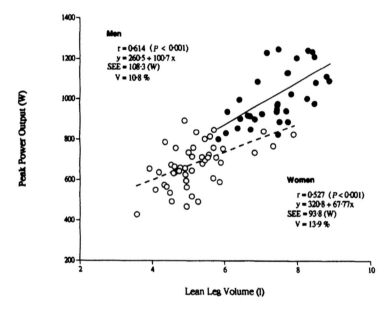

Figure 11.3 The relationship between optimised peak power output and lean leg volume in men (● ———) and women (O - - - - - -) (Winter *et al.*, 1991).

11.5.1 ANCOVA – A WORKED EXAMPLE

Table 11.1 contains data for lean leg volume and peak power output in men and women (Winter *et al.*, 1991). Figure 11.3 illustrates the regression lines and raw data plots for the two groups. Comparison of the ratio standards peak power output / lean leg volume showed that there was no difference between the groups (136, 3 WI^{-1} vs. 131, 3 WI^{-1} in men and women respectively (mean, SEM) $p > 0.05$). This suggests that there is no difference between the qualitative characteristics of the groups. In marked contrast, ANCOVA produced adjusted means of 903, 108 W in men and 748, 94 W in women (mean, SEE) $p < 0.001$. This suggests that there are qualitative differences between men and women. The technique has also been applied to study strength and cross-sectional area of muscle (Winter and Maughan, 1991) with the same outcome. It has also been used to adjust oxygen uptake values of children and adults to compensate for the large differences in body mass. Using this procedure, the difference in mass-relative oxygen uptake calculated by the simple ratio standard (ml kg^{-1} min^{-1}) at any given running speed is removed (Eston *et al.*, 1993; Armstrong *et al.*, 1997). (See Appendix A to carry out the appropriate analysis using SPSS.)

11.6 ALLOMETRY AND POWER FUNCTION STANDARDS

It would appear that ANCOVA on regression lines solves the problems associated with scaling. This is not necessarily the case. Nevill *et al.* (1992a) identified two major weaknesses in the use of linear modelling techniques on raw data:

1. Data are not necessarily related linearly.
2. Error about regression is not necessarily additive, it might be multiplicative.

Non-linear relationships between variables are well known to biologists (Schmidt-Nielsen, 1984) and curiously, although they receive attention in notable texts (MacDougall *et al.*, 1991; Åstrand and Rodahl, 1986), have not been used widely by sport and exercise scientists.

Growth and development in humans and other living things is accompanied by differential changes in the size and configuration of the body's segments (Tanner, 1989). These changes are said to be *allometric* (Schmidt-Nielsen, 1984), a word derived from the Greek *allos* which means "other". Physiological variables y are scaled in relation to an index of body size x according to allometric equations. These are of the general form:

$$y = ax^b$$

11.7 PRACTICAL 1: THE IDENTIFICATION OF ALLOMETRIC RELATIONSHIPS

The allometric principles can be illustrated by using spheres as examples and Table 11.2 contains relevant data. In spheres:

$$\text{Area} = 4\pi r^2$$

$$\text{Volume} = \frac{4\pi r^3}{3}$$

where r = radius.

For area, the numerical value of a, the constant multiplier, is 12.566, i.e. 4π, and the exponent is 2. Similarly, for volume, the constant multiplier is 4.189 ($4\pi/3$) and the exponent is 3.

1. With radius on the abscissa, draw two graphs: one for surface area and one for volume. Figures 11.4 and 11.5 show what you should have. How can these relationships be identified? The answer is simple. The raw variables are converted into natural logarithms and ln y is regressed on ln x. This linearizes the otherwise non-linear relationship and produces an expression which is of the form:

$$\ln y = \ln a + b \ln x$$

The antilog of ln a identifies the constant multiplier in the allometric equation and the slope of the line is the numerical value of the exponent.

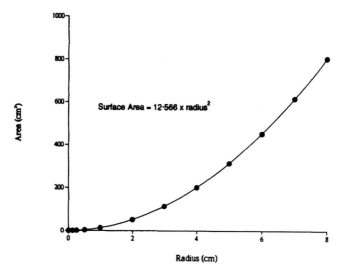

Figure 11.4 The relationship between surface area and radius in spheres.

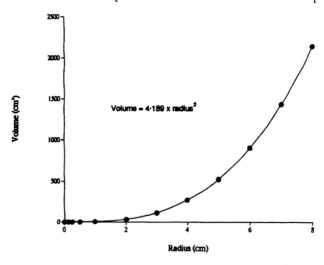

Figure 11.5 The relationship between volume and radius in spheres.

Table 11.2 Absolute and natural logarithm values (ln) of radii, surface areas and volumes in spheres

Radius (cm)	Ln radius (ln cm)	Area (cm²)	Ln area (ln cm³)	Volume (cm³)	Ln volume (ln cm³)
0.125	−2.079	0.2	−1.628	0	−4.806
0.25	−1.386	0.8	−0.242	0.1	−2.726
0.5	−0.693	3.1	1.145	0.5	−0.647
1	0	12.6	2.531	4.2	1.433
2	0.693	50.3	3.917	33.5	3.512
3	1.099	113.1	4.728	113.1	4.728
4	1.386	201.0	5.303	268.1	5.591
5	1.609	314.1	5.750	523.7	6.261
6	1.792	452.3	6.114	904.9	6.808
7	1.946	615.6	6.423	1 436.9	7.270
8	2.079	804.1	6.690	2 144.9	7.671

2. Using the values in Table 11.2, with ln radius on the abscissa, plot two graphs: one for surface area and one for volume.

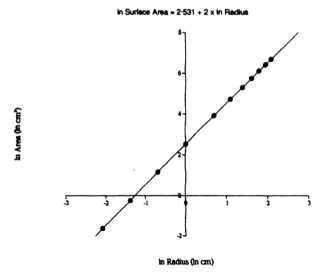

ln Surface Area = 2·531 + 2 x ln Radius

Figure 11.6 The relationship between ln surface area and ln radius in spheres.

3. Calculate the regression equations for each graph. Figures 11.6 and 11.7 show what you should have. For the graph of ln surface area regressed on ln radius, *a* (the constant multiplier in the allometric equation which relates the raw variables) is the antilog of 2.531. This value is 12.566. Similarly, the exponent is given by the slope of the log–log regression equation, i.e. 2. In the same way, the constant multiplier in the volume–radius relationship is the antilog of 1.432 = 4.189, and the exponent is 3. From these known relationships, we can explore an unknown one; the relationship between surface area and volume.

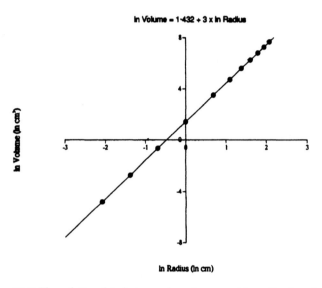

Figure 11.7 The relationship between ln volume and ln radius in spheres.

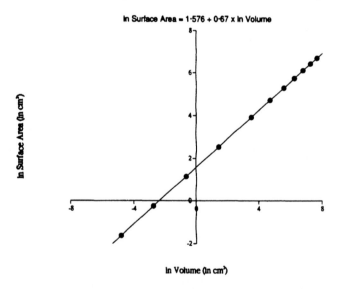

Figure 11.8 The relationship between ln surface area and ln volume in spheres.

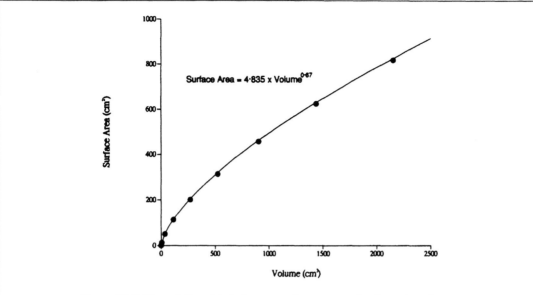

Figure 11.9 The relationship between surface area and volume in spheres.

4. Again using the data in Table 11.2, identify the allometric relationship between surface area and volume. Make surface area the dependent variable. Figures 11.8 and 11.9 show what you should have.

where:

a = constant multiplier;
b = exponent

An example is described in Practical 1.

11.8 POWER FUNCTION RATIO STANDARDS

The relationship in Figure 11.9 illustrates an important principle which is known as the *surface law* (Schmidt-Nielsen, 1984); the surface area of a body is related to its volume raised to the power 0·67. In other words, as the volume of a body increases, its surface area actually reduces in proportion. Nevill *et al.* (1992a) and Nevill and Holder (1994) have provided compelling evidence which suggests that measures such as $\dot{V}O_2$ are related to body mass raised to this 0·67 power. To scale correctly, an independent variable should be raised to a power which is identified from log–log transformations. This value is called a *power function*.

The power function can then be divided into the dependent variable to produce a *power function ratio standard*.

Another important point about allometric relationships concerns the error term. In linear models, error about the regression line is assumed to be constant. Such error is said to be additive or *homoscedastic*. Allometric models do not make this assumption; error is assumed to be multiplicative or *heteroscedastic*. In this case, error increases as the independent variable increases. This is what tends to happen with living things (Nevill and Holder, 1994).

Groups can be compared by using power function ratios and *t* tests or analysis of variance as appropriate. They can also be compared using ANCOVA on the log–log transformations. These transformations

11.9 PRACTICAL 2: A WORKED EXAMPLE

The data in Table 11.1 can be revisited. The natural logarithms of lean leg volume and peak power output can now be used to compare performance in men and women. This is the analysis reported by Nevill *et al.* (1992b).

1. With ln Lean Leg Volume on the abscissa, plot a graph with ln Peak Power Output for men and women. Calculate the regression equations. Figure 11.10 illustrates what you should have.
2. ANCOVA on these data (Nevill, 1994) confirms that for a given lean leg volume, peak power output in men is greater than in women ($p < 0.001$). (See Appendix B to implement ANCOVA using SPSS.)

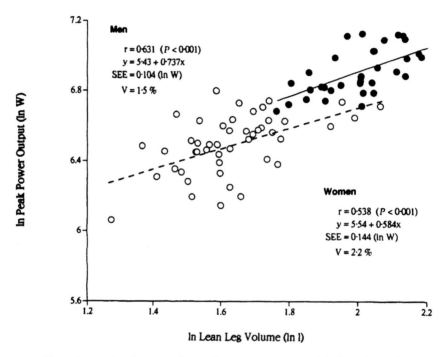

Figure 11.10. The relationship between ln peak power output and ln lean leg volume in men (————) and women (O - - - - - - -) (Nevill *et al.*, 1992b).

3. Plot the allometric relationships for men and women. Figure 11.11 illustrates what you should have.
4. ANCOVA also demonstrates that the slopes of the log/log transformations (0.737 in men vs. 0.584 in women) are not significantly different ($p > 0.05$). A common slope of 0.626 can be used for both groups. Note that this approximates to a theoretical value of 0.67 suggested by the surface law.

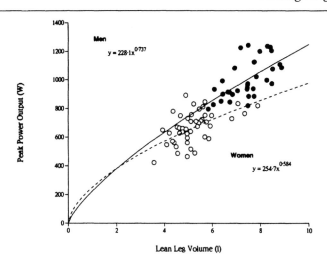

Figure 11.11. The allometric relationship between peak power output and lean leg volume in men
($\bullet$ ————) and women (O - - - - - - -) (Nevill *et al.*, 1992b).

5. Produce power function ratio standards (W $l^{-0.626}$) for men and women and compare the
   groups. This should give means, SEM of 286, 5 W $l^{-0.626}$ and 239, 5 W $l^{-0.626}$ respectively ($p <$
   0.001). *Similar results were observed in the study by Eston et al.* (1997). They also reported a
   common exponent of 0.60 to describe the relationship between lean upper leg volume
   and peak power output. Mean values, SEM were 376, 14 W $l^{-0.60}$ and 296, 13 W $l^{-0.60}$, for
   men and women, respectively ($p < 0.01$).

constrain error to be additive and so allow
the use of ANCOVA. An example is shown in
Practical 2.

11.10 SCALING LONGITUDINAL DATA

In the previous sections we investigated the difference in peak power output between men and
women having scaled for differences in lean leg
volume, i.e. by using lean leg volume as a
covariate. The study was a cross-sectional design
since the subjects, physical education and sports
studies students in their early twenties, were
measured on one occasion. To identify and separate the relative contribution of factors such as
sex or physical activity from changes attributable to growth, maturation and ageing,
'growth' data should be collected longitudi-
nally. An appropriate method for subsequent

analysis is some form of multilevel modelling
(Goldstein, 1995; Rasbash and Woodhouse, 1995).

Multilevel modelling is an extension of ordi-
nary multiple regression where the data have a
hierarchical or cluster structure. The hierarchy
consists of units or measurements that are
grouped at different levels. An example is
repeated measures data in which individuals
are assessed on more than one occasion. Here
the subjects, or individuals, are assumed to be
a random sample and represent level-two
units; the subjects' repeated measurements
recorded at each visit are level-one units. In
contrast to traditional repeated measures analysis, visit occasions are modelled as a random
variable over time for each subject. The two
levels of random variation take account of the
fact that growth or ageing characteristics of
individual subjects, such as their average
growth (or decay) rate, vary around a

population mean, and also that each subject's observed measurements vary around his or her own growth (or decay) trajectory.

Adapting these methods, Nevill *et al.* (1998) fitted allometric models to the results of two studies: the first by Baxter-Jones *et al.* (1993) that investigated developmental changes in aerobic power of young athletes and the second by Round *et al.* (1999) that investigated developmental changes in strength of school children from North London. Not only did the allometric models provide a superior fit compared with traditional ANCOVA methods, but they also provided a simpler and more plausible interpretation of the data. For example, in the first study, the body mass exponents for boys and girls were close to the anticipated theoretical values, $m^{2/3}$. More recently, Armstrong *et al.* (1999) confirmed the suitability of allometric multilevel modelling when describing longitudinal changes in peak oxygen uptake in 11–13-year-olds. (For further discussion, see Winter *et al.* (2001)).

11.11 SUMMARY

Three simple points can be stated about techniques that partition out differences in body size:

1. The a priori use of ratio standards is incorrect. These standards should only be used when Tanner's (1949) special circumstance is satisfied.

APPENDIX A: ANALYSIS OF DATA IN TABLE 11.1 USING SPSS VERSION 9.0

1. Entering the data given in Table 11.1
   1.1 Create three columns: gender, llv and OPP.
   1.2 Code the men as 1 and the women as 2 in the gender column (column 1).
   1.3 Put the llv data into column 2.
   1.4 Put the OPP data into column 3.

This codes the data according to gender.

2. Splitting the data by gender
   2.1 Single click Data on the menubar.
   2.2 Single click on Split File.
   2.3 Single click on Compare groups.
   2.4 Double click on gender so it is contained within the Groups Based on box.
   2.5 Single click on OK.

This splits the data on the basis of gender.

3. Descriptives
   3.1 Single click on Analyze on the tool bar.
   3.2 Single click on Descriptive Statistics.
   3.3 Single click on Descriptives.
   3.4 Double click on variables OPP and llv in the variable(s) box.
   3.5 Single click on Options.
   3.6 Single click on S.E. Mean.
   3.7 Single click on Continue.
   3.8 Single click on OK.

This gives descriptive data for llv and OPP in the men and women. You should have values of (mean, SEM) 7.41, 0.14 l and 1007, 23 W for the men and 5.19, 0.12 l and 673, 16 W for the women.

Remember to remove the split after you have obtained the descriptives. Do this by:
3.9 Single click Data on the menubar.
3.10 Single click on Split File.
3.11 Single click on 'Analyze all cases, do not compare groups'.
3.12 Single click on OK.

4. Calculate ratio standards
   4.1 Single click Transform on the menubar.
   4.2 Single click on Compute.
   4.3 In the Target Variable box, type a name, e.g. Oppratio.
   4.4 In the Numeric Expression box type OPP/llv.
   4.5 Single click on OK.

This calculates simple ratio standards OPP/llv in the men and women.

5. Recoding the sex variable
   5.1 Single click on Transform on the menubar.
   5.2 Single click on Compute.
   5.3 In the Target Variable box, type sex.
   5.4 In the Numeric Expression Box type 1.
   5.5 Single click on If . . .
   5.6 Single click on 'Include if case satisfies condition'.
   5.7 Type 'gender=1'.
   5.8 Single click on Continue.
   5.9 Single click on OK.
   5.10 Repeat steps above (5.1 – 5.9), but this time at step 5.4 type 0 in Numeric Expression, and at step 5.7 type gender = 2.

This recoding is necessary for the regression and ANCOVA analyses.

6. Using ANOVA to compare the ratio standards
   6.1 Single click on Analyze in the menubar.
   6.2 Single click on Compare Means.
   6.3 Single click on One-way ANOVA.
   6.4 Put Oppratio into the Dependent Box and sex into the Factor Box.
   6.5 Single click on Options.
   6.6 Single click in the Descriptives check box.
   6.7 Single click on Continue.
   6.8 Single click on OK.

This should give (mean, SEM) 136, 3 W l^{-1} for the men and 131, 3 W l^{-1} for the women (P = 0.206).

7. Creating sex interaction
   7.1 Single click Transform on the menubar.
   7.2 Single click on Compute.
   7.3 Remove the If ... command that created the sex variable by single clicking on 'If ...' and then single clicking on 'Include all cases'. Single click on Continue.
   7.4 In the Target Variable box, type 'sex_llv'.

7.5 In the Numeric expression box, type sex*llv
7.6 Single click on OK.

This might seem to be curious but we will use this interaction to compare the gradients of the regression lines.

8. Testing interaction
   8.1 Single click on Analyze in the menubar.
   8.2 Single click on Regression.
   8.3 Single click on Linear.
   8.4 Put 'llv', 'sex' and 'sex_llv' into the Independent box.
   8.5 Put 'opp' in the Dependent box.
   8.6 Single click OK.

You should see that the interaction term – sex x llv – does not make a significant contribution to the regression equation (p = 0.233) and, hence, the need for separate slopes for the male and female covariates (llv) can be rejected.

9. Regression
   9.1 Single click on Analyze in the menubar.
   9.2 Single click on Regression.
   9.3 Single click on Linear.
   9.4 Put 'llv' and 'sex' into the Independent box.
   9.5 Put 'opp' in the dependent box.
   9.6 Single click on OK.

This regression analysis is, in effect, an analysis of covariance that identifies both the covariate – llv – and the sex main effect as highly significant (p < 0.001) in both cases. This result can be confirmed using the SPSS ANCOVA commands as follows:

10. ANCOVA (Linear)
    10.1 Single click on Analyze in the menubar.
    10.2 Single click on General Linear Model.
    10.3 Single click on Univariate …
    10.4 Put 'opp' in the Dependent Variable box.
    10.5 Put 'sex' into the Fixed Factor box.
    10.6 Put 'llv' into the Covariate(s) box.
    10.7 Single click on options.
    10.8 Include sex in the Display Means For box.
    10.9 Single click on Continue.
    10.10 Single click on OK.

This completes the analysis and calculates adjusted means i.e. values for opp adjusted for differences in llv. The values should be (mean, SEM) 748, 19 W for the women and 902, 24 W for the men (p < 0.001).

APPENDIX B: ANALYSIS OF THE LOG-TRANSFORMED DATA IN TABLE 11.1

1. Log transformation
   1.1 Single click on Transform in the menu bar.
   1.2 Single click on Compute.
   1.3 In the target Variable box, type 'lnllv'.
   1.4 In the Numeric Expression box type 'ln(llv)'.
   1.5 Single click on OK.

This takes the natural logarithm of llv and creates an lnllv column.

2. Repeat for OPP

Similarly, this takes the natural logarithm of opp and creates an lnopp column.

3. Creating sex interaction
   3.1 Single click Transform on the menubar.
   3.2 Single click on Compute.
   3.3 In the Target Variable box, type sex_lnllv.
   3.4 In the Numeric Expression box, type sex*lnllv.
   3.5 Single click on OK.

As before, this creates a variable – sex × lnllv – that can be used to test for interaction.

4. Testing interaction
   4.1 Single click on Analyze in the menubar.
   4.2 Single click on Regression.
   4.3 Single click on Linear.
   4.4 Put 'lnllv', 'sex' and 'sex_lnllv' into the independent box.
   4.5 Put 'lnopp' in the Dependent box.
   4.6 Single click on OK.

As with the raw variables, you should see that the interaction term – sex × lnllv – does not make a significant contribution to the regression equation ($p = 0.515$) and, hence, the need for separate slopes for the male and female covariates (lnllv) can be rejected. A common slope can be used.

5. Regression
   5.1 Repeat 4 above but remove sex_lnllv from the Independent box.

Again as before, this analysis is equivalent to an analysis of covariance with both the covariate lnllv and sex main effect highly significant ($p < 0.001$). The analysis also identifies the allometric models that describe the relationship between OPP and lnLLV for the male and female subjects. By taking antilogs of the constant (5.475) and the constant plus the sex indicator variable (5.475 + 0.182 = 5.657), the constant multipliers – a – for the men (286.3) and the women (238.7) are obtained. Note that b, the common gradient and hence exponent in the allometric model is also obtained (0.626). So, in the men, $OPP = 286.3 \times llv^{0.626}$ and in the women, $OPP = 238.7 \times llv^{0.626}$.

6. ANCOVA (Log-linear)
   6.1 Single click on <u>A</u>nalyze in the menubar.
   6.2 Single click on General Linear Model.
   6.3 Single click on Univariate...
   6.4 Put 'lnopp' in the Dependent Variable box.
   6.5 Put 'sex' into the Fixed Factor box.
   6.6 Put 'lnllv' into the Covariate(s) box.
   6.7 Single click on Options.
   6.8 Include sex in the Display Means For box.
   6.9 Single click on Continue.

7.0 Single click on OK.

Simply by taking the antilogarithms of the two adjusted means, the difference between the men's peak power output (876 W) and women's (730) is obtained, adjusted for differences in lean leg volume. Note that if we divide these two adjusted means by the antilogarithm of the mean lnllv for all 81 subjects – 5.97 l – raised to the power 0.626, i.e. $5.97^{0.626} = 3.060$ we obtain the mean power function ratio standards for the women, 239 W $l^{0.626}$, and the men, 286 W $l^{0.626}$ as derived earlier.

2. Allometric modelling should be used to partial out differences in body size.
3. Multilevel modelling is useful in the analysis of longitudinal data.

ACKNOWLEDGEMENT

We are grateful to Patrick Johnson (Sheffield Hallam University) and Ann Rowlands (University of Wales, Bangor) for their help with the descriptions of the statistical analyses (SPSS Version 9.0) given in Appendices A and B.

REFERENCES

Armstrong, N., Kirby, B.J., Welsman, J.R. and McManus, A.M. (1997). Submaximal exercise in pre-pubertal children. In *Children and Exercise XIX: Promoting Health and Well-Being*. eds. N. Armstrong, B.J. Kirby and J.R. Welsman (E. & F.N. Spon, London), pp. 221–7.

Armstrong, N., Welsman, J.R., Kirby, B.J. and Nevill, A.M. (1999). Longitudinal changes in young people's peak oxygen uptake. *Journal of Applied Physiology*, **87**, 2230–6.

Åstrand, P-O. and Rodahl, K. (1986). *Textbook of Work Physiology*, 3rd edn. (McGraw-Hill, New York).

Batterham, A.M., Tolfrey, K. and George, K.P. (1997). Nevill's explanation of Kleiber's 0.75 mass exponent: an artifact of collinearity problems in least squares models? *Journal of Applied Physiology*, **82**, 693–7.

Baxter Jones, A., Goldstein, H. and Helms, P. (1993). The development of aerobic power in young athletes. *Journal of Applied Physiology*, **75**, 1160–7.

Eston, R.G., Robson, S. and Winter, E.M. (1993). A comparison of oxygen uptake during running in children and adults. In *Kinanthropometry IV*. eds. W. Duquet and J.A.P. Day (E. & F.N. Spon, London), pp. 236–41.

Eston, R.G., Winter, E. and Baltzopoulos, V. (1997). Ratio standards and allometric modelling to scale peak-power output for differences in lean upper leg volume in men and women. *Journal of Sports Sciences*, 29.

Goldstein, H. (1995) *Multilevel Statistical Models*, 2nd. edn. (Edward Arnold, London).

Huxley, J.S. (1932). *Problems of Relative Growth*. (Dial, New York).

Jakeman, P.M., Winter, E.M. and Doust, J. (1994). A review of research in sports physiology. *Journal of Sports Sciences*, **12**, 33–60.

Katch, V. (1973). The use of oxygen/body weight ratio in correlational analyses: spurious correlations and statistical considerations. *Medicine and Science in Sports and Exercise*, **5**, 253–7.

Kermack, K.A. and Haldane, J.B.S. (1950). Organic correlation and allometry. *Biometrika*, **37**, 30–41.

MacDougall, J.D., Wenger, H.A. and Green, H.J. eds. (1991). *Physiological Testing of the High-Performance Athlete*. 2nd edn. (Human Kinetics, Champaign, IL).

Nevill, A.M. (1994). The need to scale for differences in body size and mass: an explanation of Kleiber's 0·75 exponent. *Journal of Applied Physiology*, **77**, 2870–3.

Nevill, A.M. and Holder, R.L. (1994). Modelling maximum oxygen uptake – a case-study in non-linear regression model formulation and comparison. *Applied Statistics*, **43**, 653–66.

Nevill, A.M., Ramsbottom, R. and Williams, C. (1992a). Scaling physiological measurements for individuals of different body size. *European Journal of Applied Physiology*, **65**, 110–17.

Nevill, A.M., Ramsbottom, R., Williams, C. and Winter, E.M. (1992b). Scaling individuals of different body size. *Journal of Sports Sciences*, **9**, 427–8.

Nevill, A.M., Holder, R.L., Baxter-Jones, A., *et al.* (1998). Modeling developmental changes in strength and aerobic power in children. *Journal of Applied Physiology*, **84**, 963-70.

Norusis, M.J. (1992). *SPSS for Windows Advanced Statistics Release 5*. (SPSS, Chicago).

Packard, G.J. and Boardman, T.J. (1987). The misuse of ratios to scale physiological data that vary allometrically with body size. In *New Directions in Ecological Physiology*. eds. M.E. Feder, A.F. Bennett, W.W. Burggren and R.B. Huey. (Cambridge University Press, Cambridge), pp. 216-39.

Rasbash, J. and Woodhouse, G. (1995). *MLn Command Reference*. Multilevel Models Project, Institute of Education, London.

Rayner, J.M.V. (1985). Linear relations in biomechanics: the statistics of scaling functions. *Journal of Zoology (London) Series A*, **206**, 415–39.

Ricker, W.E. (1973). Linear regression in fishery research. *Journal of Fisheries Research Board Canada*, **30**, 409–34.

Round, J.M., Jones, D.A., Honour, J.W. and Nevill, A.M. (1999). Hormonal factors in the development of differences in strength between boys and girls during adolescence: a longitudinal study. *Annals of Human Biology*, **26**, 49–62.

Sarrus and Rameaux (1838). *Bulletin de l'Academie Royal de Medecine, Paris*, **3**, 1094–1100.

Schmidt-Nielsen, K. (1984). *Scaling: Why is animal size so important?* (Cambridge University Press, Cambridge).

Sholl, D. (1948). The quantitative investigation of the vertebrate brain and the applicability of allometric formulae to its study. *Proceedings of the Royal Society Series B*, **35**, 243–57.

Snedecor, G.W. and Cochran, W.G. (1989). *Statistical Methods*. 8th edn. (Iowa State Press, Ames, IA).

Sokal, R.R. and Rohlf, F.J. (1995). *Biometry*. 3rd edn. (W.H. Freeman and Company, New York).

Tabachnick, B.G. and Fidell, L.S. (1996). *Using Multivariate Statistics*. 3rd edn. (Harper Collins, New York).

Tanner, J.M. (1949). Fallacy of per-weight and per-surface area standards and their relation to spurious correlation. *Journal of Applied Physiology*, **2**, 1–15.

Tanner, J.M. (1964). *The Physique of the Olympic Athlete*. (George, Allen and Unwin, London).

Tanner, J.M. (1989). *Foetus into Man*. 2nd edn. (Castlemead Publications, Ware, Herts).

Thompson, D.W. (1917). *Growth and Form*. (Cambridge University Press, Cambridge).

Winter, E.M. (1992). Scaling: partitioning out differences in size. *Pediatric Exercise Science*, **4**, 296–301.

Winter, E.M. (1996). Importance and principles of scaling for size differences. In *The Child and Adolescent Athlete*. ed. O. Bar-Or (Blackwell, Oxford), pp. 673–9.

Winter, E.M. and Maughan, R.J. (1991). Strength and cross-sectional area of the quadriceps in men and women. *Journal of Physiology*, **43S**, 175P.

Winter, E.M., Brookes, F.B.C. and Hamley, E.J. (1991). Maximal exercise performance and lean leg volume in men and women. *Journal of Sports Sciences*, **9**, 3–13.

Winter, E.M., Eston, R.E. and Lamb, K.L. (2001) Statistical techniques for physiology research. *Journal of Sports Sciences*. In press.

INDEX